Time and Identity

Topics in Contemporary Philosophy

Editors
Joseph Keim Campbell, Washington State University
Michael O'Rourke, University of Idaho
Harry S. Silverstein, Washington State University

Time and Identity

edited by Joseph Keim Campbell, Michael O'Rourke, and
Harry S. Silverstein

A Bradford Book
The MIT Press
Cambridge, Massachusetts
London, England

MIT Press books may be purchased at special quantity discounts for business or sales promotional use. For information, please email special_sales@mitpress.mit .edu or write to Special Sales Department, The MIT Press, 55 Hayward Street, Cambridge, MA 02142.

This book was set in Stone and Stone Sans by Westchester Book Group. Printed and bound in the United States of America.

Library of Congress Cataloging-in-Publication Data

Time and identity / edited by Joseph Keim Campbell, Michael O'Rourke, and Harry S. Silverstein.
    p.   cm.—(Topics in contemporary philosophy)
"A Bradford book."
Includes bibliographical references and index.
ISBN 978-0-262-01409-0 (hardcover : alk. paper)—ISBN 978-0-262-51397-5 (pbk. : alk. paper)
1. Time. 2. Identity (Philosophical concept). 3. Self (Philosophy). 4. Death.
I. Campbell, Joseph Keim, 1958–. II. O'Rourke, Michael, 1963–. III. Silverstein, Harry, 1942–.
BD638.T5437   2010
115—dc22
                                                              2009041935

10 9 8 7 6 5 4 3 2 1

Contents

Acknowledgments

Earlier versions of the essays in this volume were presented in Pullman, Washington, and Moscow, Idaho, at the eighth annual Inland Northwest Philosophy Conference (INPC), held April 1–3, 2005. For administrative and financial support for the conference, we thank the philosophy departments at Washington State University (David Shier, Chair) and the University of Idaho (Douglas Lind, Chair), the College of Liberal Arts at Washington State University (Erich Lear, Dean), the College of Letters, Arts & Social Sciences (Joe Zeller, Dean) and the Provost's Office at the University of Idaho, the research offices at both universities, and the departmental administrative managers, DeeDee Torgeson and Diane Ellison. We are also grateful for a grant from the Idaho Humanities Council, a state-based affiliate of the National Endowment for the Humanities, to help fund the Public Forum.

Those who presented papers at INPC 2005 were encouraged to submit their work for possible inclusion in this volume, and, after a process of peer evaluation, only a few were selected. We regret that we had to turn down numerous quality essays. For help with the selection process and other matters, we thank William Beardsley, Ben Bradley, Andrei Buckareff, Ben Caplan, Larry Colter, Barry Dainton, Bruce Glymour, Gary Hardcastle, Katherine Hawley, Mark Heller, Paul Hovda, Charlie Huenemann, Simon Keller, Ann Levey, Marc Moffett, Mark Moyer, Joe Salerno, Steve Savitt, Christopher Shields, Russell Wahl, Lisa Warenski, Ryan Wasserman, Brian Weatherson, and Ron Wilburn.

Finally, our thanks to Delphine Keim Campbell, Rebecca O'Rourke, and Lorinda Knight for continued support and understanding!

Introduction: Framing the Problems of Time and Identity

Matthew H. Slater

Concepts Familiar yet Perplexing

Many philosophical concepts are difficult. Some, however, are doubly confounding in their apparent *familiarity*. The concepts of *time* and *identity* may top this list. The fourth-century philosopher, Augustine of Hippo, expressed his exasperation with time this way:

> For what is time? Who can easily and briefly explain it? Who can even comprehend it in thought or put the answer into words? Yet is it not true that in conversation we refer to nothing more familiarly or knowingly than time? And surely we understand it when we speak of it; we understand it also when we hear another speak of it. What, then, is time? If no one asks me, I know what it is. If I wish to explain it to him who asks me, I do not know. (*Confessions*, 11, XIV, 17)

Time is an intricate and deeply embedded part of our experience. Indeed, it would seem that the passage of time is a prerequisite for having any experiences at all. But a number of recalcitrant questions about time remain: Is time real? Does time objectively flow? Do past and future moments exist just as present moments do, or is the present in some way special?

The concept of identity also seems at once philosophically unproblematic and frustratingly difficult. It is, as philosophers have long noted, *that relation everything bears to itself and to no other thing.*[1] Of course, as Hawthorne (2003, 99) points out, this cannot be an *analysis* of identity—for '*itself*' and 'no *other* thing' already presuppose an understanding of identity. David Lewis likewise tempers his praise of identity's simplicity:

> There is never any problem about what makes something identical to itself; nothing can ever fail to be. And there is never any problem about what makes two things identical; two things never can be identical. There might be a problem about how to define identity to someone sufficiently lacking in conceptual resources—we note that it won't suffice to teach him certain rules of inference—but since such

unfortunates are rare, even among philosophers, we needn't worry much if their condition is incurable. (Lewis 1986, 192–193)

And yet philosophers face plenty of hard questions about identity. Is a statue identical with the bronze out of which it is made? Is identity ever contingent or indeterminate? How can things change and yet remain the same? What determines whether a person is the same over time—do we have privileged first-person access to the sameness of "the self"? What, in general, are the metaphysics and epistemology of persistence?

Many of these questions (explicitly or implicitly) involve time; they thus tend to inherit its complexities. What we say about persistence presumably bears on what we say about time (and vice versa). The essays in this collection attempt to make progress on some of these most baffling philosophical problems, either singly or in combination. Before getting to them, however, let us sketch some of terrain lying in the background.

Time

The Reality of Time
Perhaps the best place to begin a discussion of the philosophy of time is with the question of whether time exists or is real. The ancients seemed to have presupposed the reality of time, even if it wasn't always clear what to *say* about time—whether the "flow" of time depended on other things, whether the future is knowable or fixed, whether time is eternal, and so on.[2] It wasn't until the twentieth century—ironically, when physicists seem to gain a better scientific understanding of time—that philosophers began to question whether time was in fact real. One argument in particular (McTaggart 1993) has influenced subsequent discussion. Let's begin there, as it will also serve to introduce some of the complex and overlapping terminology employed by various philosophers of time.

McTaggart's argument began with a basic distinction between two ways of ordering events in time. The first—what he called "the A-series"—locates events relative to the present. For example, my birth is in the past and my death is in the (one hopes somewhat distant) future. But these temporal properties change: my birth was once in the future and my death will someday be in the past. The second way of ordering events in time—what McTaggart called "the B-series"—remains constant. My birth is earlier than my death but later than the death of Socrates. These temporal relations remain constant, even as the temporal properties of the A-series change. It does not matter when the proposition ordering my birth and death is uttered. Its truth-value will never change, for it concerns only the temporal *ordering* of events. We might say that A-series expressions ('tomorrow', 'now', 'yesterday', etc.) are *tensed* expressions, whereas B-series expressions ('earlier than', 'later than', 'at 1:00 PM, PST, November 25, 1977', etc.) are *untensed* (or "tenseless") expressions.

So far, so good. But here McTaggart points out that if time is real, there must be an A-series—for A-series expressions are more fundamental or more characteristic of "temporality." But unfortunately, thought McTaggart, the A-series is contradictory and thus cannot exist: As time flows, events come to have different A-series properties. But the propositions 'My birth is past' and 'My birth is future' are incompatible. Thus, because the A-series does not exist, time is unreal. Philosophers have gone several different ways responding to this argument. So-called *B-theorists* (sometimes, perhaps misleadingly, called "eternalists"[3]) object to McTaggart's assumption that B-series facts do not afford "real time." *A-theorists* (sometimes called "presentists") object to his claim that the A-series is contradictory. While these philosophers agree that time is real, they propose (purportedly) different metaphysical accounts of time.[4]

Eternalism and Presentism

We might identify two reasons for thinking with McTaggart that the B-series alone cannot provide an account of time. First, we might regard the A-series as semantically fundamental—if the B-series ordering depends on A-series properties, and those properties turn out to be incoherent, then it follows that there just *is* no B-series. Second, the B-theory can appear to be problematically "static," but time is dynamic. The present "flows" ineluctably. But one might claim that though time cannot properly be said to "pass," we can still make sense of A-series locutions as *indexicals*. Here the analogy between 'here' and 'now' becomes useful. Imagine standing in the middle of a long stretch of desert highway. "It's hot here," you whimper. Your philosopher friend tries to placate your fried nerves: "That's false! There is no spot which is objectively 'here'!" He's misguided, of course (in several ways). Your statement can be true from where you're standing, even if it's false in Siberia.

This is roughly how the eternalist thinks of 'now': although there is no particular time that is objectively *now*, utterances of the form 'I'm hot now' can perfectly well be true (and indeed translated into B-series expressions). They may go on to aver that, just as different spots in the road are no less real for being distant, events and objects at different times are equally real. Presentists disagree. They side with McTaggart on the B-series' failure to account for the *flow* of time (they point out that 'here' doesn't apparently "move locations"). They deny that the past and future are on the same ontological footing as the present: only the present *is real*. This has struck many philosophers as odd. As J. J. C. Smart put it, "Reality is not a property which anything can acquire. To be real is to be part of the universe" (Smart 1981, 142).

Though we seem to be able to put sense to the slogans of the presentist and eternalist, on reflection it is not always clear that their disagreement is genuine. Suppose we try making the foregoing slogan more precise: 'For every *x*, *x* is present.'[5] This is equivalent to 'it's not the case that there exists something *x* such that *x* is not present'. But notice the tense of the verbs: if they are present tense, the claim is trivial. It amounts to the claim that everything that currently exists currently exists. If we read 'exists' instead as "disjunctively omnitemporal," as in 'it's not the case that there existed, exists, or will exist something *x* such that *x* is not present', the claim seems trivially false: plenty of things have *existed* that no longer are present. Similar difficulties plague attempts to correctly formulate the eternalist position. Perhaps the presentist and eternalist are engaged in a merely verbal dispute.

One way of showing that the debate is in fact substantive may be to illustrate one or the other view's ability to accommodate other philosophical problems (e.g., persistence, material constitution, responsibility, welfare). Identity, in particular, appears to be an important battleground for the eternalists and presentists.

Identity

The Mission

Agent X has gone rogue and is attempting with her usual reckless zeal to expose the super-secret Identity Non-Proliferation Cabal (or "INPC"), an organization dedicated to spreading philosophical confusion. But she's captured and subjected to the Process: her physical appearance, memory, and personality are altered so that she looks and behaves exactly like Joan Rivers—indeed, believes wholeheartedly that she *is* Joan Rivers. The INPC directors find this hilarious. Just for kicks (since they hold Agent X's agency in such low esteem) they abduct the real Joan Rivers and subject her to the same procedure in the opposite direction, turning her into an Agent X look-alike/act-alike. They send Joan (as Agent X) back to the agency and Agent X (as Joan) back to Hollywood and bite their lips to keep from cracking up. Luckily, the agency sees through the ruse and drags Agent X off the Red Carpet mid-celebrity-interview. Rogue agents must be pun-ished. She protests: "Don't you know who I am!? I'm Joan Rivers! I'm not an enemy of the state!" Someone in the van (who looks very much like Agent X), stares at her feet and feels guilty.

Variations on this sort of story go back at least to Locke (1689/1975, book II, chapter 27), who imagined the consciousness of a prince and cob-bler "switching bodies."[6] This showed, he thought, that the identity of a person consists in nothing but memories and conscious experience, which are independent of the body. Many have objected to Locke's argument. Joseph Butler, for example, pointed out that the argument is only compel-ling if we can be assured that the cobber is *genuinely remembering* the deeds of the prince, but Locke cannot assure us of this unless he simply begs the question. Peter van Inwagen put essentially the same point in colorful terms (worth quoting at length):

I know a prince, Charlie, and a cobbler, Harry. One day the following seems to hap-pen: Harry without warning begins to talk and act exactly as if he were Charlie. He exhibits both an unshakable conviction that he is Charlie and perfect knowledge of the most particular and intimate details of Charlie's life. . . . (And, of course, all this happens, or seems to happen to Charlie, but the other way round: He loses his horsemanship but becomes able to mend shoes.) . . . Should I be forced by this strange occurrence to concede that a person is not after all an organism and that the organism that had hitherto been "associated with" Charlie was now associated with Harry? Well, no, I certainly wouldn't say *that*. Better to say nothing than to talk nonsense. And, really, in such a case there would be a great deal to be said for saying nothing. The only thing that would be clearly true would be that something wholly mysterious had happened. What should one say if the Eiffel Tower suddenly sprouted wings and flew away? Probably there is nothing one should say, beyond admitting that one had no idea what the explanation of this phenomenon is. (van Inwagen 1990, 187–188)

Countless further variants on these sorts of cases—not all of them so fanciful—have been discussed in the philosophical literature. They put pressure on different philosophical accounts of what it is to persist, how we can be responsible for our actions, and indeed, how we conceptualize ourselves.

Platitudes?

Something might seem fishy. If Lewis and company are correct that we never have a philosophical problem with identity, what (aside from the INPC) explains the persistence of puzzled philosophers? Perhaps our trou-ble devolves from the clashing of our characterization of identity with intuitions about how to *apply* the identity relation. We characterized identity above as the relation that everything bears to itself. This encapsulates the logical property of *reflexivity*. Identity is also *transitive*: if Jones is Jekyll and Jekyll is Hyde, then Jones is Hyde. It is also symmetric: if Jekyll is Hyde, then Hyde is Jekyll. Moreover, if Jekyll is Hyde, then whatever can be truly predicated of Jekyll can be truly predicated of Hyde.

This last principle—known variously as the *Indiscernibility of Identicals* and *Leibniz's law*[7]—has been a longstanding source of puzzlement. A simple way of putting the same idea is that we can always substitute coreferring terms for each other without changing the truth-value of sentences (*salva veritate*). Suppose the sentence 'Jekyll is tall' is true. If Jekyll is Hyde (if 'Jekyll' and 'Hyde' refer to the same person), then the sentence 'Hyde is tall' must also be true—the sentence is in effect saying the same thing or expressing the same proposition: that *this guy* (whatever we call him) is tall. But now consider the true sentence 'Mary is in love with Jekyll'. When we substitute 'Hyde' for 'Jekyll', we seem to get a falsehood: Mary is *not* in love with Hyde—she fears him, in fact! What has gone wrong? Well, perhaps nothing. We can after all make *some* sense of the thought that Mary is in love with Hyde—for she *is* in love with Jekyll . . . and Jekyll *is* Hyde (her ignorance aside). She's in love with *that guy*.[8] Other examples are more recalcitrant. Take Quine's chestnuts from "Reference and Modality" (Quine 1953b): Giorgione is Barbarelli, and Giorgione was so called because of his size; not so for Barbarelli. Nine is the number of planets; necessarily, 9 is greater than 7; but the number of planets is not necessarily greater than 7. Quine's approach to these apparent counterexamples to the Indiscernibility of Identicals was to identify certain semantic situations—typically those involving belief, modality, or where the names involved are not "purely referential"—in which the principle is fallaciously applied.[9] He called these "opaque contexts," and much philosophical effort has been exerted trying to fully understand them.

Not surprisingly, the contrapositive of the Indiscernibility of Identicals (call it the *Nonidentity of Discernibles*) has also caused many headaches. It says that for any x and y, if x has any property y lacks, then x and y must be distinct. The same sorts of problems as we encountered above still apply: Jekyll seems to possess the property *is loved by Mary* while Hyde lacks it; so the principle wrongly implies that they are distinct. Similar gambits avail themselves: perhaps we're again in an opaque context, or no genuine *property* is expressed by 'is loved by Mary'—but then we're saddled again with the problem of identifying opaque contexts or distinguishing properties from mere predicates.

The Problem of Change and Persistence over Time

The same reasoning behind the Nonidentity of Discernibles lurks behind the old and fertile dispute between Heraclitus and Parmenides. Parmenides argued that change was impossible, for if something changes by gaining or losing a property, it becomes "what it is not." But that (Parmenides thought) is impossible. Reality is *permanence*; only *appearances* change. The slogans attributed to Heraclitus—that the world is change and that one cannot step twice in the same river[10]—record prima facie disagreement.

But there is a sense in which Heraclitus *agreed* with Parmenides. We might thus accuse these two of engaging in a merely verbal dispute. Heraclitus' dictum that the world is change can seem a bit ironic: the Heraclitean world is in fact one where no object changes. It's a world of change only in the sense that there's a constant stream of *different objects* that momentarily pop into and go out of existence, one after the other. You cannot step twice in the same river because as the water flows by, new rivers constantly come into and go out of existence. By way of analogy, consider a film: does it change? If we think of the film as a whole—sitting on the shelf, say—it seems static. It is simply a collection of frames that changes when we watch it. On the other hand, perhaps this is all that change *is*: being composed by various distinct "frames."

But this thought raises a worry about our own persistence. As Quine put it, "Undergoing change as I do, how can I be said to continue to be myself? Considering that a complete replacement of my material substance takes place every few years, how can I be said to continue to be I for the more than such a period at best" (Quine 1953a, 65). Yesterday, I had the property of being sore from playing too much basketball. Today, I lack that property. Does the Nonidentity of Discernibles show that I am no longer the same person? *How can I change and yet remain the same?* The very idea looks like a contradiction.

Not so fast. We must distinguish between *qualitative identity* and what philosophers refer to as *numerical identity*. Imagine a pair of twins. Call them Rod and Todd. Rod and Todd are special in that not only are they genetically identical, they are physically identical in general down to the cell of skin and flake of dander (or anyway, we can suppose that they are at *some* point in their life). Rod and Todd are identical in the *qualitative sense*: they look exactly the same; they have all the same qualities (properties).

And yet they are different: while *qualitatively* identical, they are *numerically* dissimilar in just the sense that Rod is not the same person as Todd. The story of Rod and Todd's adventures is a tale of *two people*, not one (hence "numerical" identity). We might imagine being friends with Rod and Todd and being put in situations where we weren't sure whether we were still talking with the same person, even though we could be quite sure that whichever person this was, he had all of the same properties of Rod. Suppose, during halftime, Rod gets up to grab a beer. We might wonder of the person returning whether he is the same as Rod—whether Todd just happened to walk in a minute later with a beer. We can thus ask whether these "two" people—the person who got up and walked out and the person who walked back in (who are, for all intents and purposes, duplicates)—are really one and the same person. So numerical and qualitative sameness can come apart in at least *one* direction: qualitative identity does not imply numerical identity. But we still might wonder about the other. Does numerical identity require qualitative identity? Does the Nonidentity of Discernibles show us that nothing can change?

Most philosophers suppose not, though, as with the debates about time, they disagree as to *how* things persist through change. Ordinarily, we regard things as changing and yet not *going out of existence* all the time. My car recently got new tires. It didn't at that point cease to be my car: some of its parts merely changed over. Intuitively, it seems that things can survive *some change* but not *other (more significant) changes*. Some philosophers—most famously, Descartes—attempt to solve the problem of *personal identity* by positing an immortal and unchanging soul that preserves our identity through change. The view faces several difficulties, not least of which is its inapplicability to "unsouled" objects.[11] As Quine put it, even if we find it "agreeable to be driven . . . to believe in a changeless and therefore immortal soul as the vehicle of my persisting self-identity," that solution won't help us understand the persistence of purely physical things like my car (Quine 1953a, 65).

We might attempt to repel the arguments against persistence through change by temporally indexing the properties. I possess the properties *sore-at-t_1* and *not-sore-at-t_2* (as it were, *eternally*), but as these are different properties, there's no problem.[12] A related strategy invokes the space-time analogy mentioned above. We often ascribe incompatible properties to the same object by ascribing them to that object's parts. I ask you if you're warm enough. You reply that you're warm and cold. Contradiction? No, you explain: while your trusty boots are keeping your feet warm, your hat is way too thin for these Idaho winters. Spatial parts can possess incompatible properties. Perhaps objects persist—or as defenders of this view like to say, "perdure"—in virtue of possessing different "temporal parts." The *perdurantist* solves the apparent paradox of change in much the way we solved the apparent paradox of warm and cold: when we predicate *sore-*

ness of me, we predicate it of some of my previous temporal *parts* (and luckily withhold it from my *present* temporal parts).

So persistence through change is no problem. On this view, objects *change* simply by possessing different temporal parts (much like movies change by possessing different-looking frames). They *persist* by being extended in both space *and* time.[13] Some perdurantists thus call themselves *four-dimensionalists*.[14] Though the perdurantist has a natural ally in the eternalist, the views are separable. For instance, the "growing block" model of time (according to which the past is real and fixed and the present is open) would seem to accommodate the existence of (growing) spatiotemporal worms. Discussion continues about whether a presentist can acknowledge temporal parts (see Lombard 1999).

Many find the perdurantist solution philosophically expensive and unwarranted. It implies, for example, that I am not now "wholly present." That seems odd.[15] Things just *endure* change—they gain and lose parts as time flows by, but that does not make them "spread out through time" in some special way. These *endurantists* can reply to the problem of persistence through change by taking a page from the presentist's playbook: so long as we "have a care for tense," the Nonidentity of Discernibles does not generate a contradiction. Although I *had* the property of soreness, I am *now* not sore. These philosophers deny that change poses any real problem for persistence. Thus, like the perdurantists, though endurantists have a natural ally in the *presentists*, most regard their views as independent. And as with the debate between the presentists and eternalists, the debate between the *endurantists* and *perdurantists* (or the "3Ders" and "4Ders") has been supposed to be merely verbal. Each camp, of course, opposes this conclusion and supposes its view to deal more effectively with various metaphysical paradoxes.[16]

The Self

How do questions about the metaphysics of persistence bear on basic questions about what sorts of things we are? How do different approaches to the latter question bear on the former? This is a rich area of philosophical inquiry. We can dip into it by considering how another one of our "platitudes" about identity—this time, *transitivity*—butts up against our intuitions.

Take the ship of Theseus.[17] While at sea, its ingenious crew carries out repairs, discarding worn wooden planks and replacing them with aluminum. Equally ingenious mariners somehow salvage these cast-off parts—every last one—and eventually rebuild the wooden ship. So we have a wooden ship that has the very same parts as Theseus' original ship and an aluminum ship that seems to have survived each change to the original. Now, it certainly seems plausible that either of the resulting ships is the original ship (after all, if the wooden ship did not exist, the aluminum ship would clearly be regarded as *the same ship*; ditto for the wooden ship if the aluminum ship did not exist). But they cannot *both* be identical to original ship. For suppose they were: if the Wooden is the Original and the Original is the Aluminum, then the Wooden is the Aluminum. But that's not so: *whatever* they are identical to, *they* are not identical to each other—they are, after all, *two ships*. So which is the original ship?

There's much to say about this case—but what does it have to do with the *self*? Well, for one, just as we can imagine a ship "fissioning" into two things, we can imagine *people* fissioning. Perhaps the INPC transplants the two hemispheres of your brain to two brainless bodies, or perhaps, to use Parfit's (1984) famous example, the matter-transporter breaks down and creates two whole duplicate copies of you. Either way, you cannot be identical two *both* of them for the same reason that the original ship cannot be both the wooden ship and the aluminum ship: two people cannot be one. But if the procedure is *symmetric*, it seems intolerably arbitrary to claim that only one or the other person is you. Nor does it look very plausible to say that *neither* is you.[18]

Parfit (1984) offered the radical suggestion that identity is not "what we care about" when it comes to our survival. Because the identity relation is transitive, I cannot be *identical* to the duplicates; but I can share their memories, beliefs, desires, personalities, goals, projects, and so on. From *my* point of view, things are just as good as being identical (indeed, I might not even *know* about my "competition"). When I consider what I *care about* in survival, it is my *psychology*.

Parfit's suggestion has generated an immense literature.[19] It is itself part of an immense literature exploring the idea that the criteria for personal identity over time must be (at least partly) psychological.[20] Specifically what psychological features matter or how these features are realized are deep and interesting questions. As we mentioned above, Descartes believed that he was a constant, immaterial soul. Hume claimed to find no such evidence of this: all he could recognize were a bundle of different perceptions.

Descartes also nicely illustrates a recent concern over the psychological approach. He thought, recall, that the mind and body were distinct substances. He could doubt the existence of the latter but not the former, so by the Nonidentity of Discernibles (despite concerns already raised), they must be distinct. But then what is my relation to the organism sitting in my chair? That creature thinks, doesn't it? Are two things thus thinking these same thoughts? That is strange. Eric Olson (1997, 2002, 2003) has been leading a campaign to rid the philosophy of personal identity of psychology. He claims that we are thinking human animals—that we were once fetuses and may someday end up in a persistent vegetative state.

As with the issues of time and identity, our philosophical puzzlement about the nature of the self is itself puzzling. We ask *what is the self*? but it might seem that we can have no better *access* to anything but ourselves. For those of us who aren't quite *sure* what we are, *how can we* not *be*? Do we misunderstand the question? Are we diving into a shallow puddle, thinking it a deep pool?

Recent Work on Time and Identity: The Essays

I've claimed that the concepts of time and identity are intimately connected.[21] Nevertheless, the essays are divided (rather roughly) into four sections corresponding to their respective centers of gravity: *Time*, *Identity*, *The Self*, and *Death*. Here's a brief tour.

Time

The essays in this section address the metaphysics of time and the conceptual links between time and freedom. The first two—by Lynne Rudder Baker and Lawrence B. Lombard—express different kinds of dissatisfaction with the debate between the eternalist and the presentist.

Baker, in "Temporal Reality" (chapter 1), argues that each position alone fails to cohere with either physics or human experience. The A-theory, though in accord with our *experience* of time, appears incomplete or incompatible with modern physics.[22] The B-theory, though apparently required for physics, cannot make sense of either the inexorable "flow" of time or the fact that you have less than a year to live or that the earth is now billions of years old. Baker proposes an intriguing theory of time—the "BA-theory"—which takes the B-series as basic. She writes, "In the absence of self-conscious beings, events occur (tenselessly) at various times, and some events are (tenselessly) later than others. But there is no ongoing now" (32). Her account makes the A-series facts relative to the experiences of self-conscious beings: without such beings, "there are no A-series" (32). But rather than taking this feature as implying that the A-series is unreal or "merely mind-dependent," she argues that the existence of self-conscious beings is a genuine feature of reality that has implications for *other* general features of reality. She closes her essay with an extended discussion of the implications of the BA-theory for the relation between time and existence.

This relation looms large for Lombard, in "Time for a Change: A Polemic against the Presentism–Eternalism Debate" (chapter 2). He assimilates the ancient debate about change between Heraclitus and Parmenides to the contemporary debate between the presentists and the eternalists: perhaps they too are engaged in a merely verbal dispute. As we have seen above, it is surprisingly difficult to explicate these views in a way that generates a substantive dispute. Lombard interrogates glosses by Merricks (1995), Zimmerman (1998), and Sider (2001), concluding that they all founder on an equivocation of tense. "If all the relevant verbs [in the definitions of eternalism and presentism] are in the present tense, there is no substantive dispute between the presentist and eternalist. And if all the relevant verbs are disjunctively omnitemporal, there is again no substantive dispute" (71–72).

Another way that eternalists and presentists might attempt to spell out their differences involves the "fixity" of the future. The eternalist's claim that past, present, and future entities are all equally "real" might usefully parlay into the claim that those facts are *fixed*—a claim the presentist may deny, at least about the *future*. Whether or not this suggestion will satisfy "skeptics" like Lombard, it raises an interesting question about the relation of our metaphysics of time and our view of our freedom. Suppose the future *is* fixed; then if I sprain my ankle on the basketball court tomorrow, it is true *now* that that event will come to pass and there is nothing I can do to prevent it. So the argument for fatalism goes. A similar issue arises in discussions of time travel.[23] Kurt Gödel provided solutions to Einstein's field equations that vindicated the possibility of "closed timelike curves," elevating time travel from entertaining fiction to tantalizing possibility.[24] Many philosophers were skeptical: they worried about logical paradoxes that might follow from meddling time travelers bent on bringing about their own nonexistence. David Lewis set many minds at ease in his seminal (1976) essay: time travelers can't, say, kill their grandfathers for the commonplace reason that they *didn't*. Sider (2002) agrees, but not everyone got on board. Kadri Vihvelin (1996) argued that this treatment downplayed the strange *inability* of time travelers to do what we otherwise think them perfectly capable of doing. In "Context, Conditionals, Fatalism, Time Travel, and Freedom" (chapter 3), John W. Carroll offers a contextualist account of counterfactual conditionals designed to sort out the dispute between Lewis–Sider and Vihvelin on the abilities of time travelers and reveal the problems with the fatalist's argument. On this account, sentences like 'Tim the time traveler cannot kill his Grandfather' are *true* in some conversational contexts and false in others. Including certain historical facts into the "common ground" of our conversational context (for example, the precise date of Grandfather's actual death) does imply that Tim cannot kill Grandfather. But this, argues Carroll, doesn't suggest any "logical shackles" for the time traveler: it simply amounts to the proposition that Tim *did not* kill Grandfather.

Other worries beset the *presentist* if we take him at his word that no past and future individuals exist. How do we yet claim that Lincoln was shot by Booth and that the earth will orbit the sun? Mark Hinchliff addresses this question in his "The Identity of the Past" (chapter 4), locating "property presentism" as the principle responsible for these worries. Roughly speaking, this principle says that if something has a property, that something exists. Put that way, it seems impossible to deny. Hinchliff weakens its hold over presentists by exploring the analogous relation between *actualism* (the view that only actual entities exist) and *property actualism*. He argues that the analogy breaks down when we take a certain view about the difference between the past and the future (on some presentist's lights): whereas the future, like the merely possible, is "irreducibly general" (resisting cross-time or cross-world identifications), the past "has a full identificatory structure of particular instances underlying it" (104). This point opens the door to an extensive batch of apparent counterexamples to property presentism. And as its fortunes wane, so does the force of the problems surrounding referring to past people and events.

Identity

Identity may be simple, but as we've seen, there's plenty of room for argument over how to *apply* that concept to problems in metaphysics and the philosophy of language. We begin with the latter. Recall that one of the "platitudes" regarding identity was the principle of *substitutivity* or the *Indiscernibility of Identicals*. Although substitutivity of identicals fails in opaque contexts, it is generally thought that when names *are* "purely referential"—for example, when the names are "rigid designators" or "directly referential"[25]—the substitutivity principle is true. But things may not be so simple. In "Identity through Change and Substitutivity *Salva Veritate*" (chapter 5), Reinaldo Elugardo and Robert J. Stainton present a new puzzle about substituting coreferring names into sentences describing accidental change. The puzzle arises from the fact that an object's name often changes along with its other properties. Toronto, for example, once had small, waterlogged streets and was thus called 'Muddy York'. But its streets were drained and its name changed to 'Toronto'. We might say that 'Muddy York evolved into Toronto'. But if we grant the substitutivity principle and grant that the names 'Muddy York' and 'Toronto' refer to the same thing, we arrive at a contradiction: "Toronto both did and did not evolve into Toronto" (113).

Their solution to this paradox abjures construing "___ evolved into ___" as an opaque context as philosophically expensive and unwarranted. Instead, Elugardo and Stainton diagnose the problem as devolving from the polysemy of the names involved: we use names sometimes to refer to an object *over time* (a continuant, for example) and sometimes to an object *at a time*. The paradox thus devolves from a subtle shift in lexical role of 'Toronto' and 'Muddy York'. Though their solution professes metaphysical neutrality, it raises an important point for semantics (and thus for metaphysics by common association): the possibility of some kind of reference-shifting need not generate opaque contexts. The relation '___ evolved into ___' "just does apply to the object however conceived" (124).

At a metaphilosophical level, Ned Markosian—in "Identifying the Problem of Personal Identity" (chapter 6)—suggests that the standard way of putting the problem improperly biases the ensuing debate in favor of four-dimensionalism. Philosophers will often put the problem this way: under what conditions are person x at time t_1 and person y at time t_2 in fact the same person? But to what entities do the phrases 'person x at t_1' and 'person y at t_2' refer? Four-dimensionalists (perdurantists) have a ready answer: *to the temporal parts of person x and person y*. Three-dimensionalists (endurantists) have no truck with this—for they deny that persons have temporal parts. They prefer to ask after the conditions under which something that is a person at t_1 is the same person as something that is a person at t_2. But as we have seen, invoking sortal identity in order to state the problem incurs a heavy philosophical burden.

Drawing on a new theory of property instantiations, Markosian proposes a new way of putting the problem that he claims levels the playing field for the 3Der and 4Der. Properties, he notes, are often instantiated for extended periods of time: the sun has been hot for several billion years; leaves stay green in summer and turn red in the fall; the number seven has always been prime. Call these instantiations "episodes." Now we can ask some questions about whether this episode is the same as that. In particular, we can ask of persons, *What are the conditions under which an instance of personhood at t_1 is part of the same episode of personhood as an instance of personhood at t_2?* This characterization helps make sense of some of the vexing problems facing the 3Ders (e.g., the fission problem, the time travel problem, and the fetus/corpse problems). Though particularly welcome for the 3Der, success here should be regarded as good news all around, as it seems preferable not to presuppose one way of thinking about a problem by merely stating it (a theme Markosian sounds more than once in his chapter).

As noted above, ascriptions of moral responsibility often seem to depend on ascriptions of identity among agents. Neal A. Tognazzini in his "Persistence and Responsibility" (chapter 7) rebuts several arguments for the claim that the metaphysics of perdurance leaves no room for the existence of responsible agents. Consider our Agent X again, after her imprisonment but before she is subjected to the (Joan Rivers) Process. To be held responsible for her actions, it clearly must be the case that the prisoner *is* Agent X. But critics of perdurantism point out that the object in custody is not *all* of Agent X. Her *captured* temporal part differs from her *thieving* temporal part: they are *numerically distinct*. But if distinct, how can we hold the captured person-stages responsible for crimes they literally didn't commit? Tognazzini replies that this and other objections simply represent prejudice against the perdurantist way of conceiving of numerical identity. He writes: "The perdurantist can quite plausibly claim that what is required for an attribution of moral responsibility to be appropriate is not that 'the self-same entity' be 'wholly present' at both times, but rather that the self-same *person* be present (but not wholly) at both times" (154). And the perdurantist can easily make sense of *this* fact. In responding to this and similar objections, Tognazzini fleshes out perdurantism's ability to integrate ascriptions of moral properties to continuants.

Geoffrey Gorham, on the other hand, seeks to pin down one famous philosopher's metaphysical commitments. In "Descartes on Persistence and Temporal Parts" (chapter 8), Gorham contends that the best way to reconstruct Descartes's argument for the immortality of the soul makes use of the modern resource of perdurantism. His interpretation begins with a suggestive passage from the Third Meditation:

For a lifespan can be divided into countless parts each completely independent of the others, so that it does not follow from the fact that I existed a little while ago that I must exist now, unless there is some cause which as it were creates me afresh at this moment—that is, preserves me.

This apparent independence of different "momentary" souls strongly suggests a perdurantist reading of persistence: perhaps we should conceive of a Cartesian soul as composed of countless *temporal* parts, each dependent on some external causal influence for its existence. However, this interpretation raises some very tricky problems of interpretation for Descartes.

One might think, for example (following Bennett 2001), that a genuine substance cannot possess distinct substantial parts; that it would be a "mere pseudo-substance" (Bennett 2001, vol. 1, 98). Gorham finds precedent in Descartes for denying this doctrine. More worrisome, however, is Descartes's famous insistence on the *simplicity* of the soul—as we've seen, this simple, unchanging soul is one way of attempting to secure an agent's numerical identity in the face of qualitative change. The solution to this problem, Gorham suggests, lies in the unchanging *individual essence* behind each thinking substance. *This* is the Cartesian ego that persists unchanged—and indeed may be argued to exist out of time and thus, in a sense, to be "immortal by its very nature" (165).

The Self

The essays in this section share a focus on our first-person experience—our understanding of our *selves*. What sort of things are we? Are we immortal souls like Descartes thought? Are we instead bundles of perceptions and thoughts? Do we even need to settle these issues to enjoy a conception of ourselves?

In "Persons, Animals, and Human Beings" (chapter 9), Harold Noonan leans on an intriguing view of first-person reference to further articulate his approach to personal identity and personhood.[26] As we've seen, we might ask very generally, "What changes can a person can survive? What changes will terminate a person's existence?" Noonan argues that the *indexical formulation* of the problem is more basic: "Our interest in personal identity is fundamentally an interest in our *own* identity." On this view, persons are just the objects of first-person reference. Armed with this simple conception of persons, Noonan suggests that defenders of the psychological approach to personal identity can rebut Olson's "too many minds objection," also known as the "thinking animal" problem. Perhaps we should admit that each of us "is" an animal "in the sense of coinciding with one and being constituted of the same matter as one—but this 'is' is the 'is' of constitution, not identity" (195).[27] But even if persons and human animals coincide in this manner and both think "'I'-thoughts," it does not follow that their thoughts are about different thinkers. Noonan thus dissolves the skeptical difficulties associated with the too many minds objection—"Both the person and the animal can know that their utterance of 'I am a person' is true" (198)—for 'I'-thoughts always refer to the *person* thinking them. His essay concludes with an extended defense of this approach from Olson's (2002) objections.

Jenann Ismael also takes up the issue of first-person reference in "Me, Again" (chapter 10). She begins with Anscombe's objection to Descartes's argument that he is an immaterial thinking substance—roughly, that Descartes cannot guarantee that the same referent is picked out in different 'I'-thoughts without presupposing some criterion of identity for selves (which is what's under discussion).[28] But Ismael points out that unlike other indexicals (like 'here' and 'now'), which can be mistakenly substituted for one another, "it's hard to make sense of the idea of mistakenly intersubstituting someone else's I-occurrence for one of our own" (212). Criteria of identity "are not employed in *re*identification" (212). We may thus manage to refer to ourselves (both at a time and over time) without possessing an explicit *concept* of the self. This realization has suggested to some philosophers that the self must in fact be a *primitive*. Ismael argues that we can avoid this conclusion by seeing the concept of the self as *constituted* by these reidentifications (rather than being presupposed by them).

John Perry—in "Selves and Self-Concepts" (chapter 11)—likewise resists the thought that the self is something *mysterious*. He proposes a "straightforward theory" of the self, offering the following analogy: a *neighbor* is just a *person* thought of under the relation of *living next door* to someone; likewise, a *self* is just a *person* thought of under the relation of *identity*. "Self is to identity as neighbor is to *living next door to*" (229). On this view, philosophical perplexities about the self stem not from the self being a special kind of *object* (selves, like neighbors, are just *persons*), but by the unique epistemic structure of this concept. Normally, we integrate knowledge about ourselves gained from external sources and from "internal" sources (what Perry calls "normally self-informative ways of knowing about a person") which are usually immune to error. The first 'normally' stems from cases like the amnesiac war hero who learns about himself from written accounts without knowing that those written accounts describe *his* actions; the second 'normally' owes to the recognition that our modes of gaining information about our surroundings and such often presuppose contingent facts about how our senses are "hooked up."[29] Just how we integrate information from these sources may lurk behind the different *public identities* we assume (e.g., teacher, student, football fan, and so forth). Our *identity* consists in those parts of our self-concept that are central—those things we cannot imagine ourselves not being. This suggests to Perry a sort of "bundle of bundles" theory of the self on which different "competing centers of agency" jockey for position. Such an account, he argues, makes good sense of our not-always-coherent mental life.

A natural way of elaborating Perry's "centers of agency" is the desire satisfaction account of well-being (pursued by Parfit). We often define ourselves by our desires or long-term plans; we look forward to having those desires fulfilled—that benefits us. But our desires often change: what I wanted ten years ago is *not* what I want now. In "Ex Ante Desire and Post Hoc Satisfaction" (chapter 12), Harriet Baber addresses this problem for the desire satisfaction model of well-being, claiming that the satisfaction even of preferences I can no longer identify with *does* benefit us, even if we are not better off, even if we don't *appreciate* our desires being satisfied. This stance leaves us better able to make sense of the obscure artist who only benefits after her death. Baber defends the view that we benefit *when the desires are satisfied*.

Death

Just as we want to speak of posthumous benefits, we may want to account for posthumous harms. Rather than achieving renown after death, our obscure artist's work may be stolen or maligned. Perhaps death itself is a harm. Defenders of this position face an ancient challenge: how could there be a harm without a subject? As Epicurus famously wrote in his "Letter to Menoeceus": "so long as we exist, death is not with us; but when it comes, then we do not exist" (Epicurus 1940, 31). Many have found this paradoxical: we clearly want to say that death is an evil, but can we coherently claim that we are *harmed* even when we do not exist?

Construing death as an evil seems to place some constraints on our metaphysics: after my death, the presentist will claim that I do not exist to be benefited or harmed. Ben Bradley claims in his "Eternalism and Death's Badness" (chapter 13) that we must be eternalists to make sense of the cross-temporal relation between a person and that person's death. Although they do not exist simultaneously, they do both exist. He spends the bulk of his essay responding to arguments offered by Harry S. Silverstein (1980/1993, 2000) that death is an "atemporal" harm to the person who has died. Bradley contends in contrast (and in a spirit similar to Baber) that death is bad for a person when that person *would have* been living a good life had death not occurred.

Silverstein finds this perplexing. He addresses Bradley's criticism in his essay "The Time of the Evil of Death" (chapter 14), sharpening and expanding his previous view that the question 'when is S's death an evil for S?' has, and needs, no answer. He points out that Bradley's view seems to entail some strange conclusions: for example, that we ought to celebrate the point at which a dead loved one *would have died* had he or she not died

the death he or she *in fact* died—as we might celebrate a loved one's release from prison.

Barbara Levenbook too wishes to accommodate the intuition that death is an evil (ceteris paribus). And she makes clear what is at stake: the very intelligibility of our possessing a "right to life" plausibly depends on our ability to explain how death counts as a frustration of interests. Addressing the Epicurean challenge in the guise of what she calls "The Retroactivity Problem" (chapter 15) and also developing previous work (Levenbook 1984), Levenbook articulates a series of principles that give rise to the problem. Ultimately, the issue depends more on moral rather than metaphysical principles—in particular, a substantive theory of the "good for" and "bad for" relations. Thus, it would seem our intuitions about death carry with them more than merely metaphysical implications.

Acknowledgments

I would like to thank the editors of this volume for the invitation to write this introduction and for many helpful suggestions for improving it.

Notes

1. See, e.g., C. S. Peirce 1982, 455.

2. As with much of philosophy, Aristotle has some particularly rich discussions of time; see in particular his *Physics* (book VIII) and *De interpretatione* (chapter 9).

3. Though as we shall see below, it may not be quite right to identify these positions along these lines.

4. For an excellent discussion of McTaggart's argument and responses to it, see Le Poidevin 2003, 127–147.

5. Here I follow Crisp's (2003) formulation of the problem, also addressed by Lombard (1999) and this volume.

6. Such cases are discussed in much more detail by Williams (1970), Nozick (1981), and Parfit (1984), each of which is reprinted in Martin and Barresi 2003; Perry 1975 also collects many classic writings on personal identity.

7. Though some reserve this name for the *converse* principle: that for all x and y, if x and y are indiscernible (i.e., if they have all the same properties), then they are in fact identical; this principle has historically been regarded as more controversial—so long as we take properties to be "sparse." See Black 1952 and Hawthorne 2003, §2.2 for discussion.

8. Salmon (1981) offers an excellent discussion of cases of unknown identities. Examples like these go back at least to Frege (1969) and arguably to Eubulides' paradox of the masked man: The masked man is your father; you don't know who the masked man is; hence (paradoxically), you do not know who your father is (see Rescher 2001, 103).

9. See Quine 1953b, 140; Harold Noonan has suggested we identify a class of predicates "whose reference is affected by the subject term to which they are attached" and call them "Abelardian" after the eleventh century philosopher Peter Abelard (Noonan 1991, 188).

10. These reports (of unknown accuracy) come from Aristotle's *Physics* (8.3.253b9) and Plato's *Cratylus* (402a), respectively.

11. Perry offers a neat argument against recourse to the soul as the "vehicle" for our persistence in "The First Night" of his *Dialogue on Personal Identity and Immortality*:

> If . . . identity of persons consisted in identity of immaterial unobservable souls, then judgments of personal identity of the sort we make every day whenever we greet a friend or avoid a pest are really judgments about souls. . . . But if such judgments were really about souls, they would all be groundless and without foundation. For we have no direct method of observing sameness of soul. . . . But our judgments about persons are not all simply groundless and silly, so we must not be judging of immaterial souls after all. (Perry 1978, 11–12)

12. Well, no problem with the Nonidentity of Discernibles; some worry about the problem of "temporary intrinsics" (see Lewis 1988).

13. These spatiotemporally extended objects are sometimes called "space-time worms," though I much prefer the image of the "space-time *salami*."

14. See Sider 1997, 2001 and Hawley 2001 for extended explications and defenses of this family of views. Its popularity notwithstanding, some find the term 'four-dimensionalism' to be nonideal; for it's not yet clear that space has only three dimensions (or time only one), or even that either has a definite number.

15. See, e.g., Wiggins 1980, Lombard 1986, and van Inwagen 1990 on the desirability of things persisting "wholly present."

16. Sider (2001) offers a vigorous rebuttal of the "metaphysical skeptic" and an illustration of four-dimensionalism's virtues.

17. The problem is mentioned first in Plutarch (*Lives*) and returned to modern philosophical consciousness by Hobbes (*De corpore*); I loosely follow Chisholm's (1976, chapter 3) presentation.

18. Suppose there's a lag in the duplication: the transporter "moves" me down to the planet's surface and then five minutes later malfunctions and produces a duplicate. Do I then go out of existence? Do I suffer "death from competition" (as Perry 1978 put it)?

19. Many oppose the suggestion that survival does not involve identity. As Lewis put it:

Suppose I wonder whether I will survive the coming battle, brainwashing, brain transplant, journey by matter-transmitter, purported reincarnation or resurrection, fission into twins, fusion with someone else, or what not. What do I really care about? . . . What matters in survival is survival. If I wonder whether I will survive, what I mostly care about is quite simple. When it's all over, will I myself—the very same person now thinking these thoughts and writing these words—still exist? Will any one of those who do exist afterward be me? In other words, *what matters in survival is identity*—identity between the I who exists now and the surviving I who will, I hope, still exist then. (Lewis 1976, 55)

Lewis and Sider both solve the "fission problem" by employing temporal parts.

20. Indeed, the possibility of fission was first conceived (as early as Butler [1736/1897]) as an objection to the psychological approach to personal identity. We might think of Parfit's particular radical spin on the psychological approach to *survival* as a way of disarming this objection.

21. Dividing the essays in the present volume into sections apparently disregards this fact. Organization often has the effect of imposing more order than exists—best, then, to view these containers as porous.

22. Baker suggests that this is true of the growing block theory as well; see Hinchliff 1996 and 2000 for a defense of the compatibility of presentism with relativity.

23. The possibility of time travel raises all manner of fascinating problems (and entertaining stories) that bear on issues of time and identity. Does one have to be an eternalist to believe in time travel (see Keller and Nelson 2001; Sider 2001, sec. 7.2)? What do we say about the time traveler conversing with herself: how many people are talking? Might there be situations where a time traveler is only *indeterminately* identical with someone who steps into a time machine (Slater 2005)?

24. Palle Yourgrau has written extensively and illuminatingly on Gödel's views; see, e.g., Yourgrau 1999; cf. Earman 1995.

25. In the sense of Kripke 1980.

26. For previous statements of this view, see Noonan 1998 and 2003.

27. This would *seem* to represent a shift from Noonan's earlier views on constitution as identity (see Noonan 1993).

28. Bertrand Russell expressed a similar sentiment when he quipped:

'I think, therefore I am' says rather more than is strictly certain. It might seem as though we were quite sure of being the same person today as we were yesterday, and this is no doubt true in some sense. But the real Self is as hard to arrive at as the real table and does not seem to have that absolute, convincing certainty that belongs to particular experiences. When I look at my table and see a certain brown colour, what is quite certain at once is not '*I* am seeing a brown colour', but rather, 'a brown colour is being seen'. (Russell 1912, 19)

29. Perry's use of 'normally' here recalls Daniel Dennett's classic paper "Where Am I?" (chapter 17 of Dennett 1981) in which he describes having his brain transplanted to a vat where it controls his brainless body by remote. We might imagine performing this procedure on two patients and putting the feeds on a switch. Perhaps it would make sense for one patient to express doubt that she was experiencing her own sensations. Or compare the film *Being John Malkovich*.

References

Bennett, J. 2001. *Learning from Six Philosophers*, 2 vols. Oxford: Oxford University Press.

Black, M. 1952. The Identity of Indiscernibles. *Mind* 51:153–164.

Butler, J. 1736/1897. *The Analogy of Religion, Natural and Revealed*. London: Henry G. Bohn.

Chisholm, R. 1976. *Person and Object*. La Salle: Open Court.

Crisp, T. 2003. Presentism. In *The Oxford Handbook of Metaphysics*, ed. M. Loux and D. Zimmerman. Oxford: Oxford University Press.

Dennett, D. 1981. *Brainstorms*. Cambridge, MA: MIT Press/Bradford Books.

Earman, J. 1995. *Bangs, Crunches, Whimpers, and Shrieks: Singularities and Acausalities in Relativistic Spacetimes*. Oxford: Oxford University Press.

Epicurus. 1940. Letter to Menoeceus. Trans. C. Bailey. In *The Stoic and Epicurean Philosophers*, ed. W. Oates. New York: The Modern Library.

Frege, G. 1969. *Translations from the Philosophical Writings of Gottlob Frege*. Trans. P. Geach and M. Black. Oxford: Blackwell.

Hawley, K. 2001. *How Things Persist*. Oxford: Oxford University Press.

Hawthorne, J. 2003. Identity. In *The Oxford Handbook of Metaphysics*, ed. M. Loux and D. Zimmerman. Oxford: Oxford University Press.

Hinchliff, M. 1996. The Puzzle of Change. In *Philosophical Perspectives 10: Metaphysics*, ed. J. Tomberlin. Oxford: Blackwell.

Hinchliff, M. 2000. A Defense of Presentism in a Relativistic Setting. *Philosophy of Science* 67:S575–S586.

Keller, S., and M. Nelson. 2001. Presentists Should Believe in Time-Travel. *Australasian Journal of Philosophy* 79:333–345.

Kripke, S. 1980. *Naming and Necessity*. Cambridge, MA: Harvard University Press.

Le Poidevin, R. 2003. *Travels in Four Dimensions*. Oxford: Oxford University Press.

Levenbook, B. 1984. Harming Someone after His Death. *Ethics* 94:407–419.

Lewis, D. 1976. The Paradoxes of Time Travel. *American Philosophical Quarterly* 13:145–152.

Lewis, D. 1986. *On the Plurality of Worlds*. Oxford: Basil Blackwell.

Lewis, D. 1988. Rearrangement of Particles: Reply to Lowe. *Analysis* 48:65–72.

Locke, J. 1975 [1689]. *Essay Concerning Human Understanding*. Oxford: Oxford University Press.

Lombard, L. 1986. *Events: A Metaphysical Study*. London: Routledge & Kegan Paul.

Lombard, L. 1999. On the Alleged Incompatibility of Presentism and Temporal Parts. *Philosophia* 27:253–260.

Martin, R., and J. Barresi, eds. 2003. *Personal Identity*. Oxford: Blackwell.

McTaggart, J. M. E. 1993 [1908]. The Unreality of Time. In *The Philosophy of Time*, ed. R. Le Poidevin and M. McBeath. Oxford: Oxford University Press.

Merricks, T. 1995. On the Incompatibility of Enduring and Perduring Entities. *Mind* 104:521–531.

Noonan, H. W. 1991. Indeterminate Identity, Contingent Identity and Abelardian Predicates. *Philosophical Quarterly* 41:183–193.

Noonan, H. 1993. Constitution Is Identity. *Mind* 102:133–146.

Noonan, H. 1998. Animalism versus Lockeanism: A Current Controversy. *Philosophical Quarterly* 48:302–318.

Noonan, H. 2003. *Personal Identity*, 2nd ed. London: Routledge.

Nozick, R. 1981. *Philosophical Explanations*. Cambridge, MA: Harvard University Press.

Olson, E. 1997. *The Human Animal*. Oxford: Oxford University Press.

Olson, E. 2002. Thinking Animals and the Reference of 'I'. *Philosophical Topics* 30:189–208.

Olson, E. 2003. An Argument for Animalism. In *Personal Identity*, ed. R. Martin and J. Barresi. Oxford: Blackwell.

Parfit, D. 1984. *Reasons and Persons*. Oxford: Oxford University Press.

Peirce, C. S. 1982. *Writings of Charles S. Peirce*, vol. 6. Indianapolis: Indiana University Press.

Perry, J. 1978. *A Dialogue on Personal Identity and Immortality*. Indianapolis: Hackett.

Perry, J., ed. 1975. *Personal Identity.* Berkeley: University of California Press.

Quine, W. V. O. 1953a. Identity, Ostension, and Hypostasis. In *From a Logical Point of View.* Cambridge, MA: Harvard University Press.

Quine, W. V. O. 1953b. Reference and Modality. In *From a Logical Point of View.* Cambridge, MA: Harvard University Press.

Rescher, N. 2001. *Paradoxes: Their Roots, Range, and Resolution.* La Salle: Open Court.

Russell, B. 1912. *The Problems of Philosophy.* Indianapolis: Hackett.

Salmon, N. U. 1981. *Reference and Essence.* Princeton: Princeton University Press.

Sider, T. 1997. Four-Dimensionalism. *Philosophical Review* 106:197–231.

Sider, T. 2001. *Four-Dimensionalism.* Oxford: Oxford University Press.

Sider, T. 2002. Time Travel, Coincidences, and Counterfactuals. *Philosophical Studies* 110:115–138.

Silverstein, H. 1980. The Evil of Death. Reprinted in J. Fischer, ed., *The Metaphysics of Death,* Stanford: Stanford University Press, 1993.

Silverstein, H. 2000. The Evil of Death Revisited. In *Midwest Studies in Philosophy,* vol. 24: *Life and Death: Metaphysics and Ethics,* ed. P. French and H. Wettstein. Malden, MA: Blackwell.

Slater, M. H. 2005. The Necessity of Time Travel (on Pain of Indeterminacy). *Monist* 88:362–369.

Smart, J. J. C. 1981. The Reality of the Future. *Philosophia* 10:141–150.

van Inwagen, P. 1990. *Material Beings.* Ithaca: Cornell University Press.

Vihvelin, K. 1996. What Time Travelers Cannot Do. *Philosophical Studies* 81:315–330.

Wiggins, D. 1980. *Sameness and Substance.* Cambridge, MA: Harvard University Press.

Williams, B. 1970. The Self and the Future. *Philosophical Review* 79:161–180.

Yourgrau, P. 1999. *Gödel Meets Einstein.* La Salle: Open Court.

Zimmerman, D. 1998. Temporary Intrinsics and Presentism. In *Metaphysics: The Big Questions,* ed. P. van Inwagen and D. Zimmerman. Oxford: Blackwell.

I Time

1 Temporal Reality

Lynne Rudder Baker

Nonphilosophers, if they think of philosophy at all, wonder why people work in metaphysics. After all, metaphysics, as Auden once said of poetry, makes nothing happen (Auden 1940). Yet some very intelligent people are driven to spend their lives exploring metaphysical theses. Part of what motivates metaphysicians is the appeal of grizzly puzzles (like the paradox of the heap or the puzzle of the ship of Theseus). But the main reason to work in metaphysics, for me at least, is to understand the shared world that we all encounter and interact with. And the shared world that we all encounter includes us self-conscious beings and our experience. The world that we inhabit is unavoidably a temporal world: the signing of the Declaration of Independence is later than the Lisbon earthquake; the cold war is in the past; your death is in the future. There is no getting away from time.

The ontology of time is currently dominated by two theories: presentism, according to which "only currently existing objects are real" (Sider 2001, 11), and eternalism, according to which "past and future objects and times are just as real as currently existing ones" (ibid.).[1] In my opinion, neither presentism nor eternalism yields a satisfactory ontology of time. Presentism seems both implausible on its face and in conflict with the special theory of relativity, and eternalism gives us no handle on time as universally experienced in terms of an ongoing now. (There is a third theory, the "growing block universe," according to which the past is real but the future is not; but it also conflicts with the special theory of relativity.[2]) So, I shall bypass these theories for now and return to them later.

This chapter has two parts. Part I aims to develop a way to understand time that is adequate both to physics and to human experience. It begins with McTaggart's framework of the A-series and the B-series—the framework that underlies both presentism and eternalism.[3] I shall set out a theory (that I call "the BA-theory") that shows how the A- and B-series are related without reducing either to the other. Then, I shall draw out some metaphysical implications of the view. Part II is a discussion of time and existence; more particularly, it is a discussion of the relation between the temporal world and the nontemporal domain of the unrestricted existential quantifier. I shall argue that the world—though not the domain of the unrestricted existential quantifier—is ontologically different at different times.

I

The A-Series and the B-Series

There are two distinct ways in which we conceive of time: in a "tensed" way, in terms of past, present, and future ("You will be dead in 60 years," "It's now 4:00," "The earth is millions of years old," "The play has just started") and in a "tenseless" way, in terms of clock times ("The play starts at 8:00 PM") and relations of succession and simultaneity ("The sinking of the Titanic is earlier than the beginning of World War I.") McTaggart named these two ways of temporally ordering events the "A-series" and the "B-series," respectively.[4]

Events change with respect to their A-properties (pastness, presentness, futurity). For example, the death of Queen Anne was once in the future, then it was present, then past. So, there are really many different A-series, not just one. By contrast, events do not change with respect to their B-relations (earlier than, simultaneous with, later than). For example, if the signing of the Declaration of Independence is later than the Lisbon earthquake, then the signing of the Declaration of Independence is always later than the Lisbon earthquake. The term 'tenseless' refers to the fact that B-relations between events do not change over time: once "earlier than," always "earlier than."

Although the expressions 'past', 'present', and 'future' are characteristic of the A-series, those expressions may be used to designate B-series relations. For example, 'in the past' is an A-series term only if it's used with a shifting reference—as in 'The McCarthy era is in the past', where 'in the past' is relative to now. If 'past' is used relationally—as in 'The McCarthy era is in the past in 2005'—'past' has nothing to do with the A-series. 'The past at t' is a B-series term equivalent to 'earlier than t', a paradigmatically B-series expression. Similarly for 'in the future'. For example, 'in the future' is an A-series expression in the sentence 'In the future, call me before 9 o'clock', where 'in the future' means in the future relative to now. But 'in the future' is a B-series expression in the sentence 'In August 1939, the beginning of World War II was in the future', where 'in the future' means later than 1939. 'In the future in 1939' is a B-series expression that applies to the same times (any time later than 1939) no matter when it is used. Parallel remarks apply to 'now at t' (B-series) and to 'now' (as in 'I'm ready to adjourn the meeting now'—A-series). So, the expressions typical of the A-series actually presuppose the A-series only if they are used in ways that have different referents on different occasions of their use. The definitive difference between the A- and B-series is this: A-properties are transient, and B-relations are not.

Verb tenses, as well as terms like 'past', 'present', and 'future', are associated with the A-series. We report facts ordered by the A-series by use of tensed verbs and copulas: 'He will not be going home', 'That happened six weeks ago', 'They're off!' yelled by the announcer at a horse race. A-sentences (as I'll call them) are true on some occasions of their utterance, but not others. By contrast, B-sentences—for example, 'In 2005, Tony Blair (tenselessly) is Prime Minister of England'—is true (if true at all) on all occasions of its utterance. Unlike the tensed 'is' of the A-series that contrasts with 'was' and 'will be', the 'is' in B-sentences should be understood tenselessly.

Let me pause for a comment on eternalism: eternalism is often characterized as I noted at the beginning—as the view that past, present, and future times and objects are equally real.[5] That characterization is highly misleading for a B-theory. The B-series, which is the basis for eternalism, makes no appeal to past, present, or future at all: 'Past', 'present', and 'future' are A-series terms. (As I just pointed out, all that can be countenanced by the B-series is 'past at t', 'present at t', and 'future at t'; but these designations are eliminable in favor of B-series terms 'earlier than t', 'simultaneous at t', and 'later than t'.) Past, present, and future—along with the ongoing now—are irrelevant to the B-series. From the perspective of the B-series, nothing is really past, present, or future—just past at t, present at t, or future at t.[6] Inasmuch as eternalism calls into question the referents of A-series words, using ostensibly A-language to characterize eternalism leads to confusion.

It is tempting to think that we can dispense with either the A-series or the B-series in favor of the other. On the contrary, I am convinced that we require both the A-series and the B-series to understand all the temporal facts. Neither the A- nor the B-series can be eliminated in favor of the other.

Here are three reasons to think that the B-series is not dispensable in favor of the A-series: (1) Prima facie, the A-series is incomplete as an account of time: we need the relations 'earlier than', 'later than', and 'simultaneous with', in addition to 'past', 'present', and 'future', to describe familiar temporal facts—for example, causes are typically earlier than their effects. Indeed, the natural way to understand the past is as earlier than now, and the natural way to understand the future is as later than now. (2) Although the B-series is required for physics, the A-series is never appealed to in theories of physics. (Time's having a direction depends on physical asymmetries, like the increase of entropy; the directionality of time in no way implicates the A-series with its ongoing now.) If one is at all a realist about physics, then one will take the B-series to be essential for temporal reality. (3) Although I cannot discuss it here, I believe that attempts to ground the B-series in the A-series have failed.[7] So, I do not believe that the B-series can be eliminated or reduced to the A-series.

Nor is the A-series dispensable in favor of the B-series. Again, there are three reasons: (1) The B-series without the A-series leaves out the paradigmatic temporal properties of past, present, and future altogether, along with the ongoing nows that order our experience. (2) There are many temporal facts that the B-series without the A-series cannot recognize—for example, that this is the twenty-first century or that social services in the United States used to be more secure that they are now. The B-series offers no way for the doctor to tell you that you have less than a year to live, or for you to assure the school board that the earth is millions of years old now. (And your having less than a year to live and the earth's being millions of years old now are by no means "subjective" or a product of psychological attitudes.) (3) The A-series is required for the occurrence of many kinds of ordinary phenomena—for making and executing plans, for regret, for making sense of ourselves and the world. A-series facts are explananda that need A-series explanations. Why are you so sad today? Because someone close to you died last night. (Being sad at t because someone died at $t-1$ is not the same at all as being sad today; being sad today because someone died last night has the sting of grief that the tenseless fact of being sad at t because someone died at $t-1$ just does not have.) So, I conclude that we cannot just eliminate the A-series in favor of the B-series.

Before setting out a theory of temporal reality that integrates the B- and A-series, let me motivate the need for a *metaphysical* theory. What's the point of a metaphysical (as opposed to a merely semantic) approach to the A-series? After all, David Kaplan and others have shown how to treat indexical sentences containing 'now', and, it may be thought, no more need be said (Kaplan 1989). There is nothing special about the present: 'Now' is just a word that applies to every time t, at that time t.[8]

Although such indexical theories may be useful in semantics, metaphysicians should not stop with them. There is information that indexical theories cannot account for—for example, facts about what time it is now and which person is you and which world you live in. It seems a rather significant fact that it is now 4:00 and not midnight, or that I am L.B. and not George Washington, or that this is the twenty-first century and not the eighteenth. These are temporal facts that one may be right or wrong about. Those who accord no metaphysical import to the A-series will point out that the only propositions involved here (on the standard semantic treatment) are B-series propositions. I reply: The propositions expressed by 'This is the twenty-first century' and 'I am L.B.' and 'it is now 4:00', according to the standard treatment, are tautologies: "The twenty-first century is the twenty-first century" and "L.B. is L.B." and "4:00 is 4:00." Tautologies are trivial. But it is far from trivial that this is the twenty-first century or that I am L.B.[9] I can only conclude that nonindexical propositions do not yield a complete account of reality.

Moreover, indexical theories of the language of the A-series are mute in the face of the transience of experience, the ineluctable ordering of our lives in terms of an ongoing now. Note the dissimilarity between 'here' and 'now': The reference of 'now' shifts inexorably. Your next utterance of 'now' will refer to a different time from your preceding utterance of 'now'. But your next utterance of 'here' will not refer to a different place from your preceding utterance of 'here' unless you have moved, and you may move in any direction. There is no spatial analogue of temporal becoming—the property by which, no matter what we do, events recede away from us into the past. Our understanding of experience in terms of an ongoing now—an understanding that is universal—is not fully captured by nonindexical language, and a metaphysical theory is in order.

A Theory of Time

As I mentioned, I'll call my proposed view "the BA-theory of time." My aim is to take the B-series as basic, but to jack up the A-series so that it too reveals an aspect of the nature of time. According to the BA-theory, time has two irreducible aspects: one that depends on there being self-conscious entities (the aspect of the A-series, the ongoing now) and one that does not depend on self-conscious entities (the aspect of the B-series, simultaneity and succession). The BA-theory will show how these two aspects are related.

(I realize that some philosophers take it to be a metaphysical mistake to claim that any aspect of reality depends on there being self-conscious entities. The claim looks like a mistake only on an assumption that I do not share—namely, the assumption that what depends on us has no ontological significance. I'll return to this point later, but now let's see how the B-series and the A-series fit together.)

In the absence of self-conscious beings, events occur (tenselessly) at various times, and some events are (tenselessly) later than others.[10] But there is no ongoing now. Given that the B-series makes no appeal to what is occurring now, we must ask: In virtue of what does an event occur now, in the present?[11] Modifying the view of Adolf Grünbaum, I say that an event's occurring now depends on someone's being judgmentally aware of it now (Grünbaum 1968, 17).[12] (Judgmental awareness is "awareness that": if you are aware that you are feeling something soft, then you are judgmentally aware of feeling something soft.) Consider, for example, a sudden snap of my fingers. The following are sufficient for your hearing the finger snap's occurring now:

1. You hear the snap.
2. You are now judgmentally aware of hearing something.
3. Your judgmental awareness is simultaneous with your hearing the snap.

Because your hearing the snap is (nearly) simultaneous with the snap, the snap also occurs now. The finger snap occurs now in virtue of someone's being judgmentally aware (now) of hearing something, together with the simultaneity of the judgmental awareness with hearing the snap. You need know nothing about the clock time of the snap. If the snap is unperceived, then it may still qualify as occurring now if it is simultaneous with some other event that meets the awareness requirements.[13]

There is no conflict between this view and the special theory of relativity. The appeal to simultaneity is local—indeed, initially, it is between mental events of a single person.[14] A physical event qualifies as occurring now only by being perceived (or by being simultaneous with some other physical event that is perceived). Absence of absolute simultaneity does not deprive reality of simultaneity; it only implies that simultaneity is relative to frame. Physics still appeals to relations of 'earlier than' and 'simultaneous with'—only now these relations on standard views are taken to be relative to inertial frame.[15] Similarly, metaphysics may still use 'past', 'present', and 'future'—only now these properties should be taken to be relative to self-conscious beings.

The nowness of judgmental awareness is, I believe, primitive. So, this view is not reductive; indeed, it is circular: What I am judgmentally aware of is *now* because my judgmental awareness is (primitively) now. I do not think that this circularity is avoidable; I think that it is a mark of an inextricable link between time and self-consciousness. Everything that a self-conscious being is aware of—her own thoughts, her rememberings, what someone else is saying, that she is about to go onstage, that the driveway needs to be shoveled, what have you—everything is always experienced as being present. Indeed, it is *constitutive* of our conscious lives that they are ordered by the A-series' ongoing nows.

The BA-theory has the virtue of empirical adequacy: it is adequate both to our experience and to the demands of physics. Anything that we self-consciously experience is perforce ordered by an A-series, but the A-series cannot stand alone. The BA-theory takes the B-series to be basic—basic, but not exclusive or exhaustive. It is also part of the nature of time that any self-conscious experience has—must have—A-properties. It is because of this feature of time that we can make sense of the old Tennessee preacher who said "Time ain't as long as it used to be."

Metaphysical Implications

Superficially, I may seem to be in league with Grünbaum: Without self-conscious beings, there are no A-series. But there is a huge metaphysical gulf between Grünbaum and me: Grünbaum took his view to show that the A-series has no ontological status, that it is merely "mind-dependent," with emphasis on the 'merely'.[16]

In contrast with Grünbaum and many others, I do not take the mind-independent–mind-dependent distinction to be a basis for metaphysics. Metaphysics should concern reality. We self-conscious beings are part of reality, and we contribute to what there is. Much that exists depends—depends ontologically, not just causally—on us: pianos, cell phones, particle accelerators. If a piece of plastic that is physically indistinguishable from your Mastercard spontaneously coalesced in outer space, it would not be a credit card: Nothing would be a credit card in a world without beings with propositional attitudes and their conventions and legal and financial arrangements. We people contribute not only to material reality, but to temporal reality as well. What we contribute to temporal reality are the A-series: "nowness" is a product of self-consciousness, but no less part of the reality of time for all that.[17]

I can hear an objection: "Time as it is *in itself* is only the B-series. On the view that you just sketched, the A-series is extrinsic to time, not part of what time is." To such an objection, I reply that it is a very general and widespread mistake to think that what something is is determined wholly by its intrinsic properties. What makes something a portrait, a credit card, or a personal computer (or any other kind of artifact) are relational and intentional properties. Of course, some philosophers think that there are no artifacts; but, then, some philosophers think that there are no material objects at all. As I have said, I am concerned with the world as we encounter it, and we encounter it as full of artifacts, and as temporally ordered by ongoing nows—indeed, as saturated with A-series temporality.

Time is not something extraneous to us, or something nontransient (as the B-series alone would have it) that simply causes us to experience the world as transient. Our relation to time is much more intimate than is effect to cause. Contrast time with heat, say. The phenomenon of heat is nothing but the motion of particles; that motion causes our sensations of heat. We can readily imagine living in a world in which there were no sensations of heat; the motions that cause sensations of heat in our world could cause other kinds of sensations or no sensations at all. But time is not like that: We cannot imagine living in a world without the passage of time. We are not just contingently related to time (as we are to heat) as a cause of certain experiences. We are wrapped up in time (indeed, we are carried away by time's wingéd chariot). Passing time is the medium of our lives: To live is to get older, and to get older is for time to pass. There is something about time, not just about us, that makes our experience transient.

So, to say that the A-series requires self-consciousness does not exclude the A-series from being an aspect of time. We might say that, in the absence of self-conscious beings, A-series are dormant (or merely potential, or latent). It is an important feature of time that it has a disposition toward A-properties, which are manifest only in relation to self-conscious beings. I do not see how to make sense of the world that we encounter without metaphysical appeal to transience; and the best metaphysical theory of transience, I believe, is that its passing depends on our self-conscious experience. Now let us tackle the question of the relation between time and existence.

II

Time and Existence
As I said at the outset, I do not think that presentism or eternalism or the growing block universe view is adequate. So, I want to find a different way to understand the relation between time and existence, between being in time and existing *simpliciter*. The discussion rightly focuses on the domain of the unrestricted existential quantifier—the domain of the wide-open ∃, not restricted in any way, the most inclusive domain that includes everything that exists.[18] I'll call the domain of the unrestricted existential

quantifier 'the Domain', and I'll use '*x* is in the Domain' and '*x* exists *simpliciter*' interchangeably. The Domain is simply the collection of all the objects that exist.

My aim is to show that although the Domain is not subject to change (as eternalists hold), the world is ontologically different at different times (as presentists hold): the world does not come "ready-made."[19] My strategy is to construe certain objects as essentially existing at times but to construe being in the Domain as nontemporal (in that '$\exists t(x$ is in the domain at $t)$' is meaningless). I'll sketch a picture of how the Domain, which is subject to no temporal qualification whatever, can contain objects that exist only in time. There are two distinct ways of existing—in time (like you and me) and not in time (like numbers). To exist *simpliciter* or to be in the Domain is not to exist in some other way; it is to exist either in time or not in time. I call this the "mixed view", because it construes the world to be temporal and the Domain to be nontemporal, and it takes the Domain to depend on what exists in the world at particular times. Let's start with the idea of existing in time.

Existing-at-t is a fundamental mode of existence, irreducible to any other mode of existing. The things that we encounter in the world exist at times. If Socrates, for example, exists at all, he exists at some time. In fact, Socrates exists (or existed—tenses don't matter here) from 470 to 399 BCE and *only* from 470 to 399 BCE. He came into existence in 470 and (putting aside the possibility of life after death) went out of existence at 399. He is not an eternal or preexisting object that simply acquired a temporal location at 470. When Socrates began to exist, a completely new entity came into being. Objects like Socrates exist by being in time: They come into existence at some time and cease to exist at some later time. They cannot exist otherwise than at times. (Although Socrates is essentially in time, it is not essential that he exist from 470 to 399—he might have been executed in 404.) Existence at a time, which may be symbolized by a predicate 'Ext', is a property. Existing at some time or other is a property that Socrates has essentially; existing at 400 BCE is a distinct property that Socrates has contingently. Let us call objects (like Socrates) that exist at times 'temporal objects'.[20]

Now let's turn to the nontemporality of being in the Domain. To be in the Domain is to be within the scope of the logician's '$\exists$'. What does the Domain include? The Domain includes everything; it is the complete ontology. Since it is the complete ontology, nothing can be added to the Domain and nothing can be taken away from it. "Everything" includes both abstract objects—like times and numbers—for which it is meaningless to say that they exist at a time at all, and concrete objects—like Socrates—that exist at times. However, there are not two senses of 'exist'.[21] There are, rather, two modes or ways of existing. Some kinds of things—abstract objects like the number nine—are nontemporal and are in the Domain without existing at times. Other kinds of things—finite concrete objects like Socrates—are in the Domain because they exist at times. So, I do not regard existing-at-t (expressed by the two-place predicate 'Ext') to be just a matter of temporal location; as I said, existing-at-t is a basic mode of existing. Existing at a time does *not contrast* with existing *simpliciter*. Rather, existing at a time is one of two ways to exist *simpliciter*.

In short, the nontemporal Domain is nothing but all the temporal objects (that exist in time) and all the nontemporal objects (that exist but not in time). I am using 'nontemporal' for the Domain, about which temporal qualifications make no sense, and 'nontemporal' for abstract objects, about which it makes sense to say that there is no time at which they exist. Abstract objects exist *simpliciter*, but do not exist at a time. The Domain is not itself an object of any sort.

Since the existential quantifier is univocal and since the Domain includes nontemporal objects as well as temporal objects, our English rendering of existential quantification as 'There exists' is not a present-tense occurrence of 'exists'; rather, 'exists' is nontemporal.[22] We can see the nontemporality of '∃' as follows: For any object in the Domain, whether it is a temporal object or not, it makes no sense to say that there is some time at which it is in the Domain, and it equally makes no sense to say that there is some time at which it is not in the Domain. It makes no sense to say that an object is *already* in the Domain, or is *always* in the Domain, or is *not yet* in the Domain. Temporal qualifications just do not apply to being in the Domain. When I say that the Domain itself is nontemporal, I do not mean that all the objects in the Domain are nontemporal. (Socrates is not nontemporal.) Rather, I mean that for any object in the Domain (whether temporal or nontemporal), its being in the Domain—like 2's being less than 3 or red's being a color—is not in time at all.

Since Socrates is a temporal object, the condition for Socrates' being in the Domain (or his existing *simpliciter*) is that there is some time t such that he exists at t:

$$\exists x(x = s) \text{ iff } \exists t(Est)$$

So, Socrates is in the Domain (since there is a time at which he exists), but it makes no sense to say that he is in the Domain in 400 BCE or in 2005 CE or at any other time. (This is not to say that Socrates is in the Domain or exists *simpliciter* even when he doesn't exist. Since it makes no sense to say that there is a time t such that Socrates is in the Domain at t, it makes no sense to say that there is a time t such that: both Socrates is in the Domain at t and Socrates does not exist at t.)

But what is nontemporally expressed by '$\exists x(x = s)$' does implicate time—since the condition of Socrates' being in the Domain is that $\exists t(Est)$. Socrates' being in the Domain of the nontemporal '$\exists$' is not some nontemporal way of existing; rather, it is none other than there being a time at which Socrates exists. His existing occurs at some particular time and his existing at that time is what makes the existential generalization true. That is, his existing at 400 BCE, or at any other time between 470 and 399 BCE, makes it true that $\exists t(Est)$, and hence makes it true that Socrates is in the Domain. So, Socrates' being in the Domain depends on his existing at some time, and not vice versa. To put it another way: Socrates is in the Domain *in virtue of the fact that* there is a time at which he exists. Socrates is in the Domain as a (logical) *consequence* of his existing at some time, not as a precondition of his existing in time.

In short, the relation between a temporal object's existing *simpliciter* and its existing at a particular time is the relation between an existential generalization and a true instantiation of it. For a temporal object, its existing-at-particular-times is its *only* mode of existence; a temporal object is in the Domain only in virtue of there being a time at which it exists. Socrates comes into existence at the earliest time t at which there is a true instance of the existential generalization, '$\exists t(Est)$'. Different objects come into existence at different times. Therefore, *the world*—the flesh-and-blood temporal world that includes us in 2005, and included Socrates between 470 and 399 BCE —is ontologically different at different times. So, let us relativize the ontology of the world to time and say:

The ontology of the world at t = all abstract objects and all objects x such that Ext.

Nevertheless, the Domain of the unrestricted existential quantifier remains nontemporal:

The Domain = all abstract objects and all objects x such that $\exists tExt$.

(I am putting aside here the view that there is an eternal being.) The mixed view accepts this distinction between the nontemporal Domain and the temporal ontology of the world at t. Since different objects exist at different times, the world exhibits ontological diversity.

Let me sum up the mixed view, according to which the Domain is non-temporal, but the world exhibits ontological diversity:

1. Objects (both temporal and nontemporal) are in the Domain. 'Being in the Domain' is not subject to temporal qualification of any kind. Some things (like numbers) are nontemporal (they do not exist at times); other things (like Socrates) are essentially temporal (they exist only at times). Socrates exists only from 470 until 399 BCE —the times that satisfy 'Est'. Since $\exists t(Est)$, Socrates is in the Domain.

2. The reason that we can quantify over any object at any time is that for a temporal object to be in the Domain is for there to be some time at which it exists.[23]

"Does Socrates exist?" you may ask.—That's an incomplete question. Socrates is a temporal object, who exists at some times but not at others. (And it makes no sense to say that he exists *simpliciter* at all times or at any time; to say that Socrates exists *simpliciter* is to say that $\exists x(x = s)$.) We can complete the question 'Does Socrates exist?' in any of several ways: 'Does Socrates exist in 400 BCE?' (yes); 'Does Socrates exist in 2005 CE?' (no); 'Does Socrates exist now?' (no); 'Does Socrates exist *simpliciter*?' (yes)—This is not to say that Socrates exists in two ways—nontemporally in the Domain and temporally in the world in time. He exists in one way: tempo-rally, in time, in the world, and because of this he—the temporal Socrates—is in the Domain.[24]

3. Existing-at-a-time is a basic mode of existing, the mode we are most familiar with. Satisfaction of the open sentence 'x exists at t' is the neces-sary and sufficient condition for a temporal object to be in the Domain or to exist *simpliciter*. 'x exists at t' has ontological import. It does not merely give a temporal location for something that "already exists" in the Domain; there is no such thing as "already existing" in the Domain.

4. For temporal objects, existing-at-t is metaphysically prior to being in the Domain in that it is only in virtue of existing at a particular time that a temporal object exists *simpliciter* or is in the Domain. Socrates is in the Domain only because he existed in time. The Domain is just the collec-tion of objects nontemporal and temporal.

5. Temporal objects—all those that we encounter, those that do not exist perpetually—come into existence at some time t. To say that x comes into existence at t is to say: 'Ext & $\sim\exists t'(t' < t$ & E$xt')$'. If x comes into existence at t, then x did not exist before t. So, there is ontological novelty in the world.

Ontological Novelty
The account just given of ontological novelty in the world can be extended from the coming-into-existence of new entities to the coming-into-existence of new kinds of entities—I call them 'primary kinds'. Indeed, anyone who believes in the evolution of the universe or in the evolution of biological species must either countenance novel primary kinds or else deny that objects of apparently novel primary kinds (e.g., stars, horses) are real objects. We can understand ontological novelty as the evolution or introduction at some time or other of objects of new primary kinds—for example, the first multicellular organisms or Galileo's first telescope. Say that a primary kind K is more complex than a primary kind K' if objects of kind K' can constitute objects of kind K. Then the comparative ontological richness of the world at different times may be understood as follows:

(OR)   The world at t' is *ontologically richer* than the world at t iff there are objects of more complex primary kinds at t' than at t.

A new primary kind (natural or artifactual) is a genuine novelty whose evolution or introduction makes the world ontologically richer. This view, again, allows for ontological novelty in the world, but not in the Domain of the unrestricted existential quantifier—not in the complete ontology.

Contrasts between the Mixed and Other Views
The mixed view may at first resemble a growing-universe view, but the "growth" is in the world; there is no room for "growth" in the complete ontology. And unlike the growing-universe views, the mixed view does not imply that objects that begin in the future do not exist; it only implies—what is surely right—that they do not exist now.

The mixed view tries to take what is intuitively right about eternalism and presentism, and leave behind what seems wrong with each. Neither presentism nor eternalism distinguishes between the ontology of the world at a time and the collection of all the objects that make up the Domain. According to presentism, both the Domain and the ontology of the world are relativized to the present, and both change over time. According to eternalism, neither the Domain nor the ontology of the world changes over time. According to the mixed view, the ontology of the world changes over time, but the Domain does not.[25] So, the mixed view leaves behind the presentist's constantly changing domain of the unrestricted existential quantifier.

The mixed view shares with eternalism the claim that the domain of the unrestricted existential quantifier is fixed; it is not subject to change. Nevertheless, the mixed view differs from eternalism in several respects.

First, on the mixed view, the ontology of the world is in time and is different at different times. On eternalism, it is not. On the eternalist view (as I understand it), the ontology of the world at any time is just the collection of objects that make up the Domain.[26]

The second way in which the mixed view differs from eternalism concerns the status of temporal existence (expressed by 'x exists at t'). According to the mixed view, there are two basic ways of existing: temporally and nontemporally. Eternalists (I think) construe all existence, understood ontologically, to be nontemporal: they do not consider existing in time to be a different mode of existence from existing nontemporally. According to the mixed view, not all existence is nontemporal. For some objects (temporal objects), existence is a matter of existing at some time or other; their being in the Domain depends on existing-at-a-time. I disagree with Sider, an eternalist, when he says, "'Exists-at' is analogous to the spatial predicate 'is located at', not the logician's '∃'" (Sider 2001, 59). According to the mixed view, 'exists at' is intimately connected with the '∃'. Existing-at-t is one of two basic modes of existence.

A corollary is that since mixed viewers construe existing-at-t to be a basic mode of existence, the mixed view takes some (perhaps all) temporal objects to come into existence at times. If an object comes into existence at a time, then there are earlier times at which the object does not exist. Sometimes eternalists seem to construe 'being in the Domain' to imply the following: if x is in the Domain, then there is no time at which x is not in the Domain; hence, x is in the Domain at all times. And hence, further, if x ever exists, there is no time that x fails to exist.[27] If this is what eternalists hold, then eternalists (unlike mixed viewers) suppose that objects do not come into existence at times.

By contrast to eternalism, on the mixed view, it is meaningless to use temporal language to speak of the Domain. It is meaningless to say that x is in the Domain at all times, or that x is in the Domain before or after it exists in time: 'Before' or 'after' make no sense when applied to the Domain. The Domain is just a collection of objects, temporal and nontemporal. An object's existing at a time implies that the object is a temporal object, and being a temporal object is sufficient for being in the Domain. So, whereas the mixed view takes objects to come into existence at different times, it seems, as I said a moment ago, that eternalism does not.[28]

The third way in which the mixed view differs from eternalism concerns the metaphysical priority of Socrates' existing at a particular time to Socrates' being in the Domain. His being in the Domain depends on there being a time at which he exists; and this in turn depends on his existing at a particular time. When Sider says that "the world comes 'ready-made' with a single domain D of objects: the class of all the objects there are" (Sider 2001, xxii), it sounds as if he is taking the Domain to constrain what exists at particular times. The mixed view takes the order of priority to be the reverse: What exists in the world at particular times determines what is in the Domain (or rather, determines what is in the temporal part of the Domain).

The fourth respect in which the mixed view differs from eternalism is that only the mixed view is compatible with the BA-theory of time. Eternalism has no place for an ongoing now in its account of reality. Nor does eternalism have resources to show how temporal reality, conceived of wholly in terms of the B-series, could give rise to the appearance of an ongoing now, as opposed to successions of simultaneous events. If all there is to time is the B-series, how could our lives be so bound up in the passage of time? On the other hand, the mixed view is neutral with respect to the BA-theory.

The obvious benefit of the BA-theory over the pure B-theory is that it allows for temporal distinctions that matter to us. For example, think about your best friend, who, let us suppose for the sake of convenience of pronouns, is a woman. She exists in 2005. That is an important (B-series) fact about her. But equally important is the (A-series) fact that she exists now. She did not die last night—an A-series fact. On the B-theory alone, your friend's existing now has no metaphysical significance whatever; indeed, it is not a different fact from her existing at 4:00 on September 30, 2005. By contrast, the BA-theory, when wedded to the mixed view, gives a metaphysical (not just semantic or "conceptual") account of things' being in the past, present, and future: being now is a relation between a time and a self-conscious being. Granted, the BA account is in terms of self-conscious beings; but, as I have noted, self-conscious beings are as much a part of reality as rocks and trees. Combining the B- and A-series into a metaphysical account of time further distinguishes the mixed view from eternalism.

Whether the mixed view is a variant of eternalism or not depends on whether an eternalist would (1) distinguish two basic ways of existing, temporal and nontemporal; (2) recognize the ontology of the world at *t* as distinct from the Domain; (3) welcome the BA-theory of time; and (4) take temporal language to be nonsensical if applied to the Domain.

Conclusion

I have two main conclusions: In part I, I argued that *both* the B-series (which orders time in terms of unchanging relations like 'earlier than') and the A-series (which orders time in terms of changing properties like 'being past', 'being present', and 'being future') are needed for an adequate account of time. Neither series is dispensable, and neither by itself is a sufficient account of time: An A-theory cannot stand alone. On a B-theory alone, things just exist at different clock times: nothing moves through time; there is no passage. On the BA-theory, objects move through time, but their doing so depends on the existence of self-conscious beings. Although the B-series is the more fundamental of the two orderings, it is a deep fact about time that it can be experienced only as transient.

In part II, I argued that there is no conflict between the commonsense view that the world exhibits ontological novelty and the metaphysical view that the domain of the unrestricted existential quantifier is nontemporal. *The world* changes ontologically over time, as new objects like Socrates and new kinds like dinosaurs come into existence. Nevertheless, *the domain* of the unrestricted existential quantifier is not subject to change (because it is not temporal at all).

Let me conclude with a brief personal remark about metaphysics. It is very important to me to get on the table an alternative to the dominant metaphysical theories that accord no place in their accounts of reality for things that everyone cares about—not only concrete objects like your car keys, or the *Mona Lisa*, but also commonplace states of affairs like your being employed next year, or your having enough money for retirement. Many philosophers treat such phenomena as if they were just a matter of our concepts. I think on the contrary that they are the stuff of reality, and I want to offer a metaphysics that has room in its ontology for the ordinary things that people value. It is not enough to have familiar sentences turn out to be true under unfamiliar interpretations. I do not want to relegate what really matters to mere concepts or semantics. My aim is to find metaphysical significance in the world as we encounter and interact with it all day, every day.

Acknowledgments

I am grateful to Edmund Gettier, Gareth B. Matthews, and Hilary Kornblith for many profitable conversations on the matters discussed here. An earlier version of this essay was read in my absence at the Inland Northwest

Philosophy Conference on Time and Identity at the University of Idaho and Washington State University, March 31–April 2, 2005. I gave a much revised version at Notre Dame University on September 30, 2005. I am grateful to audiences at both venues.

Notes

1. See also Markosian 2004 and Crisp 2004. Crisp characterizes eternalism as "the view that our most inclusive domain of quantification includes past, present and future entities" (Crisp 2004, 19).

2. See Tooley 1997. In chapter 11, Tooley suggests modifying the special theory of relativity in a way that entails absolute simultaneity while maintaining consistency with experimental results. See also Broad 1923.

3. Rea (2003) notes that we cannot equate the A-theory with presentism, nor the B-theory with eternalism. Nevertheless, eternalism is *a* B-theory, and presentism is *an* A-theory, albeit a truncated one that singles out only the present as real.

4. See McTaggart 1968. I take 'earlier than' and 'later than' to denote temporal relations; hence, there is no question that the B-series is a temporal series.

5. See note 1. The term 'eternalism' seems to me to be a misnomer for *any* theory of time: According to a B-theory of time, temporal objects exist tenselessly. Something that exists eternally—e.g., God or the square root of 2 or the set of possible worlds—exists "outside" of time altogether. (E.g., to say that God exists eternally is to *deny* that God is in time; the term 'semipeternal' is used to mean that God exists at all times.)

6. It is also wrong to think that the B-series implies fatalism. As J. J. C. Smart, a four-dimensionalist advocate of the B-series (without the A-series), observed, the B-series "is compatible both with determinism and with indeterminism, i.e., both with the view that earlier time slices of the universe are determinately related by laws of nature at later time slices and with the view that they are not so related" (Smart 1963, 142). For a full discussion of the matter of determinism and indeterminism with respect to the A-series, see Grünbaum 1968, especially pp. 28–36.

7. E.g., McTaggart's attempt to define 'earlier than' in terms of A-properties is circular. See Gale 1968, p. 90. More recently, Oaklander (2003) has subjected William Lane Craig's (2000a,b) version of A-time—presentism—to a convincing critique.

8. Some philosophers speak of the reduction of the tenses by B-language. E.g., Sider (2001, 20). But what is meant by 'reduction of the tenses' is that there are tenseless truth conditions for tensed tokens: e.g., '*S* is now *F*' uttered at *t* is true just in case *S* is *F* at *t*. For example, after Kennedy was assassinated, a doctor said, "It is too late to help him; he has died." We can supply tenseless truth conditions for an utterance of 'It is too late to help him' at time *t* concerning an event (the death of

Kennedy) that tenselessly takes place earlier than t. However, those tenseless truth conditions cannot convey the tensed information that it is too late to help him. As I interpret the important papers of John Perry and others, the existence of tenseless truth conditions does not signal that indexicals and tensed language can be dispensed with. See Perry 1979.

9. I discussed these matters at length in Baker 1982.

10. The locution 'at t' is neutral between an absolute and a relational theory of time. Relationalists like Grünbaum freely use 'at t'. As Grünbaum observed, an event occurs "in a network of relations of earlier and later and thus can be said to occur 'at a certain time t.' Hence to assert tenselessly that an event exists (occurs) is to claim that there is a time or clock reading t with which it coincides" (Grünbaum 1968, 24).

11. The following discussion is from my Ph.D. dissertation (Baker 1972). At that time, I joined Grünbaum in denigrating what is "mind-dependent." I have since come to my senses.

12. Also see Grünbaum 1963, part II.

13. I have defended this view in Baker 1974–75 and Baker 1979.

14. "In the first instance, it is only an experience (i.e., a mental event) which can ever qualify as occurring now" (Grünbaum 1968, 19).

15. Anja Janernig pointed out that if I'm standing still and you jump, then we are not in the same inertial frame since you are accelerating. But I still experience your jumping as occurring in the present. So, we should loosen the simultaneity requirement between the judgmental awareness and the physical event that occurs now, and speak of near-simultaneity. (Since judgmental awareness is not instantaneous, no judgmental awareness is simultaneous, strictly speaking, with an instantaneous physical event anyway.)

16. There is even less similarity between Hugh Mellor and me. According to Mellor, temporal reality is purely B-series; but we think about it in A-series terms. We need A-series beliefs in order for our actions to be successful. Nevertheless, there are no A-series facts. See Mellor 1999.

17. That now is relative to an inertial frame only means that there is no unique now; there is no unique A-series. But this casts no doubt on there being an ongoing now relative to us—just as just as the fact that the truth of an utterance of 'It's 4:00 now' depends on time zone casts no doubt on its really being 4:00.

18. I am agreeing here with Sider that there are meaningful disagreements about what exists (Sider 2001, "Introduction"). Sider cites van Inwagen (2002), but van Inwagen makes much stronger claims than the one I am agreeing to here.

19. This term comes from Sider, who is an eternalist. See Sider 2001, xxii.

20. Temporal objects are concrete particulars, not events. Following Kim, I take events to be objects' having properties at times; I do not take events to be particulars.

21. See Matthews 1971 and 1972.

22. As every beginning logic student learns, the logician's '∃' is nontemporal. Why not paraphrase the logician's '∃' as 'there exists in the past, present, or future'? (Peter van Inwagen and Patricia Blanchette raised this question.) Not only is the standard reading nontemporal, but also it is possible that there exist numbers in a world without time. In such a world, there is no temporal reading of '∃'. (Marian David supplied the latter answer.)

23. Am I saying that we can existentially quantify over an object when it does not exist? Yes. We can quantify over any object in the Domain. Existential quantification does not entail that a temporal object *exists at the time* that it is quantified over; it entails, rather, that it *exists at some time or other* (i.e., that it is in the Domain, that it exists *simpliciter*).

24. I.e., Socrates' being in the Domain is a nontemporal fact. Are all nontemporal facts necessary? No. If there had not been a time at which Socrates existed, he would not have been in the domain.

25. Because the Domain is nontemporal (not in time at all), it is meaningless to say that an object is in the Domain only when it exists.

26. An eternalist may agree that, if he were to accept my definition of the 'ontology of the world at *t*', he would agree that the ontology of the world changes; however, I think it highly unlikely that he would accept my definition. I admit that this may be merely a semantic difference between the mixed view and eternalism.

27. There is at least a suggestion that all objects in the Domain do not begin to exist at some time in Michael Rea's characterization of eternalism like this: "Eternalists believe that all past and future objects exist (i.e., there are some past objects, there are some future objects and there neither were nor will be objects that do not exist)" (Rea 2003, 247).

28. A colleague of mine thinks it uncharitable to impute to eternalists the view that objects do not come into existence in time or that they exist at all times. Clearheaded eternalists, he says, think no such thing. So, I leave this as only a possible difference between the mixed view and eternalism.

References

Auden, W. H. 1940. In Memory of W. B. Yeats. In *Another Time*. New York: Random House.

Baker, L. R. 1972. Linguistic and Ontological Aspects of Temporal Becoming. Dissertation, Vanderbilt University.

Baker, L. R. 1974–75. Temporal Becoming: The Argument from Physics. *Philosophical Forum* 6:218–236.

Baker, L. R. 1979. On the Mind-Dependence of Temporal Becoming. *Philosophy and Phenomenological Research* 39:341–357.

Baker, L. R. 1982. Underprivileged Access. *Noûs* 16:227–241.

Broad, C. D. 1923. *Scientific Thought*. London: Routledge & Kegan Paul.

Craig, W. L. 2000a. *The Tensed Theory of Time: A Critique*. Dordrecht: Kluwer.

Craig, W. L. 2000b. *The Tenseless Theory of Time: A Critique*. Dordrecht: Kluwer.

Crisp, T. 2004. Defining Presentism. In *Oxford Studies in Metaphysics*, vol. 1, ed. D. Zimmerman. Oxford: Clarendon Press.

Gale, R. 1968. *The Language of Time*. New York: Routledge & Kegan Paul.

Grünbaum, A. 1963. *Philosophical Problems of Space and Time*. New York: Alfred A. Knopf.

Grünbaum, A. 1968. The Status of Temporal Becoming. In *Modern Science and Zeno's Paradoxes*. London: George Allen & Unwin.

Kaplan, D. 1989. Demonstratives. In *Themes from Kaplan*, ed. J. Almog, J. Perry, and H. Wettstein. New York: Oxford University Press.

Markosian, N. 2004. In Defense of Presentism. In *Oxford Studies in Metaphysics*, vol. 1, ed. D. Zimmerman. Oxford: Clarendon Press.

Matthews, G. B. 1971. Dualism and Solecism. *Philosophical Review* 80:85–95.

Matthews, G. B. 1972. Senses and Kinds. *Journal of Philosophy* 69:149–157.

McTaggart, J. M. E. 1927/1968. Time. In *The Philosophy of Time*, ed. R. Gale. London: Macmillan.

Mellor, H. 1999. The Time of Our Lives. Lecture to the Royal Institute of Philosophy, London. Delivered 22 October 1999. Accessible at: www.dspace.cam.ac.uk/bitstream/1810/753/1/TimeLives.html.

Oaklander, L. N. 2003. Presentism: A Critique. In *Real Metaphysics*, ed. H. Lillehammer and G. Rodriguez-Pereya. London: Routledge.

Perry, J. 1979. The Problem of the Essential Indexical. *Noûs* 13:3–21.

Rea, M. C. 2003. Four-Dimensionalism. In *The Oxford Handbook of Metaphysics*, ed. M. Loux and D. Zimmerman. Oxford: Oxford University Press.

Sider, T. 2001. *Four-Dimensionalism: An Ontology of Persistence and Time.* Oxford: Clarendon Press.

Smart, J. J. C. 1963. *Philosophy and Scientific Realism.* London: Routledge & Kegan Paul.

Tooley, M. 1997. *Time, Tense, and Causation.* Oxford: Clarendon Press.

van Inwagen, P. 2002. The Number of Things. In *Philosophical Issues 12: Realism and Relativism,* ed. E. Sosa. Oxford: Blackwell.

2 Time for a Change: A Polemic against the Presentism–Eternalism Debate

Lawrence B. Lombard

"It depends on what the meaning of the word 'is' is."
—William Jefferson Clinton

"No, it doesn't."
—Anonymous

Introduction

An intuitive criterion much discussed by the ancient Greek philosophers gives conditions under which an object can be said to change.[1] According to that criterion, an object changes just in case it has a property at one time that it lacks at another:

(ACC) An object, x, changes if and only if
(i)   there are distinct times, t and t',
(ii)   there is a property, P, and
(iii) x has P at t and lacks P at t'.[2]

Both Heraclitus and Parmenides, each in his own way, denied the possibility of change.

A thing, in going from having P, and thus being a P-thing, to lacking P, apparently becomes what it is not, namely a non-P-thing. Since, according to Parmenides, nothing can become what it is not, no thing can change.

Heraclitus seems to have found nothing to complain about in Parmenides' argument. Yet, he held that change was a pervasive feature of reality; he held that *changes* are constantly occurring. So, he needed to sever what seems to be a connection between the idea that *a thing changes* and the idea that *a change occurs*, a connection expressed by the claim that a change occurs just in case some thing changes.[3] The connection can be seen to be severable by noticing that the ACC requires that changing things *endure* the changes they undergo; the thing that had *P* must be the very thing that lacks it. One consequence of this aspect of the ancient criterion is that, if nonexistent things neither have nor lack the properties changes with respect to which constitute alterations, then no thing changes just in virtue of the fact that it comes into or goes out of existence. But surely, it might be said, a change occurs when a thing comes into or goes out of existence. Thus, if the *only* changes that occur are comings into and goings out of existence, then one can maintain *both* the Heraclitean thesis that change is a pervasive feature of reality *and* the Parmenidean thesis that no thing changes. The price for Heraclitus' view, however, is the abandonment of the idea that the things that come into and go out of existence are also things that can alter; one must accept the idea that no thing can endure or survive alteration. Heraclitus was a temporal parts theorist.

So, both Heraclitus and Parmenides denied that any thing could change. In an attempt to steer a course between these rival,[4] but, by my lights, equally implausible, views, Plato denied "full" reality to the world of changeable physical objects (because it was a real though contradictory world in which things become what they are not), and postulated, in addition, an "ideal" world, a "really real" Parmenidean world of entities that neither change nor come into or go out of existence.

Aristotle rejected this solution, first, by arguing that Plato's "ideal" world in fact reproduced the problems that Plato had found with the changeable world of physical objects, and, second, by arguing that there is a way to explain how it is possible for ordinary, physical things both to change and to satisfy the principle of noncontradiction, that is, to change without becoming what they are not. He drew the distinction between those features of things which they *cannot* lose without becoming what they are not (their *essential* properties) and those features of things which they *can* lose without becoming what they are not (their *accidental* properties). This distinction effectively undermines Parmenides' argument by accusing and convicting it of an equivocation. What a thing is is determined by its *essential*, not its accidental, properties. So, a thing can change with respect to its *accidental* properties without becoming what it is not. In this way, Aristotle ended the ancient debate over the possibility of change in enduring things.[5]

A New Problem Concerning Change

Although Aristotle might have ended the *ancient* debate over the possibility of change, a new version of this debate has recently made its presence felt. This new version employs a contrast between two apparently incompatible theories concerning the reality of times and the reality of the things that exist in time: *presentism* and *eternalism*.

Subject to revision and clarification, *presentism* is the view that only the present time exists, that the only things that exist are the things that exist at the present time, and that the only properties a thing has are those it has at the present time. *Eternalism* is the view that there is nothing privileged about the present time, that all times exist, and that all things, whenever they exist, are equally real. Although these formulations of presentism and eternalism may, and undoubtedly will, require clarification or refinement later on, it can be, and has been, argued that each of these apparently contrary views creates a difficulty for the idea that things change.

Trenton Merricks, for example, argued for the thesis that no possible universe can contain both things that have temporal parts and things that don't (Merricks 1995). His argument looked like this:

(M)   Eternalism entails that there are no enduring objects.

Presentism entails that there are no things with temporal parts.

Either eternalism or presentism is true (but not both).

Therefore, either there are no enduring objects or there are no things with temporal parts.

On the one hand, a world in which there are no enduring things is one in which the only (relevant) things that exist are things with temporal parts. To the extent that I can make sense of such a world, it is a world in which no thing really changes; it is, rather, a world in which things go out of existence and other things come into existence; it is a world in which the idea that things change is *simulated* but not realized. According to temporal parts theory, a thing composed of temporal parts changes by having *distinct* temporal parts that are qualitatively different. This is a view that, since it denies that any thing successively (and nonderivatively) has contrary properties, takes change to be the *replacement* of one thing, one temporal part, by another. That is what *I* mean by saying that such a view *simulates* the idea that things change—in roughly the way that a series of still photographs, when streamed rapidly before our eyes, simulates motion.

Heraclitus held that to change is to become different in the sense of becoming a *different thing* (one cannot, he said, step into the same river twice). Thus he held that, although there are changes—the goings-out-of and comings-into existence of things—no thing endures through any change. A world in which there are perduring, but no enduring, entities is Heraclitean. A thing's coming into or going out of existence is *not* a change in the thing that comes into or goes out of existence (according to the ACC), since it does not, in coming into or going out of existence, endure. A world without enduring things is a changeless Heraclitean world.

Merricks argued that, if eternalism is true, then there are no things that endure, for if eternalism is true and an enduring thing apparently changed from being *F* to not being *F*, then that object would, impossibly, be both *F* and not-*F*; this is the so-called problem of temporary intrinsics. Thus, since to be an enduring thing is to be a thing that endures through change, if eternalism is true, then there are no enduring things, and the world is Heraclitean.

On the other hand, a world in which there are enduring entities, but no entities with temporal parts, is a world in which, since *events* have temporal parts, there are no events.[6] Since a world without events is a world in which, it seems to me, nothing happens, and, since I think that the connection between the idea that things change and the idea that change occurs should not, Heraclitus notwithstanding, be severed,[7] a world populated only by enduring things is *also* a world in which no thing changes. But, in this case, the world would be Parmenidean.

If presentism is true, then, apparently, not all of the parts of a thing with temporal parts exist, since those parts do not all exist at the present time. However, Merricks thinks that the claim

(1) An object cannot have another object as a part if that other part does not exist

is obviously true (Merricks 1995, 524). Therefore, since a thing with temporal parts has as parts objects that do not exist at present, then, if presentism is true, either (1) is false or there are no things that have temporal parts. But Merricks thinks (1) too obvious to deny. Thus, if presentism is true, there are no things with temporal parts. But if there are no things with temporal parts, then there are no events. And if it is the case that, if a thing alters, then there is an event that is that thing's changing, then no thing alters, and the world is Parmenidean.

As I see things, then, Merricks has argued that the world must be changeless in either a Heraclitean or a Parmenidean way. And thus, we have a new challenge to the apparently obvious truth that things change; for it appears that, if either presentism or eternalism is true, change is impossible.

There are at least two ways in which this challenge might be met. One involves challenging the arguments that, respectively, have presentism and eternalism as premises and the denial of change (in one form or another) as conclusion. I have attempted to do that elsewhere.[8] A second involves attempting to undermine the very terms in which this new challenge to the possibility of change is framed. And that is what I would like to do in this essay. I want to argue that the contrast between presentism and eternalism, as substantive and contrary metaphysical views about time and the reality of things that exist in time, has yet to be made, and that it appears that this contrast, so understood, is spurious.[9] And so, unless further work is done which shows that presentism and eternalism are substantive and contrary views, these new arguments do not really pose any new challenge to the idea that things change.[10]

A Challenge Too Facile?

According to Merricks, presentism is

the doctrine that the present time is ontologically privileged. According to the Presentist, all that exists, exists at the present time; and an object has only those properties it has at the present time. (Merricks 1995, 524)

But, although this expression of presentism might seem, to both the view's adherents and opponents, to be adequate, it also seems, at least at first glance, difficult to take it as expressing a view that might inspire controversy.

Does Merricks's statement express the view that the present time is the *only* time that exists? Well, it is certainly the only time that exists *now*; but that is hardly controversial. Does it express the view that the present time is the only time that exists at *any* time? If so, the view is uncontroversially *false*. Similarly, it is hardly controversial that the only things that exist now are things that exist now; and the denial of that is uncontroversially false. And, if the first occurrence of the word 'has' in the claim that "an object has only those properties it has at the present time" is in the present tense, the claim seems trivially true; if the claim means that the only properties that an object *ever* has are the ones it has at the present time, the claim seems obviously false. So, presentism seems either trivially true or obviously false.

Eternalism is alleged to be the view that *all* times are on the same onto-logical footing, and that all things, whenever they exist, are equally real. Does eternalism assert that *all* times exist now, and that all things, when-ever they exist, exist now? Such a view seems obviously untrue—unless, as *presentism* appears to insist, only one time, namely the present, exists. Does eternalism assert that *all* times exist at some time or other? Now that view seems true; but it is not one that would inspire even the most argu-mentative among philosophers to object.

In the paragraph to follow, I want to play a little fast and loose with the word 'real' in order to highlight the charge of triviality. I will get more serious about it below, where it will be seen how important it is to be clear about the distinction between 'exists' and 'is real'.

Of course, both Bill Clinton and Aristotle each exist at some time or other. But are they *equally* real? On the one hand, hardly—Clinton, it might be said, *is* more real than Aristotle, for Clinton *is* (real) and Aristotle isn't (or so it seems). And though Aristotle *was* just as real as Clinton *is* (and Clinton will be just as unreal as Aristotle now is), does that make them equally real *now*? On the other hand—and this is the hand I prefer, for reasons that will emerge later—Clinton and Aristotle are, in some sense, equally real. It is not as if Aristotle, having lived and died many cen-turies ago, now has some sort of shadowy existence, one that is less sub-stantial than the existence that Clinton now has (though it is also not the case that Aristotle now has an existence that rivals Clinton's in robust-ness). There aren't two, or three, kinds of existence for contingent things—past existence, present existence, and, perhaps, future existence—which are such that objects that possess one of them, present existence, are "more real" than objects that possess the others. (Indeed, I do not think I understand the idea that is supposed to be expressed by the words 'more real' at all.) Now, is this an issue that presentists and eternalists can profit-ably argue over? I think not, but I shall be returning to the words 'exist' and 'real' in due course.

It may be argued that this reduction of presentism and eternalism to trivial truth or obvious falsehood is too facile. *If* presentism and eter-nalism meant what I have just taken them to mean, then, it might be said, the charge of triviality would be justified. However, to see the depth of the debate between presentists and eternalists and the depth of the challenge to the idea that things change, we need to see presentism and eternalism as more sophisticated than I have represented them as being.

Dean Zimmerman, for example, says something like this, admitting that there is a version of presentism that is either trivially true or obviously false (Zimmerman 1998, 209). With respect to the statement, "the only things that exist are those that exist at present," he too notes that if the occurrence of 'exist' is in the present tense, then the statement is a trivial tautology; but if it means 'did exist, exists, or will exist', then it expresses an "implausible metaphysical thesis." But, he continues, "Presentism is neither a boring truth nor an interesting falsehood" (ibid.). Rather, according to Zimmerman, the presentist holds, that

(2)   There is only one largest class of all real things, and this class contains nothing that lies wholly in the past or future (Zimmerman 1998, 210).

But this at least seems to be subject to the same kind of objection that plagues the "trivial" versions. If the "real" things are just the things that exist, Zimmerman's statement of presentism seems equivalent, if all the verbs are in the present tense, to this:

(2′)   There is now one class that contains all the things that exist now, and this class contains nothing that does not exist now.

And this seems trivially true. So, if (2) is understood in this way, it is trivially true as well. And if (2) is read with its 'exists' given a reading according to which 'x exists' means 'x existed, exists, or will exist', it is, I believe, just as problematic as Zimmerman's interesting falsehood. And so, just what is this version of presentism that is neither a boring truth nor an interesting falsehood?[11]

Now, it might be charged that I have not given Zimmerman's idea sufficient attention here. And that is true. But I will later, when the issue of the meaning of 'real' will come up again.

Ted Sider's book, *Four-Dimensionalism* (Sider 2001), is an extended defense of temporal parts. Like most philosophers involved in the discussion of presentism and eternalism, he thinks temporal parts theory is closely allied with eternalism. Thus, Sider is concerned to argue against presentism and in favor of eternalism. Here is Sider's statement of eternalism:

past and future objects and times are just as real as currently existing ones. Just as distant objects are no less real for being spatially distant, distant times are no less real for being temporally distant. . . . In the block universe, dinosaurs, computers, and future outposts on Mars are all equally real. . . . According to *presentism*, on the other hand, only currently existing objects are real. (Sider 2001, 11)

But this statement appears to make presentism obviously true and eternalism false, if its verbs are taken to be in the present tense.[12] And if what is now real is what now exists, it is simply not true that past (and perhaps future) objects are *now* just as real as presently existing ones. But, again, the issue of the meaning of 'real' will come up below.

Perhaps it will be said that I am still taking a cheap shot at the presentism–eternalism dispute, and that a more careful look at it is called for. But before doing so, I want to make a brief remark about what my skepticism about the debate between presentists and eternalists does and does not concern.

Whatever it is for something to exist is something that the presentist, the eternalist, and I can (and should) agree about. No party to this dispute thinks that Aristotle currently has a shadowy, ethereal existence, which replaced the robust existence he had when he "really" existed, with the presentist insisting that shadowy existence is not real existence and eternalist insisting that it is. The presentist denies that Aristotle exists now; but so does the eternalist, and so do I. But the eternalist claims to see in that no impediment to Aristotle's existence. My complaint is *not* that the presentist and the eternalist only appear to disagree because they equivocate on the word 'exist', in the sense of that word which currently applies to Bill Clinton, and once applied to Aristotle. According to me, 'exists' is univocal; it always expresses the property of existence. Now, the number two has this property "tenselessly" in the sense that the number two would exist even if there were no times. My computer, however, would not; it has the property expressed by 'exists' only at times. Despite this contrast, though, in worlds in which there are times, the number two exists at all of them.[13] Tenseless existence and tensed existence are *not* two kinds of existence. There is only one kind of existence, though certain entities, if they exist at all, have it tenselessly, whereas others have it tensedly.[14] My complaint concerns, not any equivocation on the meaning of the word 'exist', but rather that aspect of occurrences of the word 'exist' that has to do with their *tense* (or lack thereof). It also concerns the word 'real'.

Tensed Readings

Are there *tensed* versions of presentism and eternalism that can inspire reasonable controversy as to which is true?[15] In a way, we have already considered this in the previous section. But, to review, consider this typical statement of presentism:

(3) Everything that exists exists now.

Since in this section I am assuming all verbs to have a tense, and since (3)'s third word is 'exists', there seem to be three interpretations we can give to (3). We can interpret that occurrence as in the present tense, giving us the trivial

(3a)   Everything that exists now exists now.

We can interpret the tense of 'exists' tense as disjunctively omnitemporal; (3) would then mean

(3b)   Everything that existed, exists, or will exist exists now.

But, since it seems obvious that Aristotle did, but does not now, exist, it seems that (3b) is obviously false.[16] Third, we can interpret the first occurrence of 'exists' in (3) as "conjunctively omnitemporal," that is, as meaning 'did, does, *and* will exist'; then it means

(3c)   Everything that exists at all times exists now;

and that seems trivially true.

In a similar way, consider a central claim of eternalism:

(4)   There are things that do not exist now.

If (4)'s second word has a tense, there seem to be three ways in which it can be understood. Construing 'are' as in the present tense gives us the trivially false

(4a)   There now are things that do not now exist.

Construing it as disjunctively omnitemporal gives us the obviously true

(4b)   There were, are now, or will be things that do not now exist.

And third, (4) can be interpreted as the obviously false

(4c)   There are things that exist at all times that do not now exist.

Generalizing, it appears that typical presentist claims come out trivially *true* when construed as either present-tensed or conjunctively omnitemporal and obviously *false* when construed as disjunctively omnitemporal. And typical eternalist claims come out obviously *false* when construed as either present-tensed or conjunctively omnitemporal and trivially *true* when construed as disjunctively omnitemporal.

Surely both the presentist and the eternalist will agree about the truth-values that (3a–c) and (4a–c) have. So what is it that they disagree about? Presentists and eternalists insist that they disagree about (3)—Everything that exists exists now—the presentist holding it true, while the eternalist insisting that it's false. After all, doesn't the eternalist insist that there are dinosaurs (Sider 2001, 11)?

Yes, but surely the eternalist does *not* insist that there *are* dinosaurs, that is, *right now*. Yet he insists that, despite that fact, dinosaurs nevertheless exist. But what could this mean except that there were, are, or will be dinosaurs? So, a disagreement over dinosaurs can be fomented between the eternalist and the presentist only if we allow them to equivocate; the equivocation concerns not what it is to exist, but the *tense* of claims that assert existence. The presentist denies that there are dinosaurs in the sense of (3a), whereas the eternalist insists that there are dinosaurs in the sense of (4b). This is no real dispute.

Well, not so fast!

The Master Class and the Word 'Real'

Let us reconsider Zimmerman's formulation of presentism, for it is here that the real source of whatever disagreement there is between presentists and eternalists may very well lie:

(2)   There is only one largest class of all real things, and this class contains nothing that lies wholly in the past or future.

The suggestion that (2), like "more naive" expressions of presentism, is trivially true assumes that the largest class of all real things is the largest class that contains all and only the things that exist; and since I have been taking this last occurrence of 'exist' to be in the present tense, that largest class would seem to be the class of all things that exist *now*. Thus, that every member of that class is a presently existing thing is a triviality.

But to argue in this way is to assume something that I believe we have *no* right to assume. And I think that presentists assert, and eternalists reject, (2) at least in part because they make the same assumption. The assumption in question is this:

(5)   If a class *S* exists at a time *t*, then everything that is a member of *S* exists at *t*.

With this assumption in hand, we can see why the presentist would have to be asserting something trivial: at any time *t*, the largest class of real things just is the class all of whose members exist at *t*. So, of course, at present, everything in that class exists at present.

But what is it that warrants this assumption? As far as I can tell, *not much*.

There is the idea that the principles of class membership are, in effect, *mereological* principles (consider (1), above). Of course, all the things that are now parts of my bicycle are things that exist now; I don't think I would understand someone who told me that my bicycle *now* has a part which, perhaps unfortunately, does not now exist. Indeed, the very fact that some thing does not now exist (e.g., the rear reflector) implies that that thing is *not* now a part of my bicycle.

But why should one think that such a mereological principle governs classes? Why isn't the following principle the proper one governing class membership?

(6)   If a class S exists at a time t, then everything that is a member of S exists *at some time or other.*[17]

According to (6), the existence condition on members of classes is disjunctively omnitemporal. And so, the largest class of all real things would, then, be the class of all things that exist at some time or other. There would thus be no impediment to there currently being a class whose members include not only Bill Clinton, but also Aristotle, dinosaurs, and perhaps future outposts on Mars (but *not* Superman).

Actually, (6) needs to be amended. We need to append to (6) the words 'or would exist even if there were no times', in order to take account of things, like numbers, that are sometimes said to exist timelessly, in the sense that they would exist even if there were no times. If the sentence 'the number seven exists but does not exist now' expresses any proposition at all, then it expresses a proposition that we know a priori to be false. The proposition, if any, that it expresses is not a contradiction, for there are, I suppose, possible worlds in which there are no times. But in any possible world in which it does express a proposition, the word 'now' would have to have a referent; and in any such world the proposition expressed would be false.[18] If there are things that would exist even if there were no times, then the largest class of all real things should include them. It should be noted that, if there are times—a condition necessary for things to change—then it would be true to say, for example, that the number seven exists now. The timelessly existing things, if there are any, belong to the "Master" class.

What are the consequences for presentism and eternalism with such an understanding of class membership? Let the Master class, the class over which all unrestricted quantifiers range, be the largest class of all "real" things, that is, the class of all things that have existed, do exist, or will exist, or would exist even if there were no times. Would it then be true, as the presentist asserts, that the only things that exist are the things that exist at the present time? Well, though the Master class includes all the "real" things—not all of those entities, obviously, exist now. So, the answer to the question "Does everything in the Master class exist now?" is No.

However, the claim that everything that exists exists now, if the first of its occurrences of 'exists' is in the present tense, is true. But this is still not an interesting thesis. What makes that claim appear to be an interesting, nontrivial thesis is that the idea that some thing exists *now* can be confused with the idea that it is now *real*, that is, with the idea that it is a member of the Master class. And that there is such a thing as the Master class is permitted by the rejection of the mereological conception of classes.

The eternalist's assertion is that all things, whenever they exist, are equally real. This claim is surely true, in the sense that all such things are members of the Master class. But not all such things exist (that is, exist now). Yes, everything in that Master class is equally real. But, again, it is not a condition on a thing's current membership in the Master class that it exist now; what is required is only that a thing be real. And for a thing to be real it is enough that it exist at some time or other (or is such that it would exist even if there were no times).

Aristotle, though he no longer exists, is real. Although the claim that Aristotle is real can be understood as 'it is true at all times that Aristotle did, does, or will exist', it is also true that Aristotle is real *now*. After all, as a member of the Master class, Aristotle can be the value of a variable of unrestricted quantification. Aristotle can be referred to (indeed, he is now being referred to by me), and can be the subject of present-tensed predications (though he cannot now have any property that implies current existence). So, Aristotle is real now. But from this it does not follow that Aristotle *exists* now.

What this shows is that the words 'real' and 'exist' do *not* mean the same thing. Whereas the tensed 'exists' distinguishes Aristotle, who doesn't, from Clinton, who does, the word 'real' distinguishes Aristotle and Clinton, who are, from Superman and Sherlock Holmes, who aren't.

Thus, the claim that dinosaurs exist may be conflated with the claim that dinosaurs are real; and this conflation is encouraged by the assumption of the mereological conception of classes. Dinosaurs don't exist;[19] but they do belong to the Master class and are, therefore, real.

This issue is related to the issue of translation. Sider writes: "Since ordinary talk and thought are full of quantification over non-present objects, presentists are in a familiar predicament: in their unreflective moments, they apparently commit themselves to far more than their ontological scruples allow. A familiar response is to begin a project of paraphrase"

(Sider 1999, 325). But Sider notes that, by and large, the presentist will have not too much trouble finding paraphrases of "difficult" sentences, except for those that involve cross-time relations (Sider 2001, 25ff.).

However, the problem of paraphrasing statements involving cross-time relations, for example, 'Clinton admires Plato', disappears if there can be true singular propositions concerning things that do not exist. That there cannot be such singular propositions is held, I think, for roughly the same sort of reason that the mereological conception of sets is held. And such a conception of singular propositions—that a singular proposition that is about an object, x, exists at a time t only if x exists at t—seems just as unmotivated as a mereological conception of sets. A proposition is not a collection or mereological sum of entities (e.g., things, properties). It is, I think, enough for a singular proposition to be about an object, x, that x exist at some time or other (or would exist even if there were no times). Thus, there can be singular propositions that exist now that are about Plato, but no singular propositions about, say, Superman.

In any event, as long as both Plato and Clinton belong to the Master class, we can express propositions that say that latter admires the former. Of course, an admirer cannot admire anything at a time at which the admirer does not exist; but the objects of admiration do not need to exist at the times at which they are admired.

Even if the Master class is admitted as the largest class of all real things, that will, by itself, help neither the eternalist nor the presentist. '$(\exists x)(Fx)$' means 'from among all the members of the Master class, there exists something that is F'. And if the word 'exists' is in the present tense, the presentist's creed—everything that exists exists now—still appears to be a trivial truth, for all it means is 'from among all the members of the Master class, everything that exists (now) exists now'.[20]

Perhaps it will be insisted that the dispute between presentists and eternalists is indeed a dispute about the Master class. The presentist might be taken to be asserting that, although the Master class is, as I am insisting, the class of all things that have existed, do exist, will exist, or would exist even if there were no times, the only things that are *currently* members of that class are those that exist *now*. And the eternalist will, presumably, deny this.

All parties to the dispute between presentism and eternalism can agree that an object cannot exist at times other than the times at which it exists. This is trivially true, and implies nothing about the population of the Master class. In addition, the claim is wholly independent of the claim that objects can have properties, and bear relations to other things, at times at which they do not exist. In addition, as I shall now argue, this latter claim seems clearly true.

Class membership is determined solely by *conditions*. And here is the condition determining membership in the Master class:

(MC) $(x)(x \in \text{MC} \equiv x$ exists, did exist, will exist, or would exist even if there were no times).

The presentist claims that the Master class now includes only things that exist now. But this view seems to be generated by the idea that class membership is determined by something other than conditions.

Consider the class of things that existed in 1950. Surely that class includes Bertrand Russell. And consider the class of things that exist now. Clearly the Eiffel Tower belongs to the intersection of these two classes. Now, surely, not only does that intersection exist, but so do the classes that "intersect." Thus, the class of things that existed in 1950 exists now and now includes things that existed in 1950 but do not exist now (e.g., Bertrand Russell).

So, the question whose answer apparently separates presentist from eternalist is this: Can the condition on class membership specified in (MC) be satisfied at a time, t, by objects that do not exist at t? The presentist answers "No," because she holds that an object can satisfy a condition at a time t only if that object exists then. But this answer assumes that objects cannot have properties, or bear relations to other things, at times at which they do not exist. And this assumption is false.

Aristotle was a philosopher. The statement 'it was the case that x was (then) a philosopher' clearly expresses a property. And it is a property that Aristotle has, and, indeed, has *now*. If Aristotle does not have that property now, then it is simply not now the case that he was a philosopher. Similarly, 'it was the case that x was taught by Plato' expresses a relational property that Aristotle has, and has *now*.

The proposition that Aristotle existed is equivalent to the proposition that it was the case that the proposition that Aristotle exists was true. But take the sentence 'the proposition that it was the case that the proposition that Aristotle exists was true', and replace 'Aristotle' by 'x'. Then we have an expression—'the proposition that it was the case that the proposition that x exists was true'—that expresses a property which an object has just in case the proposition that it exists was true. But clearly, Aristotle has that property, and he has it *now*. And that is sufficient for Aristotle's being a member of the Master class, because any object that satisfies the condition expressed by 'the proposition that it was the case that the proposition that x exists was true' clearly satisfies the condition of having existed. And satisfying that condition is sufficient for being a member of the Master class, that is, for being real.

It should also be noted that it is clearly true that for some time, t, Aristotle exists at t. But the proposition expressed by the sentence 'for some time, t, Aristotle exists at t', is true at *all* times, even at those times at which Aristotle does *not* exist.

One might argue, I suppose, that the sentence 'it was the case that Aristotle existed' does not now express a proposition on the grounds that Aristotle does not now exist (see Markosian 2004, 51–60). But if that were so, then it would not now be true that Aristotle was a philosopher, that Aristotle taught Plato, that Aristotle wrote *Metaphysics*, and so on; there would now be *no* truths about Aristotle. But this is absurd. In attempting to defend presentism, Ned Markosian, in effect, accepts the view that such claims are false, but insists that there are truths that are *much like* the ones that he thinks are, owing to the nonexistence of Aristotle, false, claims like 'it was the case that there was someone whose was the referent of 'Aristotle' and was a philosopher'. But, first, it just *is* true that Aristotle was a philosopher, despite Markosian's attempts at explaining away the appearance of truth. Second, it would have been true that Aristotle was a philosopher even if there had never been anyone who was the referent of the name 'Aristotle' (after all, Aristotle's name could have been 'Fred'); 'Aristotle was a philosopher' and 'it was the case that there was someone whose was the referent of 'Aristotle' and was a philosopher' are just not close enough in meaning. And third, if, in order to formulate (and defend) presentism, we have to reject the obvious truth that Aristotle was a philosopher in favor of what seems to be a highly implausible view about what propositions expressed by sentences like 'Aristotle was a philosopher' would have to mean, if they are to come out to be "close" to true, why should one think that presentism was worth formulating and defending in the first place?

It might also be suggested that in sentences like 'it was the case that Aristotle was a philosopher', 'Aristotle' does not refer, since the tense operator, 'it was the case that', creates a context in which names within its scope are not "ontologically committing." However, though it is, of course, the case that 'Aristotle' does not now refer to anything that exists, it does *not* follow from this that 'Aristotle' does not now refer to anything.

Thus, it seems that objects *can* have properties and bear relations to other things at times at which they do not exist (see Soames 2002, 91). Of course, I am *not* arguing that Aristotle can truly be the subject of just any

old predication. Aristotle does not *now* have the property of being a philosopher or the property of getting older, for anyone who now has these
properties must exist now. But he does now have the property of having
been a philosopher, and he does now have the property of being dead.
Aristotle can now have properties that do not imply that he exists now.
The claim that objects *cannot* have any properties or bear any relations to
other things at times at which they do not exist strikes me as simply false;
and thus I do not see a serious objection to its being the case that currently nonexistent objects can satisfy the condition for membership in the
Master class, and thus be real.[21] Nor do I see a serious objection to its being
the case that currently nonexistent objects can be the subjects of singular
propositions.

If the dispute between the presentist and the eternalist is a dispute about
whether the Master class now contains things that do not now exist—with
the presentist saying "No" and the eternalist saying "Yes"—then the eternalist wins, hands down.

The dispute between presentists and eternalists is supposed to be a
metaphysical dispute about time and what exists; presentists appear to be
asserting that only what exists in the present exists, and eternalists appear
to be asserting that things other than presently existing things exist as well.
Both can agree, if they reject a mereological conception of classes, that
there is a class—the Master class—that contains exactly the objects that
the eternalist says there are: the objects that have existed, do now exist,
and will exist (and the things that would exist even if there were no times).
This class, however, contains more objects than the presentist says there
are. But this should give no comfort to the eternalist and need cause no
dismay to the presentist. The presentist will insist that not all of the entities in the Master class exist now. And, of course, in this the presentist is
absolutely right. But when the tense of that occurrence of 'exist' is interpreted as disjunctively omnitemporal, the eternalist is right; everything in
the Master class exists, did exist, or will exist (or would exist even if there
were no times). And, the presentist will have to admit that, in that sense,
there exist things that do not exist now; for the class of things that are now
real includes more than just the things that now exist.

But there is no disagreement here concerning what exists. The source of
the apparent disagreement is, at least in part, the acceptance of a mereological conception of sets. Once that conception is accepted, the presentist
will insist that the eternalist's Master class is too large—too large, that is,
to tolerate the claim that everything in that class exists (in the sense of
'exists *now*'), and the eternalist will have to insist that the presentist's Mas-

ter class is too small—too small to tolerate the claim that everything that is real is in that class. But no issue is joined. That is, no issue is joined that is about what presentists and eternalists have said they were arguing about—times and the existence of things that exist in time. The dispute might be shifted to one concerning the principles of class membership, the constituents of singular propositions, and the interpretation of quantifiers; but it is *not* about what exists.

So, if the crucial verbs are construed as being tensed (either as present tensed or as disjunctively omnitemporal), then both presentism and eternalism appear to be either trivially true or obviously false.

And if presentism is trivial in the way just suggested, then Merricks's argument for the Parmenidean denial of change collapses. The claim, crucial to the argument for the claim that presentism implies that there are no things with temporal parts—that an object cannot have another object as a part if that other part does not exist—is clearly true, when all verbs in it are interpreted as in the present tense. However, so construed, the claim does not imply that objects cannot have, at times other than the present, parts that do not exist at the present time. That is, if (1) is interpreted as

(1′) $\sim\lozenge((\exists t)(\exists x)(\exists y)(t$ is a time & at t, x has y as a part) & y does not exist at t),

the claim is clearly true; but (1′) does not imply the desired conclusion.

But if the claim is interpreted as asserting that objects cannot at some time or other have another object as a part if that other part does not exist at some time or other, it should be interpreted as

(1″) $\sim\lozenge((\exists t)(\exists x)(\exists y)(t$ is a time & at t x has y as a part) & $(\exists t')(y$ does not exist at $t'))$.

(1″) does imply the desired conclusion, but it is simply not true, so long as an object can have parts at some times and not have them at others (see Lombard 1999).

And the arguments that allegedly derive a contradiction from eternalism and the idea that enduring objects change do so only by committing scope fallacies (see Lombard 2005). Thus, the differences between presentist and eternalists seem to have no consequences for the issue of whether changeable objects persist by enduring or by perduring, or for the possibility of change itself.

Sider has insisted that there is a single sense of 'exists' in which the debate between presentists and eternalists can be framed (Sider 2001, 17). If Sider is right, then 'exist' in that sense cannot have a tense. If there are

nontrivial versions of presentism and eternalism, they will have to be formulated in a way that does not employ a tensed sense of 'exist'. It is to this
subject that I now turn.

Tenseless Formulations

There *appears* to be a dispute between presentists and eternalists concerning what exists. Eternalists appear to insist that there are dinosaurs, despite
the fact that no dinosaurs exist now; presentists appear to deny this. But,
if the eternalist means that there were, are, or will be dinosaurs, then the
presentist will readily agree, and no battle will be joined. If the presentist
means that there are no dinosaurs in existence now, then the eternalist
will (or should) readily agree, and again no battle will be joined.

Both eternalist and presentist insist that they disagree about the truth
of some existential claim. But just what existential claim it is that they
disagree about is unclear. They cannot, I have argued, be disagreeing
about some existential claim expressed with *tensed* verbs. So, the eternalist
must be claiming that 'there are (exist) dinosaurs' is true, while the presentist insists that it's not—in some univocal sense of 'are' (and 'exist') that is
not tensed. But what does the untensed 'are' (and 'exist') mean in the context of assertions of existence concerning contingent things?

While they take the concept of existence *simpliciter* to be primitive, Scott
Hestevold and W. R. Carter offer the following informal explication:

(HC₁)   *Something* exists *simpliciter* if and only if it is among the things that
the universe includes—if and only if *it* is *real*. (i) That *something* exists *simpliciter* implies neither that *it did* exist nor that *it will* exist; and (ii) that *two
things* both exist *simpliciter* does not alone imply that *they* coexist (Hestevold and Carter 2002a).

I propose that we understand this suggestion along the following lines.

Suppose that someone were to say "there's a rabbit," where the occurrence of 'there' does *not* mean anything like 'over there' or 'in that place';
rather, one is simply *placelessly* asserting the existence of a rabbit. That there
is a rabbit, in this sense, implies neither that it is here nor that it is there, and
that there are two rabbits does not imply that they are in the same place.

In a similar way, suppose that the occurrence of 'is' in 'x is red' does *not*
mean anything like 'is now', that it is tenselessly predicative. That something is red implies, on this interpretation, neither that it was nor that it
will be red; and that there are two red things does not imply that they are
red at the same time.

Similarly for the "existential" but untensed 'are' in 'there are dinosaurs'. In this tenseless sense, to say that there are dinosaurs is not to say that dinosaurs exist *now*. In this sense, 'there are dinosaurs' does not imply that they either did or will exist; and the fact that there are dinosaurs and humans does not imply that dinosaurs and humans coexist. The occurrence of 'are' in 'there are dinosaurs' is not temporal; it is purely existential.

Presentists and eternalists, in insisting that the dispute between them is genuine and substantive, must at least agree on the meaning of key expressions, particularly that of 'exist' (and its cognates). And it strikes me that Hestevold and Carter have hit on a reasonable explanation of the idea of tenseless existence. It detaches the idea of existence from the idea of existence at some particular time. In addition, it appears to allow the eternalist to insist (either truly or falsely) that both Aristotle and Bill Clinton exist (that is, exist *simpliciter*), and to allow the presentist to insist that only presently existing things exist without falling into triviality.

Presentism appears to assert that nothing exists that does not presently exist. Hestevold and Carter propose the following formulation of that doctrine:

(PR)   Necessarily, if x exists simpliciter, then x presently exists (Hestevold and Carter 2002a).[22]

(PR) seems as good an attempt as any at saying what presentism is, since it links an apparently untensed concept of existence (existence *simpliciter*) with present existence. Clearly, the eternalist will insist that there is such a concept of existence *simpliciter*, under which both Plato and Clinton fall; and, consequently, the eternalist will insist that (PR) is false. And, the presentist will argue that, even if there is such a conception of existence, only presently existing things fall under it. Thus, it appears that (PR) expresses a view that presentists accept and eternalists reject.

It seems to me that (PR) is as good an explanation of presentism as one could have. And the debate between presentists and eternalists over the truth of (PR) appears substantive and genuine. I think, however, that appearances deceive.

First, if 'existence *simpliciter*' means what I mean by 'is real', and it surely looks like that is so,[23] then (PR) implies that either Aristotle exists now or Aristotle isn't real. But both these disjuncts are false. Aristotle surely does not exist now; and Aristotle, having once existed, is real. So, if (PR) is to be true, 'x exists *simpliciter*' must mean 'x exists (now)'. But then, (PR) is trivial.

Second, it should be noted how odd principle (PR) is. Presumably, (PR) must be true at every moment, *t*, which is such that *t* is referred to by 'presently'. But, since every moment is a now at some time, past, present, or future, that is *every t*. So, if (PR) is true, then it is true at every time. But then it follows that, necessarily, every object that exists *simpliciter* exists *at every time*. This is surely *not* a result that presentists want.[24] Nor is it, by the way, a result that eternalists should welcome. After all, it is they who believe that there are objects (that is, objects that exist *simpliciter*) that do not exist now, that the present nonexistence of a thing is not an impediment to its existence. But, if (PR) is true at all times, there can be no such objects. Alternatively, the presentist may want to pick out some *really special* time, *t*, such that (PR) is true precisely when, and only when, 'presently' refers just to *t*. But which time might that be? And why is that time so special?

Third, there is another problem, a problem that arises when Hestevold and Carter's characterization of presentism, (PR), is combined with their conception of existence *simpliciter* (HC₁). Suppose that some objects, *x* and *y*, both exist *simpliciter*. Then it follows from (PR) that *x* presently exists and that *y* presently exists. And, given what 'presently exists' must mean, it follows trivially that *x and y coexist*. But that conclusion, when conjoined with clause (ii) of (HC₁) and the claim that something exists *simpliciter*, yields a contradiction.[25] So, if (PR) and (HC₁) are true, then *nothing* exists *simpliciter*.[26,27]

Thus, if Hestevold and Carter have indeed isolated a correct understanding of tenseless existence (existence *simpliciter*), and they have if 'exists *simpliciter*' means what I mean by 'is real', we should conclude that presentism, understood as (PR), is false. Victory for eternalism! However, a victory achieved by virtue of one's opponent's stipulative definition, however plausible it might be, is a tainted victory. But before victory—tainted or otherwise—is conceded to the eternalist, we need to look a bit more carefully at the concept of tenseless existence.[28]

Though it might be claimed that the purely existential 'there' is "placeless," it might be difficult to defend such a claim. If there is (in the purely existential sense) a rabbit, then there is a rabbit *somewhere*; and this is *not* an accident. After all, rabbits, being physical beings, have spatial locations. If, for every "there" (that is, for every place), it is false that there is a rabbit *there*, then it is simply false that there is any rabbit at all. And, if there is a rabbit somewhere, then there is a rabbit *simpliciter* (that is, in the purely existential sense). It appears, then, that 'there is a rabbit' (in the purely existential sense) is equivalent to 'there is a rabbit somewhere'. If it is going to be said that there is a difference between a clearly "placed" sense of 'there'—a disjunctively omnispatial sense, equivalent to 'exists somewhere or other'—and a "placeless," purely existential sense, we are, I think, owed an explanation of the difference and an account of the latter.[29]

And I should think that, if 'the barn is (tenselessly) red' is true, then, despite the fact that 'is' is supposed to have no tense, the barn must be red at some time or other; and this is *not* an accident. If, for every "now," it is false that the barn is red *now*, then it is simply false that the barn is red. And, if the barn is red at some time, then it is red *simpliciter*, that is, it is red in the tenseless sense of 'is'.

Similarly, it might be claimed that there is a purely existential, tenseless sense of 'is' or 'exists' that applies to contingent entities; but it might be difficult to defend that claim. After all, rabbits are physical beings. If there is (in the purely existential sense) a rabbit, then some rabbit exists at some time or other; and, if a rabbit exists at some time or other, then there is a rabbit (in the purely existential sense). It appears, then, that 'there is a rabbit' (in the purely existential, tenseless sense) is equivalent to 'there is a rabbit at some time or other'. If it is going to be said that there is a difference between a clearly tensed sense of 'exists'—a disjunctively omnitemporal sense, equivalent to 'exists at some time or other'—and a tenseless, purely existential sense, we are, I think, owed an explanation of the difference and an account of the latter.[30]

I just do not understand what the tenseless sense of 'is' or 'exists' is supposed to mean, as it applies to contingently existing things, unless it means what the disjunctively omnitemporal sense of those expressions means (that is, 'is, was, or will be'). But, on such a construal, there seems to be no substantive point of controversy between presentists and eternalists, and thus I do not understand how a substantive ontological debate between them is to be framed. It cannot be framed by using tensed verbs; and I just do not see what the sense of an untensed verb is supposed to be in terms of which the debate is to be conducted.[31]

Presentists and eternalists need to provide explications of tenseless senses of 'is' and 'exists' and nontrivial versions of presentism and eternalism that are formulated in terms of that notion of existence. But what could those explications and formulations be? I just don't know.

There are issues that need to be settled concerning how quantifiers, tensed and untensed, are to be understood. And, there can be a debate between those who think that presently nonexistent things can now be members of classes, and that currently nonexistent things can now be constituents of singular propositions, and that things can have some properties (and bear relations to other things) at times at which they do not exist, and those who don't think so. But, it seems clear who wins that debate. More importantly, however, it seems clear that such a debate is not about time or the existence of things that exist in time. And since, I have argued, presentism does not imply that there are no things with temporal parts, and eternalism does not imply that things cannot endure the changes they undergo, the debate seems to have no consequences either for the issue of whether things endure or perdure, nor does it constitute a new threat to the idea that things change.

A Verbal Dispute?

It has been said that the dispute between presentism and eternalism is an ontological dispute, a dispute over what there is, and that it cannot be dismissed without dismissing other existential disputes in metaphysics as well. For example, Sider insists that presentism and eternalism are metaphysical views about what there is—specifically, about what times exist, and which things that exist in time exist—on a par with other metaphysical views concerning, say, whether universals exist, whether disembodied mental substances exist, whether God exists, and whether (merely) possible entities exist; and that to dismiss the controversy between presentism and eternalism would open the door to dismissing these other, clearly substantive, metaphysical controversies (Sider 2001, 17).

Sider's argument for this conclusion rests on the idea that the dispute between presentists and the eternalists is often dismissed by accusing the parties of meaning different things by 'exist', and thus accusing the parties of "dispute by equivocation." Thus, it might be argued, if 'exists' means 'existed, exists now, or will exist', then, of course, dinosaurs exist and the eternalist is right; but if 'exists' means 'exists now', then dinosaurs do not exist and the presentist is right. But if that is how the "dispute" is framed, there is no dispute, only the illusion of one.

Similarly, Sider suggests, if 'exists' means 'actually or possibly exists', then, of course, there are possible objects (in addition to actual ones), and the modal realist is right; but if 'exists' means 'actually exists', then there are no (merely) possible objects, and the modal actualist is right. And thus, the debate between modal realists and modal actualists is spurious, depending on an equivocation for its appearance of legitimacy. And similarly, if 'exists' can mean 'mathematically exists', then there is a sense in which 'numbers exist' is trivially true, and there is no real debate between mathematical realists and their opponents.

But, it is said, the dispute between modal realists and modal actualists and the dispute between mathematical realists and their opponents are *genuine* disputes, and are not to be dismissed as "disputes by equivocation." So, it is argued, the debate between presentists and eternalists is not trivial, for it is like these other, clearly substantive, ontological disputes in metaphysics.

However, I do not accept Sider's claim that the disputes he mentions are analogous to the alleged dispute between presentists and eternalists. First, 'exists' does *not* mean 'mathematically exists'. As I understand the latter phrase, it means 'exists and is a mathematical entity'. So, there is a *real* question of whether any entity satisfies that predicate; it is *not* a triviality that numbers exist mathematically. Of course, one could *invent* a predicate that is true of an entity if and only if it is a number and exists; but it would not be a trivial matter whether anything satisfied that condition. The dispute between mathematical realists and their opponents does not involve an equivocation on the word 'exist'.

Similarly, the dispute between modal realists and modal actualists does not depend on any equivocation. Both parties to the dispute mean by 'exist' what we all mean by it (whatever that is). The modal realist does *not* think that possible entities exist in some strange or shadowy way, unlike the robustness with which actual entities exist. The modal realist thinks that possible entities are concrete things just like us and the things in our surroundings; it is just that they are spatially unconnected to us (see Lewis 1986, 2, 82). And 'exists' simply does *not* mean 'exists and is spatially connected to us'. The dispute between modal realists and their opponents is about what exists, in the only sense of 'exists' there is (or needs to be). 'Exists' does *not* mean 'either exists or possibly exists'; it means *exists*. The modal realist holds that possibilia are not *mere* possibilia; they are *actualia* relative to things spatially connected to them, *possibilia* relative to things that are not. (Thus the insistence that 'actual' is an indexical.) That is, they do not merely possibly exist; they exist in the only way that something can (only they are not spatially connected to us).[32] The dispute is (at least in part) over whether or not there are physical objects that are not spatially connected to us, and that dispute is genuine.

As for skepticism about the apparent debate between presentists and eternalists, matters are quite different, I contend. The charge of triviality is *not* grounded in a claim that the word 'exists' is being equivocated on. What is being equivocated on are the *tenses* of the word 'exist'. If all the relevant verbs are in the present tense, there is no substantive dispute between presentist and eternalist. And if all the relevant verbs are disjunctively omnitemporal, there is again no substantive dispute between presentist and eternalist. The only hope for a substantive dispute between presentist and eternalist lies with construing the relevant verbs as tenseless. But, when applied to contingent, changeable things, the tenseless 'is' and 'exist' seem equivalent to a disjunctively omnitemporal construal, in terms of which no nontrivial version of the debate can be framed. And if there is a tenseless construal of these words that is different from a disjunctively omnitemporal interpretation of their tenses and in terms of which the dispute between presentists and eternalists can be conducted, I do not believe that we have been told by the presentists and eternalists what it is.

The alleged controversy between presentists and eternalists does *not* involve, as the other metaphysical disputes mentioned by Sider do, any dispute about what exists. There may be genuine issues over which presentists and eternalists disagree; but those issues are *not* about the reality of time, the reality of what exists in time, or the nature of persistence. Nor do those issues, however they are resolved, appear to pose any threat to or force any realignment of the idea that things change.

Acknowledgments

I would like to express my thanks here to Michael McKinsey for his painstaking, extensive, and enormously helpful comments on several drafts of this essay, and to Dean Zimmerman and Ted Sider for their encouragement. I would also like to thank Wayne State University for a 2003 Summer Research Grant that enabled me to do a substantial amount of the preliminary work on this essay. The current version of this essay is a revised and expanded version of the essay I read at the 2005 Inland Northwest Philosophy Conference on Time and Identity; and I wish to thank the organizers of that conference, principally Michael O'Rourke and Joe Campbell, for all their hard work in bringing the conference into existence so successfully, and for providing me with the opportunity to present and discuss my views with the distinguished group of philosophers that they gathered together.

Notes

1. See, e.g., Plato 2005, *Theaetetus* 155a3–5, and Aristotle 1995, *Physics*, Bk. 1, ch. 7, 191a3–7.

2. There are many issues this criterion raises that I will not be discussing in this chapter, for example, its apparent commitment to the existence of properties and times, and the problem of relational or "Cambridge" change. By the way, (i) is to be understood as 'there was, is, or will be a time t, and there was, is, or will be a time t', and $t \neq t'$'.

3. For this connecting claim to be, by my lights, more plausible, it should be understood as asserting that a change occurs just in case some thing *alters* (for a thing that changes relationally, say, by becoming a widow, does not alter). I shall here understand the claim in this way.

4. They are rivals in the sense that, if it is indeed true that a thing changes if and only if a change occurs, then Parmenides' view implies that changes cannot occur, contrary to Heraclitus' view, and Heraclitus' view implies that things can change, contrary to Parmenides' view.

5. It also ended the ancient debate over the principle of noncontradiction, a principle that was believed to be threatened by the phenomenon of change; see Powers 2005.

6. Events, by their very nature, have temporal parts. See Lombard 1995, esp. pp. 347–348.

7. That is, I think that a change (i.e., an event) occurs if and only if a thing alters.

8. See Lombard 1999, in which I argue that presentism does not imply that there are no things with temporal parts, for a response to (M)'s first premise; Lombard 2005, in which I argue that the problem of temporary intrinsics cannot be generated (nonfallaciously) from eternalism and the idea that things endure change; and Lombard 2003 for responses to (M)'s second premise.

9. However, it might turn out to be the case that presentists and eternalists are disagreeing about something else.

10. A third way would be to argue that the temporal parts theorist's understanding of change does not constitute a mere simulation of change. In this essay, however, I shall not attempt either to construct an argument for that conclusion or to refute such a proposal.

11. It is certainly not this semantic thesis: an utterance of 'x exists' is true if and only if x exists at the time at which existence is attributed to x. For this is trivially true. And the companion version of eternalism—that existence can be attributed to x at times at which it does not exist—is trivially false.

12. Which is, undoubtedly, *not* how Sider meant it. Tenseless interpretations will be taken up below.

13. More on this below.

14. One reason for thinking that tenseless and tensed existence are not two kinds of existence is that certain entities, e.g., numbers, if they exist at all, not only exist in worlds in which there are no times (and thus exist tenselessly), but also exist in worlds in which there are times and in which they have properties at times.

15. What I mean by a 'tensed version' of presentism or eternalism is a version that interprets the verbs contained in them as having a tense, in the semantic sense of indicating something about the time at which some utterance is true, some state of affairs obtains, some property is exemplified, or the like.

16. A presentist might argue that the truth of the claim that Aristotle did, but does not now exist, is not incompatible with the truth of (3b), on the grounds that the extension of 'everything' in (3b) is just the things that exist now. I will take up this issue below.

17. That a slightly emended version of (6), one that takes into account "timeless" entities, e.g., numbers, is the correct condition to place on class membership will be defended below.

18. I owe this point to Michael McKinsey.

19. That is, dinosaurs do not exist *now*. But in the disjunctively omnitemporal sense, they do.

20. And 'everything exists' should be understood in the following way. If 'exists' is in the present tense, and 'everything' covers the entire Master class, then it is false. But if 'exists' means 'did exist, does exist, will exist, or would exist even if there were no times', then 'everything exists' comes out true. Alternatively, one could tense, and thereby restrict the quantifier 'everything'; with the quantifier restricted to currently existing things, and 'exists' in the present tense, 'everything exists' come out true.

21. 'All humans are bipedal', if its quantifier is unrestricted and its 'are' construed as in the present tense, is simply *false*. The unrestricted quantifier 'all humans' picks out all the humans who have existed, do exist, and will exist; 'are bipedal', with its 'are' construed as in the present tense, is true of those things that are now bipedal; and so construed, 'all humans are bipedal' is not true, since nonexistent humans are now neither bipedal nor nonbipedal. If 'all humans are bipedal' is to express a truth, either its quantifier must be unrestricted and its 'are' construed as disjunctively omnitemporal, or 'all humans' must be construed as a quantifier restricted to only present humans and its 'are' construed as present tensed.

22. '(PR)' is *my* designation of Hestevold and Carter's (2002a) formulation.

23. If some object is real, then it either existed, exists, or will exist (or would exist even if there were not times). Thus, to say of some object that it is (now) real is to say neither that it did nor that it will exist; and to say of two things that there are

(now) real does not imply that they coexist. Thus, Hestevold and Carter's (2002a) concept of tenseless existence seems clearly to match my notion of what is real.

24. The presentist might respond that this result is fine, since the present time is the only time that exists. But surely, it is the only time that exists *now*. If the presentist takes this line, we are back to a tensed and trivial version of presentism.

25. If (PR) is a *necessary* truth, then its appearance in this argument, from the claim that some objects exist *simpliciter* to the claim that those objects coexist, should not be seen as contravening clause (ii) of (HC$_1$). And it certainly seems that (PR) is a necessary truth, if a truth at all.

26. Note that if nothing exists *simpliciter*, then (PR) is trivially true, owing to the falsity of its antecedent; and it would also follow that every thing that exists *simpliciter* exists at all times.

27. My thanks to Michael McKinsey for helping me with this argument.

28. In another attempt, Hestevold and Carter retain their version of presentism (PR), but revise their explication of existence *simpliciter* as follows:

(HC2) x exists simpliciter if and only if x is among the things that the universe includes—if and only if x is real. That x exists simpliciter does not alone imply that x did exist, that x presently exists, nor that x will exist. (Hestevold and Carter 2002b, 499)

But the combination of (HC2) and (PR) will not do at all. According to (PR), that something exists simpliciter implies that it presently exists. But according to (HC2), that something exists simpliciter does not imply that it presently exists. So, if both (HC2) and (PR) are true, then the existence simpliciter of any object both does and does not imply that it presently exists. But that is impossible. So, either Hestevold and Carter's characterization of existence simpliciter or their characterization of presentism is false, or nothing exists simpliciter.

29. Here's one difference. The claim 'there is a prime number between 3 and 7' does not imply that there is a prime number between 3 and 7 somewhere or other, since the former claim is true and the latter false, if numbers have no spatial location. Thus, the 'there' in 'there is a prime number between 3 and 7' must be placeless. However, this difference is of no relevance when objects that are essentially spatial are involved.

30. It might be argued that 'there is a prime number between 3 and 7' does not imply that there is a prime number between 3 and 7 at some time or other. However, again, even if numbers are "timeless" entities, 'there is a prime number between 3 and 7 but not now' cannot express a true proposition. In any case, my challenge concerns claims that are about contingently existing things that are subject to alterations; and numbers, if they exist, are not such entities.

31. The following might be suggested. Having argued that there is a sense of 'there is' in which 'there is a rabbit' is equivalent to 'there is, was, or will be a rabbit', I have in effect argued that there is no other "tenseless," purely existential sense of 'there is' or 'exists' that applies to contingent things. But there would be such a sense if the following argument were sound:

a. Necessarily, there is a single mode of existence had by everything.

b. Possibly, an atemporal entity exists.

c. Necessarily, an atemporal entity does not have a tensed mode of existence.

d. Therefore, an atemporal entity does not have a tensed mode of existence.

Given (d), then, if (a), *contingent* entities must have an atemporal mode of existence, contrary to what I have been arguing. (This argument was offered by an anonymous donor.)

However, (a) is true if what it means is that all things that exist have a single property in common, namely, the property of existence. (b) is true in that there are entities, e.g., numbers, that would exist even if there were no times. But, (c) is *not* true. In every possible world in which there are times, it is true that the number 3 exists at all times. So, if it is true that if the number 3 exists now, then that number has a tensed mode of existence, then (c) is *false*. (And we should conclude that existence at a time is *not* a "mode" of existence.) I suppose that one might instead infer that my argument shows that the number 3 is not an atemporal entity. But if it isn't atemporal, then it is hard to see what entity would be.

32. At least that is what, I presume, most modal realists think. For those who believe in mere *possibilia*, there is, I think, a genuine question of whether their dispute with modal actualists is merely verbal.

References

Aristotle. 1995. *The Complete Works of Aristotle: The Revised Oxford Translation*. Ed. J. Barnes. Princeton: Princeton University Press.

Hestevold, S., and W. R. Carter. 2002a. What Is Presentism, and Does It Preclude Persistence? Paper presented at the American Philosophical Association, Pacific Division, April 2002.

Hestevold, S., and W. R. Carter. 2002b. On Presentism, Endurance, and Change. *Canadian Journal of Philosophy* 32:491–510.

Lewis, D. 1986. *On the Plurality of Worlds*. Oxford: Basil Blackwell.

Lombard, L. B. 1995. Sooner or Later. *Noûs* 29:343–359.

Lombard, L. B. 1999. On the Alleged Incompatibility of Presentism and Perduring Entities. *Philosophia: Philosophical Quarterly of Israel* 27:253–260.

Lombard, L. B. 2003. The Lowe Road to the Problem of Temporary Intrinsics. *Philosophical Studies* 112:163–185.

Lombard, L. B. 2005. Scope Fallacies and the Problem of Temporary Intrinsics. Paper presented at the American Philosophical Association, Pacific Division, March 2005.

Markosian, N. 2004. A Defense of Presentism. In *Oxford Studies in Metaphysics*, vol. I, ed. D. Zimmerman. Oxford: Oxford University Press.

Merricks, T. 1995. On the Incompatibility of Enduring and Perduring Entities. *Mind* 104:521–531.

Plato. 2005. *The Collected Dialogues of Plato*. Ed. E. Hamilton and H. Cairns, trans. L. Cooper. Princeton: Princeton University Press.

Powers, L. N.d. *Non-Contradiction*. Manuscript.

Sider, T. 1999. Presentism and Ontological Commitment. *Journal of Philosophy* 96: 325–347.

Sider, T. 2001. *Four-Dimensionalism*. Oxford: Clarendon Press.

Soames, S. 2002. *Beyond Rigidity*. Oxford: Oxford University Press.

Zimmerman, D. 1998. Temporary Intrinsics and Presentism. In *Metaphysics: The Big Questions*, ed. P. van Inwagen and D. Zimmerman. Oxford: Blackwell Publishers.

3 Context, Conditionals, Fatalism, Time Travel, and Freedom

John W. Carroll

In this essay, building on the work of Robert Stalnaker and David Lewis, I sketch a theory describing the context-dependence of certain modal sentences, including counterfactual sentences. Then, I reveal its potential by briefly considering its application to a familiar argument for fatalism and a recent exchange about time-traveler freedom between Kadri Vihvelin and Ted Sider. My discussion provides a new take on the flaws and the seductiveness of both the fatalist argument and the freedom paradox, a take that may even have application to arguments for incompatibilism advanced by Carl Ginet and Peter van Inwagen.

Stalnaker on Context, Lewis on Boundary

According to Stalnaker, context includes information presumed to be shared by the participants in the conversation. He proposes representing this information, *the common ground*, by a set of possible worlds, *the context set*. Intuitively, the presumed-to-be-shared information is what is true in all the members of the context set. Stalnaker takes this information to be what is presupposed. He also takes the common ground to play an important role regarding assertion. If I utter 'The king of France is bald', then, in order for me to assert that the king of France is bald, the common ground must include the presupposition of that sentence, the proposition that there is presently one and only one king of France. So, for Stalnaker, the context set must include only worlds in which there is just one such king. It is not required that the king of France be bald in these worlds. Indeed, that would undermine the point of the assertion. "Assertions . . . are proposals to change the context by adding the information that is their content" (Stalnaker 1999, 111).

I will adopt Stalnaker's account of context as just presented with two minor modifications. First, instead of representing the common ground as a set of possible worlds, I will represent it as a set of propositions. Hence, content is added to the common ground by adding a proposition rather than by eliminating possible worlds. This avoids the consequence that every proposition entailed by a presupposition is thereby a presupposition. Second, in the representation of the common ground, it will be useful to keep track of which of the propositions are *suppositions* and which are *presuppositions*. Both presuppositions and suppositions can be bits of presumed-to-be-shared information, but, as I see it, presupposing *P* includes a commitment to the truth of *P* that supposing *P* does not. As a result, and as I will illustrate below, important features of modal utterances are sensitive to the falsity of a presupposition in a manner that they are not sensitive to the falsity of a supposition. Just so, it will be helpful that I not represent the common ground (as Stalnaker does) in one uniform presuppositional lump.

In "Scorekeeping in a Language Game," Lewis suggests that, for an utterance of a sentence with modal terms, context determines the sentence's truth conditions:

The boundary between the relevant possibilities and the ignored ones . . . is a component of conversational score, which enters into the truth conditions of sentences with 'can' or 'must' or other modal verbs. (Lewis 1983, 246)

My favorite illustration of this idea is from "The Paradoxes of Time Travel":

To say that something can happen means that its happening is compossible with certain facts. *Which* facts? That is determined, but sometimes not determined well enough, by context. An ape can't speak a human language—say, Finnish—but I can. Facts about the anatomy and operation of the ape's larynx and nervous system are not compossible with his speaking Finnish. The corresponding facts about my larynx and nervous system are compossible with my speaking Finnish. But don't take me along to Helsinki as your interpreter: I can't speak Finnish. My speaking Finnish is compossible with the facts considered so far, but not with further facts about my lack of training. (Lewis 1986, 77)

Lewis uses this idea to resolve the grandfather paradox. Suppose Tim's grandfather died of natural causes in 1957. Still, Tim wishes that he had killed Grandfather. Tim hops into a time machine and emerges in 1920. After careful planning and training, Tim is well prepared to murder his grandfather in 1921.

Tim's killing Grandfather that day in 1921 is compossible with a fairly rich set of facts: the facts about his rifle, his skill and training, the unobstructed line of fire, the locked door and the absence of any chaperone to defend the past, and so on. Indeed it is compossible with all the facts of the sorts we would ordinarily count as relevant in saying what someone can do. . . . Relative to these facts, Tim can kill Grandfather. But his killing Grandfather is not compossible with another, more inclusive set of facts. There is the simple fact that Grandfather was not killed. Also there are the various other facts about Grandfather's doings after 1921 and their effects. . . . Relative to these facts, Tim cannot kill Grandfather. (Lewis 1986, 77)

I find Lewis's case for context setting a boundary between the relevant possibilities and the ignored ones convincing. I hope you will go along with me on the need for the boundary as part of the conversational score.

Here is my suggestion on how to make the boundary part of the score: The boundary between the relevant possibilities and the ignored ones is the common ground—the suppositions and presuppositions—of the context for evaluation. To see how my suggestion is supposed to work, notice that it is when we suppose that Grandfather was not killed in 1921 that it seems so natural to say, 'Tim can't kill Grandfather'. It is when we don't suppose that, and only suppose or presuppose matters local to Tim's stalking Grandfather, that we are inclined to say, 'Tim can kill Grandfather'. What I offer here is a hypothesis as to the set of facts with which a proposition needs to be compossible for that proposition to correctly be asserted to be possible. Thus, '$\Diamond P$' is true in C if and only if the content of 'P' is compossible with the common ground of C.[1] The corresponding account for necessity sentences is: '$\Box P$' is true in C if and only if the content of 'P' is entailed by the common ground of C.[2]

This account of the truth conditions of modal sentences may need to be qualified to sidestep a messy matter stemming from the possibility of false presuppositions. Suppose Smith utters, 'Jones can't get polio', and it is presupposed that Jones has had a polio vaccination. Suppose also that, unbeknownst to all the participants of the conversation, Jones has not been vaccinated and so is at risk. Then it seems very clear that Smith has not made a true assertion when he says 'Jones can't get polio', despite the fact that the content of 'Jones gets polio' is not compossible with the common ground at the time the utterance was made.

My take[3] on cases like this is that the built-in context-dependence of modal sentences generates an interesting but familiar phenomenon in a new guise. Because of this context-dependence, a false presupposition of *the context* can have effects parallel to the effects of a false sentential presupposition, a presupposition of *a sentence*. Since the elements of the common ground are already being taken for granted, they are no part of the information the speaker intends to convey by the utterance of the modal sentence, but his commitment to the truth of the conveyed information may still be sensitive to what is being taken for granted. So, for example, should Smith find out that Jones wasn't vaccinated, he would surely want to retract his utterance. It would be like saying 'The king of France is bald' with a common ground that includes the presupposition that there is a unique king of France, only to find out later that there is no such king. When we do recognize cases like the vaccination case as involving something akin to sentential presupposition failure, familiar hard questions arise. It certainly seems that no true assertion is made in the vaccination case, but are we prepared to say that a false assertion was made, or is it that the presupposition failure undercuts there being any assertion at all? Rather than pretending to settle this and other hard issues about presupposition failure,[4] I will take a safer path, sidestepping them thus: Take my account of the truth conditions of modal sentences to apply only in cases where all the presuppositions of the common ground are true.

The possibility of false suppositions is not as troublesome as the possibility of false presuppositions. If we are supposing that there is a monster in the next room, then an utterance of 'It must be scary in there' should clearly be counted as making an assertion and as true even though there is (presumably) no monster in there. No restriction of my account is needed to sidestep potential worries about false suppositions.

The Subjunctive Conditional

Consider a simple analysis of the subjunctive conditional ('$P > Q$' abbreviates 'If P were the case, then Q would be the case'):

$P > Q$ if and only if $\Box(P \supset Q)$,

with a contextualist twist developed by Ken Warmbrōd (1981) and Kai von Fintel (2001). Very roughly, as Warmbrōd describes it, context will supply what he calls auxiliary assumptions or auxiliary "suppositions," which together with P must entail Q in order for it to be true that if P were the case Q would be the case. The auxiliary assumptions function something like the cotenable propositions and laws of nature do in Nelson Goodman's work (e.g., Goodman 1983, 8–9, 15) or like what Roderick Chisholm calls "presuppositions" in his work (Chisholm 1955, 102–103).

There is a straightforward way to incorporate this approach to subjunctive conditionals into my contextualist framework, because the simple analysis basically tells us that subjunctive conditionals are a kind of modal sentence already discussed. Thus, if the presuppositions of the common ground of the context for evaluation are true and this common ground entails that the antecedent implies the consequent, then the assertion made by the utterance of the subjunctive conditional sentence is true. If the presuppositions of the common ground are true and the common ground doesn't entail that the antecedent implies the consequent, then the sentence is false. Support: In standard philosophical discussions of time travel, why do we often say, 'If Tim were to try to kill Grandfather, he would fail'? Obviously, for the same sorts of reasons that we say in these contexts, 'He can't kill Grandfather'. We are supposing that he didn't. So, it *must* be true that, *if he tries, then he fails.*

This is not the place to try to give a full defense of my approach to subjunctive conditionals. I should, however, at least address one standard example of a criticism that has been thought to undermine this idea:

(1)   If the match were struck, then it would light.

(2)   If the match were struck and wet, then it would light.

It seems that the premise is true, but, in conjunction with the proposed analysis, the premise also seems to entail an obvious falsehood. Surely, the objection goes, it might be true that, if the match were struck, it would light, even though, if it were struck and wet, then it would not light. Strengthening the antecedent is a valid form of inference for strict conditionals. But, because of examples like the match example, it is not generally regarded as a valid form of inference for subjunctive conditionals.

Fortunately, the match example is fallacious. The premise's being true and the conclusion's being false depend on there being a change of context. Though utterances of the premise sentence are true in many contexts, the conclusion sentence will usually be defective for those contexts. In a typical context in which the premise sentence is uttered, the common ground will include that the match is dry. In those contexts, the common ground contradicts the antecedent of the conclusion, and so an utterance of the conclusion sentence would have little point; on the proposed analysis, the conditional would be trivially true.[5] For just this reason, these are not natural contexts for evaluation of the conclusion sentence; when we consider the conclusion sentence, we tend to bring into play a different kind of context, one where the common ground is consistent with the antecedent. These contexts will not have as part of the common ground that the match is dry. These contexts do not present any problem either. Given the analysis, it is hard to see how the premise sentence could be true in any of these contexts precisely because it is not part of the common ground that the match is dry.

Fatalism

As a first illustration, I want to show how my contextualist framework reorients a certain familiar reply to a famous fatalist argument. I take Gilbert Ryle's "It Was to Be" as my source for the statement of the argument:

At a certain moment yesterday evening I coughed and at a certain moment yesterday I went to bed. It was therefore true on Saturday that on Sunday I would cough at the one moment and go to bed at the other. . . . But if it was true beforehand . . . that I was to cough and go to bed at those two moments on Sunday, 25 January 1953, then it was impossible for me not to do so. (Ryle 1954, 15)

Leaving out the coughing, and substituting 'necessarily' for 'impossible not', fairly enough, the argument can be put in premise–conclusion form as follows:

The Fatalist Argument

(1) Ryle went to bed on 1/25/53.

(2) If Ryle went to bed on 1/25/53, then it was true on 1/24/53 that Ryle would go to bed on 1/25/53.

(3) If it was true on 1/24/53 that Ryle would go to bed on 1/25/53, then necessarily Ryle went to bed on 1/25/53.

---

(4) Necessarily, Ryle went to bed on 1/25/53.

The argument generalizes. There doesn't seem to be anything special about Ryle's going to bed or the dates selected.

One standard reply to this style of argument (advanced, for example, in Thomas 1970) is that the statement of premise 3 is ambiguous between a wide-scope reading and a narrow-scope reading. We are told that we should distinguish:

Necessarily (if it was true on 1/24/53 that Ryle would go to bed on 1/25/53, then Ryle went to bed on 1/25/53)

from

If it was true on 1/24/53 that Ryle would go to bed on 1/25/53, then (necessarily, Ryle went to bed on 1/25/53).

The wide-scope reading is true, indeed obvious. In every possible world in which it was true on 1/24/53 that Ryle would go to bed on 1/25/53, it is also true that Ryle would go to bed on 1/25/53. The narrow-scope reading is false; it is not the case that Ryle went to bed on 1/25/53 in every possible world. This appears to give us a nice and neat account both of why the fatalist argument is seductive and how it is flawed. It is flawed because on neither of these readings of the premise-3 sentence does it turn out that the argument is sound. On the wide-scope reading, the premise-3 sentence is true, but then the argument is invalid. On the narrow-scope reading, the argument is valid, but then the premise-3 sentence is false. The argument is seductive because it can seem sound if we take the narrow-scope reading when considering the validity of the argument and take the wide-scope reading when considering whether all the premises are true.

My contextualist framework suggests that something different is going on with the fatalist argument. Consider the first premise. It is a claim about Ryle's action of going to bed on a particular day over fifty years ago. I don't know about you, but that is not something I have good information about. It is a pretty common activity, and we do have Ryle's report that he went to bed that day, but we also know that philosophers are prone not to let the truth get in the way of a good example. Still, it seems like it would be a little silly for us to worry too much about whether Ryle did go to bed that day, because, as I said, the argument generalizes; we could run a parallel argument about John Wilkes Booth's shooting Abraham Lincoln, or about some action that we all might have witnessed first hand. Just so, in considering Ryle's argument, we normally just suppose that the first premise is true and then get on with the philosophy. This supposition matters given my contextualist framework. For a context that includes the supposition that Ryle went to bed on 1/25/53, the premise-1 sentence is true. The consequent of the premise-3 sentence is also true—that Ryle went to bed is entailed by the common ground of the context—and, so, the entire premise-3 sentence is true. (In order to keep things simple, I am assuming the premise-3 sentence is a material conditional sentence.) The premise-2 sentence is a necessary truth (and is so quite independent of the context). Prima facie, the argument is valid. Therefore, with premise 1 as a supposition in the common ground of the context, the argument is sound!

Have I just endorsed fatalism? No. I have claimed that there is at least one sort of context relative to which the premise sentences and the conclusion sentence of the fatalist argument constitute a sound argument. So, I have also claimed that, in this sort of context, the conclusion sentence, 'Necessarily, Ryle went to bed on 1/25/53', is true. But, insofar as that is anything like an endorsement of fatalism, it is not a terribly worrisome one. My contextualist framework also includes an account of the truth conditions of this sentence that makes it clear that we have not been given any reason to think that Ryle was somehow fated to go to bed on that date; 'Necessarily, Ryle went to bed on 1/25/53' is true in a context with a common ground that includes the supposition that Ryle went to bed on 1/25/53 simply because that Ryle went to bed on 1/25/53 entails that Ryle went to bed on 1/25/53. Furthermore, notice that, for the argument to be sound and for the conclusion sentence to be true, it is crucial that the context include a supposition or a presupposition to the effect that Ryle went to bed on that date. (If the common ground does not entail that Ryle went to bed on 1/25/53, then my contextualist framework says that the premise-3 sentence has a false consequent. So, then, in order for the premise-3 sentence to be true, the premise-1 sentence must be false.) There are lots of ordinary contexts that don't include such a common ground; relative to these contexts, 'Ryle could have not gone to bed' is true.[6]

What of the narrow-scope–wide-scope ambiguity? My suspicion is that there is no such ambiguity, because there is no natural-language transformation of, say, 'If Ben is a bachelor, then Ben is necessarily unmarried' that reveals the so-called ambiguity (cf. Stalnaker 1999, 42, on definite descriptions and scope distinctions); we have to resort to a formal language or some context-shifting or at least slip in parentheses and then do some coaxing. All of this is to be expected on my account. If the content of 'P' is in the common ground of C, then '$\Box(P \supset Q)$' will be true in C if and only if '$P \supset \Box Q$' is true in C.[7] I think that is why we sometimes move freely back and forth between 'Necessarily, if P, then Q' and 'If P, then necessarily Q' in certain situations. There are other situations where those same English constructions don't exhibit this equivalence, but there isn't anything here to support the idea that there is a single English construction with two meanings.

Time-Traveler Freedom

For a second application of my contextualist framework, I will consider the freedom paradox. Though neither author considers the paradox in precisely the form I will, my formulation owes much to Kadri Vihvelin's (1996) "What Time Travelers Cannot Do" and Ted Sider's (2002) "Time Travel, Coincidences, and Counterfactuals." The paradox is a nice, concise, and still tempting rendering of the common concern that the real threat to the possibility of one-dimensional backward time travel is not that we could change the past, but that there would be surprising and inexplicable constraints on what a time traveler can do.

Suppose again that Tim's grandfather died of natural causes in 1957, that Tim hops into a time machine emerging in 1920, and so on. Then consider:

The Freedom Paradox

(1) Tim can kill Grandfather.

(2) If S can A, then, if S were to try to A, S would (or at least might) succeed.

(3) If Tim were to try to kill Grandfather, then he would not succeed.

(4) Tim can't kill Grandfather.

The first premise is motivated the same way that it is motivated in the grandfather paradox; Tim has what it takes, nothing stands in his way. The second premise, a principle from Vihvelin, is doing most of the real work here, but it is a principle with intuitive appeal. If I say I can make the eight-foot putt before me and it's true that I would fail to make it if I tried, then what I said was wrong. (Following Sider, I will refer to premise 2 as *Vihvelin's principle*.) The third premise is supposed to be obvious given the time-travel story we are supposing is true of Tim: We all know that Grandfather didn't die at the earlier time; in order for no inconsistency to arise, it must be the case that if Tim were to try kill Grandfather, he would fail. Prima facie, the only escape from contradiction is to abandon the possibility of time travel or admit that premise 1 is false, thereby welcoming "strange shackles" (Sider 2002, 122) on what a time traveler can do.

Speaking in favor of the possibility of time travel, Sider in effect begins a response to the freedom paradox that argues that Vihvelin's principle is false in certain contexts. Consider:

(*) If Ben were a permanent bachelor and tried to get married, then he would not succeed,

where 'permanent bachelor' is a phrase of art meaning someone who never marries. Intuitively, (*) is true. In fact, it doesn't matter how often or how hard Ben tries; if he were a permanent bachelor, it is not true that he would or even that he might marry. The evident truth of (*) in and of itself is no threat to Vihvelin's principle; the counterfactual that is relevant to whether Ben can get married and Vihvelin's principle is not (*). It is ($):

($) If Ben were to try to marry, then he would not succeed.

Sider's clever move, however, is to point out that the truth of (*) indicates that there will at least be some contexts in which ($) is true:

Constraints on the similarity metric for the counterfactual conditional can accomplish what is accomplished by the explicit inclusion of a predicate inside the antecedent of such a conditional. Imagine a similarity metric that holds constant a person's status with respect to permanent bachelorhood, and therefore counts possible worlds in which an actual permanent bachelor gets married as being very distant from the actual world. (Sider 2002, 130)

Working within the framework of Lewis's account of counterfactuals, the idea is that ($) will turn out true if the context selects a similarity metric on possible worlds such that worlds in which Ben is a permanent bachelor are all closer to the actual world than worlds in which Ben is not a permanent bachelor. Though I would tell this story a little differently than Sider, doing it in terms of what is in the common ground rather than in terms of a contextually selected similarity metric, I think Sider is essentially correct about (*) and ($) and that this is the key insight for understanding what is going on in the freedom paradox.

Now, Sider thinks that the truth of ($) in such contexts spells trouble for Vihvelin's principle. Just following my previous quote from Sider, he goes on to say,

In that case ($)[8] is true; nevertheless, actual permanent bachelors are free to marry. The truth of ($) is due to the same sort of selective attention as results in the truth of (*), only now the selective attention is accomplished by the similarity metric rather than the presence of the predicate 'permanent bachelor' inside the scope of the counterfactual. The moral is that Vihvelin's principle fails if the similarity metric for the counterfactual conditional accomplishes this sort of selective attention. (Sider 2002, 130)

I will disagree with Sider on just this point, but, before doing so, let me complete Sider's solution to the freedom paradox, which is merely a matter of reapplying what has been said about ($). In certain contexts, where the similarity metric is such that the worlds closest to the actual world are ones where Tim is a time traveler and Grandfather lived a long life, premise 2 of the freedom paradox, Vihvelin's principle, is false. In such a context, 'If Tim were to try to kill Grandfather, he would not succeed', the premise-3 sentence, is true, and yet Tim still has the ability to kill Grandfather. There are other contexts where those facts don't hold in all the closest worlds. So, some of the closest worlds would be worlds where Tim is not a time traveler and it is not true that Grandfather lived a long life. In some of these worlds, Tim tries to kill Grandfather and succeeds. So, in these contexts, the premise-3 sentence will be false. The idea is that there are no contexts in which the freedom paradox is sound. In every context, either the premise-2 sentence or the premise-3 sentence will be false.[9]

Sider makes a minor mistake. Though there will be contexts where ($) is true, this doesn't show that Vihvelin's principle is false. We should expect 'is free to', 'is able to', and 'can' to be context dependent in the same manner that counterfactuals are. In contexts selecting a similarity metric that has Ben being a permanent bachelor in the nearby worlds, not only is ($) true, but so is 'Ben is not able to marry' and 'Ben can't marry'; otherwise we are stuck with abominable conjunctions like 'If Ben were to try to marry, he would fail, though Ben can marry'. One can't undermine Vihvelin's principle by showing that its consequent sentence is false in certain contexts and then showing that its antecedent sentence is true in another context. That would be a kind of equivocation.

If I am right, then I need a different way out of the freedom paradox. I am not prepared to challenge Vihvelin's principle, and I agree with Sider that there are contexts in which the premise-3 sentence is true. So, it looks like I must accept that there are contexts where the premise-1 sentence is false. But, the negation of premise 1 looks like trouble. It says that Tim can't kill Grandfather. The strange shackles seem to be back in place. What am I to say?

Having been exposed to my contextualist framework and its application to the fatalist argument, perhaps you already see what I should say. Yes, there are contexts in which we suppose that Tim is a time traveler and that Grandfather didn't die at a young age. These are common in discussions of the grandfather paradox; that's how philosophical discussions of the case all begin. In these contexts, the premise-3 sentence is true, the premise-1 sentence is false, and I see no reason to question Vihvelin's principle; that Tim is a time traveler and that Grandfather didn't die at a young age are suppositions in the common ground for these contexts, and so sentences like 'Tim can't kill Grandfather' and 'If Tim were to try, then he would not succeed' are true. But so what? According to my contextualist framework, the falsehood of the premise-1 sentence in these contexts merely amounts to Tim's not killing Grandfather in 1921 being entailed by the supposition that Grandfather didn't die until 1957. That truthmaker does not begin to suggest that there are shackles of any kind preventing Tim from taking out Gramps. Furthermore, there are plenty of other contexts with nothing about Grandfather's death in 1957 or any of his post-1921 doings in the common ground for which 'Tim can kill Grandfather' is true. The failure of premise 1 in contexts that often arise in philosophical discussions is no more worrisome than the fact that the conclusion sentence of the fatalist argument is true in such contexts.

Freedom from Consequence

My contextualist framework has applications to other philosophical issues besides fatalism and time-traveler freedom. For example, in a recent article (Carroll 2005), I apply my conclusions about modal sentences to issues about explanation and knowledge. There is more to be done. Here is a concluding and (I hope) enticing gesture in the direction of some of the work that remains.

What is generally regarded as one of the most serious metaphysical issues about human freedom is the issue of the compatibility of free will and determinism. Consequence arguments of the sort made famous by Peter van Inwagen (e.g., van Inwagen 1983) and Carl Ginet (e.g., Ginet 1983) are the leading arguments in favor of incompatibilism. Very roughly, these arguments start by asking us to suppose that determinism is true, that there is some accurate specification of the state of the world at some distant past time, H, that in conjunction with an accurate specification of the laws of nature, L, entails that some agent, S, will perform some action, A, one that S indeed will perform. Then, we are given two premise sentences that it is natural to think are true, something like 'S can't prevent H' and 'S can't prevent L'. We are asked to conclude that S can't prevent A on the strength of the fact that the conjunction of H and L entails that S performs A. There is certainly something compelling about these arguments. It can also seem that there is something disappointing and implausible about their conclusion. Seeing this as a threat to our attributions of moral responsibility, many uphold incompatibilism and search for some account of free will on which free will is compatible with indeterminism.

Given my contextualism, the search for such account is an overreaction to the arguments: Insofar as the context for evaluation includes in its common ground the suppositions that H, that L, and that the conjunction of H and L entails that S performs A, which it quite naturally will given that these propositions are more or less precisely what we are asked to suppose, the premise sentences and the conclusion sentence will all be true. But, there is no great cause for concern. The conclusion sentence, 'S can't prevent A', turns out to be true in such contexts for a straightforward reason—namely, that the content of 'S does not perform A' is not compossible with the suppositions about H, L, and S's performing A. There are, of course, plenty of other, much more ordinary contexts with nothing about the laws of nature or states of the universe in the common ground; in these contexts, 'S can prevent A' may be true.

Acknowledgments

Thanks to an anonymous referee, David Auerbach, David Austin, Joe Keim Campbell, Stephen Crowley, Wayne Davis, Mylan Engel, Marc Lange, Ram Neta, Alistair Norcross, Duncan Pritchard, John Roberts, Jonathan Schaffer, Jason Turner, Kadri Vihvelin, and especially Mark Heller and Michael Pendlebury for terrific conversations about context.

Notes

1. My approach is similar to the approach of Chierchia and McConnell-Ginet (1990, 235–237), though in their discussion of presupposition they do not go so far as to identify any relationship between the common ground and what they call the modal base. See their discussion of the common ground *vs.* the modal base (pp. 290–291). Their modal base is Lewis's "certain facts," but they think that it should not be identified with the common ground.

2. My statement of the truth conditions of necessity sentences uses the verb 'entails'. It is tempting to take this modal term *not* to be context sensitive, perhaps as expressing some formal notion of logical consequence. That is fine for the purposes of this early sketch of my framework. It does keep matters conveniently simple. Nevertheless, I am tempted to think that 'entails' as used in the text should not be treated in any exceptional way. Parallel points apply to my statement of the truth conditions of possibility sentences and its use of the phrase 'is compossible'.

3. My first temptation (see Carroll 2005) when faced with an example like this was to change my specification of the boundary to require that the boundary only include the suppositions and the *true* presuppositions of the common ground. My thought was that Smith had actually made a false assertion. But, now, I don't think that this is the way to go. Suppose again that Jones wasn't vaccinated, but this time suppose that he is genetically immune to the disease, and so doesn't have the normal susceptibility to the disease. If Smith made a false assertion in the original case, then he made a true assertion in this variation of that case, even though Jones's getting polio is compossible with the true presuppositions and the suppositions. Thank you to Marc Lange for raising both versions of the vaccination example.

4. See von Fintel 2004 and Yablo 2006 for a taste of the complications concerning sentential presupposition failure.

5. Von Fintel (2001, 134–135) reports that Irene Heim has made the proposal that, roughly, subjunctive conditionals presuppose that their antecedent is possible. Von Fintel adopts Heim's proposal. It is in line with my contention that an utterance of

the conclusion sentence in a context that includes that the match is dry would be defective.

6. One other point about the fatalist argument: I have suggested that we normally just *suppose* that Ryle went to bed on the date reported. We don't *presuppose* that because we don't have much reason to think that it is true. So, the truth of the conclusion sentence in these contexts depends on a supposition that we don't have much reason to think is true. That's one more reason not to be troubled by the fact that 'Necessarily, Ryle went to bed on 1/25/53' will be true in such a context. We might all suppose that pigs fly, and so 'Pigs fly' would be true, but that doesn't mean we should worry about hitting one on our next airline flight. Of course, *some* events can be plugged into the argument for which participants of a conversation will be prepared to presuppose the first premise. My point is just that this won't work for every event. In particular, it won't work for a wide range of future events, the ones we don't have reason to think will occur.

7. Proof: Assume the content of 'P' is in the common ground of C. If '$\Box(P \supset Q)$' is true in C, then the common ground of C entails the content of '$P \supset Q$'. But, since the content of 'P' is in the common ground of C, it also follows that the common ground of C entails the content of 'Q'. So, '$\Box Q$' and '$P \supset \Box Q$' are true in C. That's one direction. If '$P \supset \Box Q$' is true in C, then, since the content of 'P' is in the common ground of C, '$\Box Q$' must be true in C. If '$\Box Q$' is true in C, then the common ground of C entails the content of 'Q'. But, since anything that entails the content of 'Q' entails the content of '$P \supset Q$', the common ground of C entails the content of '$P \supset Q$'. So, '$\Box(P \supset Q)$' is true in C.

8. I am putting words in Sider's mouth. He actually says what I have quoted here not about ($) and (*), but about two analogous but more complicated sentences he labels (PB1') and (PB1).

9. Here's where Sider makes essentially this point:

(KV) If Killer had attempted to kill Victim, Killer would have or at least might have succeeded.

Vihvelin's principle says that Killer is free to kill Victim only if (KV) is true. (KV) may well be false under a similarity metric that gives weight to what occurs after the confrontation of Victim by Killer. Such a metric might require Killer and Victim to be temporal parts of the same time-traveling continuant in nearby worlds, and in such worlds Killer's murderous attempt fails. But under such interpretations of counterfactuals, Vihvelin's principle is false. On the only interpretation of counterfactuals that vindicates Vihvelin's principle, what occurs after the confrontation does not affect the similarity of worlds, and therefore whether worlds match the actual world with respect to whether Killer and Victim are temporal parts of the same continuant is irrelevant. . . . (KV) is therefore true, under this similarity metric. Vihvelin's principle is no obstacle to the temporal part, Killer, being free to kill the temporal part, Victim. (Sider 2002, 131)

References

Carroll, J. 2005. Boundary in Context. *Acta Analytica* 20:43–54.

Chierchia, G., and S. McConnell-Ginet. 1990. *Meaning and Grammar*. Cambridge, MA: MIT Press.

Chisholm, R. 1955. Law Statements and Counterfactual Inference. *Analysis* 15: 97–105.

Ginet, C. 1983. A Defense of Incompatibilism. *Philosophical Studies* 44:391–400.

Goodman, N. 1983. *Fact, Fiction, and Forecast*. Cambridge, MA: Harvard University Press.

Lewis, D. 1983. *Philosophical Papers*, vol. 1. New York: Oxford University Press.

Lewis, D. 1986. *Philosophical Papers*, vol. 2. New York: Oxford University Press.

Ryle, G. 1954. *Dilemmas*. New York: Cambridge University Press.

Sider, T. 2002. Time Travel, Coincidences, and Counterfactuals. *Philosophical Studies* 110:115–138.

Stalnaker, R. 1999. *Context and Content*. Oxford: Oxford University Press.

Thomas, S. 1970. A Modal Muddle. In *Determinism, Free Will, and Responsibility*, ed. G. Dworkin. Englewood Cliffs, NJ: Prentice-Hall.

Vihvelin, K. 1996. What Time Travelers Cannot Do. *Philosophical Studies* 81: 315–330.

van Inwagen, P. 1983. *An Essay on Free Will*. Oxford: Clarendon Press.

von Fintel, K. 2001. Counterfactuals in a Dynamic Context. In *Ken Hale: A Life in Language*, ed. M. Kenstowicz. Cambridge, MA: MIT Press.

von Fintel, K. 2004. Would You Believe It? The King of France Is Back. In *Descriptions and Beyond*, ed. A. Bezuidenout and M. Reimer. Oxford: Oxford University Press.

Warmbrōd, K. 1981. Indexical Theory of Conditionals. *Dialogue* 20:644–664.

Yablo, S. 2006. Non-Catastrophic Presupposition Failure. In *Content and Modality*, ed. J. Thomson and A. Byrne. Oxford: Oxford University Press.

4 The Identity of the Past

Mark Hinchliff

The presentist, after denying that past and future individuals exist, must still account for the manifest facts about the past and the future. It is simply too extreme a view to deny that Lincoln was shot by Booth and that the Earth will orbit the Sun.

Several obstacles appear to block the presentist from giving an account of the past. A fully general problem concerns the apparent lack of truthmakers: nothing in the presentist's ontology appears to ground truths about the past.[1] A more specific cluster of problems concerns singular truths about past individuals. Individuals that do not exist do not have properties or stand in relations. If past individuals do not exist, they do not have properties or stand in relations. Moreover, we cannot *talk* about them, since reference is a relation; and we cannot even *think* about them, since singular propositions about them do not exist if they do not. These conclusions are *absurd*. Past individuals must exist. Presentism must be false.

Those who have addressed this cluster of problems have ingeniously tried to make the best of a bad situation. They have tried to find *surrogates* in the present for the past individuals, individual essences or complex properties of the world (see Bigelow 1996 and Rea 2003). They have tried to find *cutouts*, third parties that can indirectly relate present things to past things (see Chisholm 1990). And they have tried to find cases of *propositional mimicry*, propositions the presentist may countenance that closely resemble the propositions he may not (see Sider 1997, 2001; Markosian 2004; Crisp 2005).

Property Presentism Defined

But the presentist may avoid this band of surrogates, third-party cutouts, and fakes by reexamining in a tensed setting the traditional connection between predication and existence that drove our cluster of puzzles: that if a thing has a property, it must exist. To deny this connection is to court charges of Meinongianism. Yet what does it come to in a tensed setting? A first answer might be:

(1)   Always $\forall x(x$ has a property $P \to x$ exists).

But (1) follows from (2):

(2)   Always $\forall x(x$ exists),

which holds if the traditional connection between quantification and existence is carried over to a tensed setting, and what is in the domain of quantification (at a time) is what exists (at that time). In a tensed setting, the traditional connection is thus not given by (1) but by property presentism:

Property Presentism   Always $\forall x$ Always (x has a property $P \to x$ exists).

Property presentism comes in two strengths, depending on a distinction between simple or unstructured properties and complex or structured properties. Broad property presentism covers both simple and complex properties; narrow covers only the simple properties:

Broad Property Presentism   Always $\forall x$ Always (x has a simple or complex property $P \to x$ exists);
Narrow Property Presentism   Always $\forall x$ Always (x has a simple property $P \to x$ exists).

The narrow property presentist permits nonexistents to have complex properties; the broad does not. Given the close connection between properties and predicates here, linguistic formulations of these views are worth stating. If A is a simple or atomic one-place predicate and φ is a one-place simple or complex predicate, then we have the following:

Broad Predicate Presentism   Always $\forall x$ Always ($\varphi x \to x$ exists);
Narrow Predicate Presentism   Always $\forall x$ Always ($Ax \to x$ exists).

Broad covers all the predicates, simple or complex; narrow covers only the simple ones, permitting nonexistents to satisfy complex predicates, such as 'is nonexistent' formed from the open sentence 'x does not exist'.[2] On the assumption that simple and complex predicates correspond to simple and complex properties respectively, narrow and broad property presentists are narrow and broad predicate presentists. Of course, these views should be understood in their full generality to cover n-place relations and predicates, simple and complex, as well.[3]

    Broad and narrow property presentism are not always clearly distinguished in the literature, but several considerations support the claim that broad property presentism is the view being defended.[4] First, Plantinga's broad property actualism is often mentioned as an analogue of the view being formulated in the metaphysics of time (Plantinga 1983a,b, 1985). Second, some of the initial puzzles about past individuals involve complex properties or relations and thus require the broader view. And finally, broad property presentism sustains the traditional connection between predication and existence by permitting *no* property to be predicated of a nonexistent at a time, whereas narrow property presentism undermines the traditional connection by permitting a *complex* property to be predicated of a nonexistent at a time.

Property Presentism Defended

Support for property presentism has been of three kinds. First, there have been a couple of arguments that attempt to show that property presentism is a consequence of presentism (see Bergmann 1999; Davidson 2003; Yannis 2007). However, these arguments appear to be beset by the same flaws as earlier attempts to show that property actualism is a consequence of actualism (see Pollock 1985; Fine 1985; Forbes 1989; Hinchliff 1989; Hudson 1997; Salmon 1998). Another source of support has been by *appeals to intuitions*. Ned Markosian says that denying property presentism "comes with a price . . . that [he] personally [is] not willing to pay." His "pre-philosophical intuitions commit [him] not only to Presentism but also to [Property Presentism]" (Markosian 2004, 52). Michael Rea speaks of not "(absurdly) committing ourselves" to the denial of property actualism (Rea 2003, 264). Thomas Crisp calls the denial of property presentism "frivolous," "difficult to believe," and not "a serious option" (Crisp 2005, 6–7).

Lurking behind these appeals to intuition is a brief but powerful argument to which Crisp also gives voice: "The suggestion here is that Caroline [Kennedy] bears a relation R [the daughter-of relation] to JFK and Jackie, but there is nothing to which she bears R. Bizarre." I suspect this brief argument influences many property presentists at some level. The traditional connection between predication and existence is quickly buttressed by appeals to two other traditional connections. Predication is traditionally connected to quantification: if an individual has a property, it must be in the domain of quantification. And quantification is traditionally connected to existence: an individual is in the domain of quantification only if it exists. I call the argument Crisp gives the *triangle argument*, because two sides of the triangle support the third.[5] Suppose that the great racehorse Montjeu bears R to Northern Dancer because Montjeu was sired by a horse sired by Northern Dancer. Because predication is connected to quantification, Montjeu bears R to something. But Northern Dancer does not exist (by the presentist's lights). Because what is in the domain of quantification exists, Northern Dancer is not in the domain. Therefore, Montjeu bears R to nothing. A contradiction. So Montjeu cannot bear R to a nonexistent individual.

The triangle argument shows that one cannot give up property presentism without giving up another side of the triangle. I suspect that a great deal of the intuitive support for property presentism comes from the role it plays in this traditional configuration. To deny property presentism and keep the other connections in place produces incoherence. So its denial is "absurd" or "bizarre."

Yet in the standard Kripke-style possible-worlds semantics for modal languages, simple predicate actualism is denied.[6] Simple predicates are true of actual individuals at worlds in which those actual individuals do not exist. The denial does not produce incoherence or seem absurd, because those actual individuals are not in the domains of quantification at those worlds. Property actualism is denied, but so is the traditional connection between predication and quantification. The connection between quantification and existence can, however, be kept in place.[7] Against this denial of property actualism, the triangle argument loses its force because two of its sides are missing. Besides the traditional and Kripke-style configurations of predication, existence, and quantification, still other configurations are possible. What really need to be compared and assessed are these different configurations of the connections in tensed or modal settings. The issue should be which configuration best accounts for the phenomena in such a setting. What seem beside the point are defenses of particular connections from within particular configurations, using triangle arguments.

The Stock Counterexamples

In the metaphysics of modality, there is a well-worn debate over property actualism. Properties and relations like nonexistence, sethood, membership, truth, designation, and identity provide stock counterexamples to property actualism and carry over with equal force to property presentism. These counterexamples are familiar and not the subject of this essay; I will just mention them in passing. (1) The complex property of nonexistence, and others like it, poses a problem for broad property actualism. Other counterexamples involve apparently simple or unstructured properties and relations and tell against both broad and narrow property actualism. Among these properties and relations are sethood, membership, truth, designation, and identity. (2) A set appears to be necessarily a set, even if it is a set of contingent individuals and does not necessarily exist. (3) An element of a set appears to be necessarily an element of a set, even if the element is a contingent individual. (4) A singular proposition about a certain individual appears to be necessarily about that individual, even if that individual is contingent. (5) The singular proposition that Socrates does not exist appears to be true at worlds in which Socrates and the proposition do not exist. (6) The name 'Socrates' necessarily designates Socrates; even at worlds in which neither it nor Socrates exists, the name designates the man. Finally, (7) Socrates is necessarily identical with Socrates, even at worlds in which Socrates does not exist. Property actualists have not been without their replies to many of these cases; but in recent years, the debate has settled down into entrenched positions with little activity or movement.[8]

Stop the Madness

Pushing counterexamples is not the way to advance the debate over property actualism. Behind its acceptance stand some core ideas that blunt the force of any counterexamples and provide the impetus for new replies. One concern is a concern to *stop the madness*.[9] If property actualism were denied, what is to stop nonexistents from having properties in the actual world? What is to stop nonexistents from being golden mountains, or in the doorway? Broad property actualism stops this madness by permitting *no* properties to hold of nonexistents at a world. The narrow property actualist permits *some* complex properties to hold of nonexistents but stops the madness by permitting no *simple* properties to hold of nonexistents at a world. In a world in which he does not exist, Socrates is permitted to be nonexistent but not to be snub-nosed.

Why does the narrow property actualist draw the line at the *simple* properties? The thought seems to be that if a *simple* property held of a nonexistent at a world, then that would have to be a *brute* fact, not explicable or analyzable in terms of the pattern of instantiation of properties and relations among the *existents* of that world. In that case, *nothing stops* a nonexistent from having a simple property at one world and lacking it at a second that agrees with the first on the behavior of the existents. That sort of independence in the behavior of the nonexistents seems to violate a principle we hold about modal reality, a supervenience principle that Kit Fine calls *world actualism*:

World Actualism   Two possible worlds that agree on the behavior of the existents cannot differ on the behavior of the nonexistents (Fine 1981, 295).

Consider two worlds in which the same individuals exist and in which the same properties and relations hold among the existents. The two worlds are duplicates as far as the existents go. Could the two worlds differ over the behavior of the nonexistents?[10] Suppose that Socrates did not exist in either world. Could he have a property in one world that he lacked in another? It does not seem so. World actualism is the articulation of that intuition, and is one of the ideas behind property actualism. If it were false and the behavior of nonexistents could vary across worlds that were existential duplicates, then there would be little reason left to prevent nonexistents from having simple properties at worlds.

Because world actualism is true, broad and narrow property actualism derive support as explanations for its truth. The broad property actualist explains why the behavior of the nonexistents does not vary across worlds that are existential duplicates as being due to the fact that the nonexistents at a world have no properties whatsoever. The narrow property actualist explains the absence of variation in two parts: first, the nonexistents do not vary across worlds in the *simple* properties they have, because they have no simple properties; and the nonexistents do not vary across worlds in the *complex* properties they have, because the same formulas are true at worlds that are duplicates as far as the behavior of the existents go.[11] Consider a world in which Socrates does not exist. The formula 'y does not exist' is thus true at the world if the variable 'y' is assigned to Socrates. The complex predicate 'is nonexistent' is thus true of Socrates at the world.[12] So Socrates is nonexistent at the world. At a second world that is an existential duplicate of the first, the same formula is true under the same assignment, and the same complex predicate is true of Socrates. Socrates is thus nonexistent at both worlds. Broad and narrow property actualism both account for the truth of world actualism equally well; since narrow property actualism does so while avoiding some of the counterexamples facing the broader view, it is the preferred account.

Life without Property Actualism

World actualism is even weaker than narrow property actualism, though. It permits a nonexistent to have a *simple* property at a world just so long as the nonexistent also has that property at any existential duplicate of the first. Could we still account for the truth of world actualism if narrow property actualism were false? One problem with nonreductive supervenience principles is that it becomes a *mystery* why supervenience holds if a reduction or analysis of the supervening facts in terms of the subvenient facts is not in the offing. This worry is often voiced against materialism when it is formulated as a nonreductive supervenience thesis. If narrow property actualism does not account for the supervenience of the nonexistent on the existent, what does? If nonexistents are permitted to have simple properties at worlds, why does world actualism hold? It would become a mystery that it does if narrow property actualism were false. Weak property actualism *has* to be true if world actualism is to hold. That is one reason why the force of counterexamples against narrow property actualism is blunted and why new defenses are always sought. World actualism must be protected, and narrow property actualism is the last line of defense.

The supervenience of the nonexistent on the existent *would* be a mystery if the nonexistent had simple properties like being golden. But no cases support the nonexistent having simple properties like that. For the most part, the simple properties nonexistents appear to have are properties they necessarily have if at all. Consider the relation of designation that holds between the name 'Socrates' and the man Socrates, a relation that holds necessarily if it holds at all.[13] In a world in which Socrates does not exist, the name still designates that man. In a second world that is an existential duplicate of the first, the name still designates the man. The relation of designation is *strongly rigid*: if it holds among certain individuals at one world, it holds among those individuals at every world (see Fine 1977, 131). Sethood, membership, and identity are also strongly rigid properties and relations. Simple properties and relations that are strongly rigid pose no threat to world actualism. Nonexistents that have them at a world have them at every world and thus at every existential duplicate.

Truth is the one simple property from our set of stock counterexamples that is not strongly rigid. A proposition that is true at one world need not be true at every world. But could a proposition be true at one world in which it does not exist and false at a second world that is an existential duplicate of the first? It seems not. The predication of truth to a proposition is constrained by the Tarskian principle: necessarily, the proposition that A is true if and only if A. The proposition that Socrates is in the doorway is thus true at a world if and only if Socrates is in the doorway at that world. If the behavior of the nonexistent individuals does not vary across worlds that are existential duplicates, the truth of propositions about those nonexistent individuals will not vary across worlds that are existential duplicates.

Since the complex properties and the strongly rigid properties of nonexistent individuals do not vary across existential duplicates and those are the only sorts of properties nonexistent individuals seem to have, the truth of propositions about those individuals will thus not vary across existential duplicates.

Nonexistent individuals may have at least *some* simple properties and relations at a world without it becoming a mystery why world actualism holds. Weak property actualism is thus not required to explain why nonexistent individuals do not vary in their behavior across worlds that are existential duplicates. The supervenience of the nonexistent on the existent may be explained either by the complexity of the properties the nonexistents have or by the strong rigidity of their simple properties or by the Tarskian principle in the case of truth. Robbed of its role as the last line of defense for world actualism, narrow property actualism no longer *has* to be true if world actualism is to be saved, and it must now face the full force of the counterexamples against it.

World actualism accords well with intuitions we have about modal reality and the dependence of the behavior of nonexistents on the behavior of existents at possible worlds. It does not require narrow or broad property actualism for support. Because it permits nonexistents to have certain complex and certain simple properties and relations at a world, it does not face any of the stock counterexamples to broad and narrow property actualism. Though we have not looked at the several other ideas that seem to lie behind the acceptance of some form of property actualism, world actualism has emerged to contend with and perhaps even to supplant both forms of property actualism in the metaphysics of modality.[14]

The Identity of the Past

When we turn to the metaphysics of time, we might expect the analogue of world actualism also to play a significant role in the debate over the connection between predication and existence, since it is so common to exploit the analogies between modality and tense. Yet the analogies break down precisely in this area. The past differs from the possible in several ways that affect the connection between predication and existence in a tensed setting and create novel problems for the property presentist. One difference between the past and the possible is brought out by considering a not unfamiliar view of the future.

Arthur Prior thought the future was like a certain kind of promise (Prior 1960). I could promise you a horse—a particular horse—or I could promise you a horse—but no particular horse, just a horse in general. In the first case, the identity of the horse was determined before I fulfilled my promise. A question of identity could significantly be raised. You could ask, "Is *this* the horse you promised me?" In the second case, *any* horse I give you fulfills my promise. Once I give you a horse, *that horse is* the horse that fulfills my promise, but it was not the horse that fulfilled my promise until I gave it to you. In the second case, a question of identity cannot significantly be raised.

Prior thought that the future was like the second kind of promise, at least that portion of the future concerned solely with the goings-on of future individuals. I may predict that a meteor will strike the Earth. My prediction is not about a particular meteor. When a meteor hits Earth, a question of identity will not arise; it will not make sense to wonder if *this* is the meteor I predicted. We may also make predictions like the first kind of promise. I may predict that the Sun will burn hydrogen in 2999, but these predictions concern only present individuals.

Prior's point is not one about our epistemic powers, that we lack the ability to see what specific future individuals are doing in the future. We may assume, if it helps, that we are clairvoyant about the future, able to see what there is to see. Prior's point is also not about a kind of openness or indeterminacy that precludes these predictions from being true or false. We may assume, if it helps, that predictions like those above have truth-values determined not by convention but by future reality.

If we set aside the complication posed by future states of present individuals, Prior's point is that the future is *irreducibly general*. Future states of the world have a general *relational structure*, but no further structure. They have underlying the general relational structure no further structure of particular instances that permits one to raise questions of identity. Truths about the future can be general, but no truths about the future can be singular. Future states thus differ from present or actual states of the world, which do have a full identificatory structure of particular instances underlying the relational structure.

Instead, future states are similar to stories like the following brief one:

There are these two guys who meet, and the one guy asks the other, "How's Hocker?"

This story has a general relational structure but no underlying identificatory structure of particular instances. It would be a mistake to wonder if maybe it is not the one guy but the *other* guy who asks how Hocker is. It would also be a mistake to wonder if in the story maybe it is *Joe* who asks how Hocker is. The problem here is not a lack of epistemic power. We see all there is to see in the story. The problem is that the story has no further structure beyond its relational structure to permit meaningful questions of identity to arise.

We thus picture a near future in which singular patches about present individuals support some general patches but other general patches go unsupported; and a more distant future in which, as the present individuals thin out, the singular patches grow sparse and the unsupported general patches abundant.

This sort of view also seems to match our conception of the possible. The possible is irreducibly general too, if we set aside the complication of the possible goings-on of actual individuals. Possible worlds have a general relational structure but no further structure of particular instances underlying it. A possible world of two homogeneous spheres, one with a bump and one without, has the same level of structure as the story about the two guys. It is an irreducibly general possibility that there might have been two such spheres. The point is not an epistemic one about our inability to discern the further structure. The world itself lacks the further structure. Worlds with actual individuals in them do have some identificatory structure about those individuals, but the rest of it is unsupported general relational structure.

These views of the future and the possible are familiar but not uncontroversial.[15] They do seem to conflict with the four-dimensionalist and possibilist ideas that future and possible individuals are as real as present and actual individuals. I do not wish to try to establish or even to claim that these views are correct here. I only wish to use these ideas to make a contrasting claim about the past and property presentism. If these ideas turn out to be wrong, the claim about the past would still stand and property presentism would only be in worse shape. The claim is that in contrast to this sort of view about the future and the possible, the past is not irreducibly general. No matter how far back we go, the past has no unsupported general patches in it. The relational structure of the past has a full identificatory structure of particular instances underlying it. Some of that identificatory structure involves present individuals, but most of it *has* to involve past individuals.

The past individuals are embedded in that structure in the same way as the present individuals. It is a singular truth that Clinton was president. It was the case that Clinton had the property of being president. That past state involves a specific present individual. The identity of that past state depends on the identity of the specific individual involved. Consider an analogy. What makes a thought about the table before me *de re* is that the identity of the thought depends on the identity of the table before me. If the table were replaced by a duplicate, the thought would be distinct. If the thought about the table were purely general, replacing the table with a duplicate would not change the identity of the thought; it would be numerically the same thought in both situations. Replacing Clinton changes the identity of that past state that he was president. The state is a *de re* state of the past whose identity depends on Clinton. The same is true of the past state that Reagan was president, except in this case the identity of the past state depends on the identity of a *past* individual, Ronald Reagan.

If it is a *de re* state of the past that Clinton was president, then not only *was* it the case that he had the property of being president, but it *is* the case that he *has* the property of having been president. Clinton now has the complex property of having been president. If the past state is *de re*, then having been president is now a property of him. This transition is familiar in modal cases. If it is a *de re* necessity that necessarily 9 is odd, then the property of being necessarily odd is a property of the number 9. If it is a *de re* possibility that Humphrey might have won the election, then the property of possibly winning the election is a property of Humphrey. Since it is also a *de re* state of the past that *Reagan* was president, it is also the case that *he now has* the property of having been president. In other words, a past individual has a property in the present. In fact, Reagan has many such properties in the present, as do all of the other past individuals. For every property an individual had in the past, there is a corresponding complex property, which that individual has in the present.[16]

The stock counterexamples facing the property actualist were of actual individuals having properties at worlds in which they did not exist, such as Socrates' being nonexistent at a world in which he does not exist. The analogues of these counterexamples for the property presentist are of *present* individuals having properties at *times* when they do not exist. But the past differs from the possible (or a familiar picture of the possible) in a fundamental way: it has no irreducibly general patches in it. As a consequence, the property presentist faces a novel and extensive category of counterexamples of *past* individuals having properties and standing in relations *in the present*.

The Order of the Past

The past differs from the possible in a second respect that raises further problems for property presentism. Though world actualism had strong intuitive appeal in the metaphysics of modality, no analogue of world actualism appears to hold in a tensed setting. One analogue replaces the worlds with times:

Time Presentism Two times that agree on the behavior of the existents must agree on the behavior of the nonexistents.

But it seems that between two times that are existential duplicates, an individual could come into existence, have some properties, perhaps undergo some changes, and then go out of existence. At the later time the individual has the property of having existed, among many other past-tense properties, but at the earlier time it has none of these properties. Time presentism thus fails.

It fails where world actualism does not because times are ordered and worlds are not, a fundamental difference between time and modality. Because times are ordered, what is past relative to one time need not be past relative to an earlier time. If worlds were ordered, world actualism would fail in the same way. But in the metaphysics of modality, the worlds are usually taken to be universally accessible. Thus, Sinatra can have the property of possibly being blue-eyed at two worlds that are existential duplicates and at which he does not exist because there is a third world possible relative to each in which he does exist and is blue-eyed.

The Independence of the Past

Perhaps the worlds in world actualism should be replaced not with times but with *tensed* worlds in which there is a distinguished present. The existents of a tensed world are then the individuals existing in its present, and the nonexistents, for our purposes, are the individuals existing in its past, with their "behavior" being their behavior in the present. Call this view *world presentism*:

World Presentism Two tensed worlds that agree on the behavior (in the present) of the present individuals must agree on the behavior (in the present) of the past individuals.

But it seems that two tensed worlds could agree in their presents but differ in their pasts. Different routes could be taken to reach the same present. Or there could be worlds with beginnings and recurrence. In these cases, past individuals have different past-tense properties in the two presents. World presentism thus fails where world actualism does not because the past differs from the possible in a third fundamental way: the past is independent of the present, but the possible supervenes on the actual.

Two *tenseless* worlds that are existential duplicates must agree on the possibilities, and so must agree on the complex modal properties of the nonexistents at the two worlds. However, two tensed worlds that are existential duplicates may differ over what is past, and so may differ on the complex tensed properties of the nonexistents at the two worlds.

Conclusion

The prospects for property actualism are not bright. It does not follow from actualism, and the triangle argument is without force. It faces a set of stock counterexamples, and it has lost its initial appeal of explaining why world actualism holds. The truth about the connection between predication and existence in a modal setting seems to lie with world actualism itself.

Property presentism certainly fares no better. It does not follow from presentism; the triangle argument is without force; and it faces a similar set of stock counterexamples. In fact, it fares much worse because the past differs from the possible in three fundamental ways: its structure is not irreducibly general; its times are ordered; and it is independent of the present. Past individuals thus have properties in the present, and have those properties independently of the behavior of the present individuals. Nothing analogous to world actualism holds in the metaphysics of time. Property presentism thus lacks even the illusion of explanatory appeal and faces a new and extensive category of counterexamples. Its prospects are dim indeed.

As the appeal of property presentism wanes, so does the force of our initial cluster of puzzles that depend upon it. When we extinguish the last distorting effects of property presentism on our understanding of the past, we begin to see that the past does not merely replicate the structure of the possible in a temporal setting but that the past has its own nature, its own identity, which is richly deserving of our study in its own right.

Acknowledgments

I am indebted to Steven Arkonovich, Rachel Fredericks, and William Taschek for their comments, and especially to Paul Hovda for illuminating discussion of these matters. I thank Joseph Keim Campbell and Michael O'Rourke for their invitation on behalf of their schools to present this essay at the Inland Northwest Philosophy Conference in 2005, and for their help and patience in preparing it for publication.

Notes

1. See Sider 1999 and Keller 2004, among others. I discuss this argument in Hinchliff 2003.

2. See Stalnaker 1977 for one way to introduce complex predicates.

3. For example, if R is a simple n-place predicate, then narrow predicate presentism is the view that Always $\forall x_1 \ldots$ Always $\forall x_n$ Always $(Rx_1 \ldots x_n \rightarrow (x_1$ exists $\& \ldots x_n$ exists)).

4. The exception is Sider 1997.

5. I have stated the three traditional connections in conditional form because the triangle moves around the sides in that direction, but the connections seem to be understood as biconditionals, especially when the properties include complex ones.

6. Kripke 1963. In footnote 11, Kripke says that what we are here calling simple predicate actualism is a "natural" assumption, and he shows how to implement the view in his semantics. He adds, however, that he has chosen not to implement the view, because the rule of substitution would then fail to hold. For discussion see Stalnaker 1977 and Menzel 2000.

7. Kripke's semantics is strictly speaking neutral on this third connection. However, an existence predicate can be introduced that preserves it, as Kripke himself points out (Kripke 1963, 70).

8. See Forbes 1989 for a good discussion of these examples. I discuss Salmon's Nothan cases (Salmon 1987, 1998) as well as other apparent counterexamples involving cross-world relations in Hinchliff 2007a.

9. I discuss several other ideas behind property actualism in Hinchliff 2007a.

10. I assume that the nonexistents are themselves possible individuals.

11. I assume that in the semantics all the worlds are accessible to each other.

12. I assume an unrestricted principle of predicate abstraction: $\Box \forall x \Box (\varphi(x) \rightarrow \hat{y}[\varphi(y)]$ $(x))$, in which '$\varphi(y)$' is a formula in which 'y' is free and '$\hat{y}[\varphi(y)]$' is a complex predicate formed from it.

13. I distinguish designation from naming or reference. It is possible that 'Socrates' not refer to Socrates. There are worlds in which the name 'Socrates' fails to name or to refer, but in those worlds 'Socrates' still designates Socrates.

14. As mentioned previously, several other ideas also seem to lie behind property actualism, and our conclusion here must be provisional upon an investigation of those other ideas.

15. I set out these rather rough ideas about the future and the possible more completely in Hinchliff 2007b, where I give a model theory to represent them.

16. Kripke (1979) notes in footnote 7 that the equivalence of *de re* and *de dicto* modal sentences involving proper names is (roughly) equivalent to his thesis of rigidity for proper names in modal contexts. He also notes that the equivalence of *de re* and *de dicto* holds for proper names in temporal contexts, and this *de re–de dicto* equivalence is (roughly) equivalent to the "temporal rigidity" of proper names.

References

Bergmann, M. 1999. (Serious) Actualism and (Serious) Presentism. *Noûs* 33: 118–132.

Bigelow, J. 1996. Presentism and Properties. In *Philosophical Perspectives, 10: Metaphysics*, ed. J. Tomberlin. Cambridge: Blackwell.

Chisholm, R. M. 1990. Referring to Things That No Longer Exist. In *Philosophical Perspectives 4: Action Theory and Philosophy of Mind*, ed. J. Tomberlin. Atascadero, CA: Ridgeview.

Crisp, T. 2005. Presentism and Cross-Time Relations. *American Philosophical Quarterly* 42:5–17.

Davidson, M. 2003. Presentism and the Non-Present. *Philosophical Studies* 113:77–92.

Fine, K. 1977. Postscript. In A. N. Prior and K. Fine, *Worlds, Times, and Selves*. London: Duckworth.

Fine, K. 1981. Model Theory for Modal Logic—Part III. *Journal of Philosophical Logic* 10:293–307.

Fine, K. 1985. Plantinga on the Reduction of Possibilist Discourse. In *Alvin Plantinga*, ed. J. Tomberlin and P. van Inwagen. Dordrecht: Reidel.

Forbes, G. 1989. *The Languages of Possibility*. Oxford: Blackwell.

Hinchliff, M. 1989. Plantinga's Defence of Serious Actualism. *Analysis* 49:182–185.

Hinchliff, M. 2003. On the Need for Truthmakers. Manuscript.

Hinchliff, M. 2007a. Against Property Presentism. Manuscript.

Hinchliff, M. 2007b. The Developing World. Manuscript.

Hudson, H. 1997. On a New Argument from Actualism to Serious Actualism. *Noûs* 31:520–524.

Keller, S. 2004. Presentism and Truthmaking. In *Oxford Studies in Metaphysics*, vol. 1, ed. D. Zimmerman. Oxford: Oxford University Press.

Kripke, S. 1963. Semantical Considerations on Modal Logic. *Acta Philosophica Fennica* 16: 83–94. Reprinted in L. Linsky, ed., *Reference and Modality*, Oxford: Oxford University Press, 1971. Page references are to the latter.

Kripke, S. 1979. A Puzzle about Belief. In *Meaning and Use*, ed. A. Margalit. Dordrecht: Reidel. Reprinted in N. Salmon and S. Soames, eds., *Propositions and Attitudes*, Oxford: Oxford University Press, 1988. Page references are to the latter.

Markosian, N. 2004. A Defense of Presentism. In *Oxford Studies in Metaphysics*, vol. 1, ed. D. Zimmerman. Oxford: Oxford University Press.

Menzel, C. 2000. Actualism. In *The Stanford Encyclopedia of Philosophy* (spring 2007 edition), ed. E. Zalta. http://plato.stanford.edu/archives/spr2007/entries/actualism/.

Plantinga, A. 1983a. De essentia. *Grazer Philosophische Studien* 7/8:101–121.

Plantinga, A. 1983b. On Existentialism. *Philosophical Studies* 44:1–20.

Plantinga, A. 1985. Replies to My Colleagues. In *Alvin Plantinga*, ed. J. Tomberlin and P. van Inwagen. Dordrecht: Reidel.

Pollock, J. 1985. Plantinga on Possible Worlds. In *Alvin Plantinga*, ed. J. Tomberlin and P. van Inwagen. Dordrecht: Reidel.

Prior, A. 1960. Identifiable Individuals. *Review of Metaphysics* 13:684–696. Reprinted in A. Prior, *Papers on Time and Tense*, Oxford: Oxford University Press, 1968. Page references are to the latter.

Rea, M. 2003. Four-Dimensionalism. In *Oxford Handbook of Metaphysics*, ed. M. Loux and D. Zimmerman. Oxford: Oxford University Press.

Salmon, N. 1987. Existence. In *Philosophical Perspectives I: Metaphysics*, ed. J. Tomberlin. Atascadero, CA: Ridgeview.

Salmon, N. 1998. Nonexistence. *Noûs* 32:277–319.

Sider, T. 1997. Four-Dimensionalism. *Philosophical Review* 106:197–231.

Sider, T. 1999. Presentism and Ontological Commitment. *Journal of Philosophy* 96:325–347.

Sider, T. 2001. *Four-Dimensionalism*. Oxford: Oxford University Press.

Stalnaker, R. 1977. Complex Predicates. *Monist* 60:327–339.

Yannis, S. 2007. Serious Actualism. *Philosophical Review* 116:219–250.

II Identity

5   Identity through Change and Substitutivity *Salva Veritate*

Reinaldo Elugardo and Robert J. Stainton

Introduction

This chapter has three modest aims: to present a puzzle, to show why some obvious solutions aren't really "easy outs," and to introduce our own solution.

The puzzle is this. When it was small and had waterlogged streets, Toronto carried the moniker 'Muddy York'. Later, the streets were drained, it grew, and Muddy York officially changed its name to 'Toronto'. Given this, each premise in the following argument seems true. Yet the conclusion is a contradiction.

(P1)   Muddy York = Toronto

(P2)   Muddy York evolved into Toronto.

(P3)   The context '__ evolved into Toronto' is transparent, that is, it allows substitution of coreferring singular terms.

(P4)   It's not the case that Toronto evolved into Toronto.

(C1)   Toronto evolved into Toronto (by P1, P2, and P3).

(C2)   Toronto both did and did not evolve into Toronto (by P4 and C1).

Of course the puzzle isn't about Toronto. It's not even about cities: the same conundrum arises with names of people (think of the well-known case of 'Cassius Clay' and 'Mohammed Ali'), diseases ('coronovirus' and 'SARS'), and so on. Nor is the puzzle just about "evolving into": it can be generated with 'changed into', 'turned into', 'became', and so forth. Generalizing, an instance of the puzzle can be got whenever we have both accidental change—that is, qualitative change that preserves numerical identity—together with a change in name.

Before moving forward, two caveats are in order. We approach the puzzle as philosophers of language, not as metaphysicians; and our proposed solution to it is linguistic. No doubt the puzzle, being about change, time, identity, and the like, also raises metaphysical questions galore; but we take our linguistic points to be compatible with any remotely plausible metaphysical account of these.[1] Related to this, we do not put forward our solution as definitive. We think it's superior to the "easy outs" that we reject, but it's not without its problems. In particular, it does leave us with one nonobvious metaphysical commitment.

Four "Easy Outs"

We now consider four natural reactions to the puzzle.[2] Each corresponds to the rejection of a premise in the argument above. All four "outs" are initially attractive. We will try to show, however, that in each case the supposed "easy out" either requires biting a hard philosophical bullet or suffers from obvious empirical faults.

Start with (P1) and (P2), since they can be dealt with quickly. Giving up (P1) avoids the substitution of 'Toronto' for 'Muddy York' at (C1). But to deny that Muddy York is, that is, is numerically identical to, Toronto, apparently involves giving up the identity over time of the one city. That's a very significant cost, to say the least. It means, for example, that the city's residents didn't truly celebrate Toronto's bicentennial in 1993, since no one thing has lasted that long. One might say: Cities are such fluid social creations that this isn't such a cost after all. But remember: the puzzle generalizes. We mentioned people (and diseases). Thus, rejecting (P1) means, for instance, that one can't really punish the very person who did the crime, after a name change, but only some *other* person who stands in the right causal-historical relation to the renamed evil-doer. We could equally have given examples of land-masses, species, etc. It seems, then, that for any changing object that has different labels at different times, we'd have to abandon identity. Of course some philosophers might be tempted to give up genuine identity over time. But this just is bullet-biting, and we think that can be avoided. Giving up (P2) doesn't look any more promising. It seems a matter of historical fact: Muddy York evolved into Toronto. (You can look it up, if you don't believe us.) You might object that given (P4) and (P1), we simply have to reject (P2). But again, that's another bullet: this move lets metaphysical scruples trump seemingly obvious empirical observations. We hope to show that all such moves can be avoided.

Abandoning (P3) seems a far more attractive option. In fact, when we first noticed the puzzle we thought we had found a new kind of opacity, similar to 'The temperature is rising; the temperature is 92 degrees; so, 92 degrees is rising'. Careful reflection convinced us, however, that '__ evolved into Toronto' behaves differently from familiar opaque contexts. First, in familiar opaque contexts one can substitute genuinely nondenoting definite descriptions and get truths. For instance, because 'is looking for' is opaque, it can be *true* that an (unfortunate) mathematician has devoted his life to looking for the largest prime. But only genuine denoting terms can give rise to true substitution instances of '__ evolved into Toronto' and the like, so that context doesn't behave like genuinely opaque contexts do. It may be objected to this test that we do say things like 'Saint Nicholas evolved into Santa Claus'. But when this is true, the expressions *do* have some kind of denotation, so they aren't really genuinely denotationless. (To see this, note that when we are using 'Saint Nicholas' in this way, it's also true that he has a beard, is over twenty years old, etc.) It's expressions of the genuinely nondenoting kind, like 'the largest prime', that distinguish genuinely opaque contexts from others—and they do not give rise to true instances of '__ evolved into __'. Second empirical difference: It seems that evolving into (etc.) is something the object considered in itself does: it's not a guise, or a linguistic description, which determines whether the thing evolved into such-and-such or didn't. And being *de re* in that way is another hallmark of referentially transparent contexts. Third, appeal to opacity is insufficiently general. Similar sorts of things happen where there is no triggering verb at all. Consider, in this regard, a much older and more familiar puzzle: 'That cute baby is that old geezer. That old geezer has a beard. Therefore, that cute baby has a beard'. The problem *here* surely is not that '__ has a beard' disallows substitutivity *salva veritate*. So, if we can find a solution that covers this old case and also solves our puzzle, that would be preferable. Finally, opacity should not be introduced without necessity. Whatever mechanism one endorses to explain away nonsubstitutivity—reference shift, parataxis, and so on—that mechanism should be deployed sparingly. And, as will emerge below, there's no need to posit opacity here. So much, then, for solving the puzzle by rejecting (P3). That's not really such an "easy out" either, because it is empirically inadequate.

The final "easy out" is to reject (P4). To give up P4, one can follow Jennifer Saul, and suggest that although it is very odd to say that Toronto evolved into Toronto, it's not actually false. The comparison here, drawn from Saul (1997), is with (1) and (2):

(1)   Superman went into the phone booth and Clark Kent came out.

(2)   Superman went into the phone booth and Superman came out.

She suggests that if (1) is true, (2) is true as well. (How could it not be, since '__ came out of the phone booth' is patently transparent?) Still, despite this, we *hear* the two sentences as having different truth-values because of pragmatics. Ditto, one might say, for 'Toronto evolved into Toronto' versus 'Muddy York evolved into Toronto'. The key difference with our puzzle, however, is that whereas sentence (2) can *be true*, and would even *strike us as true* (e.g., if the famous gentleman went in with his cape on, and came out the same way), '__ evolved into __' is irreflexive. No object can evolve into itself, and under no circumstances does it strike us as true that one does so.[3] (Though see below for some complications.) So giving up (P4) doesn't seem consistent with an important fact about the semantics of '__ evolved into __'.

To sum up so far, we have presented our puzzle, namely that premises (P1) through (P4) seem true, though they jointly yield a contradiction; and we have canvassed four "easy outs," each corresponding to the rejection of a premise, suggesting that rejecting the premise in question either requires biting a philosophical bullet, or is empirically inadequate. The final step, which we turn to shortly, is to present our own proposal. First, however, we need to introduce and defend an idea that will play a crucial role.

Polysemy

We maintain that names of places, people, and things are polysemous in a way that can solve our puzzle. We will defend this idea in two stages. First, we explain what polysemy in general is. Then, we introduce the particular way in which, according to us, names like 'Toronto' are polysemous.

Polysemy is a kind of ambiguity, but one that is less problematic than homophony, as in 'bank [of a river]' and 'bank [where I have my checking account]'. Polysemy understood broadly is a matter of numerous related senses—with theorists differing on what it is to have different "senses." However implemented, polysemy is systematic enough that it doesn't postulate hard-to-acquire unrelated meanings. (See Apresjan 1974, Moravcsik 1998, and Pustejovsky 1998 for detailed discussion.)

Here are a series of examples. Sometimes a product name refers to the model, but in other uses it refers to a token thereof. Thus consider (3).

(3)   Rob's Ford is reliable.

One can use this sentence to say, about the kind of Ford Rob owns, namely the Focus, that it's reliable. Such a statement would be false: the Focus is notoriously unreliable. But consider a context in which Rob owns two cars, a peculiarly unreliable Honda and a Focus that, against all odds, is very reliable. Then, even if the *kind* of Ford Rob owns is notoriously unreliable, one can still speak truly with (3). This sort of example supports the idea that the phrase 'Rob's Ford' is polysemous, being used here to refer to a type and there to refer to a token. Notice that this doesn't require two independent lexical entries for 'Ford', since the phenomenon occurs with kinds quite broadly. For example, think of (4):

(4)   Every Canadian coin has a monarch's face on it.

This is true of every denomination, but false of some of the more well-worn metallic tokens. Nor is type–token the only place where "multiplicity of related senses" shows up. Consider these examples, adapted from Pustejovsky 1998 and Nunberg 1979, 1995.

(5)   'Denny's is located on the corner of 5th and Broadway' versus 'Denny's once had controversial hiring practices'.

(6)   'Mary broke the bottle' versus 'The baby finished the bottle'.

(7)   'The window is rotting' versus 'Mary crawled through the window'.

(8)   'The *Toronto Star* fired its editor' versus 'John spilled coffee on the *Toronto Star*'.

(9)   'Saul Bellow died recently' versus 'Saul Bellow would make a terrific dissertation topic'.

(10)   'Washington is a great tourist destination' versus 'Washington declared war'.

In (5), the shift is something like token–type: from a particular location to the corporation as a whole. In (6), 'the bottle' shifts from standing for the container, to standing for its contents, and in (7), 'the window' similarly shifts from the outside to the inside. In (8) and (9) one refers first to the producer, then to (something like) the product. Finally, in (10), 'Washington' is used first to refer to the city as a location, then to refer to it as seat of government. (Compare also: 'Washington beat the Maple Leafs to win the Stanley Cup'.)

Again, in contrast with the homophonous 'bank' (river versus financial institution), one doesn't have to memorize two autonomous meanings for the specific terms 'bottle', 'window', and 'the *Toronto Star*', and so on. What the language learner needs to internalize is that there is a comparatively systematic effect of multiple senses that applies generally to models, containers, figures, and products (among other cases). *That* is polysemy.

Before laying out in more detail our polysemy idea for names, it may help to foreshadow how appeal to polysemy would solve the puzzle. Recall the 'Rob's Ford' example, and consider the following argument, which parallels the one we began with:

(P1*)   The car in the driveway = Rob's Ford.

(P2*)   The car in the driveway is unreliable.

(P3*)   The context '__ is unreliable' is transparent, that is, it allows substitution of coreferring singular terms.

(P4*)   It's not the case that Rob's Ford is unreliable.

(C1*)   Rob's Ford is unreliable (by P1, P2, and P3).

(C2*)   Rob's Ford both is and is not unreliable (by P4 and C1).

(P1*) is an identity *at* a time; surely it can't be denied. (P2*) is an empirical fact: the 2000 Ford Focus, which is the one that Rob owns, is an extremely unreliable car. It has, for instance, been subject to a record number of recalls. As for (P3*), if '__ is unreliable' is opaque, then just about anything is. As for (P4*), it's an empirical fact too: Rob's Ford is even more reliable than his Honda, and Hondas are one of the most reliable cars on the road. We thus have four premises that seem true, and a conclusion that is a contradiction. Should we bite the bullet, and reject one of the premises? Clearly not. In this case, it's quite obvious what is wrong with the argument: on the sense of 'Rob's Ford' on which (P1*) (and P4*) is true, namely the token sense, (P2*) is false; and on the sense of 'Rob's Ford' on which (P2*) is true, namely the model sense, (P1*) (and P4*) is false. The trouble with the argument, then, is that its premises seem true because of equivocation on the polysemous phrase 'Rob's Ford'.

So much for introducing polysemy as a general phenomenon. That it exists at all is at least somewhat controversial (e.g., Fodor and Lepore [1998] take issue with it), but we think something in the neighborhood is real and ubiquitous, and we'll assume as much in what follows. Taking polysemy in general as a given, our idea with respect to the puzzling argument with which we began is that polysemy of an unnoticed sort occurs with names of places, people, and the like. In particular, and putting things crudely for the time being, such names have two lexically specified use-potentials: they have the linguistic function both of being used to refer to an object over time, and to refer to that object at a time.[4] Using 'Toronto' as an example, the idea is that the meaning of this name permits two literal uses: to refer to the city as a whole, across its entire history, and to refer to the city at a particular stage of its growth and development.

Two clarifications. First, the idea is not merely that 'Toronto' can be used to refer to various things. Of course that's true, because speakers can in general refer with a word *w* to lots of things that *w* does not designate. Nor, second, is the idea that there is a "meaning" of 'Toronto' for each thing it can be used literally to refer to. Since there are ever so many stages at which Toronto exists, there are every so many ways of referring to Toronto at a time: on July 22, 2005; in 1929; on VE Day; and so on—and it's clear that 'Toronto' does not have, as a matter of its linguistic job, a distinct use-potential for each of these. Rather, the idea, again crudely for now, is that 'Toronto' has two relevant senses: one for referring to the object over time, and the other for referring to that object during the contextually salient period of time.

Why think that names for people, places, things, and the like are polysemous in this at-a-time versus over-time way? Let's start with three points in favor. First, notice that 'John Graves Simcoe, having died in 1806, lived in Muddy York, not in Toronto' sounds true. More exactly, we think it can be used literally to make a true statement. But it couldn't do so if 'Muddy York' and 'Toronto' could only be used literally to refer to the entire object-over-time. Also, 'Muddy York is now overrun with SUVs and cookie-cutter houses' sounds true. Or better, we think it too can be used literally to make a true statement. But it couldn't be so used if 'Muddy York' could only be deployed literally to refer to the long-ago object-at-a-time. Thus polysemy for such expressions seems to be required on independent grounds: object-at-a-time for the former usage, object-over-time for the latter. Second, the effect is quite general. It's not just names that are here used literally to talk about objects-at-a-time and are there used literally to refer to objects-over-time. Nominals in general can be used literally with each kind of satisfier. Thus, to take an example from Ted Sider (personal correspondence), 'Some frontier towns evolved into major centers of culture' can easily be used literally to say something true, unlike 'Some major centers of culture evolved into major centers of culture'. Or, to take an example from Lenny Clapp (personal correspondence), one could point at a picture and then at a crusty oldster and say, using a demonstrative rather than a name, 'That cute baby evolved into that grizzly old codger'. That statement could be true. But 'That grizzly old codger evolved into that grizzly old codger'? So, introducing polysemy for this kind of name is not ad hoc. Third, and speaking of generality, introducing polysemy for referring terms allows us to explain away other apparent examples of opacity. Consider: 'Lunch is a tuna fish sandwich; lunch is always served at noon; therefore, a tuna fish sandwich is always served at noon'. The premises are true. The conclusion is false. Still, it's not plausible that '__ is always served at noon' is opaque. But how then is substitution failure to be explained? The obvious answer is that 'lunch' is polysemous, being used here for a daily eating activity, there for the item to be eaten on a specific day. Role-occupier cases like this turn out to be quite common. (Here's another case. 'The boss is getting younger; Samantha is the boss; therefore, Samantha is getting younger'.) Noting this, consider again the familiar example 'The temperature is rising'. Our initial thought, following Montague, was that '__ evolved into __' exemplified a variety of opacity along these lines. We were wrong about the opacity of '__ evolved into __'. But maybe we were right about the similarity. Perhaps what's going on in this more familiar example is not that '__ is rising' is resistant to substitution of coreferring terms—with the "functional sense" being contributed instead of the usual referent—but rather that 'The temperature' is polysemous: here it is used to refer to the role, there it is used to talk about the present occupier (e.g., 22 degrees). In other words, coreferring terms *can* be substituted in this context; the thing is, 'The temperature' when used to pick out the role, *doesn't* actually corefer with '22 degrees'.[5]

Consider now four objections to our polysemy hypothesis for 'Toronto' et al., and our replies. First, introducing multiple senses will strike some as a violation of "Grice's razor": do not posit ambiguities without necessity. One obvious reply is that there *is* necessity here, because there are usages that cannot be adequately described without varying senses. Though we think this reply carries some weight, we recognize that such a response will seem question-begging in the present context. Another reply, then, which skirts the necessity issue, is this. Polysemy can be understood in at least two ways. On the first, polysemous terms are assigned a *series* of contents, and context selects among these. So understood, polysemy really is full-blown ambiguity, so, for better or worse, this version does introduce extra type meanings. Happily, there's another way of spelling out the idea. On the second version, the polysemous term is assigned a single content that can permit literal reference to something more determinate on the basis of the context. To give an example, on the first account 'Ford' would mean both FORD MODEL and FORD INSTANCE; then a use of 'Rob's Ford' would exhibit one of these two preset senses. On the second account, 'Ford' would simply mean FORD; but that content would not single out tokens or types as what could be literally referred to, allowing a speaker to refer literally to either. The phrase would thus have both use-potentials determined by its one standing meaning. The cost of the second approach, if it is a cost, is that the sentence type 'Rob's Ford is unreliable' would not express a context-independent proposition. Indeed, it's consonant with this approach that sentence types in general do not have propositions as their meaning. Rather, as per Strawson (1950), their meaning allows them to be used by agents to state various propositions. The benefit is that this one sentence could be used literally to assert (at least) two quite different kinds of propositions, thereby accounting for the observed usage. For reasons of theoretical economy, and for other reasons that are quite independent of the puzzle, we happen to favor the latter option. And *it* isn't open to the objection under consideration, whether or not additional senses are required to describe the data correctly.

Here is a second objection, due to Mark Moyer (personal correspondence). Consider sentence (11).

(11)   Muddy York evolved into Toronto, and its bicentennial was in 1993.

On our view, 'its' would have to refer to the object-over-time, since that is the thing that survived for 200 years, but the only antecedents available each would be used to refer to the object-at-a-time, since it is those that "evolve into." Thus, our view seemingly predicts that (11) will be semantically anomalous. But, continues the objection, the sentence is perfectly fine. Hence, there must be something wrong with our analysis. Our reply is that polysemous terms in general just do behave this way: an anaphor doesn't always pick up the exact "sense" of its antecedent. For instance, take 'Rob's Ford has won *Car and Driver*'s Ten Best award five years in a row, but this morning it won't start'. The antecedent can be about the type while the anaphor is used to refer to the token (otherwise, every literal use of the sentence would be false). Yet we shouldn't conclude that 'Rob's Ford' isn't polysemous. Here are some other nice examples, from Nunberg 1979, 1995:

(12)   Yeats did not enjoy hearing himself read aloud.

(13)   The window was broken so many times that it had to be boarded up.

(14)   Tom sat down to read the *New York Times*, which minutes before had fired its president.

(15)   After drinking all three bottles, Scott smashed them against his head.

In short, the peculiar anaphoric behavior of 'its' in (11) does not provide evidence against 'Muddy York' and 'Toronto' being polysemous in the suggested object-at-a-time versus object-over-time way.

Third objection, due to Jill Rusin (personal correspondence). It's an obvious feature of our view that Ray could speak truly in saying (16):

(16)   Toronto did not evolve into Toronto.

The truth of this statement is precisely part of what gets the puzzle going. A less obvious and potentially problematic feature of the view is that Rob could speak truly in saying (17):

(17)   Toronto did evolve into Toronto.

That's because, on our account, 'Toronto' is not just polysemous, it is also context sensitive in another sense. Like 'he', 'Toronto' can be used on its at-a-time sense to refer to the city at different times. Thus the first 'Toronto' in an utterance of (17) might be used to refer to the city on the day of its founding in 1793, and the second might be used to refer to Toronto on VE Day. So used, the speaker (say, Rob) states something true with this sentence. (Compare 'That evolved into that': it is overtly context sensitive, and it can be used to say something true, by demonstrating first the little town and then the metropolis.) But, continues the objection, if Ray can speak truly with (16) and Rob can speak truly with (17), it seems that one could use (18) truly as well:

(18)   Ray said that Toronto did not evolve into Toronto, and Rob said that Toronto did evolve into Toronto, and what they both said is true.

But, and here is the nub of the objection, (18) just can't be used truly. This counts against our view that 'Toronto' can shift its reference: it doesn't behave like authentic reference-shifters such as 'he'. The argument is clever. Our reply, however, is that once the context is right, one *can* use (18) truly. For instance, Ray could speak normally, while Rob could say the first 'Toronto' in a small quiet voice and the second loudly and with enthusiasm. Ray would then have spoken truly, about the object-over-time, and Rob would have spoken truly about the object at a distinct time— for example, speaking truly about the evolution of Toronto the small reserved town into Toronto the vibrant multiethnic megacity. Deploying (18) would, it must be granted, typically be an odd way of reporting this event, but that doesn't mean it cannot be used to speak the truth. Besides, imagine both the speaker and addressee have had the benefit of reading the present essay, and the speaker wants to remind the addressee about the view. Then, the speaker could say (18), speak truly, and speak felicitously![6]

The final objection is that our view is metaphysically untenable. In particular, goes the objection, our "solution" introduces time slices, or temporal parts, or something like that. This is problematic on a host of fronts. For instance, it's unclear how such slices/parts relate to ordinary objects, and it's unclear how an early time slice (or part) can evolve into a later one, since the former has ceased to exist by the time the latter comes onto the stage. Our reply is that our view has no such implication, and this in two senses. First, the appeal to polysemy is about natural language semantics; it simply is not about metaphysics in and of itself. So we certainly do not intend any controversial metaphysical commitments. Second, so far as we can tell, our semantic claims do not entail any one view about the metaphysics of objects-at-a-time versus objects-over-time. That's because all our view requires is:

a. that people can refer to an object-at-a-time;
b. that people can refer to an object-over-time;
c. that there is some difference between doing these two things; and
d. that objects at a time "evolve into" (whereas objects over time "evolve").

Any metaphysics consistent with (a)–(d) is fine by us, and there are surely lots of metaphysical views that can endorse these.

We would add that any *plausible* metaphysics has got to be consistent at least with (a)–(c), because they are patently true. Starting with (a) and (b), one can, for example, refer now to Elton John at the moment that *Goodbye Yellow Brick Road* was released. Indeed, we just did. One can also refer to Elton during his entire life. We just did that too. As for (c), that there's some difference is clear from the fact that Elton on the release date, way back in 1973, has different kinds of properties from Elton over time. For instance, Elton at the moment the album was released had a height and weight, whereas Elton over time only has an *average* height and weight; Elton at the moment the album appeared in stores was surely wearing a certain pair of glasses, whereas Elton over time has worn many, many different pairs of glasses; and so on. And, of course, whereas the man over time has two names, 'Elton John' and 'Reg Dwight', the man at the time of his birth had only one name, namely 'Reg Dwight'.

The sticking point is (d). In particular, it's not obvious that what one refers to when speaking of (say) Toronto at a time is a *thing* at all, let alone a thing that "evolves into." Now, granting this, we don't immediately have to buy any specific metaphysical story about what an object-at-a-time is, such that it can evolve into: whatever the right story is, we can endorse it. Still, *that we can refer to such a thing* does seem to be a (metaphysical?) commitment of our view. As hinted at the very outset, this is a consequence we are a bit uneasy with. Still, it's better than the obvious bizarre bullets that must be bitten, if (P1) or (P2) is abandoned. That, then, is the minor bullet that we bite.

Using Polysemy to Solve the Puzzle

Our proposal is that the names of places, people, and things are polysemous. In particular, they permit literal reference either to the object-over-time, or to the object-at-a-time. We gave three arguments for this idea and responded to four arguments against it. What remains is to put the proposal to work, to solve the puzzle with which we began. The game plan is to explain, for each premise, how it turns out to be true without yielding the contradictory conclusion. Along the way, we also want to highlight an insight that lies behind each of the "easy outs."

Start with premises 3 and 4. (P3) is plain true: '__ evolves into __' just does apply to the *object itself*, however conceived. What was right about rejecting it, however, was the insight that there is reference-shifting going on. But, on our view, the reference shifting isn't of the sort Frege envisaged, that is, the kind triggered by an opaque context. Instead, it's merely a matter of one of the two use-potentials of a polysemous name (viz., the at-a-time one) being salient because the linguistic context (viz., '__ evolves into __') pragmatically calls for that kind of referent. As for (P4), it is true when 'Toronto' is used to refer univocally to the object over time. It is also true when 'Toronto' is used univocally to refer to the object at the same time. The insight we can glean from the Saul-style strategy, rejected earlier, is that pragmatics can play an unexpected role, namely to explain why one can use 'Toronto evolved into Toronto' truly, to talk of an object at different times. (E.g., 'Toronto evolved into TORONTO'.)

Turning to premises 1 and 2, we come to the heart of the solution to the puzzle. (P1) is true when 'Muddy York' and 'Toronto' are both used to refer to the object-over-time. Nevertheless, and this is an insight of the first "easy out," (P1) is false on another reading: the one where the two names are used to talk about distinct objects-at-a-time. As for (P2), it is true when 'Muddy York' and 'Toronto' are each used to refer to the city at different times. The insight of the second "easy out" is that (P2) is false on another reading, namely where both names are employed to refer to the city over time. Crucially, (P2) is false on the reading in which (P1) is true, and (P1) is false on the reading on which (P2) is true. There is thus no unequivocal way to make all the premises true. That's why the argument fails.

But why do we not notice the slide? For instance, why is the argument using (P1)–(P4) so much more puzzling than the argument that uses (P1*)–(P4*)? (No one would be even initially fooled by the latter.) The answer, we think, is that (P1) and (P2) each have exactly one *salient* reading: it's wholly natural to read (P1) as only being about the object-at-a-time, and wholly natural to read (P2) as being only about the object over time. And so read, they are both true. Thus the polysemy does not jump out at us. It takes hard work to see that (P1) can also be used to talk about the early water-logged city versus the modern metropolis—and that the statement so made would be false, because those are not numerically identical. And it takes hard work to realize that (P2) can be used to talk about the single city throughout its history—and that the statement so made would be false, because that object didn't evolve into Toronto. (It *is* Toronto.) Once the work has been done, however, we think the original argument loses its force.

The solution, in sum, is that all the premises seem true because they all *are* true on their most salient reading. Thus the right approach is not to reject any premise on its most salient reading: that only leads to bullet-biting or predictions that aren't empirically borne out. The problem, rather, is one of equivocation: 'Toronto' is being used one way in (P1), and a different way in (P2).

Acknowledgments

We would like to thank the two anonymous referees for their excellent comments and suggestions. We are grateful to Fred Adams, Michael Allers, Kent Bach, Harriet Barber, Lenny Clapp, Irwin Goldstein, Tim Kenyon, Martin Montminy, Adam Morton, Michael Rea, Jay Newhard, Ted Sider, and Catherine Wearing for comments on an earlier draft. Thanks also to Catherine Elgin for a stimulating conversation early on that helped us think through the issues. An early draft of this essay was presented at the 2004 Ontario Philosophical Society Meeting at Wilfred Laurier University. We are also grateful to the audience members, and especially our commentator Jill Rusin, for their assistance. A later version was presented at the 2005 Inland Northwest Philosophy Conference on Time and Identity. We would like to thank Mark Moyer for his comments at that meeting. We are grateful to the Social Sciences and Humanities Research Council of Canada for our research grant that enabled us to write this essay.

Notes

1. On the other hand, we don't mean to suggest that our proposal is neutral to any metaphysical theory about change. If endurantism, for instance, really does entail that one cannot talk about the young George Washington who chopped down a cherry tree but only about Washington over time, then so much the worse for it. If, in contrast, endurantism can allow for talk about objects-at-a-time and objects-over-time, then it is consistent with our approach. One who thinks that our view begs certain metaphysical questions may be assuming that linguistic referential acts are successful only if the objects of those acts exist (in the metaphysically loaded sense at work here). We are not committed to that assumption. We are, though, committed to a more modest but true claim, namely, that we have a linguistic ability to refer to all different kinds of things. See pp. 123–124.

2. One solution that we will not consider is the metalinguistic solution: the name, 'Toronto', is used nonliterally in (P2). (P2) means something like 'The city called 'Muddy York' became known as 'Toronto''. We won't consider it because it is not an "obvious" out to the puzzle. For one thing, there is no semantic hint of anything metalinguistic about (P2), and thus, there is no plausible reason for advancing that reading. (For a defense of a metalinguistic view of the semantics of proper names, see Bach 1987 and Katz 1990. Kent Bach later revised his view in Bach 2002.) For another, (P2) is not necessarily extensionally equivalent to the corresponding metalinguistic reading for familiar Kripkean reasons, assuming that names for cities are rigid designators. Thus, they are not semantically equivalent in meaning.

3. Some metaphysicians will beg to differ. For example, endurantists will take (P2) as being semantically trivially true (if (P1) is true) or trivially false (if (P1) is false). Furthermore, they will take sentences of the form, 'x became F', as being the primary form of expression of change-over-time, where 'F' is a descriptive predicate, and contend that such sentences are true just in case the object in question lacks F at some time and is F at some later time—it is numerically one and the same object (over time) that changes its properties. The idea is to treat (P2) as being semantically equivalent in meaning to 'Muddy York became Toronto', and then specify the truth conditions of the latter in a manner that doesn't countenance distinct objects-at-a-time as relata. Without getting embroiled in a metaphysical debate, we only wish to point out that, on the present proposal of understanding change, (P2) entails that Muddy York evolved into *itself* given the truth of (P1). If 'evolved into' is reflexive, then it follows that Muddy York evolved into itself only if there is a single object (over time) that at one time wasn't self-identical but which (that very same object over time) is self-identical at some later time. Given the choice between accepting this rather bizarre result and accepting the claim that 'evolved into' is irreflexive, we will gladly opt for the second. We don't deny, of course, that Muddy

York *qua* object-over-time has been evolving. We do, however, think that it is very important to distinguish the process of evolving from the relation of *x* evolving into *y*. (See note 6.)

4. Putting the point in this crude way is helpful because it shows that we are not claiming that 'Toronto' refers to objects-at-a-time primarily and to an object-over-time only derivatively, or vice versa. Quite the contrary: we think that both use-potentials are semantically on a par, which is consistent with the view, developed below, that 'Toronto' has a single semantic meaning that underdetermines what a speaker means to be referring to with 'Toronto' in different contexts of use.

5. We are by no means alone in blaming the nominal, rather than the predicate, for the failure of substitution in 'The temperature is rising'. We aren't exactly sure who noted the point first, but it goes back at least as far as Michael Bennett and Barbara Partee's work in the mid-1970s.

6. It's interesting to compare in this regard 'Toronto evolved into itself' versus 'Toronto evolved into Toronto'. Putting aside "proxy readings"—such as Ringo Starr bumping into a wax figure of the Beatles' drummer, described as 'Ringo Starr knocked over himself'—we find the former much worse than that latter; and this fits with our view that 'Toronto evolved into Toronto' can be used to talk about one thing evolving into another. (See Jackendoff 1992 for discussion.)

References

Apresjan, J. D. 1974. Regular Polysemy. *Linguistics* 142:5–32.

Bach, K. 1987. *Thought and Reference*. Oxford: Oxford University Press.

Bach, K. 2002. Georgione Was So-Called Because of His Name. In *Philosophical Perspectives: Language and Mind*, vol. 16, ed. J. E. Tomberlin. Oxford: Blackwell.

Fodor, J., and E. Lepore. 1998. The Emptiness of the Lexicon. *Linguistic Inquiry* 29:269–288.

Jackendoff, R. 1992. Mme Tussaud meets the Binding Theory. *Natural Language and Linguistic Theory* 10:1–31.

Katz, J. J. 1990. Has the Description Theory of Names Been Refuted? In *Meaning and Method: Essays in Honour of Hilary Putnam*, ed. G. Boolos. Cambridge: Cambridge University Press.

Moravcsik, J. 1998. *Meaning, Creativity, and the Partial Inscrutability of the Human Mind*. Stanford, CA: CSLI Publications.

Nunberg, G. 1979. The Non-Uniqueness of Semantic Solutions: Polysemy. *Linguistics and Philosophy* 3:143–184.

Nunberg, G. 1995. Transfers of Meaning. *Journal of Semantics* 12:109–132.

Pustejovsky, J. 1998. *The Generative Lexicon*. Cambridge, MA: MIT Press.

Saul, J. 1997. Substitution and Simple Sentences. *Analysis* 57:102–108.

Strawson, P. F. 1950. On Referring. *Mind* 59:320–344.

6 Identifying the Problem of Personal Identity

Ned Markosian

Introduction

This chapter has two main aims. The first is to propose a new way of characterizing the problem of personal identity. The second is to show that the metaphysical picture that underlies my proposal has important implications for the 3D–4D debate. I start by spelling out several of the old ways of characterizing the problem of personal identity and saying what I think is wrong with each of them. Next I present and motivate some metaphysical principles concerning property instantiations that underlie my proposal. Then I introduce the new way of characterizing the problem of personal identity that I am recommending, and I show that it avoids the difficulties facing the old ways. I also mention several vexing problems that arise in connection with certain popular views about personal identity, and I argue that if we formulate the problem of personal identity in the way that I am proposing, then each of these problems can be handled fairly easily. Finally, I show that there is an additional benefit to adopting my proposal, namely, that several other important problems facing anyone who endorses a 3D view of persistence (as opposed to the 4D, 'temporal parts' view of persistence) can all be resolved in a relatively straightforward manner by one who adopts the metaphysical principles concerning property instantiations that underlie the proposal.[1]

Five Ways of Characterizing the Problem of Personal Identity

Many philosophers, in their introductory lectures on personal identity, say something like this: "Suppose you have a person at one time and you have a person at another time. Then how can you determine whether the person at the first time is the same person as the person at the second time?" This often leads to a formulation of the problem that looks more or less like the following.

The Naive Characterization of the Problem of Personal Identity

The problem of personal identity consists in trying to provide an answer to the following question: What are the conditions under which person x at t_1 is the same person as person y at t_2?

Although the naive characterization is an intuitively satisfying way to get people onto the problem of personal identity, there are several difficulties with this way of characterizing the problem. The main difficulty is that it appears to be based on the assumption that there are such things as "person x at t_1" and "person y at t_2." But what could such phrases refer to? One who holds the 4D view of persistence might answer this question by saying that 'person x at t_1' refers to the t_1 temporal part of x, and that 'person y at t_2' refers to the t_2 temporal part of y. But of course this option is not open to the 3Der, who does not believe in temporal parts of physical objects.[2]

Philosophers are of course not so naive in their writings on the problem of personal identity as they are in their lectures. And many philosophers are happy to employ 4D-friendly terminology in their characterizations of the problem. Here is a standard way of doing so.[3]

The Standard 4D Characterization of the Problem of Personal Identity

The problem of personal identity consists in trying to provide an answer to the following question: What are the conditions under which two person-stages, S_1 and S_2, are stages of the same person?

It should be clear that this approach is quite suitable for 4Ders, who can take a person-stage to be a temporal part of a person. But what about 3Ders? Can we adopt something like the standard 4D characterization of the problem of personal identity?

It is sometimes said that 3Ders can adopt this characterization of the problem by taking a person-stage to be a stage in the life (or perhaps the life history) of a person. The idea would be that lives are events, and that 3Ders, who do not believe in temporal parts of physical objects, can nevertheless happily endorse the existence of temporal parts of certain other entities, such as times and events.

There is, however, a problem facing this proposal. If we adopt the above characterization of the problem of personal identity, and if we also take a person-stage to be a stage in the life of a person, then we automatically rule out the possibility that a person could persist after death (in the form of a ghost, for example, or a computer, or a robot, or some other nonliving entity). This is a possibility that we may have independent reasons for ruling out, but it should not be ruled out by the very way that we characterize the problem of personal identity.[4]

Perhaps because of these difficulties for 3Ders, a number of philosophers introduce the topic of personal identity by saying something about the problem of determining, with respect to something that is a person at one time and something that is a person at a later time, whether the first person is the *same person* as the second one.[5] That is, many of us give something like the following characterization of the problem of personal identity.[6]

The Standard 3D Characterization of the Problem of Personal Identity

The problem of personal identity consists of trying to provide an answer to the following question: What are the conditions under which something that is a person at t_1 is the same person as something that is a person at t_2?

The standard 3D characterization of the problem of personal identity is also an intuitively satisfying way to get people onto the problem of personal identity, and it has the virtue of being more obviously compatible with the 3D view than either the naive characterization or the standard 4D characterization of the problem. But it is nevertheless susceptible to an important objection[7] (which, by the way, also applies to the naive characterization). For the standard 3D characterization seems to presuppose that the problem concerns a certain relation—the *same person* relation—between a thing and a thing. But, the objection goes, there is no such relation. The objector will grant that there is the relation of classical identity, and that this relation often holds between a thing that is a person and a thing that is a person. But, the objector will insist, there is no relation distinct from identity that we can perspicuously call the "same person" relation.

Philosophers who make this objection to the standard 3D characterization usually endorse a stronger claim. They say that there is no such thing as "concept-relative identity" or "identity under a sortal" or "sortal identity." That is, they say that locutions of the form 'x is the same φ as y' are either nonsense or else merely express the proposition that x and y are both φs and are identical.

I take it that what is at issue in the debate over sortal identity is whether there are true instances of any of the following three sentence schemas.[8]

(S1)   *x* is the same φ as *y* but *x* is not the same ψ as *y*.

(S2)   *x* is the same φ as *y* but *x* ≠ *y*.

(S3)   *x* = *y* but *x* is not the same φ as *y*.

Those who believe in sortal identity maintain that there can be true instances of (S1), (S2), or (S3). But, according to the objection under consideration, there really cannot be.

I am sympathetic to this objection. I agree that the notion of sortal identity is problematic. But I also think that the idea of identity under a sortal, as well as the standard 3D characterization itself, can nevertheless be salvaged. In fact, I think that the idea of identity under a sortal can be salvaged in a way that also allows the 3Der to make sense of the naive characterization of the problem of personal identity. I will return to this topic below. But first, let's consider two 3D alternatives to the naive characterization and the standard 3D characterization that avoid any appearance of being concerned with the notion of identity under a sortal. The first is the approach that is adopted by Eric Olson in his book *The Human Animal*, and the second is a similar approach that Olson eschews for reasons that I won't discuss here.[9]

Olson's Characterization of the Problem of Personal Identity

The problem of personal identity consists of trying to provide an answer to the following question: What are the conditions under which something that is a person at t_1 is identical with something that exists at t_2?

A Variation on Olson's Characterization of the Problem of Personal Identity

The problem of personal identity consists of trying to provide an answer to the following question: What are the conditions under which something that is a person at t_1 is identical with something that is a person at t_2?

I have two worries about these characterizations of the problem. The first one involves examples like the following. Suppose that some person lives a long and happy life, and then dies. Suppose his body is then preserved in some unusual way—in a peat bog, say, or in a glacier, or as a petrified rock. And suppose that a million years later some powerful being finds this object and rearranges its particles in such a way that it comes to be alive, and a person, once again—although this time as a woman, who looks utterly different from the man of a million years earlier, and who has a completely different psychology from his.

Now, many of us will want to say both (i) that there is a single thing in the story that is a man at the beginning and a woman at the end, and (ii) that the man from the beginning of the story and the woman from the end of the story are different people. But if we adopt either Olson's characterization or the above variation on Olson's characterization as our characterization of the problem of personal identity, then we will be forced to say that any theory of personal identity according to which there is a single thing in the story that is a man at the beginning and a woman at the end, but also says that that man and that woman are different people, is automatically false. To me, this seems like a major strike against these characterizations of the problem of personal identity.

My second worry about Olson's characterization and the above variation on Olson's characterization involves David Wiggins's notion of a *substance concept* (Wiggins 1980). The substance concept of an object is, roughly, the answer to the question *What is it?* as applied to that object. More precisely, an object's substance concept is the concept or property, among those exemplified by that object, that determines its persistence conditions.

Now, on my view, *person* is not the substance concept of the objects that are people. Instead, *person* is, in Wiggins's (1967) terminology, a "phase sortal"—a property that is typically exemplified by a thing for only a portion of the time that that thing exists. For example, it seems clear that I was not a person in the earliest days of my existence, when I was either a newly fertilized egg, or an embryo, or a fetus, or something else (take your pick, depending on your favorite theory of when a human being typically comes into existence).[10] In fact, it seems likely that even when I was a newborn I did not yet have what it takes to be a person. Similarly, it is hard to deny that there will come a time when I still exist but am no longer a person—for some day I will be a corpse that lacks the ability to reason and deliberate, and also lacks the rights and responsibilities that go with being a person.[11]

But, given that *person* is a phase sortal rather than the substance concept of the objects that are typically people, it follows that Olson's characterization and the above variation on Olson's characterization are peculiar ways of asking the questions that they pose. For if *person* is a phase sortal, then x's being a person at t_1 (and, in the case of the variation on Olson's characterization, y's being a person at t_2) will have little or nothing to do with the question of whether x is identical to y. Instead, that will be determined by the persistence conditions of x, which will themselves be determined by x's substance concept. Moreover, since it is not possible for an object to change its substance concept over time (this follows from the stipulation that an object's substance concept determines its persistence conditions), the fact that x is going through a person-phase at t_1 (or that y is going through a person-phase at t_2) will be largely irrelevant to whether x is identical to y.

Given all of this, the questions raised by Olson's characterization and the variation on Olson's characterization really amount to asking this question: *What are the persistence conditions for the objects that sometimes exemplify personhood?* This is surely an interesting question, but it is not what Olson's characterization and the variation on Olson's characterization appear at first glance to be asking about. Moreover, this question that Olson's characterization and the variation on Olson's characterization are really asking does not seem to capture what we are trying to get at when we ask about personal identity. (In the case of Olson's characterization this worry is especially acute, since we take ourselves to be asking about which future *people* we will be identical to, not about which future petrified rocks or scattered objects we will be identical to.)

Notice that this second worry points out that the way we talk about personal identity makes it at least *sound* like we're discussing a special relation between a person and a person, and not merely a relation between a person and any old thing. But of course, if we take seriously the idea that we are asking about some special relation between a person and a person, then it looks like we will need to return to the problematic notion of a *same person* relation.

Some Underlying Metaphysical Principles

My attempt to rehabilitate the problematic notion of a *same person* relation, and the characterization of the problem of personal identity that goes with it, is based on some underlying metaphysical principles that need to be made explicit. To begin with, I assume that there are such things as *instantiations* (also known as *exemplifications*) of properties.[12] Here are some examples: your being a human being, my being under seven feet tall, the Earth's being roughly spherical, the number 2's being a prime number, and Alpha Centauri's being a star.

Note that I do not mean by 'instantiations' what philosophers sometimes mean by 'tropes'.[13] Tropes, if there are any, are "abstract particulars" like Joe Montana's greatness and the blueness of my shirt. Montana's greatness is meant to differ from, for example, Brett Favre's greatness, even though both are tropes that involve the same property. The idea is that the greatness of each great quarterback is something unique to that individual, and that, moreover, this would be the case even if two quarterbacks were great in exactly the same way. If there are such things as tropes, then each trope corresponds to a unique instantiation, but is nevertheless distinct from that instantiation.

What I do mean by 'instantiations of properties' are instances of properties, such as Montana's being great and my shirt's being blue. An instantiation of a property is a complex entity that occurs during some specific period of time and that involves, in addition to the property being instantiated, some object that is doing the instantiating.[14] Moreover, instantiations typically last for some extended period of time.

This last point—that instantiations typically last for some extended period of time—is an important and unduly neglected one. It is widely recognized that physical objects persist through time, and it is sometimes also recognized that events persist through time. But philosophers do not often explicitly acknowledge that instantiations also persist through time.[15] Nevertheless, instantiations most certainly do persist. For example, consider a typical leaf from an oak tree in western Massachusetts. First the leaf is green. That lasts all summer. Then it turns red in October, and its being red lasts for about a week. Then it becomes brown, and stays brown for the rest of its days. Or consider a basketball player with a swollen knee. She goes to a doctor, who asks, "How long has it been like this?"

Once we have noticed that instantiations persist through time, we are in a position to raise some important questions about instantiations. For example, just as we can ask questions about the identity over time of a particular object, so too can we ask questions about the identity over time of a given instantiation. If x has the property φ at t_1 and y has φ at t_2, then we can wonder whether y's being φ at t_2 is part of the same episode of φ-ness as x's being φ at t_1.

In fact, it's a bit of an understatement to say that we can ask such questions. For it is also true that there must be answers to these questions. If x has φ at t_1 and y has φ at t_2, then either y's being φ at t_2 is part of the same episode of φ-ness as x's being φ at t_1, or it isn't. (Those who accept ontological vagueness may want to add a third option here, namely, that it is an indeterminate matter whether y's being φ at t_2 is part of the same episode of φ as x's being φ at t_1. But either way, there must be an answer to the question.)[16]

An example might help to make it clearer what I'm talking about here. Suppose you see me in a blue shirt one day, and you see me a week later in a similar blue shirt. Then you can wonder whether the shirt's being blue on the second occasion is part of the same episode of blueness that you observed on the earlier occasion. If it turns out that the same shirt is involved in both cases, and if it has remained blue from the first occasion to the second, then the answer is clearly *Yes, the second instance of blueness is part of the same episode of blueness as the first one.* But if, on the other hand, it turns out that there are two different shirts involved, or if there is a single shirt that was dyed red for part of the intervening time, then it seems clear that the answer is *No, the second instance of blueness is not a part of the same episode of blueness as the first one.*

Notice that there is an analogous question involving events. Suppose you see two guys playing chess; you subsequently go away for an hour, and then you come back to find the same two guys playing chess. Then you can ask whether the chess game you see on your return is the same game that you saw before you left.

Notice also that, in the case of events, the question of whether this is the same event as the event before is not automatically resolved just by settling the question of which things are involved. For when you see the same players playing chess again an hour later, you still don't know whether you're seeing a new game on the second occasion. And even if you see different people playing chess on the second occasion, it might turn out that it's still the same game as before (but with new players having taken over for the original players).

Speaking of events, it is worth commenting on some similarities and differences between instantiations, as I understand them, and events. On one conception of events, championed by Jaegwon Kim, events are complex entities, each one of which involves some object exemplifying some property at some time.[17] Such complexes are of course no different from what I am calling instantiations. But on another conception of events, endorsed by such philosophers as Arthur Prior, events are changes in things.[18] If we understand events in this second way, then we can say that an instantiation is just about the exact opposite of an event: for whereas an event consists of a change in some thing, according to this conception of events, an instantiation consists of some thing's remaining the same in some respect (such as color, or size, or whatever).

Personally, I am inclined to think that events (at least in the ordinary language sense, in which football games and earthquakes are events) are neither property exemplifications (as Kim says) nor changes in things (as Prior suggests); but for the purposes of this essay I will remain neutral on the question of what we should call events. What I cannot remain neutral on is whether there are property instantiations. Nor can I remain neutral on whether property instantiations can persist through time. For I am committed to saying both that there are such things as property instantiations and that they can persist through time. But I don't think either of these claims should be seen as controversial.

So far I have been using terms like 'instantiation' and 'episode' fairly loosely, but it is now time to settle on some official and uniform terminology. From now on I will take *instances* to be those momentary items each one of which consists of some object's having some property at some instant of time (such as my being human at exactly noon today). I will take *instantiations* to include such momentary instances as well as their temporally extended cousins (such as my being human all day today); moreover, I will take extended instantiations to have momentary instances among their temporal parts, and to be fusions of such instances. And finally, I will understand *episodes* to be instantiations that are maximal in the following sense: instantiation E of property φ is *maximal* iff the fusion of E with any further instance of φ-ness (i.e., one that is not a part of E) is not a single instantiation of φ-ness.[19]

The metaphysical principles underlying my proposed characterization of the problem of personal identity, then, are these. First, there are such things as instantiations of properties. Second, instantiations come in episodes, which are event-like entities that can be extended in time. And third, it makes sense to talk about whether x's being φ at t_1 is part of the same episode of φ-ness as y's being φ at t_2.

The Episodic Characterization of the Problem of Personal Identity

Here's how all of this is relevant to salvaging the notion of identity under a sortal. Once we acknowledge that there are such things as episodes of property instantiations, and that it is legitimate to ask whether a particular instance of φ-ness is part of the same episode of φ-ness as a certain earlier instance of φ-ness, we have paved the way to a new conception of identity under a sortal. To say that some thing, y, that is φ at t_2 is the *same* φ as some thing, x, that is φ at t_1 is to say that y's being φ at t_2 is part of the same episode of φ-ness as x's being φ at t_1.

On this way of thinking, the *same* φ relation is really a relation between instances of φ-ness. Thus, the *same* φ relation is distinct from the relation that holds between an x and a y just in case x is φ, y is φ, and $x = y$, and it is distinct from the latter relation for one main reason: it takes different entities (instances of properties rather than things) as its relata. But note also that the above example involving a shirt (the one that is blue for a time and is then dyed red for a while before becoming blue again) demonstrates another important difference between the same φ relation and the relation that holds between an *x* and a *y* just in case *x* is φ, *y* is φ, and *x* = *y*. For in the shirt example there are two distinct episodes of the same property—blueness—that both involve the same shirt.

On this conception of identity under a sortal, when we ask whether this shirt today is the same shirt as that shirt yesterday, we are asking whether this instance of shirthood today is part of the same episode of shirthood as that instance of shirthood yesterday. (Or at least, that is one of the main things we may be asking.) And, similarly, when we ask whether this person today is the same person as that person yesterday, we are asking whether this instance of personhood today is part of the same episode of personhood as that instance of personhood yesterday.

We are now in a position to formulate my proposal.

The Episodic Characterization of the Problem of Personal Identity

The problem of personal identity consists of trying to provide an answer to the following question: What are the conditions under which an instance of personhood at t_1 is part of the same episode of personhood as an instance of personhood at t_2?

A brief look at some of the most popular theories of personal identity will help to illustrate the idea behind the episodic characterization. Consider what Olson calls the psychological approach to personal identity, according to which psychological continuity is the key to personal identity. When it is formulated as an answer to the episodic characterization of the problem of personal identity, this approach will say that in order for one instance of personhood to be a part of the same episode of personhood as a later instance, there must be some kind of psychological continuity between the two instances. Or consider what Olson calls the biological approach to personal identity, according to which biological continuity is the key to personal identity.[20] When it is formulated as an answer to the episodic characterization of the problem of personal identity, this approach will say that in order for one instance of personhood to be a part of the same episode of personhood as a later instance, there must be some kind of biological continuity between the two instances. (The biological approach, incidentally, is the one that Olson advocates. It is probably the main rival to the psychological approach.)

In general, I would go so far as to say that any respectable view about personal identity can be formulated as an answer to the question raised by the episodic characterization of the problem of personal identity.

Here is why the episodic characterization is an improvement over the other characterizations of the problem. First, the episodic characterization, unlike the naive characterization, allows the 3Der to make sense of talk about "person x at t_1" and "person y at t_2." For on the episodic characterization such talk is to be understood as talk about x's instantiation of personhood at t_1 and y's instantiation of personhood at t_2; and this kind of talk is unproblematic for the 3Der. Also, like both the naive characterization and the standard 3D characterization, the episodic characterization allows us to take seriously the notion of a *same person* relation. But unlike those other characterizations, the episodic characterization comes with a ready-made and straightforward way of understanding that notion.

Meanwhile, the episodic characterization is an improvement over Olson's characterization and the variation on Olson's characterization, for two reasons. First, the episodic characterization allows us to say, in cases like the person-turned-petrified-rock-turned-person example, that there is a single thing throughout the story, but that the person at the end of the story is not the same person as the person at the beginning of the story. For the episodic characterization allows us to say that the later instance of personhood in the story is not a part of the same episode of personhood as the earlier one (despite the fact that the same object is involved in each case).[21] And second, the episodic characterization does not turn out to involve a disguised way of asking a question (about the persistence conditions of objects that can be, but need not be, people) that fails to get at what we are really trying to ask when we ask about personal identity.

Despite all of these wonderful advantages of the episodic characterization over its rivals, there is a certain likely objection to my proposal.[22] When we ask about personal identity, it might be objected, we are asking about something that bears on our *survival*, also known as our *persistence*. I want to know, for example, whether the very thing that is now me will continue to exist after the operation; and you want to know whether the very thing that is now you will survive the transporter machine. In other words, when we ask questions about personal identity, we are asking questions that crucially have to do with the notion of *identity*. But my proposal apparently fails to capture this feature of our talk about personal identity. My proposal, it might be said, takes the identity out of personal identity.

As a first response to this objection, I would point out that there is a sense in which I have not taken identity out of the equation. For on my proposal, when we ask about personal identity, we are asking whether the episode of personhood that we see going on now is identical to the episode of personhood that we saw going on earlier.[23]

I don't expect this reply to satisfy anyone making the relevant objection to my proposal. For what the objector really wants is for identity to be in the equation as a relation between the very thing that is now instantiating personhood and the very thing that will instantiate it later.

In response to this objection (when it is put in this way), I say to the objector: If you really want identity to be in the equation, then we can do that. In fact, there are several ways to get identity back into the mix. One way would be to endorse the following principle.

A Principle about Personhood (PP)

If an instance of personhood at t_1 is part of the same episode of personhood as an instance of personhood at t_2, then the object instantiating personhood in the first instance must be identical to the object instantiating personhood in the second instance.

Another way to ensure that matters of personal identity are matters of identity would be to endorse a more general version of PP that applies to all properties, like the following.

A Principle about Property Instantiations (PPI)

For any property, φ, if an instance of φ-ness at t_1 is part of the same episode of φ-ness as an instance of φ-ness at t_2, then the object instantiating φ-ness in the first instance must be identical to the object instantiating φ-ness in the second instance.

And finally, a third way to ensure that we are really talking about identity when we talk about personal identity would be to amend the episodic characterization so that the relevant kind of identity is explicitly built into the question, as follows.

A Variation on the Episodic Characterization of the Problem of Personal Identity

The problem of personal identity consists in trying to provide an answer to the following question: What are the conditions under which an instance of personhood at t_1 and an instance of personhood at t_2 are such that (i) the two instances are parts of the same episode of personhood, and (ii) the object instantiating personhood in the first instance is identical to the object instantiating personhood in the second instance?

This variation on my proposal would have most of the advantages of the original proposal, and it would also accommodate the intuition that questions about personal identity are questions about identity. Moreover, I think this variation on my proposal is clearly still in the spirit of the original proposal. So I recommend it to anyone who is inclined to make the objection that personal identity must be about identity, but who does not want to endorse either PP or PPI.

Further Advantages of the Episodic Characterization Over Its Rivals

In addition to being preferable to Olson's characterization and the variation on Olson's characterization for the reasons given above, it also turns out that formulating the problem of personal identity according to the episodic characterization allows the 3Der to solve various problems that are otherwise not so easy to solve. For example, there is the well-known fission problem. Suppose a person's brain is bisected, and the resulting hemispheres are transplanted into two different bodies, so that each of the resulting people seems to be "the continuation" of the original person. Or suppose a single person is duplicated in such a way that it is indeterminate which of the resulting people is "the continuation" of the original. 4Ders, who believe in temporal parts of objects, and can thus say that there are two people in the story who share their earlier temporal parts, have an easy account of such cases; but 3Ders don't.

Unless we adopt the episodic characterization of the problem of personal identity, that is. For if we do, then we can say that there are two episodes of personhood in the relevant story, and that they overlap for a while (before the fission). Since the relation *being parts of a single episode of personhood* (unlike the relation of identity) can fail to be transitive, there is no contradiction in the 3Der's saying that each of the people after the fission stands in the *same person* relation to the original person, even though the two people after the fission do not stand in that relation to one another. For if we adopt the episodic characterization, this amounts to saying of the two later instances of personhood that each one is a part of some episode of personhood that includes the prefission instance of personhood, even though the two later instances are not themselves parts of a single episode of personhood.[24]

Another problem that the episodic characterization will help the 3Der to solve is the time travel problem. (This is a problem that has been discussed by Theodore Sider in his book, *Four-Dimensionalism*.[25]) When Ted travels back in time to visit his former self, there is a problem about the relation between the younger Ted and the time-traveling Ted. Are they the same person? On the one hand, they have different properties (one is sitting, for example, while the other is standing), so it appears that they must be different people. But on the other hand, if we don't say that they are the same person, then it looks like we can't describe the case as involving a meeting of Ted and his former self.

As Sider points out, the 4Der has a solution to this problem. For on the 4D view, the younger Ted and the time-traveling Ted are two distinct spatial parts of a single temporal part of Ted. They are not identical, and so they can have such different properties as sitting and standing, but they nevertheless stand in the same person relation to one another, in virtue of the fact that there is a single "space-time worm," a.k.a. Ted, that doubles back on itself, and is such that the younger Ted in the time travel scenario and the time-traveling Ted are both stages of this same worm. But it looks like 3Ders do not have available any such solution to this problem.

Unless we adopt the episodic characterization of the problem of personal identity, that is. For if we do adopt that characterization of the problem, then we can plausibly say, since this is a case in which a time traveler visits his former self, that the story involves an episode of personhood that "doubles back" on itself. This in turn allows us to say both (i) that the time-traveling Ted and the younger Ted are two distinct things, which are spatial parts of Ted at the time in question; and (ii) that the time-traveling Ted's being a person at that time is a part of the same episode of personhood as the younger Ted's being a person at that time. In short, if we adopt the episodic characterization of the problem of personal identity then we can give an account of the time-travel scenario that is perfectly analogous to the 4Der's account.

Another example of a problem that the episodic characterization can help with is the fetus problem, which is a problem for the psychological approach to personal identity that is discussed in chapter 4 of Olson 1997. Recall that on both Olson's characterization and the variation on Olson's characterization, the problem of personal identity amounts to the problem of determining what is the substance concept of the objects that can be, but need not be, people. According to the psychological approach (as an answer to the questions raised by Olson's characterization and the variation on Olson's characterization), then, *person* is our substance concept. So on this view, either (a) when you came into existence, you replaced a fetus that was in your mother's womb before you, or else (b) ever since you came into existence, you have been sharing space (and parts, and matter, and even clothes) with a thing that was once a fetus, that has never been a person, and that has always been distinct from you. Neither option seems very attractive. This is of course not a problem for 4D advocates of the psychological approach (who can say that you are a temporal part of an organism whose earlier temporal parts include a temporal part that is a fetus), but it is a big problem for 3D advocates of the psychological approach.

Unless they adopt the episodic characterization of the problem of personal identity, that is. For if they do, then they will not take the psychological approach to be answering any question about the substance concept of the things that can be people. Thus, 3D proponents of the psychological approach who endorse the episodic characterization of the problem of personal identity will be able to say that the same thing that was a fetus is now a grown-up person, even though the episode of personhood in question did not begin until that thing came to have the relevant psychological properties.

A similar problem is the corpse problem for the biological approach. According to the biological approach (as an answer to the questions raised by Olson's characterization and the variation on Olson's characterization, that is), our substance concept is something like *living organism*. So on this view, either (a) when you die, you will be replaced by a brand-new object—a corpse—that was not there before, or (b) when you die, you will go out of existence, and the particles that previously composed you will not compose anything (not even a corpse), or else (c) you are now sharing space (and parts, and matter, and even clothes) with a weird, nonliving entity that will one day be a corpse (your corpse, in fact) but that has always been distinct from you. Again, none of these options seems very attractive; and, again, this is not a problem for 4D advocates of the biological approach (who can say that you are a temporal part of a temporally extended object whose later temporal parts include a temporal part that is a corpse), but it is a big problem for 3D advocates of the biological approach.

Unless they adopt the episodic characterization, that is. For if they do, then they can say that the same thing that will be a corpse after you die is now a person, even though the episode of personhood that is going on in your vicinity right now will have ended by the time the relevant object becomes a corpse.

In general, I want to claim that adopting the episodic characterization will be a terrific boon for 3Ders. For given that episodes, like events, can plausibly be said to have temporal parts, the 3Der (who doesn't believe that objects have temporal parts, but should be willing to say that events and episodes do), can give an account of fission cases, time-travel cases, and any other cases that seem to present a special problem for the 3Der, an account analogous to the 4Der's account of those cases.

In fact, I think that this general approach to making sense of talk about identity under a sortal will help the 3Der in other areas as well. Once we adopt this way of talking, for example, we will have an easy time of dealing with such matters as the statue and the lump, without being forced to posit coincident entities. For we can say that there is a single thing—the lump of clay—that goes through a temporary statue phase, and also that the persistence conditions (and modal properties) for an episode of statue-hood are different from those for an episode of lumpiness.

Conclusion

Let me end with a couple of disclaimers. I want to be clear about the fact that I haven't solved the problem of personal identity. Nor am I even claiming that the problem is easier to solve once we adopt this new way of characterizing the problem. It is still going to be an interesting and challenging task to say under what conditions one instance of personhood will be a part of the same episode of personhood as a later instance of personhood.

What I am claiming, however, is that there are important advantages (for the 3Der) that come with this way of characterizing the problem of personal identity. And I'm also claiming that, as a kind of bonus, the general metaphysical picture behind the characterization of the problem that is recommended here also gives us a sensible way to understand talk about identity under a sortal, and to solve a host of otherwise vexing problems facing the 3Der.

Acknowledgments

Earlier versions of this essay were presented at Western Washington University, the University of Massachusetts, the Inland Northwest Philosophy Conference, and The Australian National University; I am grateful to members of all four audiences for helpful comments. I am also indebted to Stuart Brock, Andy Egan, Tove Finnestad, Mark Heller, Eric Olson, Ted Sider, Joshua T. Spencer, Brian Weatherson, and two anonymous referees for helpful comments on earlier versions of the essay.

Notes

1. On the 3D and 4D views, see Sider 2001.

2. In light of these considerations, it is perhaps a misnomer to label the naive characterization naive (since it seems to be based on a sophisticated metaphysical assumption, namely, that people have temporal parts). What is more clearly naive

in the present context is the 3Der who blithely goes along with the naive characterization as a way to capture the problem of personal identity.

3. For characterizations of the problem similar to the standard 4D characterization of the problem of personal identity see John Perry's introduction to Perry 1975, and Sider 2000.

4. An alternative approach for the 3Der who wants to endorse something like the standard 4D characterization of the problem of personal identity would be to take a person-stage to be a momentary stage in a (possibly) longer instantiation of the property of being a person. This approach seems to me to differ in important ways from what proponents of the standard 4D characterization normally have in mind; but in any case, it is an approach that I discuss at some length (and end up advocating) below.

5. For the reason mentioned in the next note, we are eventually likely to take back the stipulation that the problem always involves a person at one time and a person at a *later* time.

6. Where 't_1' refers to a time, 't_2' refers to a time, and t_1 and t_2 may or may not be identical. The idea is that most cases we will be interested in will involve two different times, but that, since we don't want our characterization of the problem of personal identity to rule out the possibility of a time traveler visiting his former self, our characterization of the problem should allow at least the theoretical possibility of that happening.

7. Several, actually. For another objection to the standard 3D characterization (different from the objection I discuss in the text), see Olson 1997, ch. 2.

8. Some qualifications are needed here. In the case of (S1), we probably want to add that x and y are both φs and also that they are both ψs. (For the claim that I am the same person as some earlier boy but not the same boy is not the kind of instance of (S1) that the sortal identity theorist and the classical identity theorist disagree over.) Similarly, in the case of (S3), we probably want to add that x and y are both φs. Also, instances of (S2) like 'Ned is the same height as Ted but Ned is not identical to Ted' suggest that what terms can go in place of φ and ψ must be somehow restricted in our characterization of the disagreement between the sortal identity theorist and the classical identity theorist. (Thanks to Eric Olson and Ted Sider for these points.) Note also that some defenders of sortal identity will insist that there is in fact no such thing as classical identity. Such philosophers will maintain that although there are true instances of (S1), all instances of (S2) and (S3) are either meaningless or false.

9. Olson (1997), ch. 2. Olson gives these characterizations of the problem different names, and formulates them in slightly different ways.

10. I am here assuming that each one of us is identical to some human being.

11. I am not proposing any analysis of the concept of a person, but am merely accepting the popular view that having certain rights and responsibilities, as well as the ability to reason and deliberate, are likely to be necessary conditions for being a person.

12. In addition to instantiations of properties, there are also instantiations of other universals: two-place relations, three-place relations, and so on. For the sake of simplicity, I will here talk only about instantiations of properties, but most of what I say would also apply to the other instantiations.

13. See Armstrong 1989, chs. 1 and 6, and Bacon 2002.

14. Some readers will wonder what the difference is between what I am calling 'instantiations' and what Jaegwon Kim calls 'events'. The answer is that there is no difference. More on this topic below. By the way, I don't believe in nontemporal instantiations (or nontemporal objects, for that matter). If you do, no worries. I am talking here only about instantiations of properties that occur in time.

15. One philosopher who discusses the question of whether instantiations persist is Douglas Ehring, in Ehring 1997, where he argues that it is in fact tropes and not instantiations that persist.

16. Notice that the claim made in the text—that either y's being φ at t_2 is part of the same episode of φ-ness as x's being φ at t_1, or it isn't—is consistent with its often being underdetermined which property is picked out by a particular use of a given predicate. For I am talking about properties and not predicates. Note also that I am not claiming that we do (or even can) always know the answer to the question of whether some y's being φ at t_2 is part of the same episode of φ-ness as some x's being φ at t_1.

17. See, e.g., Kim 1993. (As I do in the text, Kim also takes there to be exemplifications of multiplace relations but for simplicity talks mainly about exemplifications of one-place properties.)

18. See, e.g., Prior 2003.

19. Notice that an important consequence of accepting that there are instantiations, and that longer instantiations are fusions of instances (i.e., momentary instantiations), is that we have a new mereological question to address, namely, under what conditions do two or more instances of a single property have a fusion? This is the special composition question for property instances, which is an analogue of Peter van Inwagen's special composition question, which asks about the conditions under which two or more physical objects have a fusion. On the special composition question see van Inwagen 1990.

20. On both the psychological and the biological approach, see chapter 1 of Olson 1997.

21. Not that characterizing the problem in the manner of the episodic character-ization commits us to saying this. The point is merely that doing so allows us to say such a thing.

22. I am grateful to Eric Olson and Ted Sider for raising this objection in response to an earlier version of this essay.

23. Notice that there is a similar objection facing the 4Der who endorses the stan-dard 4D characterization of the problem of personal identity, together with a simi-lar reply.

24. Note, by the way, that this advantage of the episodic characterization does not apply to the above variation on the episodic characterization. For if the fission case is described in a suitable way, we will want to say that neither of the later instances of personhood involves the same object that is involved in the earlier instance of personhood; which means that we will not be able to say that either one of the later people is the same person as the earlier person. It is partly for this reason that I prefer my original proposal over the variation on it.

25 Sider 2001, 101–109. See also Markosian 2004 and Sider 2004.

References

Armstrong, D. M. 1989. *Universals: An Opinionated Introduction*. Boulder: Westview Press.

Bacon, J. 2002. Tropes. In *The Stanford Encyclopedia of Philosophy* (fall 2002 edition), ed. E. N. Zalta. http://plato.stanford.edu/archives/fall2002/entries/tropes/.

Ehring, D. 1997. *Causation and Persistence*. Oxford: Oxford University Press.

Kim, J. 1993. Events as Property Exemplifications. In *Supervenience and Mind*. Cam-bridge: Cambridge University Press.

Markosian, N. 2004. Two Arguments from Sider's Four-Dimensionalism. *Philosophy and Phenomenological Research* 68:665–673.

Olson, E. 1997. *The Human Animal*. Oxford: Oxford University Press.

Perry, J. 1975. *Personal Identity*. Berkeley: University of California Press.

Prior, A. 2003. Changes in Events and Changes in Things. In *Papers on Time and Tense*, new edition, ed. P. Hasle, P. Øhrstrøm, T. Braüner, and J. Copeland. Oxford: Oxford University Press.

Sider, T. 2000. Recent Work on Identity over Time. *Philosophical Books* 41:81–89.

Sider, T. 2001. *Four-Dimensionalism*. Oxford: Oxford University Press.

Sider, T. 2004. Replies to Gallois, Hirsch, and Markosian. *Philosophy and Phenomeno-logical Research* 68:674–687.

van Inwagen, P. 1990. *Material Beings*. Ithaca: Cornell University Press.

Wiggins, D. 1967. *Identity and Spatio-Temporal Continuity*. Oxford: Blackwell.

Wiggins, D. 1980. *Sameness and Substance*. Cambridge, MA: Harvard University Press.

7 Persistence and Responsibility

Neal A. Tognazzini

Introduction

Let me begin with the seemingly simple fact that I persist through time. If, while preparing dinner sometime next week, I accidentally cut off the end of my finger, I will survive. And not just in the ordinary sense that this biological organism will continue functioning; even in the philosopher's sense, I'll survive. That is, the person who gets rushed to the hospital will be the same person who is sitting here typing these words, with all ten fingers intact. And it's not that I'm special; you persist through time too. That persons persist through time is not in question. What *is* in question is what persistence through time amounts to. Do persons persist, on the one hand, by *enduring* through time?[1] Or do persons persist by *perduring* through time?[2] This is a genuine metaphysical dispute.

As with many important metaphysical questions, however, the consequences of this dispute reach beyond metaphysics. In this chapter, I explore the relationship between the debate over persistence and another philosophical thesis that is not in question, namely, that persons are at least sometimes morally responsible for their actions.[3] Some philosophers have thought that persons cannot properly be held morally responsible for their actions unless they endure through time.[4] On this view, if persons perdure, then no person is morally responsible for anything. If true, this would be a telling objection against the view that persons perdure.

Unfortunately, the remarks made in the literature against the compatibility of perdurance and moral responsibility, though suggestive, are often quite brief. In order to remedy this, I aim to expand on these suggestive remarks in order to see what *arguments* can be found for the incompatibility claim. Not that these arguments will turn out to be more convincing than the suggestive remarks, though. Indeed, though there are five such arguments I will be considering, we will see that the proponent of perdurance can successfully rebut them all. The upshot will be that we have yet to see a good reason to think that perdurance is incompatible with morally responsible agency.

Theories of Persistence

First, let me say a bit more about theories of persistence. There are actually a number of different theories one might have about persistence through time. The two most common are endurance and perdurance, but at least one other theory deserves to be mentioned here: stage theory.[5] I will not be discussing stage theory directly in what follows, but it will help to include it in this section so that we can better understand the philosophical terrain.[6]

Following Ted Sider, let the term 'continuants' refer to those things that we ordinarily talk about, quantify over, and (I'll add) attribute responsibility to in everyday contexts (Sider 2001, 191). This way of using the term will help us better understand the different theories of persistence. Each theory has a view about which objects are continuants, and each theory has an explanation about how those continuants persist through time. Both endurance and stage theory maintain that continuants are three-dimensional things, that is, things that are only extended in the three *spatial* dimensions.[7] According to perdurance, on the other hand, continuants are four-dimensional things extended in three dimensions of space and one dimension of time. Endurantists and stage theorists maintain, in other words, that continuants have spatial parts but no temporal parts, whereas perdurantists maintain that continuants have both spatial and temporal parts. Though the concepts involved here are notoriously difficult to pin down, we can get the intuitive idea of a temporal part as follows. Just as I have a part that I ordinarily call 'my head', which occupies the region of space from somewhere on my neck on up, perdurance says that I also have a part that we might call 'my last-year-self' that occupies the region of time from the beginning of 2009 to the beginning of 2010. What I am, on this view, is the four-dimensional object composed of all of my many temporal parts.

Now that we have each theory's understanding of continuants out of the way, let me turn to each theory's account of how continuants persist through time.[8] Up to this point, I haven't mentioned any differences between endurance and stage theory, but there's a big difference. According to endurance, continuants persist through time by being *wholly present* (another notoriously slippery concept that I will leave at an intuitive level) at each time when they exist. The very same continuant is located first at t_1, and then again at t_2, and so on. According to stage theory, on the other hand, continuants are instantaneous stages that persist by bearing important relations to distinct future instantaneous stages. The instantaneous stage that is located at t_1 is not identical with the instantaneous stage located at t_2, but it still makes sense to talk about persistence because the two stages are related to one another in the appropriate way.[9] So, what makes endurance different from stage theory is that according to the former, continuants are multiply located in time, whereas according to the latter, they are not. Finally, according to perdurance, a continuant persists by having a temporal part at each time when it exists. Though the temporal parts are wholly present at particular moments, the continuant itself is not wholly present at any one moment, but rather stretches through a four-dimensional spatiotemporal region.

Each theory gives a distinctive account of persistence. According to endurance and stage theory, continuants are three-dimensional objects without temporal parts; according to perdurance, continuants are four-dimensional objects with temporal parts. Endurance has it that continuants persist by being wholly present at each time when they exist; stage theory has it that continuants persist in virtue of the intimate relations they bear to other instantaneous stages; and perdurance has it that continuants persist by having a temporal part at each time when they exist.

The foregoing remarks are not meant to be a complete explanation of these theories of persistence by any means, but rather a rough sketch to help us get our bearings. We now have enough information to move on to the main attraction. Why might someone think that perdurance is incompatible with moral responsibility?

Objections to the Compatibility of Perdurance and Responsibility

Agency

The first objection to the compatibility of perdurance and responsibility alleges that if perdurance is true, then there are no morally responsible agents because there are no agents at all. And the reason why there aren't any agents at all if perdurance is true is that perdurance includes temporal parts in its ontology and it is absurd to think that a temporal part has what it takes to be an agent.[10] Walter Glannon raises this particular objection when he says that the perdurantist cannot offer a satisfactory account of agency necessary for responsibility. To be an agent means having the capacity for practical reasoning about action, which involves having interests, formulating long-term projects or goals, and having beliefs about the likely consequences of acting to achieve these goals. . . . It is extremely difficult to see how a four-dimensionalist account of person-stages or time-slices could capture these essential features of agency. (Glannon 1998, 234)

I won't spend much time on this objection in the current essay, however, because I think that this objection is more appropriately aimed at stage theory than perdurance. Indeed, Glannon goes on to say that *instantaneous stages* "cannot give us the diachronic conception of agency we need for responsibility." So, if this is not an objection against perdurance, why do I bring it up here?

I point it out here to show how important it is to consider perdurance and stage theory separately. I think that many who have these concerns about agency in general have conflated the two theories. In fact, though this is an objection the stage theorist must take very seriously, if anyone were to raise this objection against perdurance, it would be based on a misunderstanding. As we've seen, perdurance does *not* identify persons with instantaneous stages. Rather, persons are four-dimensional objects composed of instantaneous stages. And four-dimensional objects *do* exist at more than one time (just not wholly). One might worry whether four-dimensional objects can have the characteristics needed for *responsibility* (as we will see below), but granting *agency* to four-dimensional objects is, I think, considerably less worrisome.[11]

Numerical Identity

The second objection has to do with considerations of numerical identity. It is clear that if anyone is ever morally responsible for an action, then persistence through time must be a real phenomenon. Suppose that Shady (who will be our protagonist for the remainder of the essay) robs a bank today. In order for an attribution of moral responsibility to be appropriate tomorrow, Shady must still exist tomorrow. That is, Shady must have persisted through time from today until tomorrow, so that the person we arrest tomorrow *is* the person who robbed the bank today, where the 'is' in question is the 'is' of identity.

Some philosophers have argued, moreover, that only endurance can accommodate the intuition that the person we arrest tomorrow is numerically identical to the person that robbed the bank today. This notion of numerical identity through time is what makes for *genuine* persistence through time, and it is this notion that cannot be reconciled with the temporal parts picture of perdurance.

Let me give a couple of examples of how this argument might go.[12] Vinit Haksar, for instance, argues against perdurance in this way: "It would seem that the view that persons perdure is inconsistent with much of our moral and practical thinking. For instance, our system of moral and criminal responsibility presupposes that the person to be blamed or punished must be the very same individual that performed the past action" (Haksar 1991, 244). Though less explicit, something that Peter van Inwagen says may be interpreted in a similar manner.[13] Imagining a rather tragic but fictional example, van Inwagen says:

> If moral responsibility is real, there must be real identity across time. If I say to my father's second wife, 'I hold you responsible for my father's death', then the person I am addressing, the person denoted by my use of the word 'you', must have existed in the past; she must be identical with the person who persuaded my father to forsake conventional medical treatment. (van Inwagen 2000, 15)

Now, what Haksar and van Inwagen say sounds quite reasonable. So, let us grant for now that in order for it to be appropriate to ascribe moral responsibility to a person who is arrested tomorrow, the person who is arrested tomorrow must be *numerically identical* with the person who robbed the bank today. Why can't perdurance accommodate this claim?

Here's the thought. According to perdurance, the object that exists today and robs the bank today is not all of Shady; rather, it is a day-long (or maybe a robbery-long) temporal part of Shady. Call this temporal part of Shady 'Shady$_1$'. Additionally, according to perdurance, the object that we arrest tomorrow is not all of Shady; rather it is a day-long (or maybe a getting-arrested-long) temporal part of Shady. Call this temporal part of Shady 'Shady$_2$'. The perdurantist must admit that Shady$_1$ is distinct from Shady$_2$. That is, after all, the way perdurance works. Shady (no subscript) is a four-dimensional object, and the *today* temporal part of Shady is distinct from the *tomorrow* temporal part of Shady. So, it seems that the perdurantist is forced to say that the person who robbed the bank today (Shady$_1$) is not, after all, identical to the person who gets arrested tomorrow (Shady$_2$). But if the person we arrest is not the same person as the person who committed the crime, then how can we legitimately hold the person we arrest responsible for the crime? He didn't do anything wrong!

Though *prima facie* plausible, this objection actually misinterprets the perdurance view. Recall that according to perdurance, when we use the name 'Shady' to talk about Shady, we refer to a four-dimensional object.

Since Shady₁ and Shady₂ are mere temporal parts of the four-dimensional Shady, neither is an appropriate referent of our term 'person'. Rather, the term 'person' refers to the four-dimensional Shady. But if that's true, then perdurance has no problem accommodating numerical identity at all.

Is the person we arrest tomorrow numerically identical to the person who robbed the bank today? Yes, since it is just Shady who is arrested tomorrow and also Shady who robbed the bank today. And Shady is surely identical to himself. That is, since persons are four-dimensional objects, the person who is arrested tomorrow is identical to the person who robbed the bank today because it is the same four-dimensional object under consideration. Of course, I'm not saying that tomorrow there will be a four-dimensional object sitting in a three-dimensional jail cell. That seems like nonsense. Rather, it is just a temporal part of Shady that will be sitting in jail tomorrow. But it is in virtue of having a temporal part in jail tomorrow that we can truly say of Shady (the four-dimensional object) that he will be in jail tomorrow. And since the temporal part of Shady that robbed the bank is part of the same four-dimensional person as the temporal part of Shady that is arrested tomorrow, perdurance has a natural way of meeting the above objection. The person that robbed the bank today is numerically identical to the person that is arrested tomorrow, because that person is a four-dimensional object.

Perhaps this seems like some kind of trickery. You may protest that a perdurantist is nevertheless *still* committed to the claim that the two temporal parts of Shady are distinct objects. And perhaps you may want to claim that moral responsibility requires more than merely that the two temporal parts are parts of the same person. You may want to claim that moral responsibility requires that the person that committed the crime be wholly present at the time when we arrest him. D. H. Mellor seems to claim as much when he says, "Now whatever identity through time may call for elsewhere, here it evidently requires the self-same entity to be wholly present both when the deed was done and later when being held accountable for it" (Mellor 1980, 106). This sentiment, however, is no more than sheer prejudice against perdurance. The perdurantist can quite plausibly claim that what is required for an attribution of moral responsibility to be appropriate is not that "the self-same entity" be "wholly present" at both times, but rather that the self-same *person* be present (but not wholly) at both times. In virtue of having a temporal part today and a temporal part tomorrow, Shady (the four-dimensional person) is present both today and tomorrow. And it is only this type of *being present* that is required by moral responsibility. (Or, at least, it is not at all *evident*, as Mellor claims, that moral responsibility requires more than this. Additional argumentation would be needed.) So, the perdurantist *is* able to successfully account for numerical identity after all.

Who's Responsible?

The third objection to the compatibility of perdurance and moral responsibility asks: "Who's responsible?" Put in the form of an argument, the objection runs as follows:

(1)   If we ever make true moral responsibility attributions, then if perdurance is true, we attribute moral responsibility to four-dimensional objects.

(2)   Attributing moral responsibility to a four-dimensional object makes no sense.

(3)   Therefore, if we ever make true moral responsibility attributions, perdurance is false.

Clearly, the premise of interest here is (2). Indeed, I will argue that the perdurantist can successfully reject premise (2).

Why might it be thought unintelligible to attribute moral responsibility to persons if persons are four-dimensional objects? Here's how one philosopher has put it:

[The suggestion of attributing responsibility to me] is a rather bizarre suggestion if I am what [perdurance] says I am—namely, a very complex temporal solid embedded in a [four-dimensional] spatiotemporal matrix with other objects and events and standing in changeless causal relations to other [four-dimensional] existents. This [four-dimensional] person is not itself conscious, although many of its parts are. What would it mean to assign responsibility to such an individual? I have no idea, nor can I imagine any point in doing so. (Delmas Lewis 1986, 307)[14]

The thought seems to be that it's just plain weird to assign responsibility to a four-dimensional object. Responsibility is a notion that we use in everyday, down-to-earth circumstances, and it's just implausible to think that when we assign responsibility to persons, we are assigning responsibility to four-dimensional objects. Moreover, and perhaps more forcefully, what are the characteristics of this four-dimensional object in virtue of which it is an appropriate candidate for responsibility attributions? It seems natural to suppose that in order for anything to be appropriately held morally responsible, it has to have certain characteristics such as consciousness, responsiveness to reasons, rationality, and the like. But if (what might also seem natural to suppose) a four-dimensional object can have none of these characteristics, then in what sense can we say it is morally responsible?

Again, though these considerations are *prima facie* plausible, I think they can be resisted by the perdurantist. To the first part—the claim that it's just weird to attribute moral responsibility to a four-dimensional object— the perdurantist can point out that we do it all the time. As we saw above, perdurantists think that all continuants are four-dimensional objects. So, if perdurance is true, then we *do* attribute moral responsibility to four-dimensional objects, for we attribute moral responsibility to persons and persons are four-dimensional objects. Sure, we may not realize that we are talking about four-dimensional objects, but that makes no difference. It remains true, the perdurantist claims, that continuants are four-dimensional objects. At this point, you may object that we do not actually quantify over and talk about four-dimensional objects. This, however, is an objection against perdurance itself and not against the compatibility of perdurance and moral responsibility. The strongest claim I need is merely this: Given perdurance, it makes perfect sense to attribute moral responsibility to a four-dimensional object—we do it all the time.[15]

But the first part of the objection isn't the strongest part, anyway. What is more important, I suspect, is the claim that certain characteristics are required for a thing to be morally responsible, and that four-dimensional objects cannot have the requisite characteristics. As I mentioned above, these characteristics likely include consciousness, rationality, and responsiveness to reasons. But if a four-dimensional object cannot have these characteristics, we can conclude that no responsibility attribution is ever appropriately applied to a four-dimensional object.

In order to respond to this objection, the perdurantist needs to appeal to the difference between *tenseless* and *temporally indexed* property instantiation. Whereas tenseless property instantiation is a two-place relation between an object and a property, temporally indexed property instantiation, on the other hand, is a three-place relation between an object, a property, and a time. This distinction furnishes the perdurantist with the resources for an adequate response.

Can a four-dimensional object be conscious? The question is ambiguous. If the question is whether a four-dimensional object can be *tenselessly* conscious, then the answer is pretty straightforwardly negative. Over the course of one's lifetime, one may go in and out of consciousness. According to perdurance, this change from being conscious to being unconscious is accounted for by reference to the fact that the person has one conscious temporal part that precedes an unconscious temporal part. But given these considerations, it is clear that the question, "Is the person conscious *simpliciter?*" is misguided. The person has a conscious temporal part at t_1 (say), and an unconscious temporal part at t_2, and so we can truly say that the person (the four-dimensional object) is conscious at t_1 and unconscious at t_2. If a person is a four-dimensional object, it makes no sense to ask whether or not the person is conscious *simpliciter*. What this shows is that whereas temporally indexed property instantiation applies to four-dimensional objects, *tenseless* property instantiation does not.

The perdurantist can respond, then, by pointing out that four-dimensional persons *do*, after all, possess characteristics in virtue of which they can be appropriately held morally responsible. They can be conscious at a time, rational at a time, and appropriately responsive to reasons at a time. And what matters for responsibility, the perdurantist might continue, is merely whether a person has these properties at the relevant times, not whether a person has them *simpliciter*. After all, it seems that our attributions of responsibility must themselves be indexed to a time. A person is not morally responsible *simpliciter*. Rather, a person is morally responsible at a time for some particular action or event that takes place at a specific time.

It seems, then, that there is nothing so odd about ascribing moral responsibility to a four-dimensional person, and hence premise (2) of the above argument can be rejected by the perdurantist.

Who Gets Punished?
Two objections remain.[16] The fourth objection is related to the third. Whereas the last objection asked, "Who's responsible?," the current objection asks, "Who gets punished?" Again, this objection can be stated clearly using an argument analogous to the one in the previous section.

(1) If perdurance is true, then when we punish a person, we punish a four-dimensional object.

(2) The idea of punishing a four-dimensional object makes no sense.

(3) Therefore, perdurance is false.

We saw above that the perdurantist can plausibly claim that it does make sense to attribute responsibility to a four-dimensional object, and, as you might expect, the perdurantist's response to this objection will be similar. But first let's get clear on why someone might object to perdurance in this way.

Even if you are willing to concede that a four-dimensional object is able to have the requisite characteristics for moral responsibility, you may still be doubtful that we can ever adequately punish such an odd object. Our world is phenomenologically three-dimensional, so if perdurance is true, any punishment that a court dubs appropriate will have to be meted out to some temporal parts of a person and not others. Vinit Haksar raises worries about this as well when he says, "Who then is being punished on [perdurance]? Is it [Shady]? But [Shady] is a logical construct. A logical construct such as [Shady] does not suffer except in the sense that the items that it is made up of include the experiences of suffering" (Haksar 1991, 220). Given that we cannot change the past, one might wonder whether it makes any sense at all to claim that when we punish people, we are punishing four-dimensional objects. We don't have access, so to speak, to *all* of the person, since some of the person existed at times past. So how on earth can we punish a four-dimensional object?

The perdurantist can respond, however, by first conceding that we don't have access to *all* of the person, and then by pointing out that we don't *need* to have such access in order to punish the person. All we need to do is punish the temporal parts of the person that we *do* have access to, and the four-dimensional object is thereby punished. So, to go back to our previous example, when we arrest Shady and put him in jail, it is in virtue of the fact that Shady has various temporal parts that are punished that we can truly say of Shady that he is being punished. Of course, we can't say that Shady is being punished *simpliciter*, because Shady has some temporal parts that are punished and some that are not. Rather, Shady is being punished *at certain times*, namely those times at which he has temporal parts that are being punished. But the temporally indexed claim seems to be what we should want to say in any case.

So, according to perdurance, when we punish people, we are indeed punishing four-dimensional objects. It's just that the *way* you punish a four-dimensional object is by punishing some of its temporal parts.

Punishing Innocent People

The final objection I will consider is that if perdurance is true, then when we punish people, we end up punishing innocent people for crimes they didn't commit. According to perdurance, the objection begins, the temporal part of Shady that is arrested tomorrow is not identical to the temporal part of Shady that robbed the bank today. But then when we punish Shady tomorrow by putting him in jail, we are punishing an innocent person. After all, the temporal part of Shady that is arrested tomorrow did not itself commit the crime.

This is the naive version of the objection. For we can easily respond to this line of reasoning as we did above. It's true that the temporal part of Shady that is arrested tomorrow did not *itself* commit the crime, but that's irrelevant. Just so long as the temporal part that is arrested is part of the same four-dimensional person as the temporal part that robbed the bank, punishment is just. We are punishing the whole person in virtue of punishing one of his temporal parts.

But the rejoinder to this is not quite so naive. Granting that both temporal parts are indeed parts of the same four-dimensional person, the objector might continue as Vinit Haksar does: "But I do not find such reasoning any better than the following reasoning: It is perfectly just to punish the current members of the Smith family for the crimes of their parents because they are all parts of the same family; it is the same family that committed the crime as is being punished now" (Haksar 1991, 246). Or again, attempting to use the perdurantist's commitment to unrestricted composition[17] against him: "We could punish Reagan for the crime committed by a former President by treating the several Presidents as forming one four dimensional object. We could punish the son for the crimes committed by his father by treating them both as belonging to the history of the same four dimensional object" (Haksar 1991, 247). The idea here is that even though the two temporal parts bear some kind of intimate relation to one another (since they are both parts of the same four-dimensional person), they are nevertheless distinct objects in their own right and ought not to be punished for crimes that they did not commit.

The perdurantist must respond, I think, by pointing out that the relation that ties together a *person's* different temporal parts (the relation sometimes called 'genidentity') is a much more intimate relation than the relation that ties together a family's different members. Whereas it *is* just to punish one temporal part for a crime it didn't commit just so long as it is part of the same four-dimensional person as the temporal part that did commit the crime, it is *not* just to punish Smith's son for Smith's crimes just because they are each members of the Smith family.

I say this is how the perdurantist must respond, but I think an adequate response must be much more sophisticated than what I have just said. What this particular objection shows, I think, is how important it is for the perdurantist to spell out in detail just what this relation of genidentity is. What is it that makes the relation *being part of the same four-dimensional person* a more intimate relation than *being part of the same family* and in virtue of which standing in the former relation might get you punished

whereas standing in the latter relation would not? I suspect different perdurantists will have different answers to this question. So long as an answer
can be formulated, though, I think the perdurantist is able to respond
adequately to this last objection as well.

Final Considerations

Although perdurance emerges from the above objections relatively
unscathed, I think that our consideration of these objections highlights
the aspects of perdurance that deserve the most attention from metaphysicians who are also interested in issues about agency and responsibility. For
instance, we have seen that it is especially important for the perdurantist
to spell out just what the relation is that makes it the case that two temporal parts are parts of the same four-dimensional person. It is only with
an adequate account of this relation that the perdurantist will be able to
respond to certain pressing objections.

Another important question that deserves attention, I think, is how to
account for characteristics that, once one temporal part comes to have
them, "infect" future temporal parts of the person. Moral responsibility
seems to be such a characteristic. When Shady commits his crime at t_1, not
only is he responsible at t_1 for robbing the bank, he is also responsible at all
subsequent times for robbing the bank at t_1. How is it that responsibility
infects future temporal parts of a worm without infecting past temporal
parts?[18] All this is just to say that although perdurance so far seems perfectly compatible with moral responsibility, there are still many interesting
questions about this topic that deserve further thought. For now, though,
it appears that we thus far have not been provided with any good reason
to think that perdurance is a threat to moral responsibility.

Acknowledgments

I am grateful to my commentator at the INPC, Brian Steverson, as well as
to those who were present at my talk, especially Ben Bradley, Joshua Spencer, and Kevin Timpe. For encouragement of and helpful comments on the
ideas of this essay, thanks are due to John Martin Fischer.

Notes

1. Proponents of this view include Peter van Inwagen (1990) and Trenton Merricks
(1999).

2. Proponents of this view include David Lewis (1986) and Mark Heller (1990).

3. Or, at least, I will not question it. Some philosophers, though, do. See, for example, Strawson 1986.

4. These philosophers include Randolph Clarke (2003), Walter Glannon (1998), Vinit Haksar (1991), Delmas Lewis (1986), D. H. Mellor (1980), and Marc Slors (2000).

5. Proponents of this view include Theodore Sider (1996, 2001) and Katherine Hawley (2001). Haslanger (2003) uses the term 'exdurantism' for stage theory. There is logical space for a fourth view as well, what Gregory Fowler (2005) has dubbed 'transdurantism'.

6. Not surprisingly, many of the objections to the compatibility of perdurance and responsibility can also serve (with slight modifications) as objections to the compatibility of stage theory and responsibility. On this issue, see Tognazzini 2005.

7. This is not to say that if it turns out there are more than three spatial dimensions (as some theories in contemporary physics have it), then endurance is false. The important point is that according to endurance, objects are not extended in any temporal dimension.

8. I'm following David Lewis (1986, 202) in using 'persist' in a theory-neutral way.

9. Just what the 'appropriate way' is, however, is a large and important question. Without getting too much into the details, the important point is that the stage theorist devises a way to do justice to our everyday claims about people by situating the instantaneous stages in a complex network of relations to other instantaneous stages.

10. It's interesting to note that some of these objections to the compatibility of perdurance and responsibility (and this objection in particular) sound quite similar to objections that have been raised against the causal theory of action. The trouble for the causal theory of action is supposed to arise from the fact that the theory's explanation of what makes an agent active rather than passive with respect to her behavior isn't robust enough. Similarly, those who object to the compatibility of perdurance and responsibility seem to be driven by the thought that temporal parts of a person aren't robust enough to play the role of the agent. Not surprisingly, I'm inclined to think both sorts of objection are mistaken. I thank an anonymous referee for bringing this parallel to my attention.

11. You may be more worried about it than I am. If so, I suspect that your worry is based on considerations that I will address throughout the course of this essay. Come back to this issue at the end and see whether you are still as worried.

12. Besides Haksar and van Inwagen, this worry about numerical identity is also stated in some form by Glannon (1998), Mellor (1980), and Slors (2000).

13. I say 'may be interpreted' because I am unclear whether van Inwagen (himself an endurantist) intends these remarks as considerations against the compatibility of perdurance and moral responsibility. In any case, I think they do hint toward that conclusion, and that is why I have chosen to include them.

14. Lewis is here actually discussing reasons for thinking that the tenseless view of time is incompatible with moral responsibility. Since most (all?) perdurantists accept the tenseless view of time, the objection can be aimed at perdurance as well, and so I have made the appropriate modifications. William Lane Craig (2000, 210) agrees with Lewis here: "I think that [Lewis's] conclusion is undeniable; and since our moral judgments are plausibly not absurd, it follows that the perdurantist conception of persons is false."

15. For more on this, see the discussion of Lewis's "best-candidate" theory of content in Sider 2001, xxi.

16. These last two objections actually deal with punishment rather than moral responsibility proper. However, since the two are so intimately linked, I think it is incumbent on the perdurantist to address these objections as well.

17. Unrestricted composition is the view that any two objects, no matter how widely scattered in space and time, compose a third, which has the first two as parts. The typical perdurantist uses this view to "hook" the different temporal parts of a person together, so to speak.

18. Then again, if determinism is true, perhaps moral responsibility does infect past temporal parts of the worm as well, and perhaps a person can be punished at times prior to his committing the crime. This is another question worth taking up.

References

Clarke, R. 2003. *Libertarian Accounts of Free Will*. Oxford: Oxford University Press.

Craig, W. L. 2000. *The Tenseless Theory of Time: A Critical Examination*. Dordrecht: Kluwer Academic.

Fowler, G. 2005. *A Fourth View Concerning Persistence*. Manuscript.

Glannon, W. 1998. Moral Responsibility and Personal Identity. *American Philosophical Quarterly* 35:231–250.

Haksar, V. 1991. *Indivisible Selves and Moral Practice*. New York: Oxford University Press.

Haslanger, S. 2003. Persistence through Time. In *The Oxford Handbook of Metaphysics*, ed. M. J. Loux and D. W. Zimmerman. New York: Oxford University Press.

Hawley, K. 2001. *How Things Persist*. Oxford: Oxford University Press.

Heller, M. 1990. *The Ontology of Physical Objects: Four Dimensional Hunks of Matter.* Cambridge: Cambridge University Press.

Lewis, David. 1986. *On the Plurality of Worlds.* Oxford: Blackwell.

Lewis, Delmas. 1986. Persons, Morality, and Tenselessness. *Philosophy and Phenomenological Research* 47:305–309.

Mellor, D. H. 1980. *Real Time.* Cambridge: Cambridge University Press.

Merricks, T. 1999. Persistence, Parts, and Presentism. *Noûs* 33:421–438.

Sider, T. 1996. All the World's a Stage. *Australasian Journal of Philosophy* 74: 433–453.

Sider, T. 2001. *Four-Dimensionalism.* Oxford: Clarendon Press.

Slors, M. 2000. Personal Identity and Responsibility for Past Actions. In *Moral Responsibility and Ontology,* ed. T. van den Beld. Dordrecht: Kluwer.

Strawson, G. 1986. *Freedom and Belief.* Oxford: Clarendon Press.

Tognazzini, N. A. 2005. *On Being a Morally Responsible Stage.* Manuscript.

van Inwagen, P. 1990. *Material Beings.* Ithaca, NY: Cornell University Press.

van Inwagen, P. 2000. Moral Responsibility and Ontology. In *Moral Responsibility and Ontology,* ed. T. van den Beld. Dordrecht: Kluwer.

8 Descartes on Persistence and Temporal Parts

Geoffrey Gorham

Introduction

The subtitle of the first edition of Descartes's *Meditations* promises a demonstration of the immortality of the soul (AT 7, xix).[1] But although the "real distinction" between the mind and body is defended in the Sixth Meditation, early readers like Arnauld, and here Mersenne, were quick to point out that "it does not seem to follow from the fact that the mind is distinct from the body that it is incorruptible or immortal" (AT 7, 128; CSM 2, 91).[2] Apparently at Mersenne's urging, Descartes constructed a more detailed proof of immortality in the final week of 1640, and included it in a "Synopsis" or "Abrégé" to the already completed, and soon to be published, *Meditations*.[3] Descartes notes that the new proof depends on two assumptions not made explicit in the six meditations (these he admits are sufficient only to give mortals the "hope" of an afterlife).[4]

First we need to know that absolutely all substances, or things that must be created by God in order to exist, are by their very nature incorruptible, and cannot ever cease to exist unless reduced to nothing by God's denying his concurrence to them. Second, we need to recognize that even body, taken in the general sense, is a substance, so that it too never perishes. But the human body, insomuch as it differs from other bodies, is simply made up of a certain configuration of limbs and other accidents of this sort, whereas the human mind is not made up of any accidents in this way but is a pure substance. For even if all the accidents of the mind change, so that it has different objects of the understanding and different desires and sensations, it does not on that account become a different mind; whereas a human body loses its identity merely as a result of a change in the shape of some of its parts. And it follows from this that whereas the body can very easily perish, the soul is immortal by its very nature. (AT 7, 14; CSM 2, 10)

Although Arnauld at least was satisfied,[5] there are difficulties with both assumptions. Regarding the first assumption, Descartes defines substances as things that "must be created by God" to exist. He must mean things that need *only* to be created by God in order to exist, since modes or attributes depend on divine concurrence no less than substances.[6] This anticipates the *Principles of Philosophy* definition of substances as "things which need only the ordinary concurrence of God in order to exist" (AT 8A, 24; CSM 1, 210). Modes or attributes, by contrast, "cannot exist without other things" (AT 9B, 47; CSM 1, 210). But this fails to establish that we are immortal since for all we know God gave our souls a naturally finite life span. Descartes seems to concede this when the problem is posed to him by Mersenne: "Here I cannot refute what you say. For I do not take it upon myself to try to use the power of human reason to settle any of those matters which depend on the free will of God" (AT 7, 153; CSM 2, 109).

Regarding the second assumption, Descartes says that minds (and body considered "*in genera*") are not prone to destruction because they are not "made up of accidents" in the ways particular bodies are. The point is not that minds do not have accidents or modes, but rather that these accidents are not *parts* of the mind. That's why minds retain strict identity through modal change. The idea is nicely summarized by Peter Markie: "Bodies have parts, but minds do not. This is what is behind Descartes' contrast of the ability of minds and bodies to survive change. . . . Minds do not have parts to lose when their thoughts change."[7] And presumably the parts of particular bodies are not properly speaking parts of body taken *in genera*. Unfortunately, Descartes does not explain what it means to consider body *in genera*. A more serious problem, as I argue below, is that Cartesian minds *do* have parts, albeit temporal parts rather than spatial parts. We will see that Descartes is a *perdurantist* in roughly the manner of David Lewis or Ted Sider.[8] In fact each of these temporal parts qualifies as a distinct substance no less than do the distinct spatial parts of bodies: minds are temporally divisible in the same way that bodies are spatially divisible. So, far from being immortal, Cartesian minds do not endure even for a moment. Despite this, I will argue, there is another sense in which Cartesian minds, and even bodies considered *in genera*, retain strict identity over time and despite change in parts (which is the first assumption of the Synopsis proof). Moreover, in this sense they are incorruptible (which is the second assumption of the Synopsis proof), though we will see that this incorruptibility depends on the timeless nature of Cartesian essences rather than simply the inscrutable will of God. So the Cartesian argument for immortality can succeed, though not in the precise form intended by Descartes.

Why Cartesian Souls Lack Endurance

In the Third Meditation Descartes argues that it follows simply from "the nature of time" that one must be continuously created:

For a lifespan can be divided into countless parts each completely independent of the others, so that it does not follow from the fact that I existed a little while ago that I must exist now, unless there is some cause which as it were creates me afresh at this moment—that is, preserves me. For it is quite clear to anyone who attentively considers the nature of time that the same power and action that are needed to preserve anything at each individual moment of its duration would be required to create that thing anew if it were not yet in existence. (AT 7, 49; CSM 2, 33)[9]

The idea is that the parts of my duration or life span are completely independent in the sense that no one part can be the efficient and total cause of any other. In particular, my existence *just now* cannot be the cause or reason for my existence *right now*. Since everything (apart from God) has a cause distinct from itself, it follows that even if I have always been alive there must still be an external author of each temporal stage of my life.[10] Barring an infinite regress, "eventually the ultimate cause is reached, and this will be God" (AT 7, 50; CSM 2, 34).

Pierre Gassendi raised the following objection to the argument for continuous creation: "What difference does this dependence or independence of the parts of time make to your creation or preservation? Surely these parts are merely external—they follow on without playing any active role. They make no more difference to your creation and preservation than the flow or passage of the particles of water in a river makes to the creation or preservation of some rock past which it flows" (AT 7, 301; CSM 2, 209–210). But this wrongly assumes that Descartes conceives of time in the same "proto-Newtonian" manner as Gassendi, as an independent, flowing thing. On the contrary, for Descartes there is no real distinction between substances and their duration: "since a substance cannot cease to endure without ceasing to be, the distinction between a substance and its duration is merely a conceptual one" (AT 8A, 30; CSM 1, 214).[11] Nor can we conceive an end to all substance without an end to all duration: "I think it involves a contradiction to conceive of any duration intervening between the destruction of an earlier world and the creation of a new one" (AT 5, 343; CSMK, 373).[12] So Descartes says that any attempt to separate the attribute of duration from the enduring thing would involve "a confusion in our thought" analogous to the attempted separation of extension or divisibility from body (AT 9B, 53). Given the merely conceptual distinction between substance and duration, Descartes is correct to infer the mutual independence of the various stages of my life from the mutual independence of the parts of time in which I live. For in reality these parts of time are nothing but the stages of my life, just as the regions of space through which I extend are nothing but the various parts of my body.[13]

So a Cartesian soul is nothing but the duration of a certain thinking substance comprising countless temporal stages, all completely independent of one another. Furthermore, each of these stages qualifies as a distinct substance in its own right.[14] For, according to Descartes's theory of distinctions, "two substances are said to be really distinct when each of them can exist apart from the other" (AT 7, 162; CSM 2, 114). For example, our mind is really distinct from our body because "the mind can, at least through the power of God, exist without the body; and likewise the body can exist apart from the mind" (AT 7, 170; CSM 2, 119). And even if a given corporeal substance is never actually divided, we know its parts are distinct things if we can adequately conceive of them apart: "from the simple fact that I consider the two halves of a piece of matter, however small it may be, as two complete substances, whose ideas are not made inadequate by an abstraction of the intellect, I conclude with certainty that they are really divisible" (AT 3, 477; CSMK, 202–203).[15] That the parts of my duration are distinct in just this way is precisely what Descartes indicates: "I regard the divisions of time as being separable from one another [*mutuo sejungi posse*] so that the fact that I exist now does not imply that I shall continue to exist in a little while" (AT 7, 109; CSM 2, 78–79). And just as I might die tomorrow even though I *will not*, it seems God could easily have arranged for me to have begun to exist yesterday even though I *did not*: "the individual moments can be separated from those immediately preceding and succeeding them [*posse a vicinis separari*]" (AT 7, 370; CSM 2, 255).[16]

In Cartesian mereology, the fact that a thing has substantial parts does not preclude it from being a substance itself. This is clearest in the case of bodies: "we can be certain that, if it [corporeal substance] exists, each and every part of it as delimited in our thought is really distinct from the other parts of the same substance" (AT 8A, 29; CSM 1, 213).[17] Furthermore, there is no end to the number of distinct substances contained in any given material substance, since "the number of particles into which matter is divided is in fact indefinite" (AT 8A, 59; CSM 1, 239). The mind–body union is another substance with substantial parts: "the mind and the body are incomplete substances when referred to a human being which they make up. But if they are considered on their own they are complete" (AT 7, 222; CSM 2, 157).[18]

So the fact that the duration of the soul has substantial parts does not mean the soul is not a substance, only that it does not *endure*. That is, my soul does not exist entirely at a various different times any more than my body exists entirely at various different places. My soul has substantial temporal parts just as my body has substantial spatial parts. Moreover, like the spatial parts of my body, Descartes says that the distinct temporal parts of my soul's duration cannot overlap or "coexist" (AT 8A, 13; CSM 1, 200) and are infinitely, or at least indefinitely, divisible, that is, "countless" (AT 7, 49; CSM 2, 33).[19] So the duration of each of these countless substances is at best fleeting. Like Lewis's "person-stages" they are "more or less momentary" time slices of persons which begin and cease to exist abruptly.[20]

Allow me to summarize the argument that Cartesian souls lack endurance.

(1)   The soul is a substance.

(2)   There is no real distinction between a substance and its duration.

(3)   The countless parts of the duration of the soul are separable from one another.

(4)   If two things are separable from one another then they are really distinct substances.

(5)   Hence, every temporal part of the soul is a really distinct substance.

(6)   Hence, the soul does not endure as a simple substance.[21]

At first glance, one might suspect that the problem of endurance is easily solved. One obvious strategy would be to temporally index Descartes's criterion of real distinctness in order to block the implication that every temporal part of a substance is also a substance. The following restriction would do the job: two things are really distinct if and only if they are mutually separable *and exist at the same time*. The problem is that this fails to account for the real distinction between, for example, the soul of Socrates and the soul of Descartes. Perhaps one could say that two mutually separable things are really distinct if and only if they exist at the same time or *exist at different times and are not spatiotemporally or psychologically connected*. Such a condition seems to limit God's power to destroy an object and replace it with a numerically distinct replica immediately afterward. It would also exclude less exotic kinds of substantial change over time which Descartes wants to countenance. He frequently says, for example, that the identity condition for bodies is simply a definite shape and size, from which it follows that a body subject to continuous change would become a distinct thing: "a human body loses its identity merely as a result of a change in the shape of some of its parts" (AT 7, 14; CSM 2, 10). The resulting body is numerically distinct from yet continuous with the old.

The problem I am posing for Descartes can be usefully expressed in terms of a distinction central to recent discussions of the metaphysics of persistence: *endurance* versus *perdurance*. An object endures if it is 'wholly present' at any time that it exists. An object perdures if it is composed of temporal parts such that at any given time only one temporal part of the object exists. Perdurantists maintain a close analogy between spatial extension and temporal persistence: just as objects extend though space by having different parts at different locations, they persist or extend through time by having different temporal parts at different times. So perdurantists will say it is true in two different but equally genuine senses that 'part of North America is covered by ice', one sense owing to the existence of arctic regions and the other sense owing to the existence of ice ages.[22]

I maintain that for Descartes, individual thinking substances (and indeed all substances) can persist only by perduring. Since the duration of my life comprises countless distinct substances, including the present one, there is no substance that is fully present at any more than one given stage.[23] The current stage can no more claim substantial identity with earlier stages than some one part of my body can claim substantial identity with all the others, given that in either case the parts are each independent and separable from one another. There appears then to be a serious tension between the Synopsis proof of immortality, which assumes that the soul is naturally indestructible, and the argument for continuous creation, which assumes that the soul must be continually created or conserved owing to the independence of the parts of time. For according to the former argument mental substances remain strictly identical over time despite modal change, whereas according to the latter argument the soul is constituted by a distinct thing at each instant it exists.

Individual Essence

Why not simply concede that the Cartesian soul persists in time only as a succession of substantial temporal parts, just as a body extends in space only as a collection of distinct substantial parts? I think Descartes would reject this "Humean" view of the soul[24]—but not because the soul would then be a "mere pseudo-substance," as Jonathan Bennett has put it.[25] As noted above, there is no good Cartesian reason to deny substantiality to what has substantial parts. Such a substance (whether body or mind) could even be immortal in perdurantist terms by having no latest part. Rather, the problem with merely perduring things from a Cartesian point of view is that they are composite and divisible, whereas Descartes insists that the soul is by nature "something quite single and complete" (AT 7, 86; CSM 2, 59).[26] It is for precisely this reason that "the natures of the mind and body are not only different but in some way opposite" (AT 7, 13; CSM 2, 9–10), or "completely different from one another" (AT 7, 86; CSM 2, 59).[27] Of course, the soul is not *absolutely* simple, as Descartes admits, since it has diverse faculties. However, "these [faculties] cannot be termed parts of the mind, since it is one and the same mind that wills, and understands, and has sensory perceptions" (ibid.). On the other hand, although "we cannot conceive of half a mind . . . we can always conceive of half a body, no matter how small" (AT 7, 13; CSM 2, 9). According to the argument for nonendurance this asymmetry is illusory: the temporal parts of a soul are as distinct as the spatial parts of a body. This undermines the Synopsis claim that the soul is a "pure substance" that retains strict identity over time, and along with it Descartes's view that the numerical identity of the human body *qua* human body is guaranteed by the identity of the soul: "it is quite true to say I have the same body now as I had ten years ago, although the matter of which it is composed has changed, because the numerical identity of the body of a man does not depend on its matter, but on its form, which is the soul" (AT 4, 346; CSMK, 278–279).[28] But since the temporal parts that compose the duration of the soul have also changed, the soul cannot be what makes chunks of matter with distinct spatial parts the same human body.

In developing a solution to the problem of endurance, I begin by observing that Cartesian souls have *individual essences*. That is, the nature of my soul is not simply *thought* but rather a *particular thinking*. That there are such essences seems to follow from fundamental principles of Cartesian metaphysics. In existing things there are only particulars (universals depend on an "abstraction of the intellect").[29] And there is no real distinction between existing things and their essence or principal attribute.[30] From this it follows that each existing soul has a distinct individual essence—a *particular thinking*. Furthermore, Descartes quite explicitly invokes individual essences for two purposes. First, as we seen, Descartes thinks the soul remains the same even if all its accidents change. This identity of the soul is secured by an individual essence. Descartes gives it a technical name—the 'I' (*ego*)[31]—and says that we apprehend it directly:

The fact that it is I who am doubting and willing and understanding is so evident that I can see no way of making it any clearer. But it is also the case that the 'I' who imagines is the same 'I' [*ego idem*]. For even if, as I have supposed, none of the objects of imagination are real, the power of imagination is something that really exists and is part of my thinking. Lastly, it is also the same 'I' which has sensory perceptions, or is aware of things as it were through the senses. (AT 7, 29; CSM 2, 19)

Second, individual essences are needed to distinguish one soul from another. For bodies, individuation is entirely a matter of differences in modes of extension. Thus, "in case of the human body, the difference between it and other bodies consists merely in the arrangement of limbs and other accidents of this sort" (AT 7, 153; CSM 2, 109). More precisely, two bodies are really distinct if they occupy different 'places', that is, "different size, shape and positions, relative to other bodies" (AT 8A, 47; CSM 1, 228), as determined by the relative motions of the other neighboring bodies (AT 8A, 53–54; CSM 1, 233).[32] In contrast, the I's mere awareness of a particular thinking nature, rather than any collection of mental modes, is what distinguishes it from every other thinking and material substance: "From the mere fact that each of us understands himself to be a thinking thing, and is capable in thought of excluding from himself every other substance, whether thinking or extended, it is certain that each of us, regarded in this way, is really distinct from every other thinking substance" (AT 8A, 29; CSM 1, 213). So we have direct and certain knowledge of a particular thinking nature—"this puzzling I" as Descartes calls it (AT 7, 29; CSM 2, 20)—which both individuates our soul and secures its identity over time.

Descartes's most detailed account of the soul's individual essence is given in a letter to Arnauld, who had presented Descartes with the following dilemma. If, on the one hand, the 'thought' that constitutes the essence of the soul is a universal, then it cannot account for the fact that the soul is "singular and determinate." If, on the other hand, 'thought' is a particular act of thinking then "the essence of the mind is constantly changing," since our thoughts are constantly changing (AT 5, 213–214). Descartes answers that the essence of the soul is neither the universal 'thought', nor any particular act of thinking, but rather the efficient cause of all our thoughts:

So thought, or a thinking nature [*natura cogitans*], which I think constitutes the essence of the human mind, is very different from any particular act of thinking. It depends on the mind itself whether it produces this or that particular act of thinking, but not that it is a thinking thing, just as it depends on a flame, as an efficient cause, whether it turns to this side or that, but not that it is an extended thing. So by 'thought' I do not mean some universal which includes all modes of thinking, but a particular nature [*sed naturam particularum*], which takes on all those modes, just as extension is a nature which takes on all shapes. (AT 5, 221; CSMK, 357)

Descartes avoids the dilemma by making the individual human mind both unchanging and particular, endowing it with an individual nature.

I will mention one other explicit appeal to individual essence. In the interview with Burman, Descartes was asked what distinguishes an angel from a human mind, "given each is merely something which thinks" (AT 5, 157). His response is that although humans and angels are both finite thinking things, they may differ in kind. By this he does not mean that angels have their own principal attribute distinct from thought. For "we can think of nothing in an angel *qua* angel that we do not also notice in ourselves" (ibid.). Rather, he means that every angel and every human has his own unique essence. Thus, in explaining his position he explicitly invokes Aquinas's doctrine that every angel is "of a different kind from every other" (ibid.).[33] In Cartesian terms, thinking things are each of a different kind by virtue of having distinct individual essences.[34]

Returning to the issue of persistence, in order to avoid being divided into temporal parts themselves individual thinking natures must be in some way distinct from perduring substances. This might seem impossible since, as I have already noted, Descartes says that there is no real distinction between existing things and their essence or principal attribute. Yet, as Descartes himself cautions in a discussion of the ontological status of essences, we need to distinguish between *formal* and *objective* existence, "between things existing outside our thought, and the ideas of things which exist in our thought" (AT 4, 349; CSMK, 280). And he makes that it clear that "if by essence we understand a thing as it is objectively in the intellect, and by existence the same thing in so far as it is outside the intellect, it is manifest that the two are really distinct" (AT 4, 350; CSMK, 281). So, except in the special case of God, it is possible for an essence to exist, at least objectively, apart from the corresponding formally existing substance: "it belongs to the essence of God to exist; but the same cannot be said of a triangle whose whole essence can be correctly understood even if it is supposed that in reality there is no such thing" (AT 3, 433; CSMK, 196).

If souls have individual essences, and if essences can exist merely objectively, then the 'I' can exist apart from any formally existing thinking substance and so avoid being carved up by duration. As surprising as this may sound, there is at least one text in which Descartes handles the problem of persistence in just this way. Burman had asked whether the fact that thinking takes time implies that thought is extended and divisible (*extensa et divisibila*) (AT 5, 148; CSMK, 335). Descartes answered: "Not at all. Thought will indeed be extended and divisible with respect to its duration [*durationem*], since its duration can be divided into parts. But it is not extended and divisible with respect to its nature [*naturam*] since its nature remains unextended" (AT 5, 149: CSMK, 335). Descartes here admits that souls have parts considered as enduring substances, but insists that they remain single and complete considered as essences.

If something exists independently of time and duration then it is eternal in the strong sense of timeless or 'permanent'. Now Descartes says that essences are 'indivisible'[35] as well as 'eternal and immutable': "When, for example, I imagine a triangle, even if perhaps no such figure exists, or has ever existed anywhere outside my thought, there is still a determinate nature, or essence, or form of the triangle, which is eternal and immutable and not invented by me or dependent on my mind" (AT 7, 64; CSM 2, 44–45).[36] The Platonic connotation is clearly intended. Indeed, Descartes explicitly compares his knowledge of such essences to recollection: "it seems to me I am not so much learning something new as remembering what I knew before" (AT 7, 64: CSM 2, 44).[37] Of course, Descartes would not accept that such essences are independent even of God, given his extreme voluntarism: "I do not think that the essences of things, and the mathematical truths which we can know concerning them, are independent of God. Nevertheless I think that they are eternal since the will and decree of God willed and decreed that they should be so" (AT 7, 380; CSM 2, 261).[38]

My suggestion, then, is that real essences, including the individual essences of human minds, are created timelessly by God.[39] As such they have an existence in God (logically) prior to the existence of any finite thinking thing. What sort of existence do they then have in God? For Descartes, one thing can exist or be contained in another thing in three distinct ways: *formally*; *objectively*; and *eminently*. To exist formally in a thing is to exist "in a way which exactly corresponds" to our usual perception of the thing (AT 7, 161; CSM 2, 114). To exist objectively in a thing is to exist in the thing's idea, not formally but representatively (AT 7, 41–42; CSM 2, 28–29). To exist eminently in a thing is to exist in the thing in a way that does not exactly correspond to our usual perception, but yet "the greatness of the [containing] object is such that it can fill the role of that which does so correspond" (AT 7, 161; CSM 2, 114). For example, God contains *thought* formally, *Adam's body* objectively, and *motion* eminently. As for the individual essences of finite minds, they clearly do not exist formally in God. For then our ordinary perception of 'I' would in part correspond to our perception of God. Nor do they exist *merely* objectively in the eternal mind of God. That would violate Descartes's fundamental causal principle that "whatever reality or perfection there is in a thing is present either formally or eminently in its first and adequate cause" (AT 7, 165; CSM 2, 116). Thus, Descartes says that "he who preserves me has within himself whatever is in me either formally or eminently" (AT 7, 168; CSM 2, 118).[40] Since essences do not exist formally in God, they must exist there eminently: "it is not always necessary that this cause should contain it formally, but only eminently" (AT 3, 545; CSMK, 211). Though it is not entirely clear what eminent containment amounts to,[41] it is clear that God's greatness and power are sufficient to eminently contain all eternal essences.

I return finally to the difficulties raised in the introductory section about Descartes's Synopsis proof of immortality. First, what entitles Descartes to say that all substances taken *in genera* are "by their very nature" indestructible aside from the hope God that will continue to concur in their existence? A possible answer is that to take a substance in a general sense is to consider its principal attribute or essence. Thus, 'body' in a general sense is *extension*[42] and 'Descartes' in a general sense (apart from any particular thought or time slice of Descartes) is an individual thinking nature or 'I'. And these essences cannot be destroyed given God's decree that any essence shall exist eternally and immutably, at least as contained eminently in God. Second difficulty: Given that souls consist of temporal parts in the same way that bodies consist of spatial parts, how can souls retain strict identity over time? The answer is the same: although enduring substances have really distinct parts, essences—*I*s in the case of souls and *extension* in the case of body *in genera*—are atemporal and indivisible.[43] Reconstructed in this way, the Synopsis proof certainly does not deliver to the Sorbonne theologians what they would like, namely a guarantee of personal immortality. Indeed the upshot is remarkably close to Spinoza's infamous doctrine that "something that pertains to the essence of the mind" is necessarily eternal.[44] Nevertheless, this reconstruction does at least give an essentially Cartesian sense to the notion that the soul is both "single and complete" and "immortal by its very nature."

Acknowledgments

For comments on earlier versions of this essay, I am grateful to Lex Newman, Andrew Pessin, Jorge Secada, Tad Schmaltz, Tom Vinci, Russell Wahl, Andrew Yim, and audiences in St. Louis, Missouri, Halifax, Nova Scotia, and at the 2005 Inland Northwest Philosophy Conference in Moscow, Idaho and Pullman, Washington.

Notes

1. *Meditationes de Prima Philosophia: In qua Dei existentia, et Animae immortalitas demonstratum*. In what follows 'AT' refers to Descartes 1996; 'CSM' refers to Descartes 1985; 'CSMK' refers to Descartes 1991.

2. Arnauld: "Since our distinguished author has undertaken to demonstrate the immortality of the soul, it may rightly be asked whether this evidently follows from the fact that the soul is distinct from the body" (AT 7, 204; CSM 2, 143). Arnauld goes on to observe that most people think the souls of animals are distinct from their bodies yet perishable.

3. Descartes's letter of December, 24, 1639, indicates that Mersenne had earlier complained that Descartes had "not said a word about the immortality of the soul" (AT 3, 266; CSMK, 163). Descartes sends along his Synopsis on December 31 (AT 3, 271; CSMK, 165).

4. AT 7, 13–14; CSM 2, 10. That philosophy can at best provide the "hope" of immortality is repeated in two letters to Elizabeth: AT 4, 282; CSMK, 263 and AT 4, 333; CSMK, 277. On the other hand, in an earlier letter consoling Huygens on the death of his brother, Descartes claims to "know very clearly that they [our souls] last longer than our bodies," since we have an "intellectual memory" that is independent of the body (AT 3, 598; CSMK, 216).

5. Arnauld comments that in the Synopsis Descartes "puts forward the same solution to the point at issue which I was on the verge of proposing" (AT 7, 204; CSM 2, 144). For his part, Mersenne simply repeats in the Second Set of Objections his complaint that the *Meditations* included "not one word" about immortality (AT 7, 127; CSM 2, 91). In reply, Descartes offers a brief restatement of the Synopsis proof (AT 7, 153; CSM 2, 109).

6. See, e.g., AT 7, 188, AT 8A, 60, AT 4, 314; CSM 2, 132; CSM 1, 240; CSMK, 272.

7. Markie 1994, 83. See also Prendergast 1993.

8. See Lewis 1983, 76–77, 1986, 202–204; Sider 2001.

9. Versions of the argument and doctrine are repeated frequently. See AT 6, 35, 45; AT 8A, 13; AT 7, 109, 165, 369–370; AT 5, 53, 155; CSM 1, 128–129, 133, 200; CSM 2, 78–79, 116, 254–255; CSMK, 320.

10. For a detailed discussion of the proof, and its implications for Cartesian physics and metaphysics, see Secada 1990 and Gorham 2004. Descartes's argument, as I understand it, is very similar to one offered a hundred years later by Jonathan

Edwards for the conclusion that "God's preserving created things in being is perfectly equivalent to a continued creation or to his creating those things out of nothing at each moment of their existence" (Edwards 1970, 401). In particular both rely crucially on the necessary simultaneity of cause and effect, which prevents me from causing my future existence. Edwards draws the further conclusion, which I think Descartes must also accept, that "what exists at this moment, by this power, is a new effect; and simply and absolutely considered, not the same with any past existence, though it may be like it, and follows it according to a certain established method" (ibid., 402). However, Edwards's reasons for drawing the further conclusion are different from the reasons Descartes has, and are to my mind unpersuasive. Granted God must always create me out of nothing, why can't he always create the numerically identical me? Paul Helm points out that there is for Edwards a crucial difference between God willing the continued existence of A and God recreating A *ex nihilo*. According to Helm, the latter implies that "A's existence at a time can consist in none of numerically the same parts that A had at an immediately previous time" (Helm 1979,41). But this seems merely to push the original question down to the level of parts: why can't God recreate (out of nothing) the numerically identical parts? Perhaps Edwards thinks things are numerically distinct simply by virtue of being at different times, as he seems to indicate in a long footnote on this question (Edwards 1970, 403n). But then the numerical distinction between time slices of creation would seem to depend somehow on "the nature of time," as Descartes says, rather than on the nature of God's operation, as Edwards says.

11. For Descartes, a substance and an attribute are merely conceptually distinct when "we are unable to form a clear and distinct idea of the substance if we exclude from it the attribute in question" (AT 8A, 30; CSM 1, 214). As mentioned, Gassendi held an absolutist or proto-Newtonian conception of time. Thus, he says, "time is not something dependent on motion, or posterior to it, but is merely indicated by motion as something measured is by the measure" (Gassendi 1972, 396).

12. And in the *Rules for the Direction of the Mind*, he includes duration (along with existence and unity) among those "simple natures" common to both thinking and material things (AT 10, 419; CSM 1, 45). See also AT 7, 20; CSM 2, 14.

13. "There is no real distinction between space, or internal place, and the corporeal substance contained in it; the only difference lies in the way we are accustomed to conceive of them" (AT 8A, 45; CSM 1, 227).

14. It might be suggested that the parts of my duration are modally rather than really distinct, like the shape and motion of a stone. The problem with this is that the parts of my duration are not even modally distinct from me. I can conceive of this stone not having its shape or motion (AT 8A, 29–30; CSM 1, 214), but the parts of my duration are not modally distinct from me, since I cannot conceive of myself continuing to be (as a complete thing) while excluding my continuing duration: "a substance cannot cease to endure without also ceasing to be" (AT 8A, 30; CSM 1,

214). Moreover, a substance can be changed with respect to its modes but not with respect to its duration: "that which always remains unmodified—for example the existence or duration in a thing which exists and endures—should be called not a quality or a mode but an attribute" (AT 8A, 26; CSM 1, 211–212). Finally, if it were merely my soul's modes, rather than the substantial parts of my enduring soul, which are mutually independent, then the argument of the Third Meditation would be undermined since such modes could depend on my enduring soul, making continuous creation unnecessary.

15. See also AT 8A, 29, CSM 1, 213; and AT 8A, 51, CSM 1, 231. The fact that the different parts of matter are really distinct, and hence substances as such, does not imply that each part is an individual *body*. For Descartes, bodies are individuated by relative motion so that "if the division into parts occurs simply in our thoughts there is no resulting change" (AT 8A, 52; CSM 1, 232). Nor does it follow from the fact that my soul is divisible into substantial parts that each of these is an individual *soul* or person. What does follow, however, is that neither matter nor my soul is a simple substance.

16. See also AT 5, 53; CSMK, 320.

17. See also AT 3, 477, CSMK, 202–203; and AT 8A, 72, CSM 1, 246.

18. See also AT 7, 228; CSM 2, 160: "Someone who says that a man's arm is a substance that is really distinct from the rest of the body does not thereby deny that the arm belongs to the nature of the whole man. And saying that the arm belongs to the nature of the whole man does not give rise to the suspicion that it cannot subsist in its own right. . . . Nor do I think I proved too little in saying that the mind is substantially united with the body since that substantial union does not prevent us from having a clear and distinct concept of the mind on its own, as a complete thing." It is, of course, a difficult question whether the mind–body union qualifies as a genuine substance for Descartes. For recent discussion see Hoffman 1986 and Schmaltz 1992.

19. In the Sixth Set of Replies, Descartes distinguishes between two senses in which something can be taken to be one and the same thing. Since we clearly perceive that the same thing that is capable of taking on a shape is capable of being moved, that which has shape and that which has motion have a "unity of nature." By contrast, thought and extension in a human being have a "unity of composition" because although they are perceived differently "they are found in the same man just as bones and flesh are found in the same animal" (AT 7, 424; CSM 2, 286). Unity of nature is thus sharing a nature or form, while unity of composition is forming the whole from parts. Note that two things can be unified in both nature and composition without being substantially identical. Thus, the two halves of a homogeneous body have unity of nature and of composition, but are still distinct things. The same goes for the temporal parts of souls, according to the argument for nonendurance.

20. Lewis 1983, 76.

21. Problems similar to the one I raise have recently been discussed, though in less detail, by Clarence Bonnen and Daniel Flage (2000), p. 9, and Jonathan Bennett (2001), vol. 1, pp. 97–98. Much earlier, Pierre Bayle wrote in his *Dictionnaire*: "How do you know that this very morning God did not allow that soul, which he continually created from the very first moments of your life until now, to fall back into nothingness? How do you know he has not created another soul with modifications like the ones yours had?" (Bayle 1965, 204).

22. For an excellent introduction to the contemporary endurantist–perdurantist debate, see Sider 2001. He provides an interesting illustration of the perdurantist doctrine: "When you touch a person you only touch a part of that person—the hand, say. According to the four-dimensionalist there is another sense in which you only directly touch a part of the person. Even if you could somehow touch all of a person's spatial parts at once, you would still fail to touch all the person, for not all of the person is *then* to be touched. To touch all of a person you must hold him in an interpenetrating total embrace from his birth until his death" (2001, 3).

23. Again, it is worth noting a similarity to Jonathan Edwards. He explicitly invokes a doctrine of perdurance or temporal parts in order to account for the imputation of original sin, arguing that Adam and his posterity share in Adam's sin because they are merely parts of one thing spread out in time, rather like a tree is spread out in space: "Both guilt, or exposedness to punishment, and also depravity of heart, came upon Adam's posterity just as they came upon him, as much as if they had all co-existed, like a tree with many branches" (Edwards 1970, 389). For detailed discussion see Crisp 2005 and Helm 1979.

24. The Cartesian soul would then be similar to the Humean self: "It is still true that every distinct perception which enters into the composition of the mind is distinct and is different and distinguishable and separable from every other perception, either contemporary or successive" (Hume 1978, 259). See also Edwards 1970, 398–399.

25. Bennett 2001, vol. 1, 98.

26. See also AT 11, 364, CSM 1, 346; and AT 11, 379, CSM 1, 352.

27. See also AT 3, 422; CSMK, 189.

28. See also AT 3, 503–506; CSMK, 207–208: "Yet if the soul is recognized merely as a substantial form, while other such forms consist in the configuration and motion of parts, this very privileged status it has as compared with other forms shows that its nature is quite different from theirs. And this difference in nature opens the easiest route to demonstrating its non-materiality and immortality. . . ." See also AT 4, 166; CSMK, 243.

29. AT 8A, 27; CSM 1, 212; AT 3, 66; CSMK, 148.

30. AT 8A, 30–31; CSM 1, 215; AT 4, 350; CSMK, 280–281.

31. "... this 'I', that is, this soul by which I am what I am" (AT 6, 33; CSM 1, 127).

32. Note that I am referring to distinct *bodies*, rather distinct *material parts* of bodies. See note 15 above.

33. While endorsing St. Thomas Aquinas's position, Descartes also uses the occasion to poke fun at the "Angelic Doctor": "he described each angel in as much detail as if he had been right in their midst" (AT 5, 157). For Aquinas's statement of the doctrine see Aquinas 1952, part 1, q. 50, art. 4.

34. Another possibility is that finite minds are only modally distinct from one another. This seems to have been the view of the Cartesian Sylvain Régis. See Lennon 1994. For criticism of this way of interpreting Regis, see Schmaltz 2002, 209–210.

35. For example, in response to Gassendi he appeals to "the common philosophical maxim that the essences of things are indivisible" (AT 7, 371; CSM 2, 255–256).

36. See also AT 5, 160; CSMK, 343.

37. See also AT 8B, 167; CSMK, 222–223. For a detailed defense of a 'Platonic' conception of Cartesian essences, see Schmaltz 1991. See also Vinci 1998, 64–69.

38. See also AT 1, 152; CSMK, 25.

39. According to Tad Schmaltz, the Cartesian Robert Desgabets sharply distinguished between the 'successive duration' of our life, which is temporal and necessarily united to corporeal motions, and our 'substantial being', which is an eternal essence. Desgabets argued that Descartes's Third Meditation proof implied that the former, but not that the latter, is corruptible and in need of continuous conservation by God. See Schmaltz 2002, 99–107.

40. See also AT 7, 42, CSM 2, 29; and AT 7, 79, CSM 2, 55.

41. For a detailed discussion of this abstruse notion, see Gorham 2003.

42. See AT 8A, 42, CSM 1, 224; and AT 8A, 47–48, CSM 1, 228.

43. The relation between the individual essence and the perduring soul should be understood on the Platonic model of the relation between the eternal essence of a triangle and formally existing triangles. Just as a collection of distinct things can all be considered triangles owing to their common essence, the distinct parts of my soul's duration can each be called the same 'I' owing their common individual essence. But neither the 'I' nor the soul endures: not the former because it is atemporal, and not the latter because it is composed of temporal parts.

44. *Ethics*, part V, prop. 23. As Steven Nadler has recently argued, Spinoza's demonstration of this doctrine neither establishes, nor was intended to establish, personal immortality. At best it shows only that in this life we can transcend our own individuality and temporality by pursuing the so-called third kind of knowledge, the intuitive apprehension the formal essence God's eternal attributes. See Nadler 2002. The distinction between the eternal essences of things and their durational existence is much more explicit in Spinoza than in Descartes. Thus in the *Metaphysical Thoughts*, Spinoza distinguished between "beings of Essence," which are contained (eminently) in God, and "beings of Existence," which are the essences existing outside of God. The former "formal essences" are eternal because they "depend on the divine essence alone" (Spinoza 1985, 305), whereas the latter are divisible into temporal parts because duration is an attribute of existence and "composed of parts" (ibid., 310).

References

Aquinas, T. 1952. *Summa theologica*. Trans. Fathers of the Dominican Province. In *Great Books of the Western World*, vols. 19 and 20. Chicago: Encyclopedia Britannica.

Bayle, P. 1965. *Historical and Critical Dictionary*. Trans. and ed. R. Popkin. Indianapolis, IN: Bobbs-Merrill.

Bennett, J. 2001. *Learning from Six Philosophers*, 2 vols. Oxford: Oxford University Press.

Bonnen, C., and D. Flage. 2000. Descartes: The Matter of Time. *International Studies in Philosophy* 32:1–11.

Crisp, O. D. 2005. *Jonathan Edwards and the Metaphysics of Sin*. Hampshire: Ashgate.

Descartes, R. 1996. *Oeuvres de Descartes*, 11 vols. Ed. C. Adam and P. Tannery. Paris: J. Vrin.

Descartes, R. 1985. *The Philosophical Writings of Descartes*, 2 vols. Ed. J. Cottingham, R. Stoothoff, and D. Murdoch. Cambridge: Cambridge University Press.

Descartes, R. 1991. *The Philosophical Writings of Descartes: The Correspondence*. Ed. J. Cottingham, R. Stoothoff, D. Murdoch, and A. Kenny. Cambridge: Cambridge University Press.

Edwards, J. 1970. *Original Sin: Works of Jonathan Edwards*, vol. 3. Ed. C. Holbrook. New Haven, CT: Yale University Press.

Gassendi, P. 1972. *The Selected Works of Pierre Gassendi*. Ed. C. Bush. New York: Johnson Reprints.

Gorham, G. 2003. Descartes's Dilemma of Eminent Containment. *Dialogue: Canadian Philosophical Review* 42:3–25.

Gorham, G. 2004. Cartesian Causation: "Continuous, Instantaneous, Overdetermined." *Journal of the History of Philosophy* 42:389–423.

Helm, P. 1979. Jonathan Edwards and the Doctrine of Temporal Parts. *Archiv fur Geschichte der Philosophie* 61:37–51.

Hoffman, P. 1986. The Unity of Descartes' Man. *Philosophical Review* 95:339–370.

Hume, D. 1978. *A Treatise of Human Nature*, 2nd ed. Ed. L. A. Selby-Bigge. Oxford: Oxford University Press.

Lennon, T. 1994. The Problem of Individuation among the Cartesians. In *Individuation and Identity in Early Modern Philosophy*, ed. J. Gracia and K. Barber. Albany, NY: SUNY Press.

Lewis, D. 1983. *Philosophical Papers*, vol. 1. Oxford: Oxford University Press.

Lewis, D. 1986. *On the Plurality of Worlds*. Oxford: Blackwell.

Markie, P. 1994. Descartes' Concept of Substance. In *Reason, Will, and Sensation: Studies in Descartes' Metaphysics*, ed. J. Cottingham. Oxford: Oxford University Press.

Nadler, S. 2002. Eternity and Immortality in Spinoza's Ethics. In *Midwest Studies in Philosophy 26: Renaissance and Early Modern Philosophy*, ed. P. French and H. Wettstein. Oxford: Blackwell.

Prendergast, T. L. 1993. Descartes: Immortality, Human Bodies, and God's Absolute Freedom. *Modern Schoolman* 71:17–46.

Schmaltz, T. 1991. Platonism and Descartes' View of Immutable Essences. *Archiv für Geschichte der Philosophie* 79:129–170.

Schmaltz, T. 1992. Descartes and Malebranche on Mind and Mind–Body Union. *Philosophical Review* 101:281–325.

Schmaltz, T. 2002. *Radical Cartesianism*. Cambridge: Cambridge University Press.

Secada, J. E. K. 1990. Descartes on Time and Causality. *Philosophical Review* 99:45–72.

Sider, T. 2001. *Four-Dimensionalism*. Oxford: Oxford University Press.

Spinoza, B. 1985. *The Collected Works of Spinoza*, volume 1. Ed. E. M. Curley. Princeton, NJ: Princeton University Press.

Vinci, T. 1998. *Cartesian Truth*. Oxford: Oxford University Press.

III The Self

9 Persons, Animals, and Human Beings

Harold Noonan

Introduction

The position I defend takes psychological continuity as the sole and sufficient criterion of personal identity.[1] I here confront the suggestion recently made by a number of authors, including Paul Snowdon (1991), Peter van Inwagen (1990), and Eric Olson (1997, 2002), that *any* such psychological approach must be mistaken, because in fact the correct account of personal identity is given by the biological approach, according to which we are human beings whose identity over time requires no kind of psychological continuity or connectedness whatsoever.

The standard objection to the biological approach is that it conflicts with our intuition that in the transplant case, in which Brown's brain is transplanted into Robinson's body, with consequent transfer of psychology, the survivor Brownson is the brain donor Brown. This "transplant intuition" has been challenged by recent defenders of that approach, particularly Olson, who have also developed additional arguments against the psychological approach. The aim of this chapter is to show that the biological theorist's challenge to the transplant intuition can be met and that his additional arguments against the psychological approach are answerable.

First, however, we need a more precise statement of the biological approach.

What the biological approach claims is that *we*—you and I and any other readers of this essay—are animals of a certain kind, that is, human beings, members of the species *Homo sapiens*. Since we are persons it follows that *some* persons are human beings. The biological approach does not exclude the possibility of persons that are not human beings, or even animals, but it does insist that *we* are human animals, and as such have the persistence conditions of human animals. The second claim made by the biological theorist is that such persistence conditions involve *no* form of psychological continuity whatsoever; they are entirely biological. For psychological continuity is never either a necessary or a sufficient condition of the identity over time of an animal.

According to the biological theorist, then, things of very different kinds can be persons, and the persistence conditions of an entity that is a person of a particular kind will depend on the kind of thing it is. We are persons for whom the persistence conditions are entirely biological, but this will not be so for divine persons, or inorganic robotic persons. Thus there are no necessary and sufficient conditions for personal identity as such, of the type the psychological approach suggests, but for each kind of person there are necessary and sufficient conditions for the identity of persons of that kind.

Olson develops this point by appeal to the familiar distinction between *substance* sortals, which tell us *what* a thing is, and *phase* sortals, which merely tell us, as it were, *how* it is during a certain period of its existence. Locke's definition of a person as a "thinking, intelligent being . . . ," he suggests, is not a definition of a substance sortal at all, but merely a phase sortal. To be a person, on this account, is merely to be an entity with certain capacities, and an entity that has such capacities may have existed before it gained them and may survive their loss; 'person' is merely a functional term, like 'genius' or 'prophet'.

Olson consequently proposes that for each of us there was a time, when he was a fetus, when he existed but was not a person, and for some of us there will be times in the future, after brain damage, when we are still in existence, but merely as human vegetables, not persons. It is an important point for Olson that we accept that in such a "vegetable case" the human animal that was once a person in the Lockean sense continues to exist, though not to be a person, and that each mature human animal was once a fetus. For if we accept these things we must accept that psychological continuity is not necessary for the persistence of the human animal.

Nor, Olson insists, is it sufficient. In the familiar transplant case there may be dispute about whether the brain recipient is the same *person* as the brain donor (as the psychological approach dictates), but there is no denying that he is not the same *human animal* as the brain donor.

Or rather, on Olson's view, it *is* correct to say in this case that the brain recipient is the same human animal as the brain donor, but this is not because of the psychological continuity that obtains and is no evidence against a purely biological account of animal identity.

We have to distinguish, Olson thinks, between *whole brain* transplants and *upper brain* transplants. The upper brain is the organ of thought, the seat of consciousness, transplantation of which will carry with it full psychological continuity. But the lower brain, more particularly, the brainstem, is the biological control center of the living human animal and essential to his identity. Thus if a person's upper brain is destroyed, he, the living animal, will continue to exist as a living vegetable so long as his brainstem continues to function, but will cease to exist when the brainstem is destroyed. But if my brainstem is destroyed and replaced, and the result is a creature psychologically and bodily (except for the brainstem) continuous with me as I was before, then I do not survive. So if my whole brain, including my brainstem, is transplanted, according to Olson, it is unproblematic that the animal who is the original owner of the brain goes with it, and it would seem (although Olson does not explicitly pronounce on this) that the result would be the same if *only* the brainstem was transplanted. But transplantation of the upper brain alone, Olson thinks, is a different matter. Such a transplant, although securing that the recipient is fully psychologically continuous with the donor, will not ensure that he is the same animal as the donor.

The biological approach is therefore inconsistent with any form of the psychological approach. According to the former I will not survive upper brain transplantation, according to the latter, I will; according to the former I was once a fetus and may be someday a human vegetable, according to the latter I was never a fetus and can be assured that whatever happens I will never be a human vegetable.

Though the incompatibility of the two approaches is evident it will be useful to exhibit it in the form of an explicit argument as follows (in what follows I use 'psychological continuer' to mean 'entity whose persistence conditions are entirely psychological'):

(1)   We are human beings.

(2)   The persistence conditions of human beings are entirely biological.

(3)   Therefore, we are not psychological continuers (from 1 and 2).

(4)   We are persons.

(5)   Therefore, some persons are not psychological continuers (from 3 and 4).

In this argument the first two premises define the biological approach and the conclusion is the negation of the defining proposition of the psychological approach.

But now it is evident that that one does not have to be a biological theorist to reject the Psychological Approach, for the following argument is also valid.

(1)   We are human beings.

(2)   The persistence conditions of human beings are partly biological.

(3)   Therefore, we are not psychological continuers (from 1 and 2).

(4)   We are persons.

(5)   Therefore, some persons are not psychological continuers (from 3 and 4).

In this argument the first two premises define what I shall call 'the hybrid approach' to personal identity (it is suggested by McDowell 1997, Parfit 2007, and Wiggins 1996). If the biological approach is rejected it is the obvious next move for the opponent of the psychological approach, but I shall not have space to discuss it here. So let us now consider the merits of the biological approach.

The Transplant Intuition

The main, and at first sight compelling, argument against the biological approach is based on the *transplant intuition*: if Brownson has Brown's upper brain with consequent psychological continuity and connectedness, he *is* Brown. So if I am Brown, contemplating the transplant, I should expect that I will continue to exist as Brownson. So it cannot be true both that I am a human being and that the persistence conditions of human beings are entirely biological.

This is a very powerful argument. As Lynne Rudder Baker writes: "If sameness of persons consists in sameness of living organism, then all of these stories [all variants on the brain transplant case in the philosophical literature] would be not only fictional, but incoherent. . . . Anyone who takes hundreds of years of thought experiments as attempting to depict what is metaphysically incoherent should show how many have gone so badly wrong" (Baker 2000, 123–124).

Thus the biological theorist has to explain away intuitions, in particular, the transplant intuition, which have considerable hold on us. Until he does we have no reason to reject them. The situation is really no different form other cases in which we make judgments about persistence. We distinguish between artifacts and the masses of matter that make them up, and what makes it compelling to do so is our conviction that artifacts can undergo change of matter and that the matter constituting an artifact at one time might constitute a different artifact (of the same or different kind) at another. The fact that in the case of personal identity divergences from bodily identity of the type illustrated by transplant cases are, so far as we now know, merely possible, does not lessen one whit our conviction that if such cases were to occur, persons would have to be regarded as distinct from organisms, and hence does not in any way reduce the strength of the case for the conceptual distinction between personal identity and identity of organism.

The force of the transplant intuition can perhaps be better appreciated if it is seen as the outcome of a typical philosophical thought experiment. In general, in any area of philosophy, conceptual analysis proceeds by appeal to such thought experiments (cf. Jackson and Chalmers 2001, to which the rest of this paragraph is indebted). We can evaluate the extension of a concept in epistemically possible circumstances whether or not the circumstances are in fact actual or counterfactual, and we can do so when the circumstances are not described in ways that directly involve the use of the concept. If the circumstances are sufficiently different from those we know to obtain, we may be unable to make a judgment about the application of the concept; but this will not be a mere consequence of the circumstances described being possibly counterfactual. Thus we can inquire whether, in circumstances described in a certain way, without appeal to that concept, the concept of knowledge would have application; and we can inquire whether, in circumstances described in a certain way, without appeal to that concept, the concept of water would have application. *Mutatis mutandis*, we can ask whether, in circumstances described in a certain way, without appeal to that concept, the concept of personal identity would have application. Unless a general skepticism about conceptual analysis or philosophical thought experiments is appropriate, it is merely ad hoc to reject the transplant intuition because it concerns the application of the concept of personal identity.

Moreover, the transplant intuition is not an isolated response to one thought experiment. It coheres with our responses to closely related cases (in what follows I draw heavily on Parfit 2007, with changes made to accommodate the need to distinguish between whole-brain and upper-brain transplants).

Consider first a case in which I become paralyzed and lose sensation in all of my body below the neck. Suppose also that, because of damage to my heart and lungs, my brain is connected to a heart-lung machine. In this case, according to both the biological theorist and the psychological theorist, I would continue to exist, the same animal and the same person.

Suppose next that in a complex and brilliantly skillful operation, my brainstem is replaced by an inorganic substance gradually, bit by bit (Olson

1997, 141). There is no interruption of consciousness throughout (the surgeons use only a local anesthetic).

Suppose now that in a third operation, after the replacement of the whole of my brainstem, my head, containing the organic upper brain and the inorganic replacement for my brainstem, is disconnected from the rest of my numb and paralyzed body. Consciousness continues throughout, and the result is a conscious being indistinguishable in its mentality and physical structure from the human animal that would have existed (according to the biological theorist) if originally my entire head, including an organic upper and lower brain, had been detached from my body and kept alive.

Suppose next that the upper brain from the disconnected head together with its covering of skin and bones is grafted on to the headless body of a second person, my upper brain is connected to his lower brain, and the resultant whole brain is disconnected from the heart-lung machine and connected to his heart and lungs.

This final case is, of course, just the original upper-brain transplant case, presented as the terminus of a series of cases. But presenting it in this way makes its evident that the biological theorist cannot just blankly deny that the upper-brain recipient is the upper-brain donor. If he does so he must accept the consequences of doing so for the description of the other cases. In fact, it is clear that the second case is the crucial one. If the biological theorist is to deny that the upper-brain transplant recipient is the donor in the upper-brain transplant case, he must deny that the original personal survives in the second case. He cannot plausibly deny that *some* conscious subject is present at the end of the complex operation, since it is no part of his position that consciousness requires an organic base. Thus he must say of this case what Olson does in fact say: "The result would be a rational conscious being with your mind . . . despite appearances, the resulting being would not be you, [or] even a human being. . . . Either that being is one of those people that aren't living organisms, along with gods and angels and rational electronic computers, to whom the Biological Approach does not apply; or there is no thinking being there at all, but only thoughts and sensations that are not the thoughts *of* anyone" (Olson 1997, 141–142). A surprising conclusion, to say the least.

The case against the biological approach based on the transplant intuition is thus a formidable one. But let us see what its defender can say in response.

Rejection of the Transplant Intuition

There are two possible lines of reply. One, taken by Snowdon (1991), is simply to deny the transplant intuition; the other, taken by Olson, is to attempt to explain it away.

Snowdon's view is that though "there is no counter intuition [to the transplant intuition] that can be generated, and there are no grounds of a general sort for being suspicious of such intuitions, no independent evidence that they lead us astray . . . this is just a case where we find ourselves with what, in the light of all the evidence, has to be recognized as a deviant, although recalcitrant, intuition" (Snowdon 1991, 226).

Crucial to the defensibility of this view, however, is the claim that "in the light of all the evidence" the transplant intuition has to be recognized as "deviant." Of course, it has to be agreed that *if* the psychological approach can be refuted and the biological approach vindicated, then intuitions to the contrary, even if recalcitrant and inexplicable, must be rejected. The key question in relation to Snowdon's view, then, is whether this is the case, which is what we will be considering later in the essay.

But now we need to examine Olson's attempt to explain away the transplant intuition, which, if successful, will at least shift the burden of proof off the shoulders of the biological theorist.

The basis of Olson's explanation is Parfit's thesis that identity is not what matters in survival (Parfit 1971, 1984). In a nutshell, the explanation is as follows: we do have a strong intuition that in the transplant case the upper-brain recipient is (the same person as) the upper-brain donor. This is because the upper-brain recipient is the Parfitian survivor of the upper-brain donor (i.e., stands to the donor in the relation that matters in survival) and we mistakenly believe that identity is what matters in survival. So we are led to believe that the upper-brain recipient *is* the upper-brain donor. Olson elaborates this explanation through four sections of his book (Olson 1997, 52–70), arguing that it is the upper-brain recipient that the upper-brain donor should be prudentially concerned about in advance of the transplant, that it is the upper-brain recipient who should be held morally responsible for the upper-brain donor's deeds, and that it is the upper-brain recipient (rather than the surviving empty-headed upper-brain donor) who should be treated by others as the original person. He also suggests that we in fact use 'same person' in ordinary speech in a "practical" sense in which it expresses not numerical identity but just the holding of those relations of psychological continuity and connectedness that, according to Parfit's thesis, matters in survival (so x is the same person as y

in the practical sense if and only if x is a Parfitian survivor of y or y is a Parfitian survivor of x). Olson's "bold conjecture" is that (in a upper-brain-transfer version of Locke's prince–cobbler example: "The fact that Brainy is the same person after the operation as Prince was before it, in this practical sense of 'same person' is the main source of the Transplant Intuition' (Olson 1997, 69).

The first thing to be said in response to all this is that it stands or falls with Parfit's claim that identity is not what matters in survival. So, I think, it falls (Noonan 2003).

But a second point needs to be made. Whatever else is to be said about it, one thing that is clear about Parfit's thesis is that it is not, and was not intended to be, a platitude. What it says is that we do *not* have any non-derivative concern for our own future existence and well-being, but only for the existence and well-being of our Parfitian survivors, although we *mistakenly* think that we have such nonderivative first-person concern. Such an astonishing thesis cannot just be accepted without argument. A compulsory question for the biological theorist, then, is whether *he* can endorse the only extant argument for Parfit's thesis, the argument from fission.

The argument from fission requires (a) that it is conceivable that a situation occur in which I stand to each of two later people in such a relation that either of them, but for the existence of the other, would be straightforwardly identical with me; (b) that the correct description of such a situation is that the original person ceases to exist, but would not have done if only one of the later people had existed; but (c) that it would be quite irrational in such a situation for the original person to be concerned about the impending fission as he would be about his impending death, or to think that he could gain anything by preventing the fission by reducing the number of fission products to one.

In order to endorse this argument the biological theorist must thus accept (as required by (a)) that a "reduplication situation" is conceivable in which there are two later *human beings*, each of which stands to an earlier *human being* in such biologically describable relations that either of them, but for the existence of the other, would be straightforwardly the same *human being* as the earlier one. He also has to accept, as required by (b), in contradiction to the Only x and y principle[2] as a principle governing the concept of a human being, that the identity of a human being over time is not something necessarily determined intrinsically, but that the best account of that concept has a "best candidate" or "no rival candidate" structure, so that in the reduplication situation the original human being ceases to exist, and two new human beings come into existence, but that the original human being would not have ceased to exist if only one candidate for identity with him had existed at the later time. And, third, of course, the biological theorist has to say, as required by (c), that contemplating the prospect of fission the original human being ought, given his actual desires and concerns, regard it as quite irrational to seek to prevent what is literally his death (the fission) by ensuring that only one fission product results.

Of course, the biological theorist *can* endorse these claims. But it is important to note that they are not merely optional for him if he is to explain the transplant intuition away in Olson's way, by appeal to Parfit's thesis, and they are not claims one would not initially have thought of as particularly congenial to a biological theorist. This is particularly so for the second claim, that is, the rejection of the Only *x* and *y* principle as a constraint on the biological concept of a human being. Olson himself writes of the "nonbranching" or *uniqueness requirement* (that you survive only if you stand in some relation to exactly one future or past being): "It is a startling claim . . . but no one accepts the Uniqueness Requirement because it sounds right. The Transplant Intuition has led us into a quandary, and the Uniqueness Requirement is seen as the best way out; it is a theoretical necessity" (Olson 1997, 49). However, it is not the transplant intuition but its rejection that requires the biological theorist to endorse the uniqueness requirement, and Olson is thus committed, as much as Parfit, to this "startling claim."

So far, then, we have seen that explaining away the transplant intuition by appeal to Parfit's thesis (a) is unacceptable because that thesis is false (as argued in Noonan 2003), and (b) even if this is denied, it is at least difficult for a biological theorist given the assumptions he must take on board from Parfit to motivate his acceptance of the thesis. The third difficulty the biological theorist faces is that he in fact needs to make a greater divide than even Parfit himself does between literal survival and "what matters" if he is to explain away the transplant intuition.

Parfit's argument from fission, if accepted, establishes that contrary to what we believe, we do not have a nonderivative concern for our own future existence and well-being, that is, that the relation that a future person must have to me to be an object of the nonderivative concern we mistakenly think we have only to ourselves is *not* identity but what Parfit calls "relation R" and what I have spoken of as the relation, the holding of which between me now and a future person is necessary and sufficient for that person to be one of my "Parfitian survivors." Another way of identifying this relation is to say that it is the relation that answers the question 'If a future will be good, how, given our basic desires and concerns, should we want that future to be related to us?' (following and modifying Parfit 2007). Olson thinks that this relation is the one expressed by 'same person' in the practical sense.

Now Parfit's fission argument, if sound, establishes that a future person can be one of my Parfitian survivors, can be, in the practical sense, the same person as me, without being me. But it can *only* establish that this is so in cases such as the fission case, in which, for logical reasons such as the transitivity of identity, *literal* identity is precluded (Shoemaker 1999, 504). In other words, Parfit's argument gives no reason at all to deny that *if a future person is my Parfitian survivor then he is literally identical with me unless fission or fusion or some other circumstance obtains that precludes literal identity on logical grounds*. Equally, Parfit's argument gives no reason to deny that *if I exist at a future time I am then one of my present self's Parfitian survivors* (i.e., that my relation to my future self is that which I would want to obtain between my present self and a future one given my basic desires and concerns *if* that future was a good one). But if the first of these conditional is correct then if my upper-brain recipient is my Parfitian survivor, that is, is the same person as me in the practical sense, then he is literally identical with me. So the biological theorist, unlike Parfit, must deny the first conditional. He must also deny the second conditional. For he must hold that if Brown's upper brain is transplanted into Robinson's head and Robinson's upper brain is transplanted into Brown's head, then Robinson-posttransplant is the same person in the practical sense as Brown-pretransplant and Brown-posttransplant is the same person in the practical sense as Robinson-pretransplant, though Robinson-posttransplant remains the same human animal as Robinson-pretransplant and Brown-posttransplant is remains the same human animal as Brown-pretransplant (Brown continues to exist as the same human animal when his upper brain is removed if his brainstem remains intact, and the addition of a new upper brain can hardly take that animal out of existence and bring into being a new one identical neither with Brown nor Robinson). Consequently, Brown-pretransplant contemplating his posttransplant future must *deny* that that future belongs to one of his Parfitian survivors while acknowledging that it is indeed *his* future.

It is reasonable, I think, to take the two conditionals identified in the last paragraph as analytic of our concepts of a person and personal identity (see also Shoemaker 1999). But, however this may be, the biological theorist has not explained away the transplant intuition until he refutes them.

The "Too Many Minds" Objection

Let us now return to the basic argument against the psychological approach, the argument that we simply *are* human beings, but human beings are not psychological continuers, so we are not psychological continuers. Why must we accept that we are (literally identical with) human beings?

A bad answer is that we must accept this because it is what we *say*. But this is open to a standard and straightforward reply (Shoemaker 1999). Just as a statue constituted of bronze 'is' a piece of bronze without being identical with any piece of bronze, so each of us 'is' an animal in the sense of coinciding with one and being constituted of the same matter as one— but this 'is' is the 'is' of constitution, not identity.

Facts of usage can therefore not force us to accept that we are not merely coincident with, but are literally identical with, human animals; so, to repeat, why *must* we accept this?

The answer given by Olson (1997) (anticipated by Carter 1989, Ayers 1990, 278–292, and Snowdon 1991) is the "too many minds" objection (so called by Shoemaker 1999), or, as Olson prefers to refer to it, the problem of the thinking animal.

The basic structure of the too many minds objection is straightforward. If I am a psychological continuer, I am not a human animal. But if I am not a human animal but merely coincident with one, then, as I sit here, writing this, so does another "thinking intelligent being with reason and reflection." For human animals are surely thinking things, and if the human animal coincident with me lacks what it takes to think, so do I (it shares my brain, nervous system, sensory inputs, behavior, and all my history— although it came into existence somewhat earlier and may go out of existence somewhat later). So there are at least two rational thinking beings within my skin, a person and an animal. I am never alone (and nor are you). But the animal I share my skin with is not a person, for the psychological approach does not apply to it (so Locke's definition of a 'person' is wrong). But doesn't it think (wrongly) that it is a person? Presumably; since it shares all my thoughts it must do. But then how do I know that I am the person and not the animal? I have my reasons for thinking this, no doubt, but since the animal with which I share my skin has them too they must be insufficient, for it is *not* a person. If I were the animal and not the person I would still think that I was the person, so for all I know I *am* the animal making a mistake, and not the person. But, of course, this is all quite absurd.

Thus goes the too many minds objection to the psychological approach. The objection is that if we take the psychological approach seriously it involves an absurdly inflated ontology (we are never alone) and an outrageous skepticism (no one can ever know that he is a person). And, if that were not quite enough, its acceptance undermines the formulation of the very problem to which it is supposed to be a solution, since human animals are rational intelligent beings, that is, Lockean persons, and yet they are not psychological continuers. So the psychological approach cannot be an answer to the question it was originally advertised as an answer to, namely the question, 'What is the (single) criterion of personal identity?' In fact, there can be no answer to that question.

All this, however, should have produced a sense of déjà vu. For Locke's original account of personal identity, with its distinction between persons and thinking substances, is open to an objection with exactly the same logical structure.[3] (In developing this response I ignore two other replies, both made by Shoemaker [1999]. The first is that the biological theorist is also vulnerable to the too many minds objection, since he must acknowledge the existence of an object coincident with an animal throughout his life but not identical with it—the object that will be its corpse, or its "corpse to be." The second is that a proper appreciation of functionalism allows us to see that animals are not thinking things at all. The first reply seems unconvincing, since there seems no theoretical necessity for the biological theorist to acknowledge the existence of the "corpse to be." The second reply seems insufficiently general, since it cannot apply to Olson's [2002] problem of the "thinking person segment" mentioned below.) Locke's position is that persons are distinct from the thinking substances that "think in" them, but that the thinking substances share all the psychological properties of the persons they "think in" and so *are* persons by Locke's definition (for persons "borrow," as it were, their psychological properties from the substances that "think in" them). So no person is ever alone. Moreover, the thinking substance presently "thinking in" me must (wrongly) think that it is a person, since I do so. And since it is wrong but has just the same reasons I have, I cannot *know* that I am a person, even if I am one. Finally, since Locke's definition of a 'person' applies to thinking substances as well as to persons, Locke's solution to the problem of personal identity cannot be a solution to the problem as he formulates it. In fact, that problem can have no solution. As Locke himself says, identity is relative to the idea, but it turns out that on Locke's account the idea of a person applies to distinct kinds of thing with distinct identity conditions, so relativization to the idea in this case fails to yield a sensible question.

To defend Locke against this objection we must reject his original definition of a 'person', replace it with the concept of the *self*, or object of first-person reference, and insist that when a thinking substance thinks an 'I'-thought its reference is not that thinking substance itself, but the person it then constitutes. Thus, to Chisholm's question to Locke: "If I want my dinner does it follow that two of us want my dinner? Or does the thinking substance want its dinner and not mine?" (Chisholm 1976), the answer is that the thinking substance wants *me* to have *my* dinner, but the only way it can think that thought is by thinking: "I want my dinner."

This replacement of the Lockean concept by the concept of the self, so explained, may be justified by reflection on what the problem of personal identity fundamentally is. We can put this problem by asking: 'What are the constraints on the history of a person? What changes can a person can survive? What changes will terminate a person's existence?', or each of us can formulate the problem for himself by asking, 'What are the constraints on *my* history? What changes can *I* survive? What changes will terminate *my* existence?'[4] But, in fact, it is clear that the latter, indexical, formulation is the basic one. Our interest in personal identity is fundamentally an interest in our *own* identity (similarly, our interest in the nature of persons is fundamentally an interest in the basic Cartesian question 'What am I?'). The usual formulations of the problem of personal identity are merely attempts to capture the content of the primary indexical formulation in nonindexical terms. Thus 'person' as it occurs in the standard formulations of the problem *just means* 'object of first-person reference', that is, that which each of us calls 'I'. The replacement of Locke's definition by the concept of the self in the formulation of the problem is thus merely a correction of an error in Locke's discussion.[5,6]

Now let us return to the too many minds Objection. Since the logical structure of this objection to the psychological approach is identical to the logical structure of the objection to Locke just reviewed, the answer to the latter objection applies *mutatis mutandis* to the former. What the psychological continuity theorist must do to answer the too many minds objection is reject the original definition of a person, substitute for it the notion of the object of self-reference, and insist on a distinction between the 'I'-user and the reference of 'I'. Then he can say that when a person and a human animal coincide the animal can indeed think 'I'-thoughts, but is not thereby constituted a person, for the reference of its 'I'-thoughts is not *itself* but the person with whom it is sharing those thoughts.

The rule of reference for 'I' is thus not that the reference of 'I' is the thinker of the 'I'-thought (there is *no* unique thinker), but that the reference is the *person* thinking the 'I'-thought.[7] No other rule is needed, since whenever a human animal is thinking an 'I'-thought, so, on this account, is a person. Moreover, the animal's thought 'I am a person' is not a mistaken thought about *it*, but a correct thought about the person it coincides with (the animal *can* think about itself, however, just not in the first-person mode).[8] So although it has just the same reasons for thinking what it does that the person has, it does not follow that the person's reasons are insufficient; and the outrageous skepticism is avoided. I can know that I am a person, since if I were the animal and not the person thinking the thought I am currently thinking in thinking that I am a person, I would *still* be right (see Noonan 1998, 2001).

To elaborate a little. Both the person and the animal can know that their utterance of 'I am a person' is true. And each understands this sentence, so each knows the proposition it expresses (by contrast, a monolingual Frenchman may know that an utterance of, say, 'London is pretty' is true, but not know the proposition it expresses, that London is pretty). In virtue of knowing this, the animal knows, *of* the person, that it is a person, and the person (who, of course, knows no less) knows, *of* the person, that it is a person. So the person knows, *of* himself, that he is a person (if *x* knows *of* *x* that he is *F*, then *x* knows *of* himself that he is *F*). I know that what I express by 'I am a person' is true. Since I understand this sentence I also know the proposition thus expressed, and in doing so I know, *of* myself, that I am a person. But no more than this can be required for knowledge *de se*, of oneself, that one is a person.

The animal, on the other hand, does not know *of* itself that it is a person, since it is not. It does, however, know the thought it would express by saying 'I am a person'. Does it know that it is itself a person? Is it correct to say 'the animal knows that it itself is a person'? Yes: 'it itself' is here the indirect reflexive. It is not an expression whose reference is the animal. In fact, it does not refer at all. 'The animal knows that it itself is a person' is a report that the animal knows what it could correctly express by saying 'I am a person'.

I find it helpful to think of this in Fregean terms, following Geach (1976). The first-person pronoun 'I' has a constant linguistic meaning but expresses different senses in the mouths of different utterers. The sense of 'I' as uttered by *x* is a function of *x*; it is a different sense from that expressed by *y* if *x* is a person distinct from the person *y*. We can speak of the *ego* function which carries any *x* to the sense 'I' has in *x*'s mouth. Then, allowing Greek letters as variables ranging over senses, we may say that '*x* thinks that it itself is *F*' means 'for some α, $\alpha=ego(x)$ and *x* thinks [α is *F*]'—here the thought that [α is *F*] is the thought you would express in language by attaching the predicate 'is F' to a subject term whose sense is the mode of presentation α.

So it is true that the animal thinks that it itself is a person. But it is not true that the animal thinks *of* itself that it is a person, since the assumption required for this inference is that in all cases $ego(x)$ is a mode of presentation of x, and if x is not a person this is not so; in this case, $ego(x)$ is a mode of presentation of the person with whom x shares the first-person thought.

This is what Olson (2002) calls my "linguistic solution" to the problem of the thinking animal.[9] I now turn to his objections.

The first is that the linguistic solution to the problem of the thinking animal makes it too easy for psychological continuity theorists. They can prove, trivially, that the view that we are animals is self-contradictory, as follows:

We are whatever we refer to when we say 'I': the word 'I' refers only to psychological continuers. Thus we are psychological continuers. But human animals are not psychological continuers. Hence we are not animals. Q.E.D.

This objection fails. It is not trivially self-contradictory, if the linguistic solution is accepted, that we are human animals. It is not an a priori truth that human beings have late vegetative states or fetal states to which, in their mature stage, they are related by no relations of psychological continuity or connectedness whatsoever. So it is not an a priori truth that human beings are not psychological continuers. It is an a priori truth that human beings, unlike psychological continuers, *can* have late vegetative stages or fetal stages to which, when mature, they stand in no relations of psychological continuity whatsoever; but merely modal differences do not ensure nonidentity (witness Goliath and Lumpl, Gibbard 1975).

Olson's second objection is that if the linguistic proposal is correct I do not know I exist, even if I know that my thoughts have a thinker, since I know that I am a psychological continuer if I exist, and I do not know that there are any psychological continuers. But this objection takes me to mean more by 'psychological continuer' than I do. Psychological continuers are things whose history exhibits psychological continuity (as Olson himself puts it, on the temporal parts ontology they are maximal aggregates of psychologically interconnected stages). So if there is thinking going on (of an appropriately sophisticated kind), a psychological continuer, albeit perhaps a very short-lived one, exists. So whenever there is a thinker (of a sufficiently sophisticated kind), there is a person, even if there are several thinkers.

There is also a problem with the form of argument in Olson's second objection. It is something like the following: 'It is impossible to doubt that *P*. But it is possible to doubt that there are any psychological continuers. So, if the linguistic proposal is correct, it *is* possible to doubt that *P*. So the linguistic proposal is incorrect'. Here '*P*' is not 'I think' or 'I exist', since Olson says it is possible to doubt that I exist and I think (Parmenides, Hume, and Russell all did). '*P*' is rather 'If there is someone thinking my thoughts, I exist'. But it is a mere consequence of a fact of grammar (that 'my' is the possessive form of the first person) that this is indubitable, and the linguistic proposal is not inconsistent with this grammatical fact.

One might also wonder why Olson's argument is not just an instance of the masked man fallacy, and whether he is committed to the validity of Moore's open question argument.

Olson's third objection is that "Noonan's view implies that whether the problems [in metaphysics and epistemology at issue] arise depends on how we speak. If we speak as we thought we did [if the linguistic solution is wrong] there are problems. If we speak as Noonan says, . . . the problems do not arise. So even if we in fact face the problems, we could avoid them by changing the way we speak. . . . If there is something that as things stand we cannot know, how could merely changing our language enable us to know it? Changing our language might make it impossible to state a question. But it cannot answer the question" (Olson 2002).

I have quoted this at length because it is confused. Of course, if as things stand there is something I express by the sentence *S* which I cannot know, then I cannot come to know *that* by changing the language so that *S* now expresses some knowable truth. And if there is a problem I can now phrase by asking 'Is *S* true?' I cannot solve *that* problem by changing the language so that *S* comes to express some easily knowable truth. But I do not see that it is any part of the linguistic solution to imply otherwise. The question what I am, asked by me, is the question 'What do I refer to when I say 'I'?' If I change my language so that 'I' means something different in my mouth (say, the Eiffel Tower), what I referred to when I uttered 'I' would indeed change. But, of course, as Olson says, changing the language would not change which things we are (I would not grow taller or gain French nationality).

Olson's final objection is, as he himself says, not so much an objection as the pointing out of an immediate consequence of the linguistic proposal: namely that 'I am *the* thinker of these thoughts' becomes unwarranted (false or truth-valueless depending on whether you are Russell or Strawson). And as he adds, "whether this counts as a *reductio ad absurdum* of the linguistic proposal or merely an unfortunate side-effect depends, I suppose, on how attractive one finds these metaphysical hypotheses" (ibid.).

Confronted with the necessity of drawing the distinction between the 'I'-user and the reference of 'I' as a reply to the too many minds objection, there is indeed a temptation to regard it as a *reductio ad absurdum* of the psychological approach. It is important to note, then, that it is not just the psychological approach that is vulnerable to the too many minds objection if this line of defense fails, but *any* account of personal identity that involves the sharing of thoughts by persons and nonpersons. But as Olson (2002) indicates, any account of personal identity that regards persons as four-dimensional perdurers will inevitably have this consequence (as Olson puts it: "The puzzle of the thinking person segment admits of no psychological solution. . . . All 'four-dimensionalists' say that a temporally extended being thinks at a time by virtue of the fact that a more-or-less momentary temporal part of her located at that time thinks without qualification. . . . Without person-stages or segments there could be no thinking beings at all"). Thus, if the psychological approach is refuted by the too many minds objection, so is any account of personal identity that regards persons as four-dimensional. But such a conclusion must be too hasty, since it may be that the four-dimensional conception can be established on general metaphysical grounds prior to any considerations pertaining to the particular issue of personal identity. In short, it needs to be recognized that biological theorists cannot in good faith wield the too many minds objection as a weapon against their opponents unless they feel able to refute the arguments for four-dimensionalism.

But the ontological commitments involved in the psychological approach may still seem hard to take, and in the absence of any general proof of four-dimensionalism it may still seem that, albeit on balance and provisionally, the most intellectually responsible response to the too many minds objection is to embrace the ontological conservatism of the biological approach. What I want to argue now is that even if we set aside the question of four-dimensionalism, that conservatism comes at too high a price: the acceptance of vagueness *de re*.

The argument is straightforward. If we allow that statements of personal identity over time can be indeterminate then we must accept that, unless persons are vague objects, in any such borderline case the singular terms that occur in its description lack determinate denotation. But this can be so only if for each such term there are at least two candidates for its denotation. So if 'Brownson is Brown' is indeterminate there will be two candidates for the denotation of 'Brown', one that survives the brain transplant and acquires Robinson's body, and one that does not.

Now the key point is that the biological theorist cannot deny the conceptual possibility of cases of indeterminate personal identity, cases, that is, in which a conceptual shadow is cast over the identity of the *human beings* involved, for this would be to regard 'human being' as radically unlike any other empirically applicable term for a kind of middle-sized material object. However, if borderline cases of personal identity are possible then for all I know at some point in the future *I* may be involved in such a case (who knows what twenty-first-century biotechnology may achieve?). But if so, and if persons are not vague objects, I am not alone. I must *already* share my skin with a rival candidate for the denotation of the name 'Harold Noonan' (and the first-person pronoun 'I'). And the biological theorist who wishes to deploy the too many minds objection against the psychological theorist cannot deny that my rival, like me, is a thinking intelligent thing, with reason and reflection (he has at least as much in common with me as the human animal with whom I share my skin if the psychological approach is correct). But, of course, what goes for me, goes for you too. So the biological theorist must acknowledge that, unless there is vagueness *de re*, for all we know none of us is ever really alone.

Of course, this falls short of saying that *in fact* no one is ever really alone. But philosophically the significance of the two conclusions is the same. If none of us can rule out the epistemic possibility that there is, here and now, more than one thinker of his thoughts, then whether or not this is so, a philosophical stance such as that of the psychological theorist cannot be condemned as absurd because of its commitment to a more capacious ontology than that which common sense allows.

Anyway, the conclusion that *in fact* we are never alone if the biological theory is correct is only a short distance away, given the rejection of vagueness *de re*. For although I do not know that I will in fact get involved in any identity-destroying science-fictional shenanigans of the type just envisaged, I surely do know that there will be no determinate last moment of my existence (if anything, the biological account of personal identity serves merely to make this more evident). But if I am not a fuzzy object, with temporally indeterminate boundaries, this can only be because there are several candidates for what I now denote by 'I', differing somewhat in their total temporal extents. Once again, however, such candidates will have as much in common as I and the animal with which, if the psychological approach is correct, I coincide. So, once again, the biological theorist must acknowledge that they are *all* thinking, intelligent things with reason and reflection, or retract his objection to the psychological approach. Thus, given plausible assumptions, the biological theorist must accept that, unless there is indeterminacy *de re*, I am never in fact alone. And, of course, nor are any of you.

Finally, it is to be noted that even the acceptance of indeterminacy *de re* does not obviously save the biological theorist from this uncomfortable commitment. For if there is a vague object determinately denoted by 'I', as I use it, there are surely many others, differing only marginally in respect of the temporal extent of their indeterminacy.[10] But such objects have as much in common with one another as do I and the animal with which, according to the psychological approach, I coincide. So once again the biological theorist is himself committed to a plurality of thinkers, or his objection to the psychological approach is undermined. In short, in order to avoid the too many minds objection the biological theorist must not only reject perdurantism and accept vagueness *de re*, but must also accept that vague objects are fewer in number than there is any reason to suppose, if there are any vague objects at all.

I conclude that if there being too many minds is a problem for anyone, it is a problem for everyone.

Notes

1. More exactly it is the following. We start from this definition: a person is a certain collection of person-stages, a collection containing a member—let us call it a 'marker' for the collection—such that all and only the members of the collection are the closest psychological continuers or predecessors of that member when they exist. However, this definition is inadequate to cases of fusion followed by fission, because it does not allow one to say that there is a person involved in such a situation for each line of personal continuity, and so does not allow one to survive through the whole course of events—which is required by the Only *x* and *y* principle (see note 2). The revision required to deal with this difficulty is as follows. Call what has just been defined a 'person-set'. Then the extension of 'person' can be indicated thus. Any person-set is a person. The union of any two person-sets determined by markers *a* and *b*, where *a* and *b* are linked by personal continuity, is a person if it contains no simultaneous person-stages. If such a union of two person-sets does contain simultaneous person-stages consider all its subclasses got by omitting all but one member of any simultaneous group of person-stages. Any such subclass all of whose members are related pairwise by personal continuity is a person. Nothing else is a person.

On this definition three people are involved in a fission case (assuming just two tied continuers): two of them survive the fission and one does not. On the other hand, when there are several continuers but no tie for closeness the number of people involved is simply identical with the number of continuers, and this, I think, seems right. Now it seems reasonable to suppose that if this is our concept of a person, the reference of 'I' on a particular occasion of utterance will be that person for whom the person-stage tokening 'I' is a marker. If so, when I look forward to the prospect of my own fission I must acknowledge that I look forward to an event after which I will not exist, even though each of the survivors of the fission will be able to say truly on looking back on the fission: 'I existed before that happened'.

2. The principle, roughly, that whether later x is identical with earlier y can depend only on facts about x and y and the relations between them; it cannot depend on facts about other things (for elaboration, see Noonan 2003). This principle, explicitly endorsed by Wiggins (1980) and implicitly endorsed by Williams (1957), is intended to rule out "best candidate" or "no rival" candidate accounts of personal identity of the type put forward by Nozick (1981) and Shoemaker (1970).

3. "It is not . . . unity of substance that comprehends all sorts of identity . . . but . . . we must consider what idea it is applied to stand for: it being one thing to be the same substance, another the same man, and a third the same person, if person, man, and substance are three names standing for three different ideas, for such as is the idea belonging to that name, such must be the identity: which if it had been . . . carefully attended to, would possibly have prevented a good deal of . . . confusion . . . especially concerning personal identity" (Locke 1961, essay II, xxvii, 7). What Locke means by 'a thinking substance' is 'a thing-like item quantified over at a basic level in one's ontology of the mental realm' (see Alston and Bennett 1988).

4. Pedantically: What conditions C satisfy the following schema: 'If I exist at t and t^* then $C(I, t, t^*)$'?

5. The move from the indexical formulation to the nonindexical formulation embodies a substantial assumption, that is, that 'person', 'object of first-person reference', is a substance sortal, i.e., that there is some kind of thing for which persistence conditions can be given, such that *all* objects of first-person reference are of that kind. But this may not be so. Perhaps I can survive changes you cannot (or vice versa) if I am a human being and you are an angel or an inorganic conscious robot or one of the three Persons of the Trinity. Thus arguments for a particular account of personal identity, e.g., the psychological continuity account, must be seen as simultaneously arguments that this apparent possibility is not real.

6. The language of identity occurs neither in the indexical formulation of the problem of personal identity nor in the nonindexical formulation. So it is not a problem about identity (Lewis 1986). Of course, we can *ask* questions of personal identity using the language of identity, but this does not make them questions about identity (the question 'Am I fat?' is logically equivalent to the question 'Am I identi-

cal with something that is fat?' but this does not make it a question about identity). For example, we can ask 'If I exist at a time t and something x exists at a time t^* and x is identical with me does it follow that x is at t^* psychologically continuous with me as I am at t?' (i.e., is psychological continuity necessary for personal identity?). But this is just the question: 'If I exist at t and t^* must it be the case that I am at t^* psychologically continuous with myself as I am at t?', in which the language of identity does not occur. Or I can ask 'If I exist at t and something x exists at t^* and x, as it is at t^*, is psychologically continuous with me, as I am at t, does it follow that x is identical with me?' (i.e., is psychological continuity sufficient for personal identity?). But this is just the question whether the *sole* necessary condition for my existence at t and t^* is that I, as I am at t^*, be psychologically continuous with myself, as I am at t (a condition is sufficient if nothing else is necessary). But the answer to this question is fixed by the answer to the indexical formulation of the problem of personal identity given in the text, i.e., by the answers (plural) to the pedantic formulation of the problem in note 4, together with these being *all* the answers. We can therefore phrase the (nonindexical version of) the so-called problem of personal identity over time as follows: (1) What conditions C satisfy the following schema: (P) for any x, if x is a person then if x exists at t and t^*, $Cxtt^*$? And an account of personal identity over time (correct or incorrect) will then take the form: (2) All and only the following conditions C satisfy schema (P): {LIST}.

7. This is nontrivial. It excludes one person making a first-person reference to another. So it excludes the possibility that I constitute you a person by making a first-person reference to you and you constitute me a person by making a first-person reference to me.

8. Why can the human animal not be an object of first-person reference? Answer: It is a trivial analytic truth that the object of first-person reference is a person. It is an interesting, conceptually necessary truth, to be established by philosophical thought experiment, that persons are psychological continuers. It is an empirical contingent truth that human beings are not psychological continuers. These three truths entail that human beings are not objects of first-person reference.

9. He also considers it as a solution to "the problem of the thinking head" and to "the problem of the thinking person-segment." You face the first if you think you have a head. (Why is it not a thinker? After all, its brain is as good as yours.) You face the second if you think that you persist by perduring. (Then your temporal segments are thinkers, or if not how is your problem of temporal intrinsics to be resolved?). If, like me, you think you have arbitrary and not-so-arbitrary unde-tached parts, including a head, persist by perduring and have psychological persistence conditions, you face all three problems. Olson distinguishes metaphysical, psychological, and linguistic solutions to these problems. The metaphysical solution denies the existence of the relevant entity, the psychological solution denies that it thinks, and the linguistic solution distinguishes 'I'-referent and 'I'-user. So

the metaphysical solution to the problem of the thinking head denies that I have a head, the psychological solution denies that it thinks, and the linguistic solution says that its 'I' thoughts are not about itself.

10. Similarly, if 'Everest' determinately designates a vague object with indeterminate spatial boundaries, there must be many other, largely overlapping, vague objects, differing only in respect of the margins of their indeterminacy (for why should precise objects be so thick on the ground and vague objects so thin?) (see Noonan 2004).

References

Alston, W., and J. Bennett. 1988. Locke on People and Substances. *Philosophical Review* 97:25–46.

Ayers, M. 1990. *Locke*, vol. 2. London: Routledge.

Baker, L. R. 2000. *Persons and Bodies: A Constitution View*. Cambridge: Cambridge University Press.

Carter, W. 1989. How to Change Your Mind. *Canadian Journal of Philosophy* 19:1–14.

Chisholm, R. 1976. *Person and Object*. London: Allen & Unwin.

Geach, P. 1976. Two Kinds of Intentionality? *Monist* 59:306–320.

Gibbard, A. 1975. Contingent Identity. *Journal of Philosophical Logic* 4:187–221.

Jackson, F., and D. Chalmers. 2001. Conceptual Analysis and Reductive Explanation. *Philosophical Review* 110:315–361.

Lewis, D. 1986. *Philosophical Papers*, volume 2. Oxford: Oxford University Press.

Locke, J. 1961. *An Essay Concerning Human Understanding*. Ed. J. Yolton. London: Dent.

McDowell, J. 1997. Reductionism and the First Person. In *Reading Parfit*, ed. J. Dancy. Oxford: Blackwell.

Noonan, H. 1998. Animalism versus Lockeanism: A Current Controversy. *Philosophical Quarterly* 48:302–318.

Noonan, H. 2001. The Epistemological Problem of Relativism—Reply to Olson. *Philosophical Studies* 104:323–336.

Noonan, H. 2003. *Personal Identity*. London: Routledge.

Noonan, H. 2004. Are There Vague Objects? *Analysis* 64:131–134.

Nozick, R. 1981. *Philosophical Explanations*. Oxford: Clarendon Press.

Olson, E. 1997. *The Human Animal: Personal Identity without Psychology*. Oxford: Oxford University Press.

Olson, E. 2002. Thinking Animals and the Reference of 'I'. *Philosophical Topics* 30:189–208.

Parfit, D. 1971. Personal Identity. *Philosophical Review* 80:3–27.

Parfit, D. 1984. *Reasons and Persons*. Oxford: Clarendon Press.

Parfit, D. 2007. Persons, Bodies and Human Beings. In *Contemporary Debates in Metaphysics*, ed. D. Zimmerman, T. Sider, and J. Hawthorne. Oxford: Blackwell.

Shoemaker, S. 1970. Persons and Their Pasts. *American Philosophical Quarterly* 7:269–285.

Shoemaker, S. 1999. Eric Olson, the Human Animal. *Noûs* 33:496–504.

Snowdon, P. 1991. Personal Identity and Brain Transplants. In *Human Beings*, ed. D. Cockburn. Cambridge: Cambridge University Press.

Van Inwagen, P. 1990. *Material Beings*. Ithaca: Cornell University Press.

Wiggins, D. 1980. *Sameness and Substance*. Oxford: Blackwell.

Wiggins, D. 1996. Replies. In *Essays for David Wiggins: Identity, Truth and Value*, ed. S. Lovibond and S. Williams. Oxford: Blackwell.

Williams, B. 1957. Personal Identity and Individuation. *Proceedings of the Aristotelian Society* 57:229–252. Reprinted in B. Williams, *Problems of the Self*, Cambridge: Cambridge University Press, 1973.

10 Me, Again

Jenann Ismael

I traveled to the conference from which this volume is drawn with John Pollock, a dear and now departed friend and colleague. I dedicate this paper to him with love and respect. He is missed.

Introduction

Thought about the self raises some very special problems. Some of these concern indexical reference quite generally; but there is one, having to do with identity over time, that seems to be unique to the self. I'll be using a historical exchange between Anscombe and Descartes to raise the problem and proposing a resolution that casts light both on why self-directed thought presents a unique epistemic predicament and where Descartes's *cogito* argument—still one of the most compelling and resilient arguments in philosophy—goes wrong.

What Anscombe Said to Descartes

Descartes begins his discussion in the *Meditations* with the question "what am I?" and concludes, famously, that he is a nonmaterial substance. His reasoning turns on the thesis that nothing can be true of his nature that is not made known to him in the act of thinking.[1]

Schematically, the argument runs thus:

(1) I $=_{def}$ that thing whose existence cannot be doubted (i.e., that thing whose existence is made known in the act of doubting that it exists).

(2) I can't be identical to anything whose existence can be doubted.

(3)   I can doubt the existence of anything for which objective criteria of identity can be provided (give me a description and I can coherently doubt that it is satisfied).

(4)   Hence, I can't be identified with anything for which objective criteria of identity can be given. (Nagel 1989, 35)[2]

So construed, the argument is subject to an objection—often associated with Lichtenberg, but repeated by Russell, and given its most articulate expression by Anscombe—that is, on first encounter, devastating (Anscombe 1990).[3] The charge is that Descartes's argument fails because he pulls a bait and switch, overtly declaring the object of his inquiry is nothing other than that whose existence is made known in the act of trying to deny that it exists, but then tacitly appealing to a richer notion in allowing that it can be reidentified in different thoughts. In Anscombe's words:

People have sometimes queried how Descartes could conclude to his *RES cogitans*. But this is to forget that Descartes declares its essence to be nothing but thinking. . . . His position has, however, the intolerable difficulty of requiring an identification of the same referent in different I-thoughts. (Anscombe 1990)

It is not the proclaimed guaranteed existence of the self that is problematic, for that does indeed follow if the 'I' in an 'I'-thought is purely reflexive, that is, if it simply refers to itself. It is the combination of guaranteed and *continuing* existence that is objectionable. For, if the thinker outlives the thought—if the 'I' in one thought is even *potentially* intersubstitutable with the 'I' in others—its existence can't be revealed in the mere production of an 'I'-thought. All whose existence is so guaranteed are the individual thoughts themselves. According to the argument, Descartes is not entitled to assume the existence of an underlying continuant to supply them a common referent. On the one hand, the concept needs to be kept bare to guarantee existence. On the other hand, the bare concept doesn't seem to be enough to support reidentification. If I cannot be something whose existence is not made known in the production of an 'I'-thought, something whose existence can be coherently doubted while I am thinking of it, then I cannot be something that even potentially recurs. The unadorned reflexive 'I' of the individual thought cannot pull other 'I' occurrences under its referential scope.

'I' and Other Indexicals

The difficulty can be brought out with a comparison of 'I' with names and other indexicals. In the case of names, ambiguity aside, criteria for identification and individuation of words substitute for criteria of identification and individuation of objects.[4] The user of what Frege used to call a "logically perfect language" with a name for every object and no indexicals could be assured that the same word used on two occasions or in two expressions referred to the same object and could be intersubstituted *salva veritate*. She would never need to look beyond language to be assured of the validity of inferences or substitutions. This purity is spoiled when indexicals are added to a language. The user of an indexical uses the same word to refer to separate objects on different occasions and has to look to the world to disambiguate. Reidentification and intersubstitution requires knowing what type of object the expression picks out, and one has to apply criteria of identity associated with the type to determine when reidentification has been achieved or when intersubstitution is licensed. Spatial and temporal indexicals, for example, require application of criteria of identity for places and times, respectively. To use an expression like 'here' you have to know that 'here'-occurrences refer to places, and to make valid substitutions you have to be able to recognize that a place identified on one occasion is the same place as that identified on another.[5] Cases of demonstrative reference that we understand best have the form 'this x' and combine a reflexive component with a sortal. With indexicals, the sortal is part of the semantic meaning of the term. With demonstratives, it is either supplied verbally (as in 'this car' or 'that cup of coffee') or made clear enough in some other way by the conversational context (as when I say "that" pointing at a bookshelf and we both understand without saying that it's a particular book that I mean to be indicating). Reference, these cases, involves a division of labor. The reflexive component centers reference on a particular time, place, or object, and the sortal provides criteria for reidentification and intersubstitution.[6] Even when we don't know exactly what we're pointing at, we can say something like "that black hulk moving across the field," letting criteria for individuation of black hulks decide whether I've got my eye on the *same* thing that you do. If we adopted a Kaplanian semantics according to which demonstratives are functions, we would say that the sortal proscribes the range and the reflexive component picks out the value (Kaplan 1989a,b).

To fit 'I' into this mold, we would have to say that occurrences of 'I' refer to the selves that produce them and intersubstitution of 'I' in temporally separated thoughts involves application of criteria of identity for selves. We would have to say that each of us applies criteria of identity for selves in judging that some past or future thought is ours and that the 'I' in that thought can be intersubstituted with the 'I' in this one, as for example we apprehend and apply criteria of identity for days in judging that a 'today'-occurrence on one occasion is intersubstitutable with a 'today'-occurrence on another. But this is not the way that 'I' works. It is the singular property of 'I' that no criteria of identity for selves play a role in reidentification of the self across different thoughts, or in intersubstitution of the 'I' in one thought for the 'I' in another. There is no judgment of identity across contexts of the kind we need to make with 'here', 'today', or 'this chair', and there is no risk of mistake of the sort we can always make in those cases. We can mistakenly intersubstitute a pair of 'here'-occurrences that pick out different places and we can mistakenly inter-substitute a pair of 'today'-occurrences that fall on different days, but it's hard to make sense of the idea of mistakenly intersubstituting someone else's 'I'-occurrence for one's own. From a psychological point of view, the bonds between our thoughts and the boundaries that separate them from those of others are fundamental and unanalyzable.

There is a general recognition in the literature on the self that the self isn't picked out by an individuating conception of the kind that could serve as a Fregean sense. Shoemaker has emphasized this feature of 'I' in his own work:

My use of the word 'I' as the subject of [statements such as 'I feel pain' or 'I see a canary'] is not due to my having identified as myself something [otherwise recognized] of which I know, or believe, or wish to say, that the predicate of my statement applies to it. (Shoemaker 2001)

It has also been discussed also by Strawson, Evans, Anscombe, and others, and is often expressed by saying that no criterion of identity is employed in picking out the self as the object of a referential act. Kant recognized the fact clearly:

In attaching 'I' to our thoughts, we designate the subject . . . without noting in it any quality whatsoever—in fact, without knowing anything of it either directly or by inference. (Kant 1997, A355)

What these passages, and others like them in the literature, don't express clearly enough to my mind is the importance of the fact that criteria of identity are not employed in *re*identification. It's the lack of employment of criteria of identity in judgments of same-self relatedness across contexts that distinguishes self-identification from other kinds of indexical and demonstrative reference.

All of this can seem to lead inevitably to the conclusion that selves are primitive constituents of reality, mutually impenetrable substances in which thoughts are housed. As James puts it:

Each [self] keeps its own thoughts to itself. There is no giving or bartering between them. No thought even comes into direct sight of a thought in another [self] than its own. Absolute insulation, irreducible pluralism is the law. . . . Neither contemporaneity, nor proximity in space, nor similarity of quality and content are able to fuse thoughts together which are sundered by this barrier of belonging to different personal minds. The breaches between such thoughts are the most absolute breaches in nature. (James 1990)

'I' works just like other indexicals on this view. The reason we can't say anything informative about what makes a pair of thoughts or impressions thoughts or impressions of the *same* self is that there is nothing more informative to say. Selves are basic constituents of reality, and criteria of identity for selves can't be analyzed in any other terms. This view is probably closest to that of the man on the street. Ask a nonphilosopher what makes two occurrences of 'I' coreferential and he will tell you they belong to the same self, end of story.

That there is something more interesting going on here is indicated by several things. First, it makes possession of the notion of a self prior to the ability to reidentify oneself over time, and that doesn't seem phenomenologically right. It seems too much thought to attribute to the child, for example, who says I enjoyed the ice cream yesterday and I want to have some more. The ability to reidentify oneself over time seems to precede any grasp of the concept of a self. More importantly, it suffers from problems that beset any view that requires intersubstitution to be regulated by *judgments* of same-self-relatedness. Any judgment that spans a pair of temporally separated thoughts would seem to presuppose, and cannot therefore establish, the numerical identity of the judging self. Instead of pressing these objections, which would require looking quite deeply into the nature of judgment, I want to suggest an alternative account, starting with an example drawn from Perry (1986) and embellishing it in a way that will allow us to see how to derive the eccentricities of 'I' from a story about the mechanics of achieving reference.

Preconceptual Thought *About* and Post Hoc Conceptualization

Perry (1986) considers a fictional populace who live in a place called Z-land. Z-landers are unadventurous folk who never travel and who never meet, or have occasion to talk to, people from other places. They talk about the weather, and their weather beliefs play an important role in their practical lives; what they plan and how they act depends on their beliefs about the weather.[7] What is striking about their talk about the weather is that it never includes an explicit reference to a place. They never mention or make any reference to Z-land in their reports; the nightly news says simply "rain today, sun tomorrow, storms on Wednesday" without any mention of place, and that tells them everything they need to know in order to decide whether to cancel the picnic or carry an umbrella.

Reports for Z-landers serve as expressions of belief and we assume that they reflect the structure of those beliefs in containing the same semantically significant constituents. We should agree with Perry that the Z-landers' beliefs are about the weather in *Z-land*, even though they make no mention of place; Z-land appears in the specification of their truth conditions. It is the weather in Z-land that confirms or disconfirms them. Perry puts this by saying that Z-land is an *unarticulated constituent* of their weather beliefs. The Z-landers can make the spatial content of their weather talk explicit by adding 'here' to their reports. This is a practically trivial addition so long as they remain at home; 'here' can function grammatically as a name for Z-land, and unconstrained intersubstitution of tokens of it will preserve reference. Inferences will go through unproblematically, information will flow smoothly from Z-land to Z-lander weather beliefs and from one Z-lander to another in talk about the weather, and the sheer mechanics of the situation will ensure coordination without any need for a mediating concept of the place. If Z-landers begin to move, however, or communicate with non-Z-landers, unconstrained intersubstitution will lead to faulty inferences and they will need something in the head that can serve as a constituent of beliefs about the weather there and distinguish those beliefs from beliefs about weather elsewhere. They will need, in short, an idea of Z-land that occurs as an articulated constituent in beliefs that are sensitive to the state of, and guide behavior in, Z-land. The links between perception, belief, and action will be less direct than they were before, mediated now by a representation of place and self-ascription of location. Z-landers then will not respond immediately to reports of rain by grabbing an umbrella; they will ask *where* it is raining and they will stop to check it against the place they are *at*.

For another example of the process by which unarticulated constituents are articulated, think of the child who learns to use 'mom' and 'dad', 'mother' and 'father' to refer to his own mother and father, without understanding that motherhood and fatherhood are relations.[8] So long as he remains in the family circle, this isn't something he needs to worry about.[9] If he hears that mom is in the garden, he will know whom to find there. And if someone tells him that mom is wearing a straw hat, he will conclude correctly that there is someone in the garden who is wearing a straw hat.

'Mom'-occurrences in his restricted world will all lead to the same place, and there is no need to interpose a parameter to coordinate them either with one another, or with their common referent. For him, 'mom' functions as a singular term. As soon as he leaves the family circle, however, he will discover that 'mother' refers to other people in the mouths of his friends, he will need to keep explicit track of *who* is speaking, and he will need to know something more about motherhood. *What* he needs to know, precisely, is a complex and highly context-dependent question. The general rule is that he needs a way of getting from an utterance of 'mother' to its referent and a way of determining whether a pair of 'mother'-occurrences corefer. What this requires will depend on contingencies of his situation, for example, how many mother–son pairs he knows, and whether there are general ways of identifying speakers' mothers.[10] How much structure he needs in his own head to keep the information flowing smoothly so that information about a particular mother is collected, combined, kept safely separate from information about others, and brought to bear in the right way in his interaction with her, will depend on which other mothers he gets information about, and how. Mom-talk in the child's environment, and mom-thought in the child's head, while he is confined to the family circle, like Z-lander weather reports, have a hidden contextual parameter[11] that can remain hidden so long as he remains in a context in which it has a fixed value but that needs to be articulated when he is exposed to contexts across which its value varies.

Focus on the process of replacing unarticulated constituents with representations. Recall how things went with the Z-landers. They began by talking freely of the weather without overt acknowledgment of the spatial relativization of weather talk. Making the spatial relativization explicit proceeds in two stages; they learn first to attach a 'here' to their weather reports as a caution against unconstrained intersubstitution. The 'here' signaled to them that they shouldn't infer disagreement from differences in reports, for the reporters might live in different places. But before they can begin to use weather talk again in inferences, before their weather thoughts can be properly integrated into the web of belief, and before they can coordinate their own weather reports with weather reports of their neighbors, they will need to replace 'here' with a parameter that explicitly represents, by varying in value with, their own location. Before they can be used effectively in reasoning, that is to say, weather reports and weather beliefs that concern different places will have to be made *internally* distinguishable. Indexicals are a perfectly legitimate way of securing reference and they have the critical advantage of securing it in a way that bypasses the ordinary route through ideas, placing less conceptual burden on their users. You don't have to have an individuating conception of a place to refer to it indexically. But they have the disadvantage of concealing relations of intersubstitutivity. One cannot tell from an internal perspective—by inspection, so to speak, of the beliefs themselves—whether a pair of 'here', 'this', or 'today' occurrences are intersubstitutable. From the inside, one 'here' or 'today' thought looks like any other.

This second stage, at which the indexical is replaced with explicit representation, is highly nontrivial. To pull it off, Z-landers will have to come to appreciate and employ criteria of identity for places. They will have to learn to identify and individuate places, and they will need a general concept of places that are not their own, something that they didn't need in order to refer to them successfully using 'here'. The same story could be told about sheltered children. Once they have left the family circle and can no longer rely on the context to coordinate reference, if they are to use 'mother' effectively in reasoning, they will need to develop an understanding of familial relations and learn to apply criteria of identity in deciding whether distinct 'mother'-occurrences are intersubstitutable. As soon as they begin to move around, Z-landers no longer have the kind of built-in, invariant informational link to a place that allows it to act as an unarticulated constituent in their thought and they need something a little higher up in the representational hierarchy, something with a looser connection to experience, to hang their Z-land thoughts on.

Return now to bridging the gap between Descartes's starting point and reference to a temporal continuant. Recall the terms of the problem. He started with an implicit definition of the object of inquiry as that thing, whatever it is, whose existence is made known in the production of an 'I'-thought. This prohibits him from appealing to any constraints on the nature of selves but those that are conditions of the possibility of 'I'-use. I want to suggest that we learn to use 'I' by a mechanical procedure: producing tokens, and allowing unconstrained intersubstitution, relying on the external relations among the tokens to preserve reference. Reference is thus secured without explicit representation of criteria of identity—indeed, without invoking concepts of any kind. This reverses the ordinary direction of determination. We do not introduce the concept of a self governing intersubstitution of 'I'-tokens; it is the *de facto* relations among tokens that get intersubstituted by application of the mechanical procedure that determines the criteria of identity for selves. It is thus, and only thus, that we can refer to ourselves not only without having an individuating idea of our own selves, but without knowing what selves *are*, without knowing what makes two thoughts thoughts of the *same* self. This makes it wholly unique among indexicals. In all other cases, the rules of use for the indexical invoke criteria of identity applied in reidentification and intersubstitution. Competence with the terms requires apprehension of such criteria. You have to possess criteria of identity for days and mothers to sort 'today'- and 'mom'-occurrences into intersubstitutability classes. No conceptualization of this sort is provided by the rule of use for 'I'.

Many in the contemporary literature have emphasized that conceptualization is, however, essential to being properly ascribable a genuine idea of self. Evans, for example, holds that in order for 'I' to be recognized as a semantically significant component of thought,

one's Idea of oneself must also comprise, over and above [unmediated links to perception and action], a knowledge of what it would be for an identity of the form 'I = ?' to be true, where ? is . . . an identification of a person which—unlike one's 'I'-identification—is of a kind which could be available to someone else. . . . (Evans 1982, 209)[12]

Kant made the same point in distinguishing the 'I think' that is the empty accompaniment of every thought from meaningful self-ascription. For Evans, the requirement is an instance of a general condition on identifying thought that gets its justification from an understanding of the role of thought in mediating perception and action. He writes:

sensory input is not only connected to behavioral disposition in the way I have been describing . . . but also serves as the input to a thinking, concept-applying, and reasoning system. . . . it is only those links which enable us to ascribe content (conceptual content now) to the thoughts.[13]

He's absolutely right about that. Reasoning with a term requires a practical understanding of how it interacts inferentially with other terms. To represent oneself in the sense of being able to take oneself as an *object* of thought requires more than the ability to produce mental tokens of 'I'. Those tokens have to function as semantically significant constituents; they have to be connected in an inferentially articulated network of concepts. We have to be able to associate them with other singular terms, use them in inferences, and distinguish them from other objects and from one another. We have to be able to entertain thoughts not only about our own selves, but those of others. We have to know, in sum, what would make true an identity of the form 'I = g', where 'g' is an arbitrary name or identifying description.

The repeated pattern is the one that we saw with the Z-landers: there is a suppressed parameter with a fixed value that is first expressed indexically and later replaced with a referring term. We get a closer analogy if we embellish. Instead of Z-landers, imagine a population of conscious, weather-sensing trees: Tree-landers. Tree-landers can tell sunny weather from rain, and each has a repertory of actions suited to weather in its own locale. Perhaps, for example, they open their leaves in rainy weather and close them in sun. They get information about rain in other locales only indirectly via reports from birds that bring news from distant lands. Their weather thoughts and reports start out, like the Z-landers, without explicit spatial content. They learn to attach 'here' mechanically, allowing unconstrained internal intersubstitution but refraining from substitution in connection with reports from outside. The conceptualization needed to integrate their here-thoughts properly into the web of belief occurs at a later stage, if it occurs, and involves apprehension of objective criteria of identity for places.

In apprehending criteria of identity for selves, we face the something like the task that Tree-landers face in apprehending criteria of identity for places. Ideas of other locations are for them, in the beginning, slots where they funnel information about weather that is not weather *here*, that is to say, weather that doesn't make itself felt in *this* way and have a direct, regulative bearing on the opening and closing of leaves. And just so, ideas of other *selves* are, in the beginning, for each of *us*, places where we house thoughts and experiences that are not our own, that is to say, thoughts and experiences other than *these*, thoughts and experiences that don't make themselves felt in this way and have a direct regulative bearing on activity. They are whatever lies at the other end of the linguistic chains that bring us news of such thoughts. There is nothing inherently mysterious, if we focus in this way on the sheer mechanics of securing reference, in the fact that each of us can refer to one object in thought in a way that is immune to failure of reference (i.e., whose existence is ensured and reference to which is secured in the very production of the thought), which is nevertheless distinct from (because it possibly outlives) the thought, and yet with no conception of what kind of thing we are referring to.

This account gives us:

1. Identification without application of criteria of identity
2. Immunity to failure of reference
3. Reference to a continuant

Moreover, since no criteria of identity are employed in reidentification, apprehension of criteria of identity, if and when it is made, will present itself as a *discovery* and show all of the psychological signs of contingency. Here's what I mean by saying it will show the psychological signs of contingency. Suppose R is the relation that turns out to unite the thoughts and experiences of a self, which is to say, the relation that 'I'-occurrences which get intersubstituted by application of the mechanical procedure bear to one another. It doesn't matter what R is; so long as it doesn't make explicit and ineliminable reference to a self, the proposition 'S and S^* belong to the same self iff S Rs S^*' will not look like a conceptual truth.

1. It will be dubitable.
2. Being told that S Rs your present thoughts will seem to leave it as an open question whether S is nevertheless *yours*.
3. It will seem as though you can imagine scenarios in which all of the objective R relations remain fixed but the gaze of your consciousness cross-cuts them, alighting now here, now there, at will.

These facts, when they are stated in general form, will seem to rule out any reductive candidate for a constitutive relation between temporal parts of a self. All of them have their roots in the fact that judgments of owner-ship and co-ownership of mental states over time are not mediated in the ordinary way by application of concepts. This is what makes 'I' wholly unique, even among indexicals. We might say that in this case, unlike other indexicals, we are constitutively confined to a context in which inter-substitution preserves reference. (1)–(3) have provided the basis for explicit philosophical arguments against reductive analyses and they are unques-tionably implicated in the intuitive conception of the self as a primitive locus of mental life, a metaphysical free variable only contingently con-nected with the material contents of the universe. As Nagel has said:

> the very bareness and apparent completeness of the concept [of the self] leaves no room for the discovery that it refers to something that has other essential features which would figure in a richer account of what I really am. Identification of myself with an objectively persisting thing of whatever kind seems to be excluded in advance. (Nagel 1989, 35)[14]

And earlier:

> My nature . . . appears to be at least conceptually independent not only of bodily continuity but also of all other subjective mental conditions, such as memory and psychological similarity. . . . at the same time it seems to be something determinate and nonconventional. That is, the question with regard to any future experience, "will it be mine or not?" seems to require a definite yes or no answer. . . . (Ibid., 34)

> This seems to leave us with the conclusion that being mine is an irreducible, unana-lyzable characteristic of all my mental states, and that it has no essential connec-tion with anything in the objective order or any connection among those states over time. (Evans 1982, 34)

I am suggesting that there is a mundane explanation that avoids this conclusion.

Drawing the Boundaries around the Self

So let's return to the question of what makes one I-thought fall within the referential scope of another on the assumption that no criteria of identity are employed by 'I'-users in reidentification. Or, to put it in a way that evokes Sartre, what makes this the case on the assumption that the self is constituted in, rather than presupposed by, the act of reflective self-consciousness? Anscombe thought that Descartes's argument foundered on what she calls the "intolerable difficulty" that if the thinker outlives the thought—that is, if the 'I' in one thought is even potentially intersub-stitutable with the 'I' in others—its existence can't be revealed in the mere production of an I-thought. Her worry was that the notion of an I, in a sense that allows *different* occurrences of 'I' to refer to the *same* self, must be prior to and independent of—and cannot be *constituted* by—the mere production of those thoughts.

We have seen now why Anscombe's difficulty is not after all so intolera-ble. There are two ways to define an intersubstitutability context: implicitly and explicitly. Explicit definition does indeed require prior conceptualiza-tion of the referent, but if we can learn how to use 'I' by a purely mechani-cal procedure, one that can be described without any explicit reference to or conceptualization of its target, we can let the de facto relations among tokens that in fact get intersubstituted when 'I' is used in accordance with the procedure implicitly define the referent. Reference—even reference to a continuant—can in this way *precede* apprehension of criteria of identity. Apprehension of such criteria will be unnecessary for purposes of coordi-nation and if it is ever made, it will present itself as a discovery. We don't need semantic links between terms (or their mental analogues, ideas) and their objects where there are architectural links in place. It is only when we break architectural links by moving to different contexts that we require mediating concepts. That was the insight in Perry's original example, but it has been extended here to apply to the links between the parts of the self in a way that explains some of its most intractable peculiarities. It shows how it can turn out to be news to us that the thing we've been identifying and reidentifying all along is really one whose parts are, unbeknownst until now, held together by such and such connections. If we specify the rules of use ("attach 'I' indiscriminately to all thought and experience, allow unconstrained intersubstitution") and let the criteria of identity be implicitly defined by the rules of use, then finding out what selves are, and in particular, what *I* am, will be a matter of determining what turns out to unite occurrences that get intersubstituted by the procedure specified in the rule of use. The crucial insight here is that we don't need to represent those relations in order to reidentify the self.

What do we get if we apply this strategy? We get—I propose—external informational relations, the direct causal links inside the head that permit information to flow without passing through perceptual or linguistic channels. These are what tie the events that lie along a single stream of consciousness to one another and separate them from events in the psychological histories of others. Selves are nothing more than sealed pockets of world-representing structure, communicating with one another and with the environment through controlled channels, mediated by experience. Each of us applies 'I' mechanically by attaching it as grammatical subject to internal states and only later, once we have worked up a rudimentary picture of the world, do we raise questions about its own nature. It is really the existence of these sealed pockets—Humean bundles, connected by external relations that let information flow directly between them—that provide the contexts of intelligibility for 'I'-use. The intelligibility of 'I'-use doesn't depend on the existence of simple enduring substances for thoughts to inhere in; it requires nothing more than the various I-thoughts, the experientially unmediated informational relations they bear one another, and ordinarily enough internal unity and informational segregation from the environment to make 'I'-use relatively unproblematic.

It is crucial to this way of understanding things that the kind of connectedness in question is an external relation, one that doesn't supervene on the internal character of such states and that is indiscernible from the inside. It is true that 'I' can meaningfully occur only in the context of articulated world-representing structure, that this requires a certain amount of continuity of content, and that given certain assumptions about how world-representing structure is formed, that in its turn may require continuity in qualitative character. And it is also true that causal connectedness of the sort that permits experientially unmediated flow of information ordinarily has the *effect* of imposing a kind of continuity in content, but internal continuity, if I am right, plays no role in individuating selves, and—again—is in no way constitutive of the relation *belongs-to-the-same-self-as*. We might want to say that internal criteria are important and relevant to *personhood*, for that is a social and moral status. The notion of a person is entangled with concepts of agency and responsibility. The existence of persons, in this richer sense, is not guaranteed by the production of an I-thought, but only external criteria are constitutive of the identity of Cartesian *selves*.

This brings out a critical divide among forms of psychological reductionism often overlooked in the literature on personal identity. If we call views that share this feature pure Lockean views, and views that include internal criteria among the conditions of selfhood, Parfitean, after their most conspicuous exemplars, Locke and Velleman hold Lockean views. As does James, who writes:

My present Thought stands . . . in the plenitude of ownership of the train of my past selves, is owner not only de facto, but de jure, the most real owner there can be. Successive thinkers, numerically distinct, but all aware of the past in the same way, form an adequate vehicle for all the experience of personal unity and sameness which we actually have.[15]

According to James, the self or subject

is a Thought [mental state], at each moment different from that of the last moment, but appropriative of the latter, together with all that the latter called its own. All the experiential facts find their place in this description, unencumbered with any hypothesis save that of the existence of passing thoughts or states of mind.[16]

As a theory of the self, only a pure Lockean view—that is, one that allows no admixture of internal criteria into the constitutive relations between the parts of a self—can explain how we can identify and reidentify ourselves over time without application of any criteria whatsoever. Only the pure Lockean view explains the fact, wholly unique to self-identification and critical to Descartes's argument, that we can make repeated identifying reference to ourselves in thought without having (or needing to have) any conception of what unites our temporal parts.

What unites the states of a subject, on a pure Lockean view, are external relations that allow for perceptually unmediated communication. This is so both synchronically and diachronically. I have perceptually unmediated access to my own past and present thoughts and experiences. The only access I have to those of others is mediated by the production of publicly observable symbols or behavior. They have to talk, write, or behave in ways that I can see, ways that are designed to clue me in. Although there is no contradiction in supposing these kinds of consciously unmediated informational connections cutting across the boundaries of bodies, in fact, the body provides the physical context in which they are realized, maintaining the direct channels for the propagation of information and sealing them off from the external environment in a way that forces information from the outside to be funneled through experience. The only way you can work your thoughts into mine is by the production of observable behavior or information-bearing symbols. My own thoughts, by contrast, feed directly into one another. There are immediate connections among the mental states of a single subject, but immediacy in this sense is shorn of the traditional encumbrances of transparency and certainty, and compatible with the kind of complicated action behind the scenes (processing that is invisible to the subject, processing that doesn't get represented *in thought*) that Dennett emphasizes in his critiques of the Cartesian Theater, and importantly, it can accommodate the kinds of pathologies and internal divisions of self that we know to arise when psychological boundaries inhibit the flow of information.[17]

There is room in this for both indeterminacy and legislation. How indirect and artificial can the causal relations in question be? If there is a difference between recovering memories of one's own and acquiring someone else's by artificial means, there have to constraints on the causal process by which I come to have them, that is to say, the route by which they come to be represented in my thought. Obvious counterexamples will tell us what kinds of constraints need to be added, and borderline cases will simply be evidence of vagueness in the concept. It might be that under certain conditions—for example, if fission or amnesia becomes common enough, or memories can be bought and uploaded with no internal signs of inauthenticity—the notion of a temporally extended self, as we know it, will no longer have application. We will need a more articulated set of concepts that accommodates the full range of relations one can bear to downstream descendents of one's thoughts.

What is special about 'I', wholly unique to it as a term in thought, is that the facts that govern intersubstitutability of 'I'-occurrences are external to, and need not be represented in, thought. To employ a Wittgensteinian image, we don't represent our boundaries so much as bump up against them. I don't have to know what I am to know which thoughts, memories, experiences, hopes, are mine. I don't have to know anything *about* my future self, that is, the downstream descendents of my present thoughts, experiences, and so on, to have thoughts about, make decisions on behalf of, have hopes and fears, and so on, centered on *her*. Whatever ideas I have about my future self play no role in determining which of the world's future inhabitants is me. If I think that I will be the first woman president of the United States, but Marla Maples beats me to it, that doesn't make my present thoughts about my future self thoughts about Miss Maples. Whoever gathered these memories and sent them to me along the discriminating internal channels that Nature has provided inside the head, with whatever internal embellishments and emotional resonances that past self added, that was me. And whoever receives these thoughts and experiences along the same channels will be me as well. Am I a thing? I am a thing in the same way that a river is a thing. When I talk or think about myself, I talk or think about the connected, and more or less continuous, stream of mental life that includes this thought, expressing the tacit confidence that that is a uniquely identifying description (in the same way I might speak confidently of 'this river' pointing at a part of it, expressing the tacit assumption that it doesn't branch), but it need not be. *Belonging-to-the-same-subject-as*, in this sense, is not an equivalence relation, and if that means that subjects are not objects, then there is no object in the world to which the Cartesian 'I' can be said to refer. But that doesn't mean there are no selves.

To sum up, we have a term in the language of thought that functions like a singular term, introduced by the mechanical procedure 'attach indiscriminately to mental states, intersubstitute freely'. And if we let the procedure implicitly determine criteria of identity, we end up saying that particular tokens of it refer to connected streams of world-representing structure in which they are situated. This positive view of identity over time is not new. It has a long history and has been eloquently and ably defended in recent literature by Velleman.[18] The story told here derives it from a general semantic framework in which thought about the self can be situated alongside other indexicals together with thought that conforms more closely to the Fregean model. The framework develops Perry's notion of an unarticulated constituent in a different direction than it has been taken in the literature,[19] but closer to the spirit of the original proposal. Unlike Perry's own explicit account of thought about the self, however, which makes the notion of a person a constituent of the self-concept, it allows reference to *precede* conceptualization. That is crucial to understanding the peculiar epistemic predicament that 'I' presents, so vividly rendered in the appended quotes from Nagel and James, and exploited by Descartes in the argument of the Second Meditation.

We can say quite precisely where that argument goes wrong. Descartes began with the question: What is this thing identified in the mere thinking of an I-thought and (here making explicit what he tacitly assumed and what Anscombe argued he was not entitled to) *re*identified with every reflective thought and experience? The argument departed from the observation that we have a way of referring to ourselves that is guaranteed reference and that leaves the nature of the self entirely open. And it turned on the thesis that nothing can be true of one's self that is not made known in the act of thinking (premise 2 in the formulation above):

(2)   I can't be identical to anything whose existence can be doubted.

In Augustine's version of the argument, (2) takes the form of the claim that the mind "is certain of being that alone, which alone it is certain of being" (Augustine 2002, book X). The Tree-landers gave us a concrete understanding of how it *could* be possible to form thoughts about oneself without having any conception of what kind of thing one is, that is, how we manage to refer in thought to an object of whose existence we are assured, and *know* that we are assured, but of whose nature we are *entirely* and *completely* ignorant. And all of this without the self being anything but a perfectly mundane sort of thing.

The recognition of unarticulated constituents is a deep and consequential emendation of a Fregean view of reference, but I believe it is correct, and that nothing less is needed to get the right account of thought about the self. Descartes's mistake is to go from the *epistemic* basicness of judgments of same-self identity in the first-personal case to ontological basicness, that is, to elevate the fragile boundaries that separate selves—the contingencies that support reidentification without application of criteria of identity over time—to the status of "absolute breaches in nature" (James 1950).[20]

Notes

1. "Now it is very certain that this notion, thus precisely understood, does not depend on things whose existence is not yet known to me" (Descartes 1984, 103).

2. Nagel is expressing, but not endorsing, the view in this passage.

3. I'll be sidestepping most exegetical questions, assuming a fairly standard reading of the argument of the *Second Meditation* and interpreting Anscombe's remarks quite freely.

4. Natural languages are, of course, massively ambiguous, and wholesale eradication of ambiguity may not be practically possible. Still, each particular instance of ambiguity is in principle eliminable.

5. In the best case, you would have an understanding of what Evans called the fundamental ground of difference between places, criteria for individuating places across all possible worlds. For practical purposes, however, a relatively reliable guide for reidentification that provides a basis for substitution suffices. What counts as reliable enough, and which circumstances reliability is relative to, will depend on what the practical purposes are.

6. There can be vagueness. 'Here' and 'now', for example, are notoriously vague, even when we take account of all potentially disambiguating features of conversational context. When I say to you in Sydney "Let's meet back here in an hour," we both probably know that Calcutta isn't included in the extension, but there is probably no determinate fact about which exactly of the indefinitely many surveyable regions of space centered on our location I referred to. It is not that reference must be determinate, but that it is not *more* determinate than the boundaries supplied by any explicitly or tacitly provided sortal.

7. We suppose that the weather is uniform across Z-land.

8. In formal terms, the process of articulating unarticulated constituents is that of representing ones frame of reference. One makes concepts drawn from different frames of reference communicable by plotting them jointly in a frame that includes a dimension in which their relations can be made explicit. The new constituents are values of parameters in added dimensions.

9. Supposing that he doesn't get information from other sources (books, radio, television), or at least that those sources don't use the terms 'mom' and 'dad'.

10. If sons never leave their mothers' sides or if sons were always the spitting images of their mothers, the task would be easier than in a world like ours, in which there are no foolproof visual ways of recognizing mothers.

11. Not hidden in the sense that it corresponds to anything in his head, but in the sense just described: it plays an unacknowledged role in coordinating his thought with its intentional object.

12. Conceptualizing oneself, for Evans, means conceiving of oneself as one among a range of entities, any of whom can bear the properties that one ascribes oneself immediately on the basis of experience.

13. The condition, which he calls the Generality Constraint, formulates the conditions under which an internal symbol makes a contribution to content, and can be said to stand for, or *represent*, a thing. In its general form, the condition requires us to see "the thought that a is F as lying at the intersection of two series of thoughts: the thoughts that a is F, that a is G, that a is H, . . ., on the one hand, and the thoughts that a is F, that b is F, that c is F, . . ., on the other" (Evans 1982, 209).

14. Nagel is not endorsing the view he is articulating here.

15. See James 1950, 1.360, and James 1990.

16. See James 1950, 1.400–401, and James 1990. See also James 1950, 1.338–342.

17. For an account of immediacy also shorn of those traditional encumbrances, see Moran 2001.

18. See "Self to Self" and "Identity and Identification" in Velleman 2005. I owe much to Velleman's masterful exposition of the view.

19. See, e.g., Recanati 2001 and Stanley 2002.

20. The themes in this essay are also developed in my book, Ismael 2006.

References

Anscombe, G. E. M. 1990. The First Person. In *Mind and Cognition*, ed. W. Lycan. Oxford: Blackwell.

Augustine. 2002. *On the Trinity*. Ed. G. B. Matthews, trans. S. McKenna. Cambridge: Cambridge University Press.

Descartes, R. 1984. Meditations on First Philosophy. In *The Philosophical Writings of Descartes*, vol. II. Ed. and trans. J. Cottingham, R. Stoothoff, and D. Murdoch. Cambridge: Cambridge University Press.

Evans, G. 1982. *Varieties of Reference*. Oxford: Oxford University Press.

Ismael, J. 2006. *The Situated Self*. Oxford: Oxford University Press.

James, W. 1950. *The Principles of Psychology*, vol. 1. New York: Dover.

James, W. 1990. The Stream of Consciousness. In *Mind and Cognition*, ed. W. Lycan. Oxford: Blackwell.

Kant, I. 1997. *Critique of Pure Reason*. Trans. P. Guyer and A. Wood. Cambridge: Cambridge University Press.

Kaplan, D. 1989a. Demonstratives. In *Themes from Kaplan*, ed. J. Almog, J. Perry, and H. Wettstein. Oxford: Oxford University Press.

Kaplan, D. 1989b. Afterthoughts. In *Themes from Kaplan*, ed. J. Almog, J. Perry, and H. Wettstein. Oxford: Oxford University Press.

Moran, R. 2001. *Authority and Estrangement*. Princeton: Princeton University Press.

Nagel, T. 1989. *The View from Nowhere*. Oxford: Oxford University Press.

Perry, J. 1986. Thought without Representation. *Supplemental Proceedings of the Aristotelian Society* 60:263–283.

Recanati, F. 2001. Literal/Nonliteral. *Midwest Studies in Philosophy* 25:264–274.

Shoemaker, S. 2001. Self-Reference and Self-Awareness. In *Self-Reference and Self-Awareness*, ed. A. Brook and R. C. DeVidi. Amsterdam: John Benjamins.

Stanley, J. 2002. Making it Articulated. *Mind and Language* 17:149–168.

Velleman, D. 2005. *Self to Self*. Cambridge: Cambridge University Press.

11   Selves and Self-Concepts

John Perry

1   Introduction

Some philosophers think of selves as rather mysterious things. Sometimes selves are identified with the souls of Christian theology, or the essential natures that are passed along in reincarnation, or as noumenal objects that exist beyond normal space and time, outside of the causal realm, and join, in some Kantian way, with the primordial structure of reality to create the world as we know it. And Hume famously could find nothing to serve as his self, except a bundle of perceptions.

I am inclined to think that most of these deep thoughts are not required to understand the self. I am inclined to think that a self is just a person, thought of under the relation of identity. I am also inclined to think, however, that Hume had something importantly right with his bundle theory. In this chapter, I will explore both ideas.

2   The Straightforward Theory

Consider what it is to be a neighbor. A neighbor is just a person, thought of as having the relation of *living next* to some person in question. A teacher is just a person, thought of as having the relation of *teaches* to some student. A father is just a person, thought of under the relation of *father of.* People play important roles in other people's lives, and we give these roles titles: neighbor, teacher, father, spouse, boss, and so forth.

But we each play an important role in our own life. I have a relation to myself that I don't have to anyone else: *identity.* Self is to *identity* as neighbor is to *living next door to.* It is a way we think of ourselves. The self is not a special kind of object, but the concept of self is a special kind of concept, one that we each have of ourselves as ourselves. It is the unusual structure

and special causal and informational role of our self-concepts that underlies the philosophical problems about the self.

2.1 Castañeda's War Hero

Sometimes the best way to find something is to first consider a case where
it stands out because it is abnormal. Now a sort of paradigm case of someone who doesn't know who he or she is, and in that sense lacks an ordinary sense of identity, and has a diminished self-concept, is someone who
has amnesia. Here I am thinking of a certain kind of amnesia, which may
only exist, in its most perfect and full-blown state, in fiction and in philosophical examples. This is a person who, as a result of a bump on the head,
has no idea who he or she is. One assumes that the knowledge is somewhere still in the brain, waiting to be released by another fortuitous bump
on the head, or perhaps surgery, or perhaps simply time. Such people do
not lose their "know-how." They can still use language, feed themselves,
walk, and the like.

I'll use an example from the great late philosopher Hector-Neri Castañeda (1966). He imagines a soldier—call him Bill—who, having performed
many brave deeds in a great battle, is injured, loses his dog-tags, wanders
far from the scene of his heroics, falls into a coma, and awakens with
amnesia. Not only does he not know who he is, no one else does either. He
is clearly a solider, however, and clearly due all the rights pertaining
thereto, so he is hospitalized, cured of everything but his amnesia, and goes
to Berkeley on the GI Bill. In the meantime, Bill's feats during the battle
have become well known. People don't know what became of him and
assume he died in battle, as this seemed inevitable given the situation he
was in when last seen. He is awarded many medals posthumously.

For the time being let's concentrate on Bill, lying in the hospital, just
awakened from his coma, before he is even told how he was found at the
scene of the great battle. Now of course there is a sense in which he does
know who he is. He can say, "I am me." Suppose Bill feels a pang of hunger, and sees a piece of chocolate cake on the tray in front of him. Does he
wonder into whose mouth this morsel should be put, in order to relieve his
pang of hunger? No. He knows that *he* is the person who is feeling the
pang of hunger, and the person whose arm he can control more or less at
will, and the person who has a mouth which he can't see right below the
nose the tip of which he can see, and he knows how to direct the fork and
the cake into that mouth. He knows that he is sitting in a room on a bed,
with a window out onto a lawn, maybe with a radio and some magazines
on the stand beside him. So, he really knows a great deal about himself.

Still, compared to the rest of us, he has a very diminished sense of self. He doesn't have memories from which he can construct a narrative about why he is where he is. He doesn't know what values, what commitments, what beliefs, what actions led him to this hospital room.

Since he doesn't know his own name, he can't exploit public sources of information about himself. He picks up the edition of *Stars and Stripes* on the table beside his bed, and reads all about the hero who has just been posthumously awarded many medals. He does not feel pride in, but only admiration for, all of the brave things which he, in fact, did. At this point he has two concepts of the person he in fact is: his concept of the war hero, and his self-concept.

Normally, we rely a great deal on such public sources of information about ourselves. If I forget my phone number, I look it up in the directory. I find out something about myself in exactly the same way as you would find out the same fact about me. Indeed, there are lots of things that make it into the public conception of us, which we can't discover in any other way. To find out the time of my talk at the Inland Northwest Philosophy Conference, I looked at the program on the Internet. I found out when John Perry's talk was scheduled the same way everyone else did.

In contrast, all of the knowledge Bill has about himself in the hospital (or almost all), he acquires by what I will call, somewhat ponderously, "normally self-informative ways of knowing about a person." That is, when you see an object by holding your head erect and opening your eyes, the object you see will be in front of someone. Who? You. Normally, at least, this is a way of finding out what is going on in front of the person who is doing the seeing. You feel a pang of hunger: someone is hungry, and will have his hunger relieved if food enters his mouth and makes it to his stomach. Who? You. This information is, in Shoemaker's words, immune to error through misidentification.[1] If you think you see a tree, you may be wrong. Perhaps it is a large bush, or a skinny man. But you won't be wrong about whom the thing you are wrong about is in front of. It will be in front of you. Why do I say "normally self-informative"? Perhaps someday brain scientists will invent a little device that will send a message from one person's eyes to another person's optic nerves, so that the second person can directly see what is front of the first. This might have some military utility. Old, frail, jittery, demolition experts can guide the movements of young, healthy, steady, inexperienced ones, as they defuse bombs. These experts will then have a cognitive burden that is not placed on most of us. They will have to keep track of whose environment they are visually obtaining information about. Most of us don't have to do that. They will have lost immunity with respect to one way of getting information. Technology can do that.

Some ways of knowing about ourselves are not only normally but necessarily self-informative, or so it seems. Our veteran demolition expert, if he gets confused, may make a mistake and think the pompous general in front of him is really in front of the novice. He may say something he shouldn't about pompous generals. But could he be wrong about who has a headache that he feels? Well, no sooner do we admit that something seems necessary than some cleverer philosopher will come up with a scenario that shows that it isn't.

Now consider Bill's act of extending his arm, grabbing his fork, breaking off a piece of cake, and shoving it in his mouth. I'll call that a "normally self-effecting way of acting." Moving in that way is a way anyone can shove a piece of cake they see in front of them in their own mouths, a way of feeding themselves. Again, *normally*, because we can dream up cases where it wouldn't work.

I'll repeat my favorite example here. At the end of Alfred Hitchcock's movie *Spellbound*, Leo G. Carroll holds a gun pointed at Ingrid Bergman, who is leaving his office, having just exposed his plot to frame his patient, Gregory Peck, for murder. We know whom Carroll will shoot if he pulls the trigger: the person in front of him. Shooting a gun pointed like that is a way of shooting the person in front of you. Then we see Carroll's hand turn the gun around. The front of the gun barrel fills the whole screen. He fires. Whom does he shoot? Himself. Firing a gun held like that is a normally self-shooting way of acting. But suppose that Carroll had a donut-shaped head. Then it would be a way of shooting the person behind him. It's only a contingent fact that we don't have donut-shaped heads. That's why we need to say "normally."

Note, however, that even if he had not turned the gun around, and had gone ahead and shot Bergman, Carroll would have performed some normally self-effecting actions. To kill Bergman he fires the gun, and to fire the gun, he pulls the trigger. He brings it about that his trigger finger moves, in the normal way we do such things, by just doing them. In this sense, every action begins with an *executable* action, a movement of the agent's body or some part of it, a movement the effects of which will, if things go right, lead to the goal for which the action was done.

So Bill, even with his amnesia, has a good deal of self-knowledge, in a perfectly reasonable sense.

Bill proceeds to Berkeley, where he ends up getting a graduate degree in history, writing, for his dissertation, a biography of the war hero who gained his fame at the very same battle from which Bill woke up with amnesia. He doesn't figure out for quite a while—after he's earned his Ph.D.—that he must be the war hero, that his dissertation is actually auto-biography. Now the point of this is that Bill knows a great deal about a person, who happens to be him. In a sense, he knows a great deal about himself, for he knows a great deal about a certain person X, and he is X. But that's not what we would ordinarily say. We would say something like this: Bill knows a great deal about the person he happens to be, but he doesn't know much about himself. We have to distinguish between self-knowledge proper, and knowledge that happens to be about oneself, knowledge of the person one happens to be.

2.2 First-Person Memory

In fact, even when Bill finally figures out that it is him he is writing about, we might be reluctant to call what he is writing an autobiography. One important thing John Locke[2] and Shoemaker emphasize is that we have a special access to our own past thoughts and actions. We remember them—but we can remember the *past* thoughts and actions of others, too. I can remember that Elwood used to think that poison oak was edible; I can remember the time Elwood ate some poison oak.

But in the case of my own thought and action, I not only remember that someone did something, or that someone thought something. I remember thinking and doing things. Shoemaker calls this "first-person memory" and "remembering from the inside." Our access to our own past thoughts and actions is phenomenologically and logically different from our memories about what others have thought and done. Remembering doing something is not *like* remembering someone else doing something. And in the case of others, there is always the questions of *who*? I remember someone eating poison oak, but was it Elwood? But if I remember *eating* poison oak, it was me that was doing the eating. Maybe it wasn't poison oak but poison ivy or just some cilantro I had an allergy to. But at least it was me that did the eating. Immunity carries over into first-person memory.

Of course, some combination of technology and imagination might undermine this too. Perhaps between the eating and the remembering the person who did the eating, the person I used to be, split into two people, neither of which can exactly claim to be the very person that did the eating. Then I only quasi-remember (Shoemaker's term again) the eating. Or suppose that memories were stored in the blood. Suppose Bill Clinton donated to a blood bank and I was given some of his blood. All of a sudden I am having flashbacks to afternoons spent with Monica Lewinsky and thoughts of Paula Jones. Let's not go further in this direction. (I have a feeling the memories-in-the-blood idea also came from Shoemaker's fertile imagination, but not the Clinton example.)

Once Bill figures out that he is the war hero, he can assimilate all the facts he has learned about his own to past into his own self-concept. But he still won't be related to these things in the normal way, the way we expect of an autobiographer. He will know that he did these things, and after a while he will remember that he did these things, but he won't remembering doing them.

A similar distinction applies to our knowledge of what we will do in the future. I can know, or at least have a pretty well-grounded belief, what you intend to do, and what you will do. But when I know what I am doing, what I am trying to do, what I intend to do, and in those ways, what I will do, it is based on a different way of knowing, a way each of us knows something of his own future; again, it is knowledge from the inside.

A case like Bill's is pretty fantastic, but the underlying moral is generally applicable. It is a fact about the complex informational world we live in that we have lots of ways of getting information about ourselves that are not normally self-informative.

Self-knowledge, in the ordinary sense, is knowledge of ourselves that is part of our self-concept. Knowing facts about the person you happen to be, as Bill did when he wrote his dissertation, isn't enough.

3   Knowledge from a Perspective

We really need to recognize a third kind of self-knowledge to complete the picture. Any animal picks up information from a perspective and acts from a perspective. Its only way of picking up information will be in normally self-informative ways. It has no real need of a self-notion to keep track of facts about itself. Except for occasionally stumbling across a still pond or a mirror, it doesn't pick up information about itself in normally other-informative ways. This primitive sort of self-knowledge I'll call *knowledge from one's own perspective.*

Now we might say that such a being has no self-knowledge. I'd rather say it has a primitive self-knowledge. The animal itself is what I call an *unarticulated constituent* of its whole system of knowledge of the world around it.

Here is what I mean by this. I think of propositions as abstract objects that we use to *classify* states and events that have contents, paradigmatically thoughts and utterances. In the case of beliefs and statements, the propositions capture truth conditions. Often we expect an isomorphism of sorts between whatever mental or linguistic representations are involved and the propositions we use to classify the states. If you say, "Brutus stabbed Caesar," your statement has the content that Brutus stabbed Caesar. The constituents of the propositions, Brutus, Caesar, and stabbing, correspond to words in the sentence you used. The belief that you were expressing involved your concepts of Brutus and Caesar and stabbing.

Sometimes we just leave out words when we do have the concepts. If you ask me the time, I'll look at my watch and say "It's two." If my wife asks me the time, when we are talking long-distance, I might say "It's two o'clock here" or "it's two o'clock Eastern time." I am aware that "o'clock attributes" are relations between times and places and not just properties of times, but I don't bother to note that relativity when it's obvious to what place my report is relative. When it isn't obvious, as in the conversation with my wife, I do explicitly note it.

But sometimes the constituent is not simply unexpressed but also unthought. I ask Jamaica-Unique, my 7-year-old granddaughter, what time it is. She looks at the clock and says, "It's 11 o'clock." "That's right," I say. What makes her statement true is the fact that it was 11 o'clock Pacific Standard Time. The time zone is the unarticulated constituent.

It might be misleading to say that she *expressed* the proposition that it was 11 o'clock Pacific Standard Time, or that that is what she said. But that fact is what made her statement true. If I were talking to Jamaica over the phone from New York, perhaps really needing to know the time since my watch has stopped, I would learn that it is 2 o'clock Eastern Standard Time. It is my knowledge of the relation between the time zone that makes her statement true and the time zone I am in that makes this inference possible. Where a constituent is unarticulated in both speech and thought, I'll say that the thought "concerns" it, as opposed to being straightforwardly about it. Jamaica's thought that it was 2 o'clock concerned California.

Classifying the truth conditions of beliefs and utterances with propositions that are not articulated in those beliefs and utterances is often an important part of explaining how those beliefs and utterances work to provide the agent with information, or reflect the information they have. Jamaica has the ability to look at an accurate clock set for the time zone in which it resides, and report accurately what time it is in that time zone. She has a way of getting knowledge about what time it is, a method that is normally informative about the time zone one is in. If Jamaica had extraordinarily acute vision, or lived in a house on the border of two time zones, this ability would be undercut—like that demolition expert we considered earlier, she would have a cognitive burden on her use of clocks to tell the time that most of us don't have.

Just as Jamaica doesn't need to keep track of the time zone relative to which she is telling the time, animals don't have to keep track of which animal's environment they are getting information about. It's always their own. It seems that the cognitive, informational needs of many animals would not gain much by having the sort of conceptual architecture we have for dealing with self-knowledge.

Such an animal has primitive self-knowledge, and we can, if we want, say that its whole cognitive system, everything it perceives and believes and wants, constitutes its self-concept. Such a self-concept wouldn't be a component of thoughts, however. Such an animal wouldn't have a self-concept part of which was a concept of the animal it happened to be, similar to its concept of other things. A simple animal will think of everything via the role that thing plays in its present experience: object in front, object to be eaten, and so on. A more sophisticated animal may have detached concepts of particular things, certain other animals and things that it can recognize and respond to in terms not only of its presently manifested properties but in terms of properties the animal has perceived them to have in the past.

What many animals don't have is a concept of themselves that is like these other detached or detachable concepts it has. It doesn't take itself to be one of the animals among others in the way we do. We do so by having a concept of the person we happen to be, linked to our primitive self-concept, to normally self-informative methods of knowing and normally self-effecting ways of acting. I would not want to claim that language is a necessary condition for needing such a concept. But it is clearly involved in the necessity for our having such a concept. For as we noted, we get information about ourselves not only in normally self-informative ways, but also in normally other-informative ways, largely in virtue of language. If we had a developed a protocol language to express primitive self-knowledge, it would have sentences like "Tree in front" and "Move paw toward food in front." Once we have a self-notion, we can perform inferences into and out of that language that amount to "I-introduction" and "I-elimination." From "Tree in front" we infer "Tree in front of me," and from "Tree in front of me" we infer "Tree in front." This latter sort of inference suggests how information from our self-notion gets translated into action, even for sophisticated animals like ourselves with self-concepts. The self-concept is the concept formed by connecting to this more primitive kind of self-knowledge a concept of the same type as the concepts we have of others.

Now if we simply put in our explicit self-concept, through I-addition, the things we gain from self-informative perception and memory, and then take them back into our primitive self-concept, through I-elimination, it would seem a pointless exercise. But because we have other ways of knowing about ourselves, it is not. I learn, using a normally other-informative method, that John Perry is supposed to lecture at noon. I know that I am John Perry, so I can infer that I am to lecture at noon. Then, by I-elimination, I get: Lecture at noon. The opposite process allows me to make information, gained in normally self-informative ways, available to others. I feel an urge I might primitively express as "Want a beer now." I-introduction is helpful in a bar: "I want a beer." For room service in a hotel, that won't do. I have to say, "John Perry, room so-and-so, wants a beer." Any architecture that allows us to get to our lectures on time and order a beer from room service clearly has a lot going for it.

All actions, however distantly their intended results extend, begin with movements of our own bodies and their parts, intended to have effects on objects playing roles in our lives at the moment of action. I want to send a fax to Norway; the result I have in mind is getting Dagfinn Føllesdal to fax me back a draft of an article he is writing. It is getting this request in front of Dagfinn that is the motivating intention, the one thing I want to accomplish. I could do it by calling, or shouting if I had a loud enough voice, or sending smoke signals, or e-mailing; faxing is just one way to bring about the result. So this intended result doesn't dictate much in the way of bodily movement. But once I have built my plan down to the point where it is *executable*, I need to move my body to get it started. I need to stick my note in the fax machine and poke the right buttons with my finger.

It is only by being attached with our self-concept, and hence with knowledge from a perspective, that our beliefs and knowledge about the world at large are of any practical use to us, as forming the basis for initiating action. I desperately need Dagfinn's paper. I know the paper exists, that Dagfinn is authoritative, that I will be able to understand what he says about Husserl, and that he will be willing to let me see the draft. I carry this information about Dagfinn around in my head even when I am not with him, or on the phone with him, even when I have no knowledge where this inveterate world traveler might be. I don't think of him via a role he plays in my life. Perhaps that is overstating it, but at any rate I don't think of him via a role that leads back to executable action. There isn't much I can do. But if I know he is in his office in Norway, I can send him a fax. I can think of him as a person who will read the fax that I send by typing certain numbers into the fax machine in front of me. He is attached, however tenuously, to my self-concept; he is the person who is playing a certain role in my life that provides the possibility of interaction, as the person who will read the fax I will send by moving my fingers in a certain way.

This structure of our self-concepts, linking concepts about the person we happen to be (or at least take ourselves to be) with our primitive self-concept, and hence with what we perceive and what we do, is very basic to human life. We incorporate what others notice and know about us into our own self-conception. We do this all the time. And in fact most of us are very concerned about our *public identities*: the conceptions of us that others have, what our mothers and fathers and sons and daughters and colleagues and students think of us. It is what is written next to our names in the newspaper or the college catalog, or on the vita on our Web page. It is what presidents of the United States worry about when they worry about their place in history. For many issues, it is a better source of information about ourselves than any normally self-informative method of knowing.

For most of us, some very important building blocks of our own identity, our own self-conception, come from the outside, from assimilation into the "I" of the "me"; that is, by adopting as part of our self-concept opinions about ourselves that originated with the insights, or mistakes, of others. My parents tell me that I am like my grandfather, that I am a thinker, not a doer, and that becomes part of my self-conception. Through a series of accidents I become a philosophy professor, and slowly the expectations the world has of philosophy professors seeps its way into the core of my self-conception. I quit worrying about attributes that once seemed to be faults: flakiness, irreverence, inappropriate use of humor, procrastination, difficulty with the more practical aspects of life. I begin to take pride in them.

Public identities may take on a life of their own. Thus Borges:

I know of Borges from the mail and see his name on a list of professors or in a biographical dictionary. . . . It would be an exaggeration to say that ours is a hostile relationship; I live, let myself go on living, so that Borges may contrive his literature, and this literature justifies me. . . . my life is a fight and I lose everything and everything belongs to oblivion, or to him. (Borges 1964, 246–247)

We may have several public identities. I may be one person in the eyes of my surviving cousins, who meet every so often in Nebraska and reminisce about our grandmother and grandfather, uncles and aunts, and each other. My interest in Nebraska football, rainfall, and whooping cranes then comes to the surface. It's not an act; it's just a motivating complex coming off the shelf, in response to the situation. It goes back on the shelf when I get back to Stanford.

So I have a sense of my own identity. Here we see another use of the term "identity," perhaps more ordinary than the one philosophers use. What is my identity? For some psychologists it is the most central part of my self-concept, the things I think are not only true of me, but in some sense define me. Perhaps I can imagine myself as being a woman, or a Canadian citizen, but I can't imagine not being a philosopher; it is unthinkable. Then being a philosopher is part of my identity in this sense.

4 Notions and Bundles

As I conceive of beliefs, desires, and concepts, they are not abstract contents, not properties, not Fregean senses, not propositions, but cognitive structures in particular minds that have causes and effects. Concepts *have* contents; that is, we classify them by things they are of or about. A concept is not a concept *of* a certain thing because that thing fits its content. It is a concept of a thing because that is the thing it is used to hold information about, and guide behavior toward. To make sense of this picture, we need to recognize *notions* of particulars and *ideas* of properties and relations.

I think of notions as file folders, into which information of various sorts is put, and I often explain them in this way. A student comes into my office who has been assigned as my advisee. I take out a file folder and dedicate it to the job of storing information about this student. I put the various documents that come to me about the student, the work he gives me, my notes concerning his progress or lack thereof toward a degree. The whole thing is like my concept of the student; the file folder is what makes it of *him*—even if, in my careless and slothful way, I get things misfiled, and the folder is full of misinformation about him.

The stuff that's put in the file folder provides the "what" of my concept of the student, the file folder itself the "who." Together they constitute what I believe about him and what if anything I desire for him.

Now consider our friend Bill, working away at his dissertation on the war hero. He has two concepts of Bill. One is a concept of Bill because it is the concept assigned to keep track of a certain person, the one Bill read about in *Stars and Stripes*. His other concept of Bill, his self-concept, is a concept of Bill because it is Bill whom it stores normally self-informative information about, and because it is Bill's executable and other self-effecting actions that it motivates. The more primitive part of his self-concept was created to keep track of Bill only in the sense that his whole cognitive system was created, along with the rest of him, with the function of keeping track of what was going on in the world from his perspective, and initiating actions that made sense given this information. The other part of his self-concept began its life when Bill was in the hospital, with amnesia, and had to begin anew building up a concept of the person he happened to be, to link with his primitive self-concept, and to provide a place to put information he got in other ways—what the nurse told him about where he was found, and so forth.

Let's push the file-folder metaphor a bit further. Think of Bill's mind as a filing cabinet on wheels. It is full of file folders for the persons, places, and things that Bill has encountered, read about, and otherwise come to be acquainted with, however indirectly, to the extent that it has been worthwhile to form more or less permanent concepts of them. These file folders are notions; they have histories; they were introduced when Bill met, read about, saw, or otherwise encountered objects worth keeping track of. Lots of these files will include information that will allow Bill to recognize the objects these files are of, should he encounter them again. Sometimes people he hasn't encountered, like General Smith, include information that will allow Bill to recognize them when he sees them for the first time. General Smith, according to the file, is a big ugly fellow with puce-colored hair and lots of medals.

On top of the filing cabinet are two boxes, the inbox and the outbox. All the notes in these boxes are in protocol language. The inbox has entries like "Mild headache, now" and "big ugly fellow in uniform with medals and puce-colored hair in front." The outbox has "walk forward and extend hand," and "utter 'I've always wanted to meet you, General Smith.'" The first file in the top drawer has entries that correspond to those in the inboxes and outboxes, like: "I have a headache," "There is a big ugly fellow in uniform with medals and puce colored hair in front of me." This file is Bill's self-notion, and the file plus what is in it is his self-concept. Included will be lots of information about Bill—what he has come to believe about himself since awakening from his coma—that he was once a soldier, that he has amnesia with respect to events before coming out of the coma, that he is a Ph.D. student at Berkeley, and so forth.

By the time he is well into his dissertation, Bill will have a pretty big file on the war hero. So he has two notions of himself. One is connected causally to him, through the story he read in *Stars and Stripes*. Another is of him, because it is connected by I-addition and I-deletion to his input and output buffers. When Bill finally figures out who he is, he merges his war-hero folder and self-folders.

The file-folder metaphor has its limits. Mark Crimmins (1992) develops some other metaphors or models of concepts that are better for many purposes. Our notions and ideas seem to provide us with something more like a relational database, a richer informational structure than file folders provide.

But those issues don't bother me too much today, so I'll stick with the file-folder metaphor, at least long enough to get clear about another aspect of it that seems misleading.

File folders are very passive things. We do things with file folders; open them, read them, perhaps plan our actions around the information in them. But who would the "I" be that read the file folder that constituted his self-notion?

On the straightforward theory, the self is the person, the agent, the subject, the flesh-and-blood human being, or something very close to the flesh-and-blood human being, differing only perhaps in the way we would individuate it through time in certain puzzling cases that the great philosophers of personal identity, especially Locke and Shoemaker, have induced us to worry about. Does the person then consult his own self-concept? Sometimes. I might search my mind for a memory of a trip that I know I took as a kid. But the person who consults his own self-concept is already someone with beliefs and desires. I believe I took the trip and I want to know more about it. Usually the beliefs and desires in my self-concept just effect what I do; I don't have to search for them.

If we think of our self-concept as a big relational database, then we can also suppose that somewhere in our cognitive apparatus is a sort of processor with the ability to scan data and do something with what it finds, maybe several of them, busily scanning files and rewriting them in response to what they find and new input from sensors. But the processor works the same way in me as it does in anyone else. Its operations are not governed by my beliefs and desires; rather its operations are part of what is involved in those beliefs and desires being more than mere data, but being the basis of action. The processor is not me; it doesn't do what I do, although its working the way it does is part of me doing what I do. It is part of my cognitive apparatus, but it is not me.

It seems better to think of the self-concept—the self-notion and its associated ideas—as what I'll call a *motivating complex*. A motivating complex has two sides. On the one hand, the cognitions themselves cause movements. On the other, the contents of the cognitions provide one sort of reason for the actions that the movements constitute. Such cognitive complexes are physical, active networks in the brain, that make the body move in ways that will promote the desires that are part of the complex if the beliefs that are part of it are true.

Now, when we think of things in this way, Hume's bundle theory, or something like it seen through modern eyes, seems attractive. Even if my self is just boring old me, thinking about myself as myself brings in my self-concept, a network of ideas associated with my self-notion. But what is this self-notion? It might seem that buried somewhere in my self-concept must be some characteristics that *make* the folder a folder of *me*. My self-notion plays the role, semantically, of a rigid designator or directly referential term. The thoughts and beliefs, the memories, anticipations, and fantasies I have with the self-notion as a component are thoughts, beliefs, and fantasies about me. But what makes them about me? Not any information about myself that is so intimate and essential to me that it finds me in any possible world no matter how different I might be there than how I am now. What makes this file a self-notion is its connection with my primitive self-notion, with the inbox and outbox in terms of the file-cabinet analogy.

One idea that I think we should resist is that it is the presence of the word "I" in the file, or in the expression of my self-thoughts, as uttered to others or to myself, that makes the file a file of me. The word "I," like all words, gives us a way of doing something. "I" gives us a way of referring to ourselves. Saying "I," like moving one's hand to the top of one's head and moving one's fingers, scratching one's head, is a normally self-directed way of acting. The one is a way of scratching our heads, the other is a way of referring to ourselves. A person who has a notion that is related in the right way to self-informative perceptions and self-directed actions will use the word "I" to express beliefs about him- or herself. And this way of using "I" is what gives it its meaning, or sustains it, once it has it.

Just the bundle itself, or maybe the baling wire used in bundling it, or the file folder, nothing more transcendent, more pure, less bound by the confines of space and time and causation, than that.

Suppose that my office at Stanford were actually quite a bit better organized than it is. The university has hired efficiency experts to set up professors' offices, as the problem of absent-mindedness has become serious. All the information relevant to all of my tasks is carefully organized into file folders stored away in file cabinets in an orderly way. There is also a special set of file folders in a bin on the desk. There is no name on the bin.

In the first bin is a section for all of the tasks I have agreed to perform, and a section with my long-range goals and shorter-range intentions and desires of the day, and also a section with my vita and some other personal information of importance. There is a huge John Perry file in the cabinet with all the other files, and a bright red ribbon between it and the bin on the desk. That's to remind me who I am. In terms of the basic architecture, that's the only real difference between my office and, say, my colleague Michael Bratman's; in his the red ribbon goes from the Bratman file to the bin on his desk.

In the morning I go in, look over the bin on the desk, and start working through the tasks. I am like the character in the movie *Memento*,[3] who has lost his ability to consolidate short-term memory. Trying to solve a murder in this condition, he must write stuff all over his body so that when he wakes up he will know what he has discovered so far and what he must do next. This is quite unlike the relationship I have with the data stored in my head, with my self-concept and with all of the other pieces of information with which it is connected.

Now suppose that a new kind of manila folder and a new kind of filing cabinet and some new office equipment are invented, and they are all wired together or perhaps they just wirelessly communicate with one another. They are integrated into a system called the "Virtual Professor." I am no longer needed at all. The little red ribbon between the bin on the desk and the John Perry file is replaced with a red cable. The university is willing to invest in Virtual Professor systems because efficiency experts tell them the system will work better than the present one involving real people, and besides it saves providing parking. My Virtual Professor doesn't quite claim to be me; it claims only to be VPJP, the Virtual Professor replacement for John Perry. It takes over all my students and committee assignments and the like. The information about me, which comes via the red cable, is presented as if it is information about VPJP, with an occasional disclaimer: "For certain purposes, as part of the university's commitment to keep tuition increases as low as possible, and provide students better parking, I pretend to be John Perry, the professor I replaced."

Every morning at 8:00 or so the office just comes alive. The first task in the task bin lights up. A process of automated reasoning begins. The first task and the related goals, desires, and values start feeding information into a deliberation buffer, automatically pulling up information from all the various files, including my own, as it seems to be needed. Maybe it checks the Internet or makes phone calls when information is needed that is missing. Maybe it Googles "+John +Perry -Barlow" every morning in case I have become famous.[4] Little video cameras feed in information about the students who come to office hours; they are recognized and responded to appropriately. The deliberation buffer sends a message to the volition buffer, which starts the various machines working. Papers are graded, emails are sent, utterances made to the students, and so forth. And, importantly, in response to phone calls, e-mails, consultations with the calendar, and the like, new goals are formulated, prioritized, and put in the bin. The office just churns away until 5:30. Then the office pours itself a big glass of Irish whiskey and takes itself off-line until 8:00 the next morning. My dynamic office isn't just a bundle of things, but a dynamic bundle of things, which changes in response to information and affects the rest of the world in various ways.

I am unlike the Virtual Professor in a number of ways, including having sensations and being conscious of having them, and having a somewhat richer emotional life, and of course being much less organized and single minded, and in need of parking. Still, it seems to me that the way my cognitions work is very much like a Virtual Professor's. My beliefs and desires (using those terms very generally, for all kinds of doxastic attitudes and pro-attitudes) combine to produce various executable actions. My self-concept is an active bundle of cognitions that converts information and misinformation of various sorts into action.

5 Two Pictures of the Self

I will end by discussing one very important way that I, and I think most people, are quite different from the Virtual Professor. This difference contributes to our sense that the real self, the real "I," is somehow elusive.

I want to contrast two pictures of our motivating self-concepts. One seems to be held by many philosophers and perhaps also by economists. Some of the people who hold it may instantiate it for all I know. I call this the *rational agent* picture. The other seems more accurate to me; I officially call this the "bundle of cognitive complexes" picture, but for short I call it the *impulsive self.*

My Virtual Professor and Mr. Spock of *Star Trek* seem to be rational agents. When Mr. Spock is faced with a decision, he deliberates, taking into account all of the goals he has and all that he believes. His desires are ordered by their importance; his beliefs by his degree of confidence in them, and that degree of confidence corresponds to the evidence he has for them. He rationally computes what the best thing to do is, that is, the thing which has the optimal chance of promoting his most important goals, given the beliefs in which he is most confident.

In other words, his self-concept forms a single, ordered, cognitive complex, and this complex motivates his actions. Emotions of course play no part in Mr. Spock's decisions, because he has no emotions; if he did happen to have one, I suppose he would wait for it to subside, or just ignore it. My conception of the impulsive self is based mainly on myself, but I think it fits almost everyone I know somewhat better than the rational agent picture. My goals and beliefs combine into clusters, often with many common elements, that vie for control of my various systems of effectors. Victory is seldom complete.

For example, suppose I'm at a department meeting. Someone says something which I interpret as a put-down. I become angry. But part of me, a little inner voice, urges restraint: "Calm down. You can be almost certain you won't lose anything by shutting up. Etc. Etc." This part of me continues thinking, even as I am uttering angry words. It has no control of an important part of my agency, that part of it that controls speech. Another cognitive cluster is in charge of that.

Some goals that are quite important to me, like not appearing foolish, not alienating colleagues, not saying things that will be counterproductive to the deliberations of the department, play no role in this second cluster, which has seized control of my mouth. They are present; they are motivating the ineffective little voice, but can't gain control of anything else, and in particular they don't control what I am saying. The goals in control are ones that are not very important to me, or so I would have thought, things like making sure people know how I feel, defending myself from criticism, and the like.

What we seem to have here is two different complexes of desires, beliefs, habits, and so on, each associated with the same self-notion, each parts of the same self-concept, producing different actions with different goals at the same time. The one is producing verbal behavior; the other is simultaneously producing articulate and reasonable inner thoughts and trying to take over the verbiage. Where am I in all of this? Looking back on it, I may feel like yet a third center of motivation, adjudicating between the two. But at the time, there are just the two centers.

Another familiar case, at least to me, is procrastination. One center of agency is busily making decisions about what to watch on TV, and controlling the remote and the rest of the body, which is sprawled out on the couch. The other part controls a corner of active thought, saying "Papers to grade, Papers to grade." Maybe, at some point, for some unknown reason, I move toward my study with its deskful of papers. The one complex of desires and beliefs has managed to get control of my body, while the other is limited to plaintive questions that pop up unbidden in the imagination: How did Elaine get out of the jam? Did Steinbrenner fire George? And Kramer, what did he do about the car he wrecked?

It would not be correct to say that these centers are multiple selves. There is a constant activity of trying to maintain coherence and order. Most of us, most of the time, keep some kind of order among our competing centers of agency. But we shouldn't think of ourselves as somehow separate from them, adjudicating between them. The competition may produce a third center of agency, a new coalition of beliefs and desires, led by the goal of producing inner equilibrium. But this new center is not the real me, but one more part of me vying for control.

Emotions are feelings that often divert us from single-minded rationality. It seems likely that emotions often serve to in effect divert us from deliberation, and move us more quickly to action. They are perhaps ways we tell ourselves that the case is too clear, or the time too pressing, for deliberation: act. Sometimes this is helpful. He who hesitates is lost. Sometimes it is not helpful. Fools rush in. At other times emotions empower one complex and weaken another. Sometimes they are like the elusive momentum in a football game, shifting inexplicably from one team to another. Guilt in particular pops up unexpectedly, too late to stop the sin, but in time to ruin full enjoyment of it.

6 Conclusion

Some philosophers will think the straightforward account of the self insufficiently mysterious or profound. Some will find my picture of self-concepts as bundles of competing bundles as at best a good description of a certain kind of neurotic, whose inner life falls far short of some rational ideal of personhood. I rather enjoy just being me, and take great pride and comfort in the occasional bursts of rationality that I see in myself and other humans.

Notes

1. A number of Shoemaker's important papers on personal identity can be found in Shoemaker 1984.

2. In Locke 1972, Bk. II, chap. 27.

3. Christopher Nolan, director; see http://www.imdb.com/title/tt0209144/.

4. But not as famous as John Perry Barlow; hence, it's best to add the '-Barlow' when searching.

References

Borges, J. 1964. Borges and I. In *Labyrinths: Selected Stories and Other Writings*. New York: New Directions.

Castañeda, H. 1966. 'He': A Study in the Logic of Self-Consciousness. *Ratio* 8: 130–157.

Crimmins, M. 1992. *Talk about Beliefs*. Cambridge, MA: MIT Press.

Locke, J. 1972. *An Essay Concerning Human Understanding*, 2nd ed. Ed. P. Nidditch. Oxford: Clarendon Press.

Shoemaker, S. 1984. *Identity, Cause, and Mind*. Cambridge: Cambridge University Press.

12 Ex Ante Desire and Post Hoc Satisfaction

H. E. Baber

Seven years, My lord have now past since I waited in your outward Rooms or was repulsed from your Door, during which time I have been pushing on my work through difficulties of which it is useless to complain, and have brought it at last to the verge of Publication without one Act of assistance, one word of encouragement, or one smile of favour. . . . The notice which you have been pleased to take of my Labours, had it been early, had been kind; but it has been delayed till I am indifferent and cannot enjoy it, till I am solitary and cannot impart it, till I am known, and do not want it.

—Dr. Johnson to Lord Chesterfield

L. W. Sumner argues that the informed desire satisfaction account of welfare is unsatisfactory because, since desires precede the states of affairs that satisfy them, satisfying desires may fail to satisfy their agents (Sumner 1996).

I argue that the temporal gap between our desires and the states of affairs that satisfy them poses no special problem for the desire theory. Even if getting what we want fails to satisfy us, we are, ceteris paribus, better off for having got it.

1 Desires for States That Aren't Like Anything for Us

According to desire satisfaction accounts of welfare, a state of affairs is good for a person to the extent that it satisfies her (informed, rationally considered) desires. The rationale for rejecting hedonistic accounts of well-being in favor of desire theories is the intuition that states of affairs that aren't "like" anything for us can harm and benefit us. Many of us would hesitate to jump onto Nozick's Experience Machine because we believe that living in a fool's paradise is not a good thing. Life on the Experience Machine may be better than a life of palpable misery but it is not so good as a life of genuine activity and achievement, we believe, because we desire things other than feely psychological states and, intuitively, getting those things contributes to our well-being.

On the desire satisfaction account, "feely" psychological states also contribute to our well-being to the extent that we want them. Most of us want the knowledge that we have achieved our goals and the pleasant phenomenal state that goes along with that as well as the fact of achievement. "Good feels," even without achievement, are good to the extent that we desire them, and achievement without good feels is good insofar as we desire it; but good feels together with achievement are best of all. A minority of subjects aver that they would plug into the Experience Machine, but we cannot conclude that this is an expression of their hedonistic intuitions: they may just rank good feels very highly in their preference orderings and be prepared to incur substantial opportunity costs to get them.

The desire theorist in any case holds that states of affairs that do not include any phenomenal component, including those that are wholly extrinsic to us, can benefit us. We can desire any possible state of affairs, and perhaps even some logically impossible ones, including the admiration of people we do not know and a place in history after our deaths. According to the desire theorist the satisfaction of such desires benefits us.

The desire theorist's intuition that states of affairs that make no difference to our experience can harm or benefit us is not universal. Sumner, however, suggests that even if we grant the desire theorist's fundamental assumption that they can make a difference to our well-being, the prospective character of desire, which opens a temporal gap between desires and the states of affairs that satisfy them, undermines the account. States of affairs that satisfy my desires may not satisfy *me*. (1) Getting what I wanted may turn out not to be like what I thought it would be like for me, so that even though my desire is satisfied I am disappointed. (2) Worse still, my tastes, preferences, and goals may change so that by the time I get what I wanted I might wish that things were otherwise.[1] (3) Worst of all, my desire may come to be satisfied only after I am dead and not around to get any satisfaction out of it at all.[2] These cases are putative counterexamples to the desire theory, which identifies welfare with desire satisfaction.

Prima facie the difficulties posed by the prospective character of desire are a linguistic artifact. Even if we cannot desire things we have or states of affairs that obtain, we can *prefer* them to other alternatives. Nevertheless, even if preference is not necessarily prospective, some preferences are, and in a range of cases the satisfaction of our preferences does not satisfy us, either because the objects of our preferences turn out to be disappointing when we get them or because our tastes have changed in the interim. So these putative counterexamples to the desire theory pose difficulties even if the account is formulated in terms of preferences: what are we to say about the satisfaction of preferences that we no longer have?

I argue that even if the satisfaction of our preferences does not satisfy us or leave us *on net* better off, it does benefit us. And this is all the desire theorist needs. Our inclination to believe that we do not benefit in these cases comes from the residual hedonist intuition that no state of affairs can benefit us unless it involves a feely psychological component. If we reject this assumption, as desire theorists must, the temporal gap between desires and their satisfaction poses no special problem for the desire theory.

2 Putative Counterexamples to the Desire Theory

2.1 Disappointment

Even where we are adequately informed, duly deliberative, and, by any reasonable account, desire that a given state of affairs obtain at a future time, we may still be disappointed when we discover what that state of affairs is like. When I desire S, I anticipate that S will satisfy me. But I can be mistaken: "Between the idea and the reality . . . Falls the Shadow," and it lodges in the temporal gap between my desire and the state of affairs that satisfies it.

The obvious move is to close the gap by stipulating that my desire for a state, S, does not count as informed unless I correctly anticipate what S will be like for me and know that I will find S satisfying when I get it. Sumner, however, suggests that to close the gap by including knowledge about what the desired state of affairs will be like for us undermines the fundamental motivation of the desire theory:

The gap could be closed by stipulating that a desire does not count as informed—and thus its satisfaction does not count as making me better off—whenever the desired state of affairs turns out upon later experience to be disappointing or unrewarding. However, to take this step would be to confirm the desire theorist's suspicion that, once our experience of states of the world is admitted as relevant, then whether or not these states satisfy antecedent desires on our part is on the way to becoming irrelevant. For it would be tantamount to conceding that what matters so far as our well-being is concerned, it is *our* satisfaction and not merely the satisfaction of our desires. (Sumner 1996, 132)

The thought here is that including prior knowledge of what the objects of our desires will be like for us implicitly builds in an experience requirement for well-being: a desired state of affairs contributes to our well-being only if our experience of it does not turn out to be disappointing. Moreover, having granted this much, Sumner suggests, it is hard to see why the character of our experience should not be sufficient as well as necessary for its contribution to our well-being.

Suppose I and my duplicate-at-t_2 are both enjoying S at t_2 but that whereas I desired S at t_1 my duplicate did not: she had no idea in advance just how nice S would be. As Sumner suggests, however, pleasant surprises benefit us: intuitively, all other things being equal, we're equally well off. Events that occur at other times might make a difference: I may have unlimited access to S in the future whereas my duplicate is doomed to an S-less future and is worse off for having tasted it, but it is not clear that that makes her worse off *at* t_2. In any case, past history, in particular whether or not we desired S at t_1, does not seem to make any difference. The desire theorist can certainly stipulate that S doesn't count as benefiting my duplicate in virtue of the absence of any earlier desire for S without any logical impropriety, but this move seems at best ad hoc.

I suggest, however, that although the phenomenal character of S contributes to my well-being at t_2 it does so precisely because it is an object of my desire. I did not just want to get S. I also wanted to get a good feel out of it. Most of us have a standing desire to get good feels, and we can assume that my duplicate, who was not born yesterday or created instantaneously for the sake of the thought experiment, had that standing desire as well. When we enjoy S both of us benefit from the phenomenal state we get from S. Arguably, however, I am better off than my duplicate because I, in addition, satisfy the desire to get S as such.

I have a special interest in the history of late antiquity in the eastern Mediterranean, and one of my life's ambitions is to see Hagia Sophia. I travel with a friend who has never particularly wanted to go there. Nevertheless, both of us are equally thrilled by the architecture, ornament, and atmosphere of the place. Still, it seems to me that in virtue of my history and past desire I benefit more from the visit than my friend does.

It is easy enough to say that that is so because, in virtue of my historical interests and past desire, my experience is different in character. But this move is ad hoc, motivated perhaps by the question-begging assumption that well-being is a function of our phenomenal state—which the desire theorist denies. Even if my friend were my duplicate in all respects other than my historical interests and desire to see Hagia Sophia, and was at the time of our visit in exactly the same brain state, neuron by neuron and atom by atom, the case can still be made that going there contributed more significantly to my well-being. Visiting Hagia Sophia benefits both of us because it satisfies our shared desire for aesthetic pleasure, a phenomenal state that both of us achieve. For me, however, it satisfies an additional desire, and to that extent I am better off.[3]

I can, of course, imagine an individual who *didn't* have a standing desire for good feels. Such beings are rare in the state of nature and our intuitions go awry when they turn up in thought experiments. Fictional cases, however, pump out intuitions. Consider Tolstoy's Father Sergius, "a handsome prince who everyone predicted would become aide-de-camp to the Emperor Nicholas I and have a brilliant career, [who] left the service, broke off his engagement to a beautiful maid of honour, a favourite of the Empress's, gave his small estate to his sister, and retired to a monastery to become a monk" (Tolstoy 1873). Brilliant, ambitious, and well-connected, Sergius, even after leaving the world, is dogged by success, including monkish success as a spiritual adept, and by good feels which he does not desire. Whether we buy Tolstoy's notions about the value of humility and benevolence, it's pretty clear that Sergius' achievements and concomitant good feels don't do a thing for him and, indeed, undermine his well-being. What a pity all those good feels are wasted on a monk, we think—*we'd* sure know what to do with them.

If my duplicate had no standing desire for good feels (or, a fortiori, if she, like Father Sergius, actively wished to avoid them), then I doubt seeing Hagia Sophia would contribute to her well-being at all.[4] As for me, I wanted both to get good feels and to see Hagia Sophia. If each of these desires is satisfied, the satisfaction of each contributes independently to my well-being.

Suppose, however, that I am disappointed on seeing Hagia Sophia. Even knowing all that I do and having seen pictures, the experience leaves me cold. Moreover, given the opportunity costs, I am worse off on balance for having gone there: the side trip to Istanbul cost me the chance to see Venice, which I would have enjoyed much more.

Arguably, however, even if I am disappointed, visiting Hagia Sophia contributes to my well-being because it is something I wanted to do. The fact that I ended up worse off *on net* as a consequence of satisfying my desire to see it does not establish that satisfying that desire failed to benefit me at all. It shows only that the visit did not make me as well-off as I had hoped because I did not get the concomitant experience I anticipated, and moreover that I was worse off *on balance* because I did not satisfy my desire to see Venice, which would have produced a better experience. I would have been even worse off if I had not gotten either to Istanbul or to Venice.

I reflect, philosophically: "Well, I didn't like Hagia Sophia—but at least I got there."

2.2 Changing Tastes

Sometimes, even when we get what we want, having correctly anticipated what it would be like, it does not satisfy us because our tastes have changed by the time we get it. I have always wanted to travel around Europe, but by the time I have the money to do it I am too old to enjoy it and would rather stay at home puttering around in my garden. By the time I get the chance to satisfy my desire, doing so would make me on net worse off.

The relatively ephemeral character of desire poses difficulties for any desire theory of well-being.[5] Suppose that at t_1 I desire S, at t_2 I do not desire S, and shortly thereafter S obtains. Does S contribute to my well-being? If so, when? Not, it seems, at the time that I desire it, because then I haven't yet got it; not when I get it, because by then I have stopped wanting it. This is suspiciously reminiscent of Epicurus' take on the evil of death. When is death an evil for us? Not when we're alive, because death is not there; not when we're dead, because we are not there.

Sometimes this worry is easy to dismiss because, on closer examination, it turns out that the state I attain is not in fact the state I desired. It may be that t_1 I desire S-at-t^*—not S-at-t_2—or that at t_1 I desire that S obtain at a time when I desire S so that S's obtaining at t_2 does *not* satisfy my earlier desire. Such time-bound desires and desires that are contingent on their own persistence do not pose serious difficulties for desire theories.

Consider Dr. Johnson's predicament. Johnson wanted, and needed, Lord Chesterfield's help when he began work on his Dictionary. After the Dictionary was finished he did not need or want Chesterfield's approval or patronage. There was *no* time at which he benefited from Chesterfield's support—whether at the beginning of his labors when he wanted but did not get it, or at the end when he got it but did not want it. The content of Johnson's desire was time bound and never, in fact, changed: he did not want Chesterfield's patronage as such—he wanted Chesterfield's help in time to facilitate his project, and that was something that he never got. Johnson did not benefit from Chesterfield's belated support because it was not something that he *ever* wanted. Johnson's predicament therefore should not trouble the desire theorist: there was *no* time at which he wanted what Chesterfield eventually delivered and hence no time at which he benefited.

In most cases, however, our desires are not time bound. As a child I wanted to live in the South but changed my mind long before I ended up spending a year in Tuscaloosa. I did not want to spend some particular part of my life in the South, and my desire was not conditional on its own persistence. My desire to live in the South at some time or other was satisfied, but it is not clear when, if ever, living in Tuscaloosa contributed to my well-being. When did living in Tuscaloosa benefit me? Not as a child, because I was not there; not when I lived in Tuscaloosa, because then I did not want to be there.

Nevertheless, arguably, there is no compelling reason why we should deny that in virtue of getting what I wanted, even though my desire was long dead by the time it was satisfied, I benefited, even though I was not *on net* better off. On balance, living in Tuscaloosa made me worse off because I incurred substantial opportunity costs. Once my desire to live in the South was extinguished and I developed compelling interests in incompatible states of affairs, my past desire did not provide any compelling self-interested reason for me to move there. Nevertheless, even though I missed out on a lot while living in Tuscaloosa and was, *on net*, worse off than I would have been if I had spent that year somewhere else, I did benefit in virtue of the satisfaction of my past desire.

I reflect, philosophically: well, I didn't want to live in Tuscaloosa when I was there and I didn't like it, but at least I got there.

When it comes to the satisfaction of dead desires in cases like this, the vexed question is not *when* we benefit but how we weight such desires against live preferences with which they are inconsistent and which, we think, contribute more heavily to well-being.[6] Even assuming that our past and current preferences are equally informed and rationally considered, and equally intense, we do not believe that they should be given equal weight. It does not, however, follow that they have no weight at all or that we do not benefit when they are satisfied.[7]

Suppose that as a girl I had an all-consuming desire to collect miniature souvenir spoons from all fifty states. My desire for a complete spoon collection is long dead, and in fact I now think that collecting spoons reflects adversely on the taste and mental competence of collectors. But I still have a display case in my attic with an almost-complete collection: only Wyoming is missing. Vacationing near Yellowstone National Park I happen to stop at a roadside stand where I see the spoon that will complete my collection. Intuitively, buying it would contribute to my well-being, and, arguably, it would make me better off solely in virtue of my past desire. Complete spoon collections are worth very little, so it will not be worth my while to advertise it on eBay; my spoon collection has no sentimental value for me, and I have no interest in passing it down as an heirloom; moreover, I do not want to be the sort of person that has a complete collection of souvenir spoons. It is only in virtue of my long-dead desire to assemble such a collection that completing the set makes my life, admittedly in a very minor way, better.[8]

Cases like this are rare: current desires normally trump past preferences when it comes to deciding what we shall do. We weigh current desires more heavily than past ones because we, in most cases quite rationally, discount the future: a bird in the hand is worth two in the bush. Regarding my past desires, I consider how satisfying them now would have looked from my past perspective, and in most cases, given a reasonable discount rate and figuring in my current preferences, striving to satisfy them is not worth it.

Ten years ago I wanted to visit Vienna. Now that I have the opportunity to see Europe, I no longer want to go: among other things, I discovered since then that in spite of passing the departmental language exam in grad school I cannot understand a word of German. I would much rather go to France where my best friend's sister has a horse farm and the language is less inflected.

Even from my earlier perspective, given my discount rate, a trip to Vienna ten years in the future might not have been worth very much, particularly if my desire was informed by a realistic assessment of my future linguistic capabilities. Satisfying that desire now will benefit me—but the benefits will be minimal, and, in light of the opportunity costs, I will be on net worse off. In general, we weigh current preferences more heavily than past desires, and give more consideration to recently past desires than to remote ones because in assessing what their satisfaction will do for us we adopt the perspective of the time at which they were current and discount the future.

Sometimes, however, even discounting the future, those past preferences carry enough weight to trump current preferences. When I was a child building my spoon collection was a very big deal and I would have been ecstatic had I learned that I would eventually get that last spoon. Even at fairly steep discount rates the future satisfaction of such desires weighs heavily. If I run across that last spoon fortuitously and can buy it for pocket change, in spite of the fact that I no longer want to complete my collection, I am still better off getting it.

It's a crying shame that I didn't find that spoon sooner, when I would have enjoyed getting it. According to the desire theory, however, although pleasant experiences, including the *experience* of desire satisfaction, benefit us because we want them, they are not the only states of affairs that benefit us. Any state of affairs that we desire benefits us, even if it obtains after we have ceased to desire it, and indeed, as I shall argue, even if it only obtains after our deaths when we are beyond all desire and the experience of its satisfaction.

2.3 Retroactive Prudential Improvement

The intuition that posthumous states of affairs can harm or benefit individuals is fragile and far from universal:

Wise men also die and perish together, as well as the ignorant and foolish, and leave their riches for other.

And yet they think that their houses shall continue forever, and that their dwelling-places shall endure from one generation to another; and call the lands after their own names.

Nevertheless, man being in honor abideth not, seeing he may be compared unto the beasts that perish. . . .

For he shall carry nothing away with him when he dieth, neither shall his pomp follow him.

(Psalms 49: 10–12, 17)

Nevertheless, the desire theorist is committed to the view that states of affairs that do not enter into our experience, including posthumous states of affairs, may, in and of themselves, benefit us. The benefits that come from posthumous desire satisfaction, however, pose special problems: it is not just that there is no time at which we shall be in a position to learn that we have benefited from posthumous desire satisfaction—it is not clear that there is any time at which we benefit.

Posthumous benefits, and harms, pose a trilemma for the desire theorist. If we benefit from the posthumous satisfaction of desires, then either (1) we benefit timelessly so that, though the satisfaction of our desires does not produce any "momentary well-being," our lives overall go better; or (2) we benefit at some time during our lives, prior to the satisfaction of our desires; or (3) we benefit posthumously, presumably at the time that our desires are satisfied. Though none of these accounts poses serious logical difficulties, I argue that in a range of cases it is most plausible to suggest that the momentary well-being that comes from satisfying our desires occurs posthumously. After dealing with each of these possibilities in turn I shall grasp the third horn of the trilemma.

2.3.1 The benefit we get from the posthumous satisfaction of some desires is momentary
Some of our desires are such that their satisfaction does not produce any momentary well-being: these desires are global, and there is no moment, either during our lives or afterward, at which they are satisfied. Among the goods we desire are what Broome (2004) has called "pattern goods": we want our lives, or at least some stretches of our lives, to go a certain way or exemplify a particular narrative. Velleman (1991), for example, suggests that most people prefer "uphill" to "downhill" lives—even given the same sum of momentary well-being through their lives in toto, they would choose lives that improve over time, preferably through their own efforts.[9] When it comes to such desires, because of the nature of their objects, there is no time during our lifetimes at which they are satisfied and no moment at which we benefit, even though in virtue of their being satisfied we should say our lives in toto go better.

The satisfaction of other desires, however, yields momentary well-being: I wanted my paper to be accepted, and when the decision was made to publish it I benefited, even though at the time of that decision I did not experience felt satisfaction or acquire any relevant "non-Cambridge" properties: I became better off when the decision was made in some remote conclave long before I received the letter of acceptance and experienced the pleasure of achievement. If my paper had been accepted posthumously I would have benefited in virtue of that desire also—but when?

If I had had a global desire to publish a certain body of work during my lifetime I should perhaps have benefited timelessly from the publication of my paper. But that is not what I wanted: to the extent that I have any preferences regarding my life in toto I just want to get what I want (whatever it happens to be) on as many occasions as possible. I have no interest having my life exemplify any particular narrative or in leaving an intellectual legacy: I just like writing papers and when I write a paper I want to get it published. Conjuring up global desires to be timelessly satisfied here is an ad hoc attempt to circumvent the question of when I benefit from posthumous desire satisfaction.

So we cannot escape by grasping the first horn of the trilemma: some posthumously satisfied desires are not global—their satisfaction is momentary, and we cannot evade the question of when we benefit by assimilating these cases to those in which we either benefit timelessly, throughout our whole lives, or nonmomentarily, through some stretch of our lives.

2.3.2 There is no time during an individual's lifetime to which the benefit of posthumous desire satisfaction should be pinned

Assigning any time during my life to the apparently momentary well-being that comes from posthumous desire satisfaction is fishy. Feinberg, for example, suggests that an individual is harmed or benefited by a posthumous event that thwarts or satisfies his antemortem desire "at some point well before his death when the person had invested so much in some postdated outcome that it became one of his interests" (Feinberg 1984, 921). This is odd. Suppose I write a paper that is only accepted for publication after I am dead. I put my heart into writing that paper and invest so much in the postdated outcome of my efforts that getting it published becomes one of my interests long before it is accepted. Shall we say that even if I had lived to see my paper accepted I would have benefited at the same time, when I had invested so much in getting it published that it became one of my interests, or shall we say that if I had lived I would only have benefited later, when the paper was accepted? Does death intervening between the time publication becomes one of my interests and the time my paper is accepted make a difference to when I benefit, or not?

Suppose death does not make a difference, and whether we live or die we benefit from a postdated outcome when we have invested so much in it that it becomes one of our interests. On this supposition, where x desires S and at some time, t_1, has invested so much in working to bring it about that it is then in his interest that S obtain, it is at t_1 that x benefits from S's obtaining in the future, whether he's around or not.

But, suppose S obtains at a time t_2 during x's lifetime. When S came about something good happened to x: the project in which he'd invested came to fruition. Moreover, he would have benefited at t_2 even if he did not find out about it then. In a remote gulag, x does not learn that the revolution has succeeded: t_2 is just another day in the salt mines for him, even though, unbeknownst to him, it's the best day of his life: he has been vindicated, and everything he dreamed of, worked for, and sacrificed for has come to pass. We would never say in circumstances like this: "Pity x invested so much in S at t_1 that it became in his interest back then, so that he got that shot of momentary well-being at t_1 rather than t_2: if he'd saved that well-being for later he would have had an uphill life." Intuitively, x benefits from S at t_2. If we want to remain faithful to that compelling intuition we shall have to say that where a person's interest is satisfied during his lifetime, he benefits when it is satisfied. So if we want to take Feinberg's suggestion about when we benefit from posthumous outcomes we will have to say that death *does* make a difference to when we benefit.

Now suppose that when an individual's interest in some state of affairs, *S*, is satisfied posthumously he benefits "at some point well before his death," either when he comes to desire *S* or, as Feinberg suggests, when he has invested so much in *S* that it becomes one of his interests, but that if he survives he only benefits later, when *S* obtains. Then we have to explain why premortem desire satisfaction or interest fulfillment benefits people when it happens but posthumous desire satisfaction or interest fulfillment benefits them earlier on, when they acquire the relevant desires or interests. There are two lines we can take.

One possibility is that, whereas in normal cases, where a person's desires or interests are satisfied during his lifetime, he benefits when they are satisfied, our folk-psychological concepts of desire, well-being, and the like do not give us any inkling about what to say in abnormal cases when they are satisfied posthumously. On this account, in such abnormal cases we should either throw up our hands and say there is no answer or pick some premortem time and, by convention, decide that it will count as the time that the individual involved benefits.

This response is reminiscent of concerns some philosophers have about the use of puzzle cases to elicit "our" criterion for personal identity. We've never had to deal with fission or fusion, brain-zaps, Star Trek machines, or brains in vats, so it may be that our concept of a person does not convey any identity criteria to deal with these cases. There is, however, an important difference between worries about the more bizarre puzzle cases of personal identity and the cases under consideration: posthumous desire satisfaction is not "abnormal." It happens all the time. So even if it is plausible to suggest that our concept of a person does not give us any guidance when it comes to elaborate science-fictional scenarios that do not happen and likely cannot happen in the order of nature, it is far less plausible to take this tack when it comes to posthumous desire satisfaction.

The other option, again inspired by the literature on personal identity, is to adopt a "best candidate" account for selecting the time at which a person benefits from the satisfaction of his desires or interests. According to such accounts there are some concepts that convey diverse criteria for application, some of which dominate others. So, while our dominant criterion for identifying artifacts through time is spatiotemporal continuity, where that fails we fall back to a secondary criterion: sameness of parts. In the most familiar case, the Ship of Theseus survives as the Continuously Repaired Ship, a vessel that is spatiotemporally continuous with the original even though after decades of reconstruction it does not have any of the same parts. If, however, the Continuously Repaired Ship hadn't survived, we should identify the Plank-Hoarders Ship, composed of all and only the planks cast off from the Ship of Theseus during its ongoing refurbishment, as the Ship of Theseus because, absent the Continuously Repaired Ship, it is the best candidate.

The problem of posthumous desire satisfaction lends itself to this treatment because, according to the desire theory, there are two conditions that have to be met for an individual's well-being to increase—his desiring S and S's obtaining—and these conditions may be satisfied at different times. So maybe we should say that while the dominant criterion for dating the momentary well-being that accrues to an individual is the time of satisfaction, where this fails, we fall back on a secondary criterion: the time of desire or the time at which an individual has invested so much in an outcome that it becomes one of his interests. Assuming that individuals cannot benefit posthumously we say that if x survives to t_2, when S obtains he benefits at t_2; if he does not survive then the best candidate time is t_1, so that is when he benefits.

This is a peculiar counterfactual, but best candidate theories always throw up peculiar counterfactuals. In the case of the Ship of Theseus, given the best candidate treatment, where only the Plank-Hoarder's Ship survives, we say, "Good thing the Continuously Repaired Ship got zapped, because if it hadn't *this ship* wouldn't be the Ship of Theseus," and if both ships survive, we say of the Plank-Hoarder's ship, "Good thing the Continuously Repaired ship is up and running, because if it hadn't survived, *this ship* wouldn't exist." Best candidate theories are always fishy.

The best candidate solution to the problem of posthumous desire satisfaction is, however, even fishier than usual, because there is no reason to think that the time an individual acquires a desire or the time at which a desire becomes of interest is even a second-best candidate for the time of benefit: they are not candidates at all. When it comes to the Ship of Theseus there is some motivation for hoarding planks: a prudent plank-hoarder with an interest in historical preservation may want to keep an extra ship as a backup: "If anything happens to that ship out on the high seas, at least we've still got this one." But there is no comparable motivation for forming desires or trying to bring it about that some state of affairs is in one's interest.

Suppose I know that I have only a month to live and that I will not survive to see a whole raft of my desires satisfied. I will not regard my current desires or interests as backups. I am not going to take comfort in the thought that because I will not live to see these desires satisfied they *now* contribute to my well-being. I am certainly not going to try to work up desires for more states of affairs that will only obtain after my death or invest more in postdated outcomes to the extent that they become interests for me in order to secure additional well-being for myself now. If anything, what I will do is divest myself of desires for future states, cash out my investments in outcomes that will only obtain after my death, and abandon long-term projects. Principled individuals with moral agendas may behave differently, but insofar as I am after my own well-being I will seize the day.

The best candidate solution is not logically incoherent. There is no general problem with accounts according to which later events bring about earlier ones so long as we recognize that not all bringing-about is causal: grades are changed retroactively, marriages are annulled, and medals are awarded posthumously. The problem is that these accounts yield counterintuitive results because, whichever way you cut it, if there is any time at which an individual benefits from the satisfaction of his desires it is the time at which they are satisfied. So, assuming that there is a time at which individuals benefit from posthumous desire satisfaction, it must be after their deaths. And, I shall argue, that is not as crazy as it sounds.

2.3.3 Individuals benefit from the posthumous satisfaction of their desires posthumously When does a state of affairs benefit us? Understood in one way, it benefits us at the time that we commence being better off in virtue of it; understood in another way, it benefits us when it makes us better off. Posthumous states that satisfy our desires benefit us in the latter sense after our deaths—and that, I argue, is the relevant sense when we want to know about "momentary well-being."

In general, if we ask when an object, x, comes to have a property, P, there are two events we could be asking about—the event which brought it about that x has P and the start of the stretch of x's history during which it has P. "Becoming P" is ambiguous between *being made P* and *commencing to be P*, events which may be, but need not be, simultaneous. I became a mother at the time that I gave birth to my first child. This event made me a mother and coincided with the commencement of my motherhood. Sometimes, however, there is a temporal gap: I was hired for my present position in April but started work in September. The event that *made* me a member of the faculty occurred in April, so if the question is one of when the event that, eventually, conferred that status on me occurred, it is in April: the stretch of my life during which I was a member of the University of San Diego philosophy department did not *commence* until September. My contract gave September 1 as its starting date.

When an event brings it about that an object commences to have a property in this way it does not *cause* the object to acquire that property. The departmental hiring decision conferred a status on me: it *entitled* me to a salary, office, and benefits starting the following September. It did not *cause* me to get the paycheck, the Kaiser card, or the office key. Causation requires a mechanism and intervening events, but the conferring of entitlements and bringing about of other Cambridge changes can leap both spatial and temporal gaps, as was the case when the hiring decision in April brought it about that I became a member of the University of San Diego philosophy department in September. Moreover, whereas causation goes only goes one way, from earlier to later events, the bringing about of Cambridge changes goes every which way. Grades are changed retrospectively and awards are conferred posthumously: the Congressional Medal of Honor is almost always conferred posthumously, since just about everyone foolhardy enough to do what it takes to get it is killed in the process. When a grade or award is conferred ex post facto the event that *makes* an individual have a property postdates his commencing to have that property.

In typical cases, when an individual's desire for some state, S, is satisfied during his lifetime, he commences to be better off at the same time that S makes him better off, namely the time at which S comes about. At t_1, x wanted S; at t_2 he got it. At t_2 the start of S's obtaining made x better off. T_2 also marks a boundary between a stretch of x's history when he was less well off and a stretch of his history when he was better off: it is the moment he commenced being better off.

Sometimes, however, the objects of our desires are necessarily nonmomentary. I want the conference that I'm planning to go well, with good papers, good discussion, lots of schmoozing. I will benefit if it goes well, but there is no *moment* at which the satisfaction of that desire makes me better off. The start of the conference doesn't make me better off; the end of the conference doesn't make me better off—if anything, it makes me worse off because that is when the fun comes to an end; and no momentary event in between makes me better off. I commenced being better off at the start of the conference, but what happened then is not "momentary well-being" like the slug of momentary well-being I got when my paper was accepted or when, after years of yearning, I finally got a dog. This is characteristic of the well-being we achieve when we satisfy our desires for "pattern goods" and suggests that the distinction between the nonmomentary well-being we achieve when our lives, or some stretch of our lives, go well and momentary well-being concerns the character of the state that *makes* us better off rather than the *commencement* of our elevated level of wellbeing. Sometimes, indeed, when the objects of our desires are global, when we want our lives in toto to go a certain way, there is *no* time during our lives when we commence being better off. We are, nevertheless, better off for satisfying such desires—and what makes us better off is the totality our lives.

So it is not implausible to suggest that when we ask for the time that a person benefits from the satisfaction of his desires, we are asking about the time—whether a moment or a stretch of time—at which the object of his desire *makes* him better off rather than the time during his life, if any, when he commences to be better off. If we take this suggestion, the problem of posthumously satisfied desires has an easy, intuitive solution: an individual benefits from posthumously satisfied desires when, after his death, the states he desires come to be. If my paper is accepted for publication after my death, the posthumous time of the decision is the moment at which I benefit.

3   The Problem of Ex Ante Desire Solved

I have argued that the temporal gap between our desires and the states of affairs that satisfy them does not pose any insurmountable difficulties for the desire theory. We benefit from the satisfaction of our desires when the states of affairs we desire make us better off, even if by then our desires are dead, and even if we ourselves are dead.

Epicurus' argument is a sophism: we don't have to be "there" to be harmed by death. But we may take some consolation in the fact that we don't have to be "there" to be benefited by posthumous desire satisfaction, either.

Acknowledgments

I am grateful to participants at the session of the Inland Northwest Philosophy Conference on Time and Identity, where an earlier version of this essay was read, for their comments, and most particularly to the anonymous referee for this volume.

Notes

1. We are, all of us, prone to dynamic inconsistency: all of us have lost desires we used to have and are, in many cases, indifferent about their satisfaction. According to Derek Parfit (1984), from the standpoint of our self-interest we have no reason to care whether our PI desires (past desires to which we are now indifferent) are fulfilled, and no reason to fulfill them were the opportunity to arise. Intuitions about this matter, however, differ: Kryster Bykvist (2001, 42) maintains that "when past preferences are replaced by new ones, it seems absurd to say that we ought to respect the preferences we once had." Other writers, however, suggest that even if present desires outweigh or trump past desires, ceteris paribus, the satisfaction of past desires, in particular those which we have not intentionally repudiated, contributes to well-being. See, e.g., Luper 2005.

2. See, e.g., Pitcher 1984 and Feinberg 1984 on posthumous harms.

3. Simon Keller (2004) argues that the investment we make in working to achieve goals contributes to their benefit for us once we achieve them, and that indeed seems to figure in cases like this one. I have been accumulating frequent flyer miles for years to get that trip to Istanbul. But I do not think that it is required to back our intuition that Hagia Sophia does more for me than for my duplicate. Even if I have not made any effort to achieve my goal I may have the standing desire that my life go a certain way as regards experiences, e.g., to assemble a collection of experiences of the world's most significant works of architecture as part of my life history.

4. If this intuition seems off, consider a comparable situation where *bad* feels are involved. Patients given some drugs report that they still feel pain but no longer mind it—the sensation is the same but the aversion is gone. It is not implausible to suggest that absent the aversion the sensation does not diminish the subject's well-being. It is moot whether, in the absence of aversion we should characterize a sensation as "pain," and, by the same token, whether we should regard any unwanted feels, regardless of their qualitative character, as *good*. Arguably, however, in both cases it is not the phenomenal character of the experience that contributes to well-being or undermines it, but the desire or aversion.

5. See, e.g., Luper 2005 for a discussion of the "lost desire thesis," the doctrine that we have no self-interested reason to care whether past desires about which we are currently indifferent are fulfilled.

6. For an extended discussion see, e.g., Bykvist 2001.

7. Vorobej (1998) suggests that philosophers may be inclined to deny the normative power of past desires because they assume that if past desires count at all they must be given the same weight as other desires and so overlook "non-egalitarian temporal neutrality theses." Parfit, he suggests, moves illegitimately from the intuitions suggesting that past desires ought not to be given the same weight as current ones to the conclusion that they ought to receive no weight at all.

8. Brandt (1984 [1979], 249–250) wonders about the following case. Your six-year-old son has a present desire to celebrate his fiftieth birthday by taking a roller-coaster ride. You know that by his fiftieth birthday that desire will be long dead. Reflecting on this case, Bykvist (2001, 20) suggests plausibly that it seems wrong to count this preference: "why should this preference be respected when your son will unavoidably lose all interest in roller-coasting? If you satisfy this preference, then he will end up later doing what he then does not want to do."

This is not a particularly compelling example because it is easy enough to write off your son's desires as uninformed or irrational insofar as he likely believes that he will enjoy a roller-coaster ride on his fiftieth birthday as much as he enjoyed it on his sixth. It does not in any case follow that there are no cases in which earlier preferences trump current ones.

9. Velleman (1991) argues compellingly that overall well-being is not a function of momentary episodes of well-being during a person's lifetime: some of the goods that make our lives go well are "pattern goods" (Broome 2004). Some of us, at least, want our lives to exhibit a certain narrative structure; e.g., as Velleman notes, even where the same amount of overall utility is involved, we prefer that our lives go better over time than that they start off well and go worse.

References

Brandt, R. 1984 [1979]. *A Theory of the Good and the Right.* Oxford: Oxford University Press.

Broome, J. 2004. *Weighing Lives.* Oxford: Oxford University Press.

Bykvist, K. 2001. What Is Wrong with Past Preferences? In *Value and Choice*, vol. 2, ed. W. Rabinowicz. Lund: Lund Philosophy Reports.

Feinberg, J. 1984. *Harm to Others.* Oxford: Oxford University Press.

Keller, S. 2004. Welfare and the Achievement of Goals. *Philosophical Studies* 121:27–41.

Luper, S. 2005. Past Desires and the Dead. *Philosophical Studies* 126:331–345.

Parfit, D. 1984. *Reasons and Persons.* Oxford: Oxford University Press.

Pitcher, G. 1984. The Misfortunes of the Dead. *American Philosophical Quarterly* 21:183–188.

Sumner, L. 1996. *Welfare, Happiness, and Ethics*. Oxford: Oxford University Press.

Tolstoy, L. 1873. *Father Sergius*. Christian Classics Ethereal Library. http://www.ccel .org/ccel/tolstoy/sergius.ii.html.

Velleman, J. 1991. Well-Being and Time. *Pacific Philosophical Quarterly* 72:48–77.

Vorobej, M. 1998. Past Desires. *Philosophical Studies* 90:305–318.

IV Death

13 Eternalism and Death's Badness

Ben Bradley

Suppose that at the moment of death, a person goes out of existence.[1] This has been thought to pose a problem for the idea that death is bad for its victim. But what exactly is the problem? Harry Silverstein says the problem stems from the truth of the "Values Connect with Feelings" thesis (VCF), according to which it must be possible for someone to have feelings about a thing in order for that thing to be bad for that person (Silverstein 2000, 122). But in order for a person to have feelings about a thing, the person and the thing must coexist in some way. Thus Silverstein feels compelled to endorse a metaphysical view he calls "four-dimensionalism," but which I prefer to call "eternalism": the view that purely past and purely future objects and events exist.[2] I agree with Silverstein that the badness of death entails eternalism. But the reason is different. Eternalism must be true in order for there to be a time at which death is bad for its victim. Death is bad for its victim at all those times when the victim is worse off for having died: namely, the times when he would have been living a good life had that death not occurred.[3] Silverstein rejects this view; he thinks there is something wrong with the very question of when death is bad for its victim. In what follows I argue that Silverstein has not shown the relevance of eternalism to VCF or the badness of death, and I defend my view about the time of death's badness against Silverstein's arguments.

1 Eternalism, Values, and Feelings

Epicureans hold that death is not bad for us; they point to the fact that death does not cause its victim to feel bad. Thus they assert a connection between values and feelings: something is bad for a person only if it causes that person to feel bad. Though Silverstein rightly rejects this strong thesis, he thinks it contains a nugget of truth; he accepts a weak version of the

VCF thesis according to which, in order for something to be good or bad for A, it must be *possible* for A to have a good or bad feeling about that thing. And "if a posthumous event does not exist, it can hardly be an object of feeling or experience" (Silverstein 1980, 110). This is where eternalism enters the picture. The eternalist holds that past and future objects and events coexist with present ones in a four-dimensional manifold. Other times are treated relevantly like other places; objects and events that exist in the past or future, but don't exist *now*, nevertheless *exist*, in just the way that objects that don't exist *here* nevertheless exist if they exist in a faraway place. By contrast, presentists hold that only present things exist. If we adopt eternalism, we can say that people coexist with their deaths, and therefore that our deaths can be the objects of our feelings.

But there are three things puzzling about this. First, why accept VCF? Silverstein briefly suggests one reason. He says that VCF explains the difference between posthumous harm and posthumous reference: "those who reject VCF owe us an explanation of why, for example, the problem of posthumous harm seems to be a 'real' problem in the way that posthumous reference is not" (Silverstein 2000, 122). This demand for explanation is puzzling for two reasons. First, there is an obvious way in which posthumous harm is more problematic than posthumous reference: unless we accept a certain sort of axiology (e.g., preferentism), posthumous harm involves backward causation. Posthumous reference does not. Perhaps Silverstein had in mind not posthumous harm, but the harm of death itself, which need not involve backward causation no matter what axiology we accept; perhaps Silverstein thinks that the harm of death seems more problematic than posthumous reference. But posthumous reference *does* seem to be a problem, at least for presentists, since at least some presentists take their position to entail that we cannot refer to purely past things (Markosian 2004). Posthumous reference and the harm of death seem equally problematic to a presentist.

Suppose we accept VCF. The next puzzle is, why think that an event must exist in order to be the object of feelings? Stephen Rosenbaum points out that people often fear events that never transpire (Rosenbaum 1986, 130). Silverstein admits that nonexistent events can be the objects of feelings in one sense, but insists that in the sense he has in mind, what he calls the *de re* conception of objects of psychological states, events must exist in order to be the objects of feelings (Silverstein 2000, 123). But this merely relocates the problem: why think that VCF is any less plausible given a conception of objects of thought that doesn't require objects of thought to exist? If the problem is that events exist only if they actually occur, then why not formulate VCF in terms of states of affairs, understood as necessarily existing, abstract objects that can obtain or fail to obtain, rather than events? States of affairs can be the objects of feelings at a time whether they obtain at that time or not.

Finally, suppose we admit that there is a true version of VCF according to which the objects of thought must exist or obtain. It is not clear that this commits us to eternalism. A presentist can say that although the event consisting of my death does not exist, since it does not exist now, there is nevertheless a related fact that obtains now: the fact that *it will be the case that I die*. And this fact can be the object of feelings such as fear or grief.[4] There may be independent reasons to think that this answer is insufficient— for example, that tensed facts must be "grounded" in nontensed facts—and that presentism is therefore unacceptable. But such reasons do not derive specifically from VCF or any problem having to do with death or posthumous harm.

2 Eternalism and the Time of Death's Badness

So I do not think eternalism is relevant to the badness of death in the way Silverstein suggests. But I think it is relevant in another way. We must be eternalists if we want to say that death is bad for its victims at times after they die. Why believe such a thing? The main reason is a consideration about value theory more generally. Bad events other than deaths seem to have their bad effects at some times but not others. This holds for events that cause intrinsically bad things to happen, such as toe-stubbings; the time of the bad effect of the toe-stubbing is just the duration of the pain. Once the pain is gone, the toe-stubbing ceases to be bad. It also holds for events that prevent intrinsically good things from happening. Suppose that Ned secretly leaves tickets to a baseball game in my mailbox, that I would enjoy going to the game, and that were I not at the game, I wouldn't enjoy myself at all during the time of the game; suppose Hud steals the tickets without me ever finding out about it. Hud's theft causes me to be worse off during the baseball game than I would have been; its bad effects on me occur during the game.

It would be nice if we could treat death like these other bad events. Some say we can't: if death is bad, it is a timeless or atemporal evil.[5] This view has a cost. It requires us to single out one particular sort of harmful event, and to say that it is bad in a different sort of way from the way other events are harmful. But the harm of death seems very similar to the harm in the baseball game example. If Hud had killed me instead of stealing my tickets, he would have harmed me in a similar way with respect to the game. (Of course, he would have harmed me in other ways too.) And I think similar harms should be treated similarly, so I say his killing me would have been bad for me during the game (and of course at many other times as well). But perhaps there is some reason to think the cases are different in a respect that matters.

Epicureans note one difference that might seem important: death marks the end of existence.[6] Failing to enjoy a baseball game because I'm bored at home instead can be bad for me during the game, because I exist then; but nothing can be good or bad for a nonexistent person. The Epicurean says that in order for an event to be bad for a person, there must be some time such that the event is bad for that person at that time. But in order for an event to be bad for a person at a time, the person must exist at that time. Since people don't exist after they die, nothing can be good or bad for them then; so death is not bad for anyone. This is a version of the "no subject" problem.

Silverstein characterizes the Epicurean argument in the following way. He makes a distinction between "life–life" comparisons and "life–death" comparisons. A life–life comparison is a comparison between the values for a person of two lives: one that he actually lives, and one that he would have lived had he not died. Such comparisons are unproblematic. A life–death comparison is a comparison between the value for a person of being alive and the value for a person of being dead. That comparison is problematic, he says, because no value can intelligibly be assigned to being dead (Silverstein 1980, 103). As before, the reason no S-relative value can be assigned to S's being dead is the no subject problem: when S is dead, S no longer exists.

Silverstein thinks Epicurus really does have a convincing argument against deprivation accounts of the evil of death that treat death like other deprivations, as my account does. Silverstein suggests that what is bad about being deprived of something good is *existing in a deprived state*, and that ordinary deprivations are bad for people at times because there are times when those people exist in a deprived state (Silverstein 2000, 120). But death is not like ordinary deprivations; since it causes nonexistence, it does not cause its victim to exist in a deprived state. The moral Silverstein draws is that death must be viewed as an atemporal evil, unlike other evils of deprivation.

I answer the Epicurean and Silverstein in the following way. Like Silverstein, I endorse eternalism. Unlike Silverstein, I deny that in order for an event to be bad for a person at a time, the person must exist at that time.

It is necessary that the person *exist* in order for an event to be bad for him at a time, but not necessary that the person exist *at that time.*[7] Death is bad for a person S at time t just in case the following proposition is true: If S had not died, S would have been enjoying a good life at t. Since this proposition is directly about S (perhaps S is a constituent of the proposition), its existence, and hence its truth, seems to require S's existence. Eternalism gives us S's existence. The proposition does not require S's existence *at t* for its existence or for its truth, in something like the way it can be true that I own property in Montana even if I do not exist in Montana.

I also reject Silverstein's account of ordinary evils of deprivation. It is question-begging to characterize those evils as causing their victims to exist in a deprived state; this rules out, by fiat, the possibility of depriving someone of goods by causing her not to exist. I say that in general, an event E is instrumentally bad for S iff E causes S to be worse off than S would have been if E had not occurred; more specifically, an event E is an evil of *deprivation* for S iff E is instrumentally bad for S, at least partly in virtue of the fact that E prevents some state of affairs that is intrinsically good for S from obtaining. This account of deprivation allows for the possibility that an event can be an evil of deprivation in virtue of causing someone to stop existing.

Thus, unlike Silverstein, I find life–death comparisons unproblematic. They are relevantly like the comparisons we make when thinking about ordinary evils of deprivation.

In "The Evil of Death Revisited," Silverstein says he won't defend his previous account of what it is to be deprived of a good, but still thinks we cannot compare a person's actual welfare level at a time after he dies with that person's welfare level at some other possible world where he continues to live. The reason is that no welfare level, even zero, can be assigned to a person at times after he dies (Silverstein 2000, 119). Silverstein is not alone in holding this view.[8] But there are good reasons to reject it.

A theory of personal well-being should identify those states that are basically intrinsically good for a person S and those that are basically intrinsically bad for S.[9] It should tell us how to determine the value of a person's life overall, and it should tell us how well things are going for the person at particular times. For example, a hedonist about welfare should say that states consisting of S experiencing some pleasure are intrinsically good for S, and states consisting of S experiencing some pain are intrinsically bad for S. We might say that the intrinsic-value-for-S function, IV_s, takes states of affairs as arguments and yields numbers as values; the hedonist says that IV_s maps S's pleasure states to positive numbers, S's pain states to negative numbers. The hedonist might add that S's overall welfare level is the sum of the values of IV_s for all arguments, and that S's welfare level at t is the sum of the values of IV_s for all arguments obtaining at t.

But this leaves open what we should say about states that are not S's pleasure or pain states. There are two possibilities for such states. Either IV_s is undefined for such states (the Undefined View), or it maps them to zero (the Zero View). So what reasons can be given in favor of one of these views against the other? Here is a quick and dirty argument: we should go the way that gets us the intuitively acceptable results in the case of death. The Zero View allows us to treat the evil of deaths like other evils, because we can derive S-relative values for times after S exists. (The value will always be zero if hedonism is true.) The Undefined View does not allow this. Better to go with the Zero View. It results in a simpler, more elegant, and unified account of extrinsic value. In other words: to choose between the views, we must look at cases where they give different results, and see which gives better results. The Zero View and the Undefined View get all the same results, except in cases where a person goes out of existence. In those cases, the Zero View gets better results. So the Zero View wins.

I suspect that argument will leave some unconvinced. Some will insist (feet stomping, fist pounding) that you just can't have a welfare level at times you don't exist! Not even zero! The Zero View is incoherent! So let me try another argument against, or perhaps rather issue a challenge to, the feet-stompers. IV_s cannot be undefined for *all* states that are not S's pleasures or pains. Consider the state consisting of me sitting in my chair. That state is neither a pleasure state nor a pain state. But on one point all agree: when I am sitting in my chair, I do have a welfare level, even if I am not feeling pleasure or pain. According to the hedonist, my welfare level is lower than it would be if I were enjoying myself, and higher than if I were in pain. So IV_{me} must be defined for the state consisting of me sitting in my chair; it must map that state to zero.

So hedonists must say that IV_s is defined for some states that are not S's pleasure or pain states. If IV_s is defined for states that obtain after S exists, then we can get a welfare level for S for times after S exists: namely, zero. The challenge, then, is to say just why IV_s should not be defined for states obtaining at times when S does not exist.

Perhaps it could be argued that IV_s should be defined only for states that are directly about S, or have S as a constituent. But this won't help Silverstein, for given the truth of eternalism, there are many such states that obtain at times when S does not exist, such as "S once existed."

Another possibility is that IV_s is defined only for states of affairs that involve S having some intrinsic property; since S can have intrinsic properties only when S exists, this proposal would entail that IV_s is undefined for all states obtaining at times when S does not exist. But there are many axiologies, such as preferentism, according to which how well someone's life goes depends on whether certain things happen outside her body. The intrinsic property proposal would force us to reject all such axiologies. Furthermore, consider the fact that S once had a mass of 50 kg. This sort of fact obtains at times when S no longer exists, but is not ruled out by the intrinsic property proposal.

I won't speculate further about ways one might try to draw the necessary distinction. I leave this as a challenge to those who deny that people have a welfare level at times after they die: draw a principled distinction between those states for which IV_s is defined and those for which it is not defined, such that IV_s is undefined for all states of affairs obtaining after S dies.

I now turn to one final objection. Silverstein denies that death is bad at a time; he thinks the question "When is A's death bad for A?" is "inapplicable" (Silverstein 2000, 131n6). According to Silverstein, the "whole truth about time" concerning A's death is constituted by the following three claims:

1. The time at which the evil itself—namely, A's death—occurs is immediately following A's life.
2. Since ascribing this evil to A requires the four-dimensional framework, it is an "atemporal" evil in the sense defined in "The Evil of Death."
3. The time during which this evil can be an object of A's negative feelings (and its being an intelligible A-relative evil requires that it be capable of being such an object) is the time during which A is alive. (Silverstein 2000, 131n6)

If these claims exhaust the truth about time concerning A's death, then there is no room for truths of the form "A would have been enjoying herself at t had A not died when she did." And there clearly are such truths. On my view, those truths are the grounds for truths of the form "A's death is bad for A at t."

Why does Silverstein deny the existence of such truths? Perhaps the answer can be found in his discussion of an example given by David-Hillel Ruben (1988, 212):

Suppose that someone now (in 2000) is eulogizing Napoleon . . . and consider the question: "*When* does Napoleon exemplify the property of being eulogized?" The puzzle is that (a) since the eulogy is occurring in 2000, the "natural" answer to this question seems to be "in 2000"; yet (b) Napoleon does not exist in 2000—and how can A exemplify properties at a time when A himself does not exist? . . . My solution . . . [is] to say that the question "When does A exemplify property P?" is inapplicable where P is a posthumous property. Specifically, my response to the question about Napoleon is:

Napoleon lived from 1769 to 1821; he is being eulogized in 2000; and that's the whole truth about "when" in this case. There *is* no further question as to "when" Napoleon exemplifies the property of being eulogized. (Silverstein 2000, 133n13)

This is a puzzling response to the question. Silverstein must be making heavy weather over the word "exemplifies," because he is happy to say that Napoleon is being eulogized in 2000, but not that Napoleon exemplifies the property of being eulogized in 2000. I wonder what the difference between these two claims is supposed to be.

In any case, it seems as if Silverstein is suggesting that it is problematic to say that something can exemplify a property at a time when it does not exist. ("How can A exemplify properties at a time when A himself does not exist?") My proposal evidently entails this problematic sort of property exemplification. But I cannot see why Silverstein thinks this is a problem. Recall that Silverstein thinks that the time during which A's death "can be an object of A's negative feelings . . . is the time during which A is alive" (Silverstein 2000, 131n6). This seems to suggest that A's death exemplifies a property—namely, the property of being an object of A's negative feelings—at a time when A's death does not exist—namely, during A's life. So Silverstein does not really have a problem, in general, with things exemplifying properties at times when they don't exist. He must think that there is some important difference between the property of being extrinsically bad for S and the property of being an object of S's negative feelings, in virtue of which the latter can be exemplified by S's death at times when S's death does not exist but the former cannot be exemplified by S at times when S does not exist. I do not see what the difference could be.

There is an interesting issue here, even if it is not quite the one Silverstein is interested in. How can something exemplify a property at a time without existing at that time? I do not have a good answer to this question. Perhaps it is misleading to talk of people *exemplifying properties* after they die. What I really want to say is that there are relations between people, deaths, and times. In particular, there is the "is-bad-for-at" relation, which relates a death D, a person P, and a time t if and only if D is P's death, and P would have been living a good life at t if D had not occurred. In order for this relation to hold, must P exemplify any properties at t? To be sure, when a death D, person P, and time t instantiate the is-bad-for-at relation, we can also say that P exemplifies the property of being an x such that D is bad for x at t. P exemplifies this property in virtue of not existing at t (and, therefore, having a welfare level of zero at t), and in virtue of the truth of counterfactuals involving D, P, and t. That sort of property exemplification does not seem problematic.

I conclude that there is no good reason to deny that a person's death harms her at times after she dies, and that insofar as we care about theoretical unity, we have reasons to treat the harm of death as a timeful harm like other ordinary harms. So the balance of reasons supports the claim that death is bad for us after we die. It is the acceptance of this claim, not VCF, that requires us to accept eternalism.

Acknowledgments

Thanks to Andre Gallois, Barbara Baum Levenbook, Harry Silverstein, and the participants at the 2005 Inland Northwest Philosophy Conference for helpful comments.

Notes

1. Feldman denies this, on materialist grounds (in Feldman 2000a), but I won't take up this controversy here. For the purposes of this essay I assume Feldman is wrong.

2. See Silverstein 1980, 2000, and Bradley 2004. "Four-dimensionalism" is at least sometimes used to name the view that objects have temporal parts (Sider 2001 xiii). That view is not relevant to the issues in this essay, which is why I prefer not to use that term.

3. I defend this view in Bradley 2004. Similar views have been defended by William Grey (1999), Neil Feit (2002) and Kai Draper (2004). It might be tendentious to say that the times when a person would have been better off are the times when he would have been living a good life, for this presupposes that one cannot have a nonzero welfare level at times when one is not alive. Some believers in posthumous benefits and harms might disagree. This dispute should have no serious impact on the arguments of this essay.

4. Andre Gallois made this point to me.

5. See Nagel 1970, 77, and Feldman 1991, 221, for views of this sort.

6. For a much more detailed exposition of an Epicurean argument along these lines, see Johansson 2005. I cannot do justice to Johansson's intricate argument in this brief essay.

7. See Bradley 2004. Also see Draper 2004, 102, for a similar view.

8. Bigelow, Campbell, and Pargetter (1990, 120) and Draper (2004, 95) are among those who hold this view.

9. On basic intrinsic value, see Harman 2000 and Feldman 2000b. Henceforth I will drop 'basic' for convenience.

References

Bigelow, J., J. Campbell, and R. Pargetter. 1990. Death and Well-Being. *Pacific Philosophical Quarterly* 71:119–140.

Bradley, B. 2004. When Is Death Bad for the One Who Dies? *Noûs* 38:1–28.

Draper, K. 2004. Epicurean Equanimity towards Death. *Philosophy and Phenomenological Research* 69:92–114.

Feit, N. 2002. The Time of Death's Misfortune. *Noûs* 36:359–383.

Feldman, F. 1991. Some Puzzles about the Evil of Death. *Philosophical Review* 100:205–227.

Feldman, F. 2000a. The Termination Thesis. In *Midwest Studies in Philosophy*, vol. 24: *Life and Death: Metaphysics and Ethics*, ed. P. French and H. Wettstein. Malden, MA: Blackwell.

Feldman, F. 2000b. Basic Intrinsic Value. *Philosophical Studies* 99:319–346.

Grey, W. 1999. Epicurus and the Harm of Death. *Australasian Journal of Philosophy* 77:358–364.

Harman, G. 2000. *Explaining Value*. Oxford: Clarendon Press.

Johansson, J. 2005. Mortal Beings: On the Metaphysics and Value of Death. PhD Dissertation, Stockholm University.

Markosian, N. 2004. A Defense of Presentism. In *Oxford Studies in Metaphysics*, vol. 1, ed. D. Zimmerman. Oxford: Oxford University Press.

Nagel, T. 1970. Death. *Noûs* 4:73–80.

Rosenbaum, S. 1986. How To Be Dead and Not Care: A Defense of Epicurus. *American Philosophical Quarterly* 23: 217–225. Reprinted in J. Fischer, ed., *The Metaphysics of Death*, Stanford, CA: Stanford University Press, 1993. References in the text are to the Fischer volume.

Ruben, D. 1988. A Puzzle about Posthumous Predication. *Philosophical Review* 97:211–236.

Sider, T. 2001. *Four-Dimensionalism: An Ontology of Persistence and Time.* New York: Oxford University Press.

Silverstein, H. 1980. The Evil of Death. *Journal of Philosophy* 77:401–424. Reprinted in J. Fischer, ed., *The Metaphysics of Death*, Stanford, CA: Stanford University Press, 1993. References in the text are to the Fischer volume.

Silverstein, H. 2000. The Evil of Death Revisited. In *Midwest Studies in Philosophy*, vol. 24: *Life and Death: Metaphysics and Ethics*, ed. P. French and H. Wettstein. Malden, MA: Blackwell.

14 The Time of the Evil of Death

Harry S. Silverstein

The "Epicurean view" (EV) is, roughly, the view that death cannot intelligibly be regarded as an evil for the person who dies because the alleged evil lacks a subject or "recipient." The basic argument underlying this view was briefly, but eloquently, articulated by Epicurus in a famous passage from the *Letter to Menoeceus* (1940, 31):

. . . so death, the most terrifying of ills, is nothing to us, since so long as we exist, death is not with us; but when death comes, then we do not exist. It does not concern either the living or the dead, since for the former it is not, and the latter are no more.

In brief, one who is still alive has not suffered the evil of death; but after one has died one no longer exists to be the recipient of goods or evils. Hence, according to EV, the contention that death is an evil for the person who dies is not simply false, but conceptually confused or incoherent. And the problem raised by EV can clearly be generalized to all (alleged) posthumous goods and evils. If Ann doesn't exist to be the recipient of the evil of her death, then she likewise doesn't exist to be the recipient of the evil of posthumous slander, the good of posthumous fame, and so on. Moreover, the problem of posthumous goods and evils at least *appears* to be a serious, substantive, problem in a way that the problem of posthumous reference, for example, is not.[1] And the reason for this, I have argued, is that for x to be good or evil for some recipient, R, it would seem that it must at least be possible for x to have an appropriate connection with relevant experiences and feelings of R. If, for example, R cannot even in principle have negative feelings or experiences in virtue of x—as would appear to be the case if x entirely postdates R—then it is hard to see how x can intelligibly be regarded as an evil for R.

In two published papers (Silverstein 1980, 2000) I have attempted to refute EV—and, thus, to show that, and how, death can intelligibly be regarded as an evil for the person who dies. My argument against EV—an argument presented in 1980, and then defended against objections in 2000—has two key components. The first is an account of the "Values Connect with Feelings" (VCF) requirement, according to which (1) the connection need not be *actual*, but merely *possible* (which allows me to agree with Nagel [1979], Levenbook [1984, this vol.]—and others—that, for example, even undiscovered infidelity is an evil for the unsuspecting spouse); and most importantly (2) the requirement is satisfied provided that the relevant object, state, or event is a possible *object*, even if (as in the case of future events) it is not a possible *cause*, of the relevant feelings. The second key component is the employment of a four-dimensional (4D) framework, a framework that allows us to claim that *temporally* distant (and, in particular, future) events (states, etc.), like spatially distant events (etc.), exist, and thus are possible objects of relevant feelings.[2] In neither essay, however, did I focus seriously on the question: "*When* is death an evil for the person who dies?" In this chapter I try to rectify this omission. In the first section I argue that the correct response to this question—a response suggested briefly in a footnote in the 2000 essay—is to claim that it has, and at any rate needs, no answer. In the second section I criticize a notable recent alternative response, a response defended by Ben Bradley in 2004 and again in this volume, namely, that death is an evil for the person who dies at "the times when he would have been living a good life had that death not occurred" (this vol., 271).

1

Suppose that Ann was born at noon on 1/1/1951 and died at noon on 1/1/2001; and suppose further that we all agree that Ann's death is an evil for her. My response to the question "When is Ann's death an evil for Ann?" is essentially as follows:

(1) The time of Ann's life extends from noon on 1/1/1951 to noon on 1/1/2001.

(2) The time during which Ann is dead begins at (or immediately after) noon on 1/1/2001 and continues indefinitely from that point.

*(3) Claims (1) and (2) above comprise the *whole relevant truth* about time in this case.[3]

In short, whereas "when" questions can be answered unproblematically for both that which is an evil—namely, Ann's death—and the person for whom it is an evil—namely, Ann—there is no further relevant "when" question that needs to be answered concerning the "when" of "Ann's death's being an evil for Ann."

My defense of this view requires that I provide some background—background taken largely from my 2000 essay—which consists in a brief, introductory comparison of three frameworks: (1) my four-dimensional (4D) framework;[4] (2) what I take to be the standard three-dimensional (3D) framework; and (3) a "zero-dimensional" (0D) framework—the latter, of course, being an artificial, *gedanken*-experiment framework not actually used by anyone. As I conceive it, the 4D framework abstracts from both "here" and "now—or to put it another way, it has neither "here" nor "now" built in. The 3D framework, by contrast, has "now"—but not "here"—built in; and the 0D framework has both "here" and "now" built in. Thus, on the 0D framework, the sentence "Ann exists" asserts that Ann's existence is both here (roughly, at the place the sentence is asserted) and now (at the time of the assertion). Hence, whereas the sentence "Joe Campbell exists" is true on this framework (since Joe is here, now[5]), the sentences "Abraham Lincoln exists" and "George W. Bush exists" are both false (the former because Lincoln does not exist *now*, the latter because Bush does not exist *here*). On the 3D framework, by contrast, the sentence "Ann exists" asserts that Ann exists now, but leaves open the place of her existence—and is thus true so long as Ann exists anywhere. On this framework, both "Joe Campbell exists" and "George W. Bush exists" are true, but "Abraham Lincoln exists" is false. And on this framework, any of these sentences that is true *anywhere* is true *everywhere*. Finally, on the 4D framework the sentence "Ann exists" leaves both the time and place of Ann's existence open, and is thus true so long as Ann exists anywhere at any time. On this framework, all three of the other sample sentences are true; and any of these sentences that is true *anywhere* at *any time* is true *everywhere* at *every time*. (Furthermore, of course, these points are not restricted to sentences with the predicate "exists." On the 3D framework, for example, if I say "Joe Campbell has a New Jersey accent," I am asserting that Joe Campbell has a New Jersey accent *now*; and if this sentence is true somewhere, it is true everywhere—hence, since it *is* true here, it is also true in, e.g., Beijing.)

On the 4D framework, then, the sentence "Abraham Lincoln exists" is eternally, or atemporally, true. But it must be emphasized that this does not imply that Lincoln's existence *itself* is eternal, or lacks temporal boundaries, any more than the fact that, on the 3D framework, the sentence "George W. Bush exists" is true everywhere implies that Bush's existence *itself* extends throughout all space or lacks spatial boundaries.[6] Thus, just as the sentence "Bush exists, but he does not exist *here*" is unproblematic on the 3D framework, so the sentence "Lincoln exists, but he does not exist *now*" is unproblematic on the 4D framework.

Moreover, when I say that "now" is built into the 3D framework, I do not of course mean that we can't talk about the past and the future on that framework. But we can do so only from the perspective of the present—and thus, only through the use of past and future tenses, tenses that have an essential reference to *now*. (To say, for example, "Lincoln exist*ed*"—a sentence that *is* true on the 3D framework—is to say that Lincoln's existence was *before now*.) And this all means that, when compared with the 4D framework, the 3D framework is primitive and cumbersome in important respects. For example, when we want to describe something's existence as extending from the distant past to the distant future, we can do so, on the 3D framework, only via a cumbersome, tripartite expression—an expression of the sort nicely illustrated by the church phrase "was, is now, and ever shall be." And of course the 0D framework is as primitive and cumbersome in comparison with the 3D framework as the latter is in comparison with the 4D framework; just as the 3D framework can deal with times other than now only via tenses, so the 0D framework can deal with spatial locations other than "here" only through what I'll call "spenses," spenses that have an essential reference to "here." I shall suppose, to adopt the simplest possibility, that, in addition to its foundational "here" spense, the 0D framework has one additional spense: an "out there" (i.e., *away from here*) spense. And if we stipulate that the "out there" form of "exists"[7] is "exouts," then, though "George W. Bush exists" is false on the 0D framework, "George W. Bush exouts" is true.

I can now turn to the defense of my view. Suppose that, here and now, Ann is hitting her husband Dan over the head with a frying pan. In this case the claim that this head-bashing is evil for Dan would seem to cause no trouble for the 0D framework. (And likewise, there seems to be no problem with saying that this head-bashing is evil for Dan *here*, and is evil for him *now*.) But suppose that that which is allegedly evil for Dan is spatially distant from him. Suppose, for example, that his wife Ann is having an affair with a business associate named Van, that Dan never leaves Seattle (which is where he and Ann live), but that Ann's affair with Van is consummated only in Spokane. In this case the 0D framework would seem to have the same sort of problem making sense of the claim that Ann's spatially distant affair is an evil for Dan that the 3D framework has making sense of the claim that a temporally distant event is an evil for him. For from the perspective of Seattle (i.e., if Seattle is "here") Ann's affair does not exist; and from the perspective of Spokane, Dan does not exist. In short, just as, on the 3D framework, there is no time at which both "Dan exists" and "Dan's death exists" (or: "Dan is dead") are true (this being the basis for EV), so, on the 0D framework, there is no place at which both "Dan exists" and "Ann's affair exists" are true. And just as the switch from the 3D to the 4D framework allows us to make sense of the claim that Dan's death is an evil for him by allowing us to say that both he and his death exist, so the switch from the 0D to the 3D framework allows us to make sense of the claim that Ann's affair is an evil for Dan by allowing us to say that both he and Ann's affair exist.

But now consider this question: does the 3D framework provide—and does making sense of the claim that Ann's affair is an evil for Dan require us to provide—an answer to the question "*Where* is Ann's affair an evil for Dan?" I submit that the answer is a clear "no." I submit, that is, that we are all at least reasonably comfortable saying that, so long as we know where the affair is (viz., Spokane) and where Dan is (viz., Seattle), then we know all there is to know about "where" in this case, that there is no relevant additional "where" question that needs to be answered concerning the "where" of "Ann's affair's being an evil for Dan."[8] In short, even if it is true that all evils that are straightforwardly intelligible on the 0D framework can straightforwardly be assigned both a time and a place, it is not true that all spatially distant evils whose intelligibility requires a move up to the 3D framework can straightforwardly be assigned a place. And since the 3D framework abstracts from "place," this fact—that the 3D framework allows room for goods and evils to which a place cannot straightforwardly be ascribed—should not, I think, be surprising. But similarly, then, it would seem perfectly reasonable to make the comparable claim about time with regard to temporally distant evils that require the 4D framework—that is, to claim that, even if all evils that are straightforwardly intelligible on the 3D framework can straightforwardly be assigned a time, it is not true that all temporally distant evils whose intelligibility requires a move up to the 4D framework can be assigned a time. And that is exactly what I want to say with respect to the evil of death.

Moreover, I think this point is supported by a consideration of what Bradley and I both (and others, such as Fred Feldman [1991, 1992]) think justifies the contention that claims like "Ann's death is an evil for Ann" are not merely intelligible but typically true, namely, a comparison, made possible by the 4D framework, of alternative temporal life-wholes. Suppose, then, that we say Ann's death is an evil for her because her actual

50-year life-whole is less desirable overall than the possible 85-year life-whole which we decide is the appropriate basis for comparison. The crucial point is that, though this comparison essentially answers the question of *why* Ann's death is evil for her (the alternative 85-year life-whole contains more of life's goods, etc.), there is nothing in it that answers, or even addresses, the question of *when* Ann's death is an evil for her. And though it does not explicitly rule out attempting to provide an answer to this question on other grounds—a point illustrated by the fact that Bradley, Feldman, and I, who all endorse this sort of comparison, give three different responses to this question[9]—it does support the view that, contrary to what Bradley clearly seems to suppose, accounting for the evil of death does not *require* an answer to this question. But if that is so—and if, as I think, none of the likely ways of answering this question is very plausible—then my view would seem to be the best option.

But that brings us to a consideration of Bradley's view.

2

Bradley's view, again, is that death is an evil for the person who dies at "the times when he would have been living a good life had that death not occurred." But this view seems, at least to me, to be very implausible and counterintuitive, and thus acceptable only if (contrary to what I've been arguing) we have no other viable alternative. To begin with, Bradley's view has some (to my mind) strange implications. For example: my mother died, at age 86, in June of 2000; and her death was at least an indirect result of, though it did not immediately follow, a serious auto accident she had had the preceding winter. If, then, we compare her actual life-whole to the life-whole which would have obtained if she had not had the accident, which would seem to be an appropriate alternative life-whole to choose for the comparison; and if we consider the likely duration of that alternative, given (among other things) the history of female longevity in my family; then it would seem plausible to say that that alternative life-whole would have extended five years longer to, say, June of 2005. Well, if that is so, then on Bradley's view it would seem to have been appropriate for my sisters and me to plan a family party for some time in, say, July 2005, to celebrate the fact that, though our mother's death *had* been an evil for her through the preceding five years, it now no longer was. And this—to me, at least—seems "exceeding strange." To turn to another kind of case, consider posthumous evils other than death—the breaking of deathbed promises, the posthumous destruction of one's reputation, and so on. Specifically, suppose that Ann was a writer who wrote several novels that were both critically acclaimed and extremely popular—novels of such stature that she could have expected to be admired for centuries after her death, in the way that, for example, Jane Austen has been—but that, some time after her death, her country is taken over by a brutally repressive regime whose leaders hate her books and manage to purge them from the culture so thoroughly that subsequent generations have no knowledge whatever of her or her work. In my view, insofar as it is reasonable to view this unfortunate purge as evil *for Ann* at all, it is just as reasonable to view it as evil for her if it occurs, say, fifty years after she dies (at a time when there is no appropriate alternative life-whole on which she would still be alive) as it is if occurs ten years after she dies (at a time when she would still be alive on an appropriate alternative life-whole). But on Bradley's view, it would seem, we would have to say that the purge is an evil for her if it occurs at the earlier time, but not if it occurs at the later time. And, again, that seems strange.

To be sure, Bradley might deny that his view concerning the time of the evil of death is intended to apply to other posthumous evils.[10] But if he takes this way out, I think he goes from the frying pan into the fire. For if, as his discussion would seem to imply, any "posthumous evil" claim requires that an answer be provided for the corresponding "when" question; and if, as the current line suggests, this answer will vary from evil to evil; then it would appear that, for every different, or at least every different kind of, posthumous evil, he will have to articulate and defend a different specific answer to the relevant "when" question. By contrast, I can just apply my "the question needs no answer" response to the whole business; thus, whenever the purge of Ann's work occurs, I can simply say (using the 4D framework) "The purge of Ann's work is an evil for her; her temporal duration extends from 1951 to 2001; the purge occurs in 2051 (or 2011, or whenever it is); the total ignorance of Ann and her work begins at, and continues indefinitely from, that time; and that's the whole relevant truth about 'when' in this case—there is no further 'when' question which needs to be answered concerning the 'when' of 'the purge's (and/or the ignorance's) being an evil for Ann.'"

Moreover, I think Bradley's view faces a deeper problem. As he acknowledges, it requires that we be able to say that the period from the time Ann dies to the time when she would have died on the alternative life-whole has a value-for-Ann of 0, or indifference (for it is only by comparing that value to the higher value-for-Ann in the alternative life-whole during that time period that we can justify the claim that her death is an evil for her during that time period). And, as he suggests—rightly—I would, and do, object that this is essentially incoherent; for when Ann does not exist to be the recipient of goods or evils, she likewise does not exist to be the recipient of middle, or indifference, values. While Ann exists, then just as things can be good for her (e.g., sipping champagne while watching a brilliant performance of *Othello*) or bad for her (e.g., eating moldy bread while watching a Nazi propaganda film), so they can be in between, or indifferent (perhaps, e.g., sipping mediocre beer while watching a *Perry Mason* rerun); but just as nothing can be good or bad for her *at a time that she does not exist*, so nothing can be indifferent for her *at that time*. Bradley's central response to this objection is that it's based on presentism, and, thus, that rejecting presentism—that is, employing, and consistently sticking to, a 4D framework—is all that is necessary to solve the problem. But I think this is a mistake. For, as I emphasized earlier, though "Ann exists" is true on the 4D framework, "Ann exists *now*" is not; "Ann exists *now*" is no more true on the 4D framework than it is on the 3D framework (just as "George W. Bush exists *here*" is no more true on the 3D framework than it is on the 0D framework). Thus, the claim that something can be good, bad, *or indifferent* for Ann *at a time when Ann does not exist* is as problematic on the 4D framework as it is on the 3D framework.[11]

There's one final issue I'd like to discuss briefly. More than once in his *Noûs* paper Bradley appeals, in support of his view, to fact that regarding *prenatal* evils as evils for the subsequent person seems to be unproblematic. But this appeal is quite puzzling. For there is of course a crucial disanalogy between prenatal and posthumous events in this context, namely, that prenatal events, unlike posthumous events, can *cause* misfortunes during one's life. Thus, if Ann is born blind because of a drug her mother took three weeks before she was conceived, there is no problem with the claim that her mother's taking the drug was an evil for Ann, for it *caused* her to suffer the misfortune of sightlessness *during—indeed, during all of—her life*. Relatedly, the question "*When* is a prenatal event an evil for the relevant person?" typically has a straightforward answer, namely, *during the period of the person's life when he or she is suffering its causal effects*. And this of course is the reason that typical prenatal evils can be accounted for even on a 3D framework, and thus pose no problem for supporters of EV.

This answer to the "when" question for typical prenatal evils is of course *not* analogous to Bradley's answer to the "when" question for posthumous evils (which is another reason I find his appeal to the prenatal case puzzling). And this brings me to my final point, namely, that *if we must* provide an answer to the question "*When* is death an evil for the person who dies?" the best—that is, the least implausible—answer, it seems to me, is the answer that *is* analogous to the comparable answer for prenatal evils, namely, "during the time of the person's life." For this, and this alone, is the time during which the person's death is a possible object of his or her negative feelings. Indeed, one might plausibly contend that a claim such as "The time during which Ann's death is a possible object of Ann's negative feelings falls entirely within the time of Ann's life" should be added to my list of relevant time claims pertaining to Ann and her death. Similarly, I think, if we *must* provide an answer to the comparable "where" question in the case of Ann's affair, I think the least implausible answer is "in Seattle; where Dan is"; for that is where Dan would (or could) be *suffering* from the affair. But it remains the case that the above time claim does not itself specify, and does not require that we specify, a time of Ann's death's being evil for her—just as the claim that the place where Ann's affair is a possible object of Dan's negative feelings is Seattle does not itself specify, and does not require that we specify, a place of Ann's affair's being an evil for Dan. And just as it remains my view—and I suspect the view of most of you—that the best response to the question "Where is Ann's affair an evil for Dan?" is that it has, and needs, no answer, so it remains my view that the best response to the question "When is Ann's death an evil for her?" is that it has, and needs, no answer.[12]

Acknowledgments

Thanks to Barbara Baum Levenbook, Ben Bradley, and participants at the University of Idaho/Washington State University Philosophy Colloquium—especially Michael O'Rourke and Joe Campbell—for helpful comments on earlier drafts.

Notes

1. I.e.: virtually no one questions the intelligibility of a sentence such as "Ann is being eulogized at her funeral" despite the fact that the apparent referent of the word "Ann" does not now (at the time of the eulogy) exist; the only issue is how this intelligibility is to be explained. By contrast, many people do seriously question the intelligibility of claims such as "Ann's death is an evil for her." To be sure, some presentists, as Bradley points out, "take their position to entail that we cannot refer to purely past things" (this vol., 272). But that does not affect my point here. For surely even such presentists must admit that the "eulogy" sentence, as uttered in ordinary circumstances, is perfectly intelligible; they simply have to

explain this intelligibility in a way that does not require "Ann" to be used in a standardly referential way. Yet it remains the case, again, that many people—including people not "infected" by philosophy—do question the intelligibility of claims asserting death to be an evil for the person who dies.

Further, I reject Bradley's claims in the same passage that (a) apart from a specific axiology, posthumous harms require backward causation, and (b) death is different from (other) posthumous harms in this regard. Since one's death postdates one's existence just as other posthumous events and states do (one is not dead until one has ceased to exist), I fail to see why the backward causation issue does not apply to death as much as it does to other posthumous harms. But the main point is that my view makes all posthumous harms, including death, intelligible *without* requiring backward causation; for on my view the intelligibility of a posthumous harm requires only that the harming event or state be a possible *object*, not that it be a possible *cause*, of one's negative feelings while one is alive. (This point is defended in Silverstein 1980 and 2000, and summarized briefly later in this essay.)

2. Noting Rosenbaum's observation that we can have negative feelings about events that never occur (Rosenbaum 1986, 130), Bradley asks (this vol., 272), "Suppose we accept VCF. . . . why think that an event must exist in order to be the object of feelings?" And he continues:

Silverstein admits that nonexistent events can be the objects of feelings in one sense, but insists that in the sense he has in mind, what he calls the *de re* conception of objects of psychological states, events must exist in order to be the objects of feelings (Silverstein 2000, 123). But this merely relocates the problem: why think that VCF is any less plausible given a conception of objects of thought that doesn't require objects of thought to exist?

But this misses the point. Of course we can have feelings about future (including posthumous) events that, as it turns out, never occur; moreover those feelings may be exactly the same as, and every bit as reasonable as, the feelings we have regarding future events that do occur—consider, to use Rosenbaum's example, the fears of Britons in the early 1940s concerning a Nazi invasion of Britain. But the question at issue in this context—viz., whether posthumous events or states can intelligibly be regarded as good or bad for the relevant persons—concerns only *actual* events and states; and the intuition underlying VCF is that an *actual* event or state, E, can intelligibly be said to have an *actual* value (i.e., to be good, bad, or indifferent) for a person, P, only if it is at least possible that there be an *actual* connection between E and P's feelings. And where E is posthumous for P, I think that the only plausible candidate for such a connection, apart from backward causation, is that provided by the combination of my 4D framework and a *de re* conception of objects of psychological attitudes. It would be absurd, for example, to say that the Nazi invasion of Britain actually was an evil, posthumous or otherwise, for anyone; and it would likewise be absurd to suppose that there could be an actual connection between that invasion and anyone's feelings. For there never was such an invasion; hence, nothing (of the relevant sort) ever existed to have value for, or to be connected to the feelings of, anyone. Yet a *de dicto* claim of the form "*P* fears that there exists (or will exist) an *x* such that *x* is a Nazi invasion of Britain"—unlike a *de re* claim of the form "There exists (or will exist) an *x* such that *P* fears *x* and *x* is a Nazi invasion of Britain"—could be true. Hence, a *de dicto* conception is not sufficient for VCF. By contrast, where there is an actual event—e.g., an actual posthumous slandering of *P*—then given the 4D framework, a relevant *de re* claim—e.g., "There exists an *x* such that *x* is a posthumous slandering of *P* and *P* has negative feelings regarding *x*"—could be true. And to say that such a claim could be true is just to say that, as the intuition underlying VCF requires, an *actual connection* between this *actual* slandering and *P*'s feelings is at least possible.

Readers who remain puzzled or skeptical should consider that exactly the same points apply, unproblematically, to spatially distant events and states (cf. my response to what I call the "phenomenalist" objection—Silverstein 1980, note 15, 375 [from 111]; repeated in Silverstein 2000, note 8, 132 [from 123]). Suppose, e.g., that *P* is distraught because he believes that his sister was just killed in an automobile accident while traveling through Europe. If *P*'s belief is false—if his sister is still very much alive and happily lounging on the beach on the south coast of Spain—then of course we cannot say "*P*'s sister's dying in an automobile accident while traveling through Europe was an evil for *P*" for there was no such dying. Yet *de dicto* claims such as "*P* is distraught by the belief that there exists an *x* such that *x* is *P*'s sister's dying in an automobile accident while traveling through Europe" remain true. It is only where the dying actually occurred—and thus only where *de re* claims such as "There exists an *x* such that *x* is *P*'s sister's dying in an automobile accident while traveling through Europe and *P* is distraught over *x*" can be true— that the dying can be an evil for *P*.

In my view it is difficult to overestimate the importance, for the issues under consideration, of the parallels between time and space—parallels emphasized, for example, by Nagel in his comment that "For certain purposes it is possible to regard time as just another sort of distance" (Nagel 1979, 66). These parallels were central to the arguments of my two earlier "death" essays, and are central again in this essay—see especially pp. 286–288, 290–291, including note 12, below.

3. Near the end of the essay (this vol., 291) I qualify this by saying "one might plausibly contend that a claim such as 'The time during which Ann's death is a possible object of Ann's negative feelings falls entirely within the time of Ann's life' should be added to my list of relevant time claims pertaining to Ann and her death."

Bradley (this vol., 277) complains that "If these claims exhaust the truth about time" in such a case, "then there is no room for truths of the form 'A would have been enjoying herself at *t* had A not died when she did.' And there clearly are such truths. On my view, those truths are the grounds for truths of the form 'A's death is bad for A at *t*.'" I agree, of course, that there are such truths; I simply deny that they are *relevant* truths with respect to the question of when A's death is an evil for her.

For, contrary to what Bradley's view requires, I deny that, at times when A no longer exists, she can be the recipient of *any* values, including middle or indifference values; as I argue below (and argued in my previous "death" essays, especially Silverstein 1980), "just as nothing can be good or bad for her *at a time that she does not exist*, so nothing can be indifferent for her *at that time*" (this vol., 290).

4. For those who might find this phrase ambiguous, I'm concerned here with the "time" issue/debate, not the "identity" issue/debate.

5. To be sure, Joe is not looking over my shoulder and making acid comments as I write—i.e., he is not actually "here, now" as I revise this essay for publication—but he was "here, now" when I presented the conference version of the paper at the Inland Northwest Philosophy Conference. So the reader should think of the time and place of that presentation as "here, now" for the purposes of this discussion.

6. It is precisely because I think Bradley's (and others') term "eternalism" makes this confusion more likely that I prefer terms like "four-dimensionalism" or "four-dimensional framework."

7. More accurately: the "out there," present tense, form of "exists." Since the 0D framework has both "here" and "now" built in, it must of course have both spenses and tenses.

8. I am aware that there may be some of you who think this question can be answered—your proposed answer, I would guess, being either "Seattle" (since that's where Dan is, or could be, suffering from the affair) or "Spokane" (since that's where the affair itself is). But I would also guess that your commitment to your answer to this question is much more tentative and hesitant than your belief that the affair is evil for Dan; and this suggests that even you should concede that giving a positive answer to the question "*Is Ann's affair evil for Dan?*" does not *require* giving an answer to the question "*Where* is Ann's affair an evil for Dan?"

9. Feldman's view, as expressed, e.g., in Feldman 1991, 320–321, is essentially that one's death is bad for one *eternally*, that is, at every time. I discuss this view, as it is expressed by Feldman, in Silverstein 2000, 119–121.

10. And, indeed, there are some posthumous evils—evils (such as the breaking of deathbed promises, or the implementation of fraudulent wills) that, by definition, cannot occur while one is still alive—to which his "evil of death" view cannot coherently be applied.

11. Consider, as an analogy, the question of Ann's financial status. While Ann is alive, her financial status might be positive (i.e., she might have net assets), negative (she might have net debits), or at the "zero" point, with neither net assets nor net debits. But just as it makes no sense to say that Ann's financial status (as opposed to, say, the financial status of her estate) is either positive or negative when she is dead, so makes no sense to say that it is at the zero point. (If, e.g., Ann lost a

bundle in the stock market last week, reducing her from having net assets of $100,000 to the zero point, it would be appropriate to say something like "Did you hear about Ann? She's $100,000 poorer than she was last week at this time!" But if instead of losing a bundle last week she died last week, saying something like this would be absurd.) And it seems obvious that this point is not affected by the employment of the 4D framework.

12. Bradley claims that the goal of "theoretical unity" supports his view (this vol., 279). But even if we ignore the problems his view faces, I think that various features of my view—especially, perhaps, the space/time parallel I've been emphasizing (the fact that my view's response to the "time" question "When is Ann's death an evil for her?" exactly matches the most plausible response to the "space" question "Where is Ann's affair an evil for Dan?")—justify the claim that my view satisfies this goal at least as well as Bradley's.

References

Bradley, B. 2004. When Is Death Bad for the One Who Dies? *Noûs* 38:1–28.

Epicurus. 1940. Letter to Menoeceus. Trans. C. Bailey. In *The Stoic and Epicurean Philosophers*, ed. W. Oates. New York: The Modern Library.

Feldman, F. 1991. "Some Puzzles about the Evil of Death." *Philosophical Review* 100: 205–227. Reprinted in J. Fischer, ed., *The Metaphysics of Death*, Stanford, CA: Stanford University Press, 1993. References in the text are to the Fischer volume.

Feldman, F. 1992. *Confrontations with the Reaper: A Philosophical Study of the Nature and Value of Death*. Oxford: Oxford University Press.

Levenbook, B. 1984. Harming Someone after His Death. *Ethics* 94:407–419.

Nagel, T. 1979. Death. In T. Nagel, *Mortal Questions*. Cambridge: Cambridge University Press. Reprinted in J. Fischer, ed., *The Metaphysics of Death*, Stanford, CA: Stanford University Press, 1993. References in the text are to the Fischer volume.

Rosenbaum, S. 1986. How To Be Dead and Not Care: A Defense of Epicurus. *American Philosophical Quarterly* 23:217–225. Reprinted in J. Fischer, ed., *The Metaphysics of Death*, Stanford, CA: Stanford University Press, 1993. References in the text are to the Fischer volume.

Silverstein, H. 1980. The Evil of Death. *Journal of Philosophy* 77:401–424. Reprinted in J. Fischer, ed., *The Metaphysics of Death*, Stanford, CA: Stanford University Press, 1993. References in the text are to the Fischer volume.

Silverstein, H. 2000. The Evil of Death Revisited. In *Midwest Studies in Philosophy*, vol. 24: *Life and Death: Metaphysics and Ethics*, ed. P. French and H. Wettstein. Malden, MA: Blackwell.

15 The Retroactivity Problem

Barbara Baum Levenbook

Can the dead be harmed, or suffer misfortune? The usual view is that there seems to be a "no subject" problem if one answers in the affirmative. If death is the end of the existence of a person, then when something occurs after Smith's death, it cannot happen to him, because at the time of the event there is no Smith existing to whom it occurs. Most philosophers who think that misfortune or harm can befall the dead solve this problem by saying that it is the antemortem person to whom these things occur, thus providing an existing subject.

But this solution gives rise, according to conventional philosophical wisdom, to a retroactivity problem. If some event or act occurs after the death of Smith, it is puzzling how it can harm him, since it would seem that to be harmed is to have one's life in some way altered or affected negatively, and by hypothesis his life has ceased.

Those of us who gamely want to pursue the idea that events occurring after a person's life can harm him must solve the retroactivity problem or explain why it is a pseudo-problem.

Is there a retroactivity problem in posthumous harm or misfortune? I want in this short essay to consider what that retroactivity problem would amount to, and what it wouldn't. I want, in other words, to clarify the alleged retroactivity problem.

What gives rise to the retroactivity problem? I am going to suggest that it is the result of making several assumptions jointly, many of which are initially plausible but none of which, as far as I can tell, are actually defended. The first of the assumptions, which I find quite plausible, I shall call *Worse-Off*:

Worse-Off An event harms a person only if it makes him worse off than he would have been if the event had not occurred.

A second assumption is that Worse-Off implies:

Welfare   An event harms a person only if it makes it the case that his welfare is lower than it would have been if the event had not occurred.

But how does an event make it the case that one's welfare is at a particular level? Some people may assume that an event does so by causing an effect. The effect is the harm, or constitutes the harm. So, for instance, if striking Joe on the jaw is harmful to Joe, the event of Joe being struck on the jaw causes some effect or effects (his being in pain, his jaw being temporarily incapacitated, and so on) that constitute the harm to Joe. Striking Joe on the jaw harms him because it causes effects that constitute harm to him. Given this additional assumption, a retroactivity problem for posthumous harm seems to arise once one adds the *No Backward Causation* principle, or NBC:

NBC   An event that happens at a time cannot cause an effect at an earlier time.

NBC seems to explain why something I do in 2005 does not cause an effect on or in Napoleon's early nineteenth-century life. However, NBC presents a problem for the coherence and logical possibility of time travel and, in particular, the possibility of reverse causation in time travel. It renders incoherent a type of scenario some philosophers maintain is coherent, such as the following:

Suppose that while I'm sitting in the time machine in the year 2000 about to travel back to 1920, someone ties my shoelaces together. I arrive in 1920, attempt to step out of the time machine, and fall down and hit my head. (Hanley 1997, 218)

Perhaps NBC ought to be modified to exclude the case of time travel. Supporters of the idea that it is logically possible to harm someone after his death do not typically depend on assuming that time travel is involved in the story. So any purported difficulties NBC has with the implications of time travel are beside the present point.

How much of an obstacle to posthumous harm is posed by NBC? Three points are in order. First, it should be clear that NBC cannot be applied in one very direct way. A harming is not a causal consequence of a striking of a jaw, a stabbing, a discriminating, a betrayal of trust, and so on. The harm to Joe is not a causal effect of my striking Joe on the jaw. By striking Joe on the jaw I harm him, but there is a noncausal relation between my striking Joe and my harming him. (See Kim 1974.) Nor is the harm to him an effect of his being in pain, which itself is an effect of my striking him on the jaw. By discriminating against Joe I might restrict or radically alter the available options for his autonomous choice, thus harming him. Perhaps the restricted options constitute the harm. But restricting or radically altering the available options is not usually a casual effect of the discrimination. Restricted alternatives usually bear a noncausal relation to the discrimination.

Second, misfortune needn't be understood in terms of causality. To say that something is a misfortune for someone is to evaluate it with respect to that person's good. It isn't hard (at least, for someone with Kantian predilections) to believe that some event can be bad for me without it causing anything particular in my life. For example, it can be bad for me that you have broken your promise to me (unjustifiably). What is bad is that I have been wronged by you. No particular effect is required. So if Worse-Off is correct, there must be something in addition about harming to make causality so central.

Third, NBC causes a problem for posthumous harm only if harming can be linked in some central way to causality and the harming does not occur to the person harmed until the cause has produced its effect. For instance, harming might be thought to be always a case of what Alvin Goldman called *causal generation* (Goldman 1970, 21–25). Then (a) Smith's harming Brown always consists in Smith's causing an effect, and (b) the time that Brown is harmed by Smith is when Smith causes the effect. These conditions would clearly be met if being harmed required experiencing (and suffering) something—some unpleasant emotion, for instance, or pain. However, harm does not seem to require this, as examples about undiscovered infidelity or embezzlement attest. Moreover, claim (a) is doubtful. It is difficult to see what effect is relevant in the case of, say, undiscovered infidelity. No doubt a sex act has causes and effects, but it would appear that adulterous Mr. Brown's harming Mrs. Brown consists, if anything, of the sex act by Mr. Brown and his paramour. It is by virtue of this act that Mrs. Brown is harmed; the causes and effects of the act are not relevant to the harm, though some of the effects may be additionally harmful.

Those who believe in the possibility of posthumous harm or misfortune can be expected to reject not only claim (a) but (b). An analysis of harm is needed to settle the question of the truth of claims (a) and (b); the question cannot be begged, either by those who reject the idea of posthumous harm or by those who favor it.

In any event, more than NBC is required to build the case that there is a retroactivity problem with posthumous harm.

Suppose, then, that harming is more like misfortune, for which causality is not central. A retroactivity problem may be generated for posthumous harm as long as one assumes Worse-Off. It is generated if in addition one accepts the *No Backward Evaluation* principle, or NoBE:

NoBE   Nothing that happens at a time can affect the evaluation of an earlier life or event.

Unfortunately, there are many counterexamples to NoBE. Consider the following evaluations:

The Great Escape was the best adventure movie of its kind.

Ty Cobb was the greatest baseball player of the twentieth century.

Kennedy's decisions during the Cuban missile crisis were pivotal during the cold war.

In all of these evaluations, what comes later than the subject candidate affects the evaluation: later movies, later baseball players, later decisions and events. So NoBE is false and shouldn't be accepted.

    The skeptic about posthumous harm might note that the evaluations I offered to falsify NoBE are comparative. These comparative evaluations smuggle in a class that extends forward (and also backward) in time from the time of the subject candidate. The real question concerns "good for him" and "bad for him" evaluations. One can imagine the skeptic substituting a more specific principle, *No Backward Evaluation for Good*, or NoBEG:

NoBEG   Nothing that happens at a time can affect the evaluation of an earlier event as good for or bad for a person.

However, there seem to be counterexamples to NoBEG, too. An old story from Europe goes something like this: One day, a farmer discovered that his only horse, a stallion, was missing. "Oh, this is bad!" he exclaimed. But the next day, his horse returned with a mare. "Oh, this is good," said the farmer, expecting foals. The farmer's nineteen-year-old son tried to tame the mare, was thrown, and broke his leg. "Oh, this is bad!" said the farmer. But the next day, war was declared. The King's soldiers came to round up all able-bodied men. Since the farmer's son was incapacitated, they passed him over. "Oh, this is good," said the farmer. The point of this story seems to be that the evaluation of events—for example, the breaking of the son's leg—can be affected by subsequent events, for example, war's being declared and the draft being enforced. (Hence the adage, "Count no man happy until he dies"?[1]) One could deny this by claiming that the event, the breaking of the leg, remained unfortunate, but the subsequent state of affairs, being disabled during a draft, was fortunate—that is, by chopping the story of what happened to the son into discrete pieces (events and states of affairs), whose evaluations do not change in the face of subsequent events. But there doesn't seem to be much plausibility in such ontological niceties. It just doesn't ring true to say that the breaking of the leg remained unfortunate for the son, once the war was declared—at least, not unfortunate, all things considered. That very event, the breaking of the leg, had consequences that, all things considered, outweighed the usual unfortunate consequences of leg-breaking. It, the breaking of the leg, may very well have saved the son's life.

I conclude that NoBEG, like NoBE, is false, and cannot be used to raise a retroactivity problem in an account of posthumous harm or posthumous misfortune. But other principles remain that can, depending on the account one offers of posthumous harm. Twenty-five years ago, Ernest Partridge criticized an account given by Feinberg according to which people can be harmed after their deaths because their interests can be invaded after their deaths (Partridge 1981). One way to put Partridge's criticism is that Feinberg's account is subject to a retroactivity problem if one holds the following principle, NFFI (*No Free-Floating Interests*):

NFFI If there is an interest invaded at a particular time, there must be an interest-bearer at that time.

This principle is attractive until one reflects that a plausible interest to postulate for many human beings in many situations is the interest in remaining alive. (Some would hold that the right to life depends on the existence of such an interest.) But here is an argument that human beings cannot have an interest in remaining alive according to NFFI: There can be no interest if nothing can count as its frustration or invasion. And what would count as the frustration or invasion of the interest in remaining alive? That interest would be frustrated, according to this argument, only by dying, and would be invaded only by being killed or allowed to die. Since by hypothesis death entails the nonexistence of a person, if we accept NFFI, it follows that at the time the very thing occurs that would, if Sam's interest in remaining alive existed, count as the frustration of that interest (namely, Sam's dying) or its invasion (namely, the killing of Sam), Sam's interest in remaining alive does not exist.

One strategy to escape this argument is to postulate other kinds of frustrations and invasions of the interest in remaining alive: it is invaded when I wound Sam fatally, even though it takes him hours to die of his wound, or frustrated when something else causes death imminently and inevitably even though the death occurs a bit later or the dying is a process. All of this assumes there is a clear termination point to the dying process, at least sometimes—an assumption that is controversial but can be conceded without prejudice at this point. The trouble with this strategy is that the interest is one in remaining alive, not in avoiding death being both imminent and inevitable *while one is still alive* (or alive to some degree), though doubtless a case can be made that there are interests many people have in remaining alive completely or at any rate to a much greater degree than at any time during the dying process. The proposed frustrations and invasions, in short, do not appear to touch the object of the postulated interest in remaining alive.

Another strategy for avoiding the argument against NFFI is to claim that no one has an interest in remaining alive *simpliciter*. Rather, people often have interests in remaining alive provided the life they would live is worthwhile or worth having by some standard we can leave open. We can call this *an interest in a future life worth living*. This interest can be frustrated long before death—for example, by a paralyzing accident, the onset of a painful and debilitating illness, and so on. However, the point remains that in the absence of such events death, or dying, cannot frustrate this interest if NFFI is true.

But suppose killing or letting die is something that takes place over an interval of time. Then a better strategy is to hold that the interest in question is (sometimes) invaded over an interval, the same interval taken by the killing or the letting die. This interval terminates in death, but it begins with the person alive. It may be milliseconds or years long. One can get a retroactivity objection to Feinberg's account of posthumous harm by postulating this variant of NFFI:

NFFI$_2$ If there is an interest invaded over a particular interval, there must be an interest-bearer at some time during that interval.

Suppose we provisionally accept NFFI$_2$. (Some desire-based accounts of interests make NFFI$_2$ very plausible.) Pitcher (1984) might be credited with having raised NFFI$_2$ objections to Feinberg's interest-invasion account of posthumous harm. Ironically, after Pitcher's article, I gave an account of posthumous harm (Levenbook 1984) to which, as Don Marquis pointed out (Marquis 1985), a retroactivity objection could also be directed. One simply need maintain the very plausible NFFL (*No Free-Floating Losses*) principle:

NFFL   If there is a loss at a particular time or over a particular interval, there must be a loser at that time or at some time during that interval whose loss it is.

As I understand him, Harry Silverstein maintained then (Silverstein 1980), and would continue to maintain (Silverstein 2000, this vol.), NFFL. So would I, now.

Notice that you can't get around $NFFI_2$ or NFFL by postulating four-dimensionalism, which Harry Silverstein does. Even if people are four-dimensional spacetime worms, a slice of which exists at a given time, the problem with posthumous harm is that the harming event occurs at a time during which there are no person-slices of the worm that is the allegedly harmed person. $NFFI_2$ and NFFL can be recast in four-dimensional language, and the problem of retroactivity resurfaces on these accounts of harm. Indeed, the problem of retroactivity resurfaces anyway if you assume that events occurring temporally outside of a person-worm cannot harm a person-worm (as in EHILS, a principle to be explored below).

What I've been leaning toward lately is the view that posthumous misfortune, and posthumous harm, can be explained by postulating that the evaluative frontier for purposes of harming extends beyond biological life.[2] Given Worse-Off, this implies that the relations "good for him" and "bad for him" don't end when he does, not on everything. It seems implausible to think that the frontiers extend indefinitely, however. A promising view may be that the frontiers end when someone's agency life ends. Agency life does not end at death. Several philosophers, including Dorothy Grover, have made the point that events that happen after someone's death affect what he or she was doing before death. (See Grover 1989.) They are, in Grover's words, "relevant to [the] determination of what action is or was performed" (1989, 337). For example, a shooting becomes a killing if the victim dies, yet the death of the victim may postdate the death of the gunman.

The view that the frontiers of harming someone do not end with his or her death will be flatly rejected by those who hold both Welfare and accounts of welfare such that welfare neither extends beyond biological life nor is affected by postmortem events. But it is a mistake to think that the strategy of defending posthumous harm stands or falls with the plausibility of extending welfare or the arena of the welfare-affecting beyond one's biological life. For there are reasons to doubt the truth of Welfare. A great deal depends on the correct analysis of welfare, which is too large a topic to be tackled here. Scanlon raises the example of a woman whose internal organ has been harmed in some way, although this does not yet affect her experience "or the achievement of goods connected with her aims" (Scanlon 1998, 124). He then imagines that she dies in an accident before the harm manifests itself in these ways. On certain conceptions of welfare, the physical harm does not affect the woman's welfare; it has the potential to affect it, but because of her untimely death, it fails to do so. It seems to me, however, that she has been harmed, physically. If, for instance, the organ is injured and malfunctioning because she has been given poison, it would be counterintuitive to say that fortunately, the poison hadn't harmed her. She is, before her death, in the position of the deceived husband whose wife is cheating on him; she has been harmed, though she doesn't know it yet.

The rejection of Welfare does not suffice, of course, to clear the way for posthumous harm. So long as one assumes Worse-Off, one can generate a retroactivity problem by adding the *No Moral Relatedness* principle, NMR:

NMR Someone cannot be one of the relata in a moral relation with an event that postdates him.

It seems to me, however, that NMR has counterexamples. One can break one's promise to someone who is now dead, and thereby betray him. He is betrayed by the breaking of the promise, which seems to me to be a (quasi-)moral relation between him (the antemortem person) and the posthumous event. One can wrong someone who is now dead, by slandering him, for instance. He is wronged by the slandering, a posthumous event.[3] One may even be able to disrespect him by ignoring the terms of his will for no good reason. So I think NMR is false. It may be that a person cannot be one of the relata in the particular relations "good for" and "bad for" with events that occur after he dies, but that will be because of these particular relations, not because of restrictions on moral relations in general.

I'm inclined to believe that the problem of whether the ideas of posthumous harm and posthumous misfortune are intelligible is not going to be settled by metaphysics. Retroactivity objections, if relevant, I expect to be consequences of something else that must be settled first: substantive moral theory, in particular, a theory of the relations "good for" and "bad for" and their connection, if at all, with welfare. It would then follow that a symposium in metaphysics is the wrong place in which to wrestle with the question of the intelligibility and possibility of posthumous harm. But I will try one or two more reasons for thinking the contrary.

Some people, I think, assume another principle that, if accepted, creates a retroactivity problem for the claim that there can be posthumous harm or posthumous misfortune. I call this putative metaphysical claim *Every Harm Is a Living State*, or EHILS:

EHILS   Harm or misfortune to a person is constituted by a state of affairs obtaining during that person's existence.

However, there are reasons to reject EHILS. I will mention one now, and one later. EHILS has a problem with prenatal harm, on several plausible theories of personal identity. EHILS may be able to account for *some* prenatal harm on the theory that identifies the person with his body. On that theory, it would follow that no one can undergo prenatal harm until the stage of fetal development in which he has a body. (In the embryo stage, for instance, it is doubtful that there is a body, let alone that it is the same body that the person will have later. The blastula, a collection of cells, seems rather to be the source of a future body, the stuff of which the object, body, will be constructed. In such a case, the embryo that will be me may be harmed, but on EHILS and this theory of personal identity, I will not yet have been harmed.) EHILS may be able to account for prenatal harm on the "same soul" theory, but this theory has enough problems on other grounds to undermine confidence in its support for the retroactivity problem.

A supporter of EHILS may be very comfortable with the idea that prenatal damage is not harm to a person. He can claim that the prenatal damage causes harm to a person later. It harms him when he's, for example, born blind, or when he goes through life without an arm, or when he tries to master language and can't. However, it's less plausible to claim that prenatal damage can't be bad for a person. For this and another reason I will shortly discuss, I am not convinced that a retroactivity problem for posthumous harm and posthumous misfortune is well based on EHILS.

With one or two highly plausible premises, EHILS will yield the *Every Harm Needs a Condition* principle, or EHNAC:

EHNAC   If someone is harmed or if some event is a misfortune for him, he must be in a harmed or unfortunate condition during his existence.[4]

EHNAC, it should be noted, doesn't have even the appearance of a problem with prenatal misfortune or prenatal harm. That is one advantage it has over EHILS.

In an article written twenty-five years ago (Pitcher 1984), George Pitcher accepts EHNAC, which if true presents a retroactivity problem for posthumous harm and misfortune. Pitcher then attempts to solve the retroactivity problem by postulating that during one's lifetime, one can "suffer" the misfortune that a particular event is going to occur (after one's lifetime). So, to use one of his examples, Bishop Berkeley suffers the misfortune during his lifetime that his beloved son William will die young, though William does not die until after his father does. With a little variation, Pitcher's answer can be adopted to surmount the retroactivity problem posed by EHILS.

But Pitcher's solution to the retroactivity problem produced by EHNAC (and EHILS) leads to difficulties. Imagine that the Bishop's wife survives both him and their son William, and that she, too, has a major interest in the continued life of William. Does she, like the Bishop, suffer the misfortune that William will die young, the same misfortune allegedly suffered by her deceased husband? It would seem so, since there are the same grounds for both alleged misfortunes. But William's death at a young age must itself be a misfortune for her; for if it isn't, how can the fact that it will occur be? Pitcher is willing to admit that William's death at a young age can be a misfortune for someone alive at the time of his death, such as his mother; William's death cannot, however, be a misfortune for someone then dead, such as Bishop Berkeley. However, the same question can be asked with regard to Bishop Berkeley: if William's death at a young age is not a misfortune for him, how can the fact that it will occur be? I can't see any sensible answer to this question other than the obvious: the fact that it will occur cannot be a misfortune for Bishop Berkeley.

I have indicated that I recant much of my earlier solution to the problem of how to account for posthumous harm. One thing I don't recant is my opposition to EHNAC. EHNAC, as I argued twenty-five years ago, implies that one's death cannot be a misfortune for one. I don't want to rehearse the arguments I gave then; suffice it to say that, just as in the Bishop Berkeley example, if being in a condition in which my death is both imminent and inevitable is bad for me, it must be bad principally because dying, that is, ceasing to exist, is bad for me. Perhaps something similar can be said about harm. With very little variation, this same line can be used against EHILS.

EHILS and EHNAC, if accepted, pose retroactivity problems for the possibility of posthumous harm and posthumous misfortune. So does NBC, given a certain assumption. As Pitcher's failure shows, these problems are not easy to overcome. To my knowledge, no one has both accepted EHILS and EHNAC and successfully overcome the problems they raise. I have argued that EHILS and EHNAC should be rejected, at least for misfortune. The question is: Should any of the three principles (NBC, EHILS, or EHNAC), suitably revised and coupled with the assumptions that jointly bar posthumous harm, be accepted? I leave the answer to be developed in future discussion.

Notes

1. The adage originated with the ancient Greeks: "count no man happy till he dies, free of pain at last" (*Oedipus the King*, 1678–1684). Solon is reputed to have said, "One should count no man happy until he is dead" (Solon, *apud Hdt.* 1.32.9). According to legend, Solon also said it to wealthy King Croesus of Lydia, who, when affronted that Solon did not name him as a happy man, demanded to know why. Solon's reply: "I count no man happy until his death, for no man can know what the gods may have in store for him" (http://allaboutturkey.com/croesus.htm; accessed March 13, 2005).

2. In this, I am using language very close to that used by Joel Feinberg (1977, 304).

3. James Stacey Taylor has recently suggested that the dead cannot be wronged. Instead, there is wrongdoing that refers to the dead, elliptically. I find this view counterintuitive. At any rate, it is a tricky position for Taylor, since (a) he is willing to admit that the dead can be betrayed, and (b) he seems willing to assume that undermining the autonomy of someone both wrongs and harms him. As pointed out above, someone's autonomy exercised before his death can find its terminus, as it were, after his death. It can also be interfered with after his death. See Taylor 2005.

4. This principle is also a consequence of NBC.

References

Feinberg, J. 1977. Harm and Self-Interest. In *Law, Morality and Society: Essays in Honour of H. L. A. Hart*, ed. P. Hacker and J. Raz. Oxford: Clarendon Press.

Goldman, A. 1970. *A Theory of Human Action*. Princeton: Princeton University Press.

Grover, D. 1989. Posthumous Harm. *Philosophical Quarterly* 39:334–353.

Hanley, R. 1997. *The Metaphysics of Star Trek*. New York: Basic Books.

Kim, J. 1974. Noncausal Connections. *Noûs* 8:41–52.

Levenbook, B. 1984. Harming Someone after His Death. *Ethics* 94:407–419.

Marquis, D. 1985. Harming the Dead. *Ethics* 96:159–161.

Partridge, E. 1981. Posthumous Interests and Posthumous Respect. *Ethics* 91:243–264.

Pitcher, G. 1984. The Misfortunes of the Dead. *American Philosophical Quarterly* 21:183–188.

Scanlon, T. 1998. *What We Owe to Each Other*. Cambridge, MA: Harvard University Press.

Silverstein, H. 1980. The Evil of Death. *Journal of Philosophy* 77:401–424. Reprinted in J. Fischer, ed., *The Metaphysics of Death*, Stanford, CA: Stanford University Press, 1993.

Silverstein, H. 2000. The Evil of Death Revisited. In *Midwest Studies in Philosophy*, vol. 24: *Life and Death: Metaphysics and Ethics*, ed. P. French and H. Wettstein. Malden, MA: Blackwell.

Taylor, J. 2005. The Myth of Posthumous Harm. *American Philosophical Quarterly* 42:311–322.

V Postlude

16 Love Conquers All, Even Time?

Andrew Light

"There are several different accounts that we get from philosophy and physics on the nature of time," he said, starting a substitute lecture in his colleague's undergraduate class in metaphysics. Andy had just started a new position in the philosophy department at the University of Portland. His new colleague Wendy was out of the country at a conference in Australia and had asked him to take over a week's worth of lectures. Though metaphysics was not his specialty, he wanted to make an impression on his new colleagues that he was a good faculty citizen. That, and he knew that since he traveled so much he would need someone to take over his classes in the future too, and so, anticipating a possible tit-for-tat, agreed to step into the breach for Wendy. Looking around the room, though, he was starting to have second thoughts. It was late in the day and the students seemed weary and not very attentive. Nonetheless, he pressed on: "But on almost any view of time there are several puzzles that arise concerning personal identity over time."

Andy felt the fifty minutes left to go, well, really forty-two or so now since he had arrived a bit late and started the class off with some pleasantries and house-keeping of sorts. Essentially, though, he had a whole period to fill up, and as usual he was waiting for a story.

It was a strange method of teaching, so far as he knew, but it had evolved over the years and he had convinced himself that it worked well enough, while also providing a ready-made excuse to not overly prepare and write out formal lectures. *Lectures*. He hated the word. Sounding so much like a thing to be forced on someone rather than listened to with anything like attention. If you want people to listen to you, tell a story. And it had better be a good one.

The story method was developed early on in his career in ethics classes, to which he was rapidly realizing it might be uniquely suited. He had stumbled across it in his first tenure-track job in Wyoming. As a novice to the teaching game, and in rooms full of students with whom he had little in common, the method snuck up on him. He couldn't remember the exact topic of the first lecture where he started doing it except that it had something to do with Aristotle's account of the virtues. In the middle of some exposition of courage or friendship or justice he found himself talking about himself, sharing some story that was entirely inappropriate for a 150-seat lecture hall in Laramie. But suddenly, as if he had finally pushed a sluggish revolving door on its axis, he was through to the other side and the students seemed to be actually listening, pens down, staring up at him from notebooks and looking with a mixture of astonishment, curiosity, and consternation. It wasn't all of them, to be sure, but there were more than he had seen in a while paying attention.

As he continued talking he then started moving, walking back and forth as he hit the rhythm of his story. He started talking with his hands, as he would with friends in a bar, and didn't for a moment consider avoiding an aside or digression. After that initial success he kept trying to recreate the same conditions. From then on, if the argument to be covered was a utilitarian account of individual welfare, he had a story about the happiness he experienced tormenting his younger brother when they were both children. If it was a duty-based approach to lying, he had a story about cheating on his taxes. And if the point was that the pursuit of understanding the good, the true, and the beautiful only resulted in an imperfect set of concepts that only approximated the world as it was lived by imperfect humans—like himself—he had many, many stories. Most of them involving Internet dating.

Though he sometimes repeated the same stories over the years, he never wrote them down in his lecture notes. A rather intense Israeli friend in graduate school had told him once that the best way to teach was simply to enter the classroom and "do philosophy" in front of the students. "Show them how *hard* it is to think through a problem on your feet." He had tried that, but though effective for a few converts, most of the younger students didn't appreciate the picture that resulted. Although the culture of philosophy had been dominated for half a century by a tortured classroom style propagated by Wittgenstein and his followers, those on the outside mostly found it embarrassing to watch.

But still, there was something to novelty, to each class becoming a fresh occasion for new thoughts; and telling stories to get a point across could benefit from spontaneity as well. After all, when you go out with friends, the stories are best which come as a flash of associative insight. Rehearsed stories could be dry and boring, even to the storyteller. It's like that moment in *I Heart Huckabees* when the Jude Law character is confronted with evidence from the existential detectives, Lily Tomlin and Dustin Hoffman, that he is telling the same story about tricking a vegetarian pop star into eating chicken salad over and over and over. Horrified with how predictable he has become, the next time he is asked to repeat the story, in a meeting of his corporation's board of directors, he vomits.

Andy's stories had not failed him so far. He would walk into class and within a few minutes of beginning he would have more than enough stories to take up the period. But so far, in this class, metaphysics was proving resistant to the method. Maybe it was his lack of familiarity with the material, but the right story just wasn't coming. Fortunately, his colleague Wendy had assigned some very good reading, a chapter on personal identity over time by NYU philosopher Ted Sider from a coauthored introductory text on metaphysics (Sider 2005). He spent the next twenty minutes going through the chapter with the class.

In a bit over ten pages Sider lays out the basics. He starts out with an example of a person put on trial for committing a murder five years ago. The defense, however, is unorthodox. The person claims to remember committing the murder, but argues that "the murderer is not the same person as me, for I have changed. That person's favorite rock band was Led Zeppelin; I now prefer Todd Rundgren. That person had an appendix, but I do not; mine was removed last week. That person was 25 years old; I am 30. I am not the same person as that murderer of five years ago. Therefore you cannot punish me, for no one is guilty of a crime committed by *someone else*" (Sider 2005, 7). Certainly no court would buy such a defense, but it does raise the question of whether a person who changes over time, either physically or psychologically, remains *the same person.*

Such an observation allows a distinction between qualitative and numerical sameness. When a person changes in any way—such as a person yesterday before a haircut and a person today after the haircut, or a person yesterday before seeing the light and becoming a Buddhist and a person today wearing saffron robes—they are not the same person. They are qualitatively different. But in another sense, the sense that we walk around with every day which helps us to understand concepts like responsibility for our past actions or anticipation of future events that we will take part in, we are numerically the same. As Sider puts it (2005, 8), the closing arguments at the trial confuse the two kinds of sameness. Even if the murderer is qualitatively different since committing the crime, no one else murdered the victim. No one is numerically distinct from the murder.

After going through this opening example, a sharp-eyed young woman with dreadlocks in the third row raises her hand. "So, this is what philosophers mean when they are talking about personal identity, numerical identity over time?" Andy thinks, indeed sharp, but maybe not doing the reading.

"What's your name?" he asks.

"Emily."

"Well, yes Emily, that's exactly as Sider puts it in the next paragraph. All of us change over time, from big changes—losing limbs, having babies—to little changes—clipping nails and the like. Since physical changes don't seem to especially matter for our identity over time, the problem of personal identity is to figure out what does matter."

From there he goes through the different options presented by Sider. One option is that we are the same over time because of the existence of a permanent, unchangeable soul. Another option is spatiotemporal continuity theory, claiming that the essence of personal identity is our continuous series of discrete locations in time and space. And finally, there is psychological continuity theory, which holds that a past person is numerically identical to a future person if the two share memories, character traits, and so on. Normally we don't have to worry much about the problem of actually identifying persons. We can use simple observations to distinguish between one person and another in order to attribute responsibility, or anything else that we normally do in relation to attribution of identity. But this doesn't solve the problem of which of these views is true, because there are cases that demonstrate the limitations of each school of thought.

The intuition pump that Sider identifies that helps people to sort out which view they prefer is the problem of duplication, derived from a range of hypothetical science-fiction examples. If we were to take a person and divide him in two, creating two identical entities, using some surgical procedure or an accident with a matter transporter of the sort found in a *Star Trek* episode, which of the two would count as the continuation of the original person? If personal identity is numerical sameness then the problem is that by either of the continuity theories we don't know which twin continues the line of the original, if indeed either does, and hence we have a puzzle of two numerically indistinct persons. In another article Sider says that if he were divided in two, into Ed and Fred, then "The puzzle . . . is that we cannot say that I am identical to both Fred and Ed, for by the transitivity and symmetry of identity the absurdity that Fred = Ed would follow. Nor can we identify me with exactly one of Fred or Ed, by the symmetry of their candidacy" (Sider 2000, 85).

Looking up from his notes after going through this material it appeared that those who had read the chapter were on board. The text is well written, highly accessible, and very engaging. Those who hadn't read the chapter were lagging back. Looking up at the ceiling he muttered to himself and waited for an insight, something that would pull the rest of them in, or at least provide a ready excuse to release the class early.

"Um, Professor Bright."

"Huh?" Looking down he sees a tall sandy-haired guy in the first row.

"What about fate?"

"What?" Andy recognizes the student from one of his classes last term as Bill. "What *about* fate?"

"Well, if I were to be split into two, say, 'Bill 1' and 'Bill 2,' what about all that stuff that is supposed to happen to me?"

"I'm not sure I'm following."

"I understand this problem that if I am duplicated then it might be bad because I would cease to exist since I can't be both Bill 1 and Bill 2. But Sider says this guy Parfait claims that personal identity goes along with psychological continuity. . . "

"Parfit."

"Right, Parfit, sorry. Anyway, Parfit says being split isn't bad, like dying, because though I might not exist I'll just psychologically continue as both Bill 1 and Bill 2."

"Correct. This is a big challenge to some of the premises we started off with, especially that personal identity is important because it is connected to anticipation, regret, and punishment, as Sider puts it at the end of this chapter. But I don't get what this has to do with fate?"

"Well, just that if there are things that are supposed to happen to me as I go through life, but then there are two of me, will those things still happen or will they happen to only one of me, or what?"

Still puzzled, Andy asks: "Why would you think this is important?"

A bit exasperated that Andy does not see the point, Bill continues: "It's like in that Gwyneth Paltrow movie *Sliding Doors*, I saw a rerun of it the other night on cable. She leaves her apartment in London one morning, goes to work, and then gets fired."

"Right. I saw that film the other night too. She gets fired, and then . . ." Andy looks around and notices that those who had been dozing off are now paying attention. It's not his story, but it is a story, and though he expects that the discussion is going to stray from the topic it certainly is something that they can identify with. Why didn't he think of this before? In an instant he recalls loads of films that have to do with time and identity, or some combination of the two, which could have been used in today's class.

"Yea," Bill continues, "she gets fired at the beginning of the film and then she goes into the subway and the film divides her in two. One time line has her making her train and she comes home to find her live-in boyfriend in their bed with his American ex-girlfriend."

"Jeanne Tripplehorn."

"Yea, she's hot. And the other time line has her miss the train, get bonked on the head, and arrive home later in the afternoon after Tripplehorn has left. The first Gwyneth Paltrow, Gwyneth 1, dumps the boyfriend, gets this really cool haircut, opens her own business, and then falls in love with this Scottish guy with a crazy accent.

"John Hannah."

"He's hot!" says someone from the back of the class, followed by giggles all around.

"Uh, right, and then the second Gwyneth Paltrow, Gwyneth 2, has to support the boyfriend by getting two waitressing jobs and then winds up crushed when she eventually finds out about the American girlfriend."

"And the point about fate?"

"At the end of the film, both Gwyneth 1 and 2 get hit by a car. I can't remember if it's the same car but it doesn't matter. Then both go to the same hospital and the time line of Gwyneth 1 sort of abruptly stops and Gwyneth 2—the one who was still with the creepy boyfriend—wakes up in the hospital and dumps him. Then, in the final scene, Gwyneth 2 walks out of the hospital and meets the same Scottish guy in an elevator that Gwyneth 1 had fallen in love with. And then, they have like this moment so we know that they are going to fall in love even though Gwyneth 2 has never noticed this guy before. So, in the film these problems about identity are kind of resolved because no matter what happens after you're duplicated what's going to happen to you is still going to happen to you. You might even say that love conquers all!"

Andy looks around and sees many heads nodding in agreement. It seems that many of these undergraduates believe in fate of this sort, or at least want to believe in it. He thinks briefly about telling a story about a recent blind date who asked him if he believes in fate but decides against it.

"Okay," Andy continues, "that's an interesting example. But even though we might think of this as a case of duplication, similar to *Run Lola Run*, is it really?"

Emily, from earlier, raises her hand. "No," she says.

"Why not?"

"Well, for one thing, these fission examples that Sider is talking about have the two duplicates continuing in the same frame of time *and* space. It's like that Schwartzenegger film where Arnold, sorry, *Governor* Arnold, gets duplicated with some kind of clone who is an exact copy of him physically and mentally and then they end up working together to save the planet or something."

"Right, go on."

"And in this film what you have is Gwyneth 1 and 2 living in some kind of parallel universe or something, though it all gets resolved somehow in the end. They can't actually meet each other in the same world and raise the same kind of problems that Sider is talking about in the chapter."

"Good, that's one important difference. There are indeed some interesting things about time and identity in *Sliding Doors*, but they might better help us to think through some puzzles that philosophers raise over the logic and metaphysics of possibility and actuality. Maybe what the film shows us is two very different possible scenarios, or possible worlds, for Paltrow's character, and then asks us to think about the relations between the two, especially the problem of how one's life could be very different depending on seemingly innocuous everyday events, like missing a train. Then we could think about what it means to talk about such possible scenarios. Is it to assert the actual existence of an alternative time line, like the film seems to portray, or would it be something else? Perhaps this film will be a better one to see later in the term when your regular professor gets back and she covers those issues in class."

Bill chimes in again. "But what about the fate thing? You still haven't answered that question."

"All right, why is this still an issue?" Silence. Bill seems hesitant to go further, looking down with a worried look on his face. From the back of the room someone shouts out, "Because it's scary!"

"What's scary?"

Bill again: "It's scary because all this stuff about identity makes me worried about my future. I think everything happens for a reason. That's what my mom always told me. And this stuff about continuity of identity and duplication and all that makes it seem like there's too much chance in life. I mean, if I were split into two Bills, or Bobs, or whatever, I still don't know if the right things will happen to me. I guess that's why I like how this movie ends."

"What do you mean?"

"At the end of the film Gwyneth Paltrow winds up with the Scottish guy she fell in love with in the time line that ended. Since we know that her original boyfriend was a jerk it's, I don't know, comforting that she found the guy she should have been with all along."

Andy was the one taken aback now. Yeah, he thought to himself, metaphysics can be scary. But what's worse is how some bits of popular culture which have a chance to raise some interesting, even profound questions, go for a cheap, happy ending and dissolve the potential lesson into absurdity. Maybe this is why he should have come up with his own story *before* coming to class. He could have controlled the moral. Then he remembered something from another class he had audited in grad school. There were, after all, more films than he had stories to tell.

"Any of you know where the plot line for *Sliding Doors* came from? No? It's actually based on a film by the Polish director Krzysztof Kieslowski from the mid-1980s called *Blind Chance*. It's set against the backdrop of Communist Poland before the transitions there. The main character is a medical student named Witek, who, like Paltrow's character, runs after a train, and three alternative time lines follow from either catching or missing it. In the first one he catches the train, meets an aging member of the Communist Party who he admires, quits medical school, joins the party and the establishment, reconnects with an old girlfriend and falls in love with her. In the second time line he runs into a railway guard after missing the train, is arrested, gets sent to a labor camp where he meets a member of the opposition, quits medical school and becomes an anti-Communist militant. In this time line he also meets a sister of a friend he lost track of when he was ten and again falls in love. Both of these time lines, however, end in frustration as in both he loses his respective girlfriend, and in both is denied a passport to leave the country to go to Paris, which is something he has always wanted to do. In the third time line, though, he again misses the train, runs into a female colleague from medical school on the platform, settles down with her, has kids, and leads a peaceful life as a doctor unwilling to get mixed up in politics. So, what's different between this film and *Sliding Doors*?"

"There's no magic," says Emily.

"Please explain."

"Well, it's like what Sider says about the soul. Some philosophers and religious thinkers hold that what makes for a real person over time, even though things change in us physically and psychologically, is that we have an immortal soul. But Sider doesn't spend much time on how positing the existence of a soul could solve these problems because there's just no proof that there is a soul. You can only have faith that there is one and hope that solves the problem. But how do you even argue with a position like that? Bill's belief in fate is similar. How do we know that there is such a thing? This other film by this Polish guy doesn't take the easy way out."

Astonishing, Andy thought to himself. Emily had just earned herself a recommendation letter for whatever graduate program she cared to apply. And thankfully, class was over. While they had strayed from the original topic of the lesson, he was pleased to have stumbled into a demonstration of the utility of metaphysics for understanding everyday life.

On the way out, Bill lingered. Andy looked at him, and Bill asked: "There's something that still bugs me about Emily's answer. What about that Witek guy? I mean, in the final time line he meets the girl that he probably should have been with all along, and he goes on to have a happy life out of politics. This European film isn't any better than *Sliding Doors.* Everything did turn out best, right?"

Andy sighed, "No, actually, in the last time line in Kieslowski's film, after he meets the girl, gets married, and becomes a doctor, he finally gets to travel abroad to Paris and the plane he's on explodes in midair shortly after takeoff. Then the film abruptly ends."

"Scary," said Bill.

"Yeah."

References

Sider, T. 2000. Identity Over Time. *Philosophical Books* 41:81–89.

Sider, T. 2005. Personal Identity. In *Riddles of Existence: A Guided Tour of Metaphysics,* ed. E. Conee and T. Sider. Oxford: Oxford University Press.

Contributors

H. E. Baber University of San Diego

Lynne Rudder Baker University of Massachusetts Amherst

Ben Bradley Syracuse University

John W. Carroll North Carolina State University

Reinaldo Elugardo University of Oklahoma

Geoffrey Gorham Macalester College

Mark Hinchliff Reed College

Jenann Ismael University of Arizona

Barbara Baum Levenbook North Carolina State University

Andrew Light George Mason University and Center for American Progress

Lawrence B. Lombard Wayne State University

Ned Markosian Western Washington University

Harold Noonan University of Nottingham

John Perry Stanford University and University of California, Riverside

Harry S. Silverstein Washington State University

Matthew H. Slater Bucknell University

Robert J. Stainton University of Western Ontario

Neal A. Tognazzini The College of William & Mary

Index

Abelard, Peter, 20
Action(s), 5, 15, 90, 149–150, 152–157, 161, 232, 236–237, 239, 241–242, 244–246, 303, 313
  executable, 232, 237, 239, 244
  normally self-effecting, 232, 236, 239
  responsibility for, 5, 15, 90, 149–150, 152–157, 313
Actualism, 13, 97–102, 105–107, 108
  predicate, 98, 108
  property, 13, 97–102, 107, 108
  world, 99–102, 105–107
Agency, 17–18, 151–152, 160, 221, 245–246, 303
  centers of, 17–18, 245–246
Alston, William, 204
Ambiguity, 86, 116–125, 225
Anscombe, G. E. M., 17, 209–210, 212, 220, 224, 225
Apresjan, Juri, 116
Aquinas, Thomas, 173, 180
Aristotle, 19, 20, 50–51, 54, 56–57, 59–60, 62–64, 67, 72, 74, 312
Armstrong, David, 146
Arnauld, Antoine, 165–166, 172–173, 176
A-series, 2–3, 11, 27–34, 41–44
Auden, W. H., 27
Augustine of Hippo, 1

Awareness, judgmental, 32–33, 44
Ayers, Michael, 195

Bach, Kent, 126
Bacon, John, 146
Baker, Lynne Rudder, 44, 188
Barresi, John, 19
Bayle, Pierre, 179
Bennett, Jonathan, 16, 170, 179, 204
Bergmann, Michael, 97
Bigelow, John, 95, 280
Black, Max, 19
Blanchette, Patricia, 45
Bodies, 5, 165–166, 168–169, 172, 175, 176, 178, 180, ch. 9 *passim*, 222, 237
Bonnen, Clarence, 179
Borges, Jorge, 238
Boundary, 79–81, 91, 202, 206, 212, 220–225, 226, 285–286
Bradley, Ben, 279, 280, 284, 287, 288–291, 292, 293–294, 295
Brandt, Richard, 266
Broad, C. D., 43
Broome, John, 258, 266
B-series, 2–3, 11, 27–34, 41–44
Burman, Frans, 173–174
Butler, Joseph, 5, 21
Bykvist, Kryster, 265, 266

Campbell, John, 280
Carter, William, 66–68, 74, 75, 195